# Philosopher of the Heart

# Philosopher of the Heart

*The Restless Life of Søren Kierkegaard*

## CLARE CARLISLE

Farrar, Straus and Giroux

New York

Farrar, Straus and Giroux
120 Broadway, New York 10271

Copyright © 2019 by Clare Carlisle
All rights reserved
Printed in the United States of America
Originally published in 2019 by Allen Lane, Great Britain
Published in the United States by Farrar, Straus and Giroux
First American edition, 2020

Library of Congress Cataloging-in-Publication Data
Names: Carlisle, Clare, 1977– author.
Title: Philosopher of the heart : the restless life of Søren Kierkegaard / Clare Carlisle.
Description: First American edition. | New York : Farrar, Straus and Giroux, 2020.
Identifiers: LCCN 2019055663 | ISBN 9780374231187
Subjects: LCSH: Kierkegaard, Søren, 1813–1855. | Philosophers—Denmark—Biography.
Classification: LCC B4376 .C37 2020 | DDC 198/.9 [B]—dc23
LC record available at https://lccn.loc.gov/2019055663

Our books may be purchased in bulk for promotional, educational, or business use.
Please contact your local bookseller or the Macmillan Corporate and Premium
Sales Department at 1-800-221-7945, extension 5442, or by e-mail at
MacmillanSpecialMarkets@macmillan.com.

www.fsgbooks.com
www.twitter.com/fsgbooks • www.facebook.com/fsgbooks

1   3   5   7   9   10   8   6   4   2

*To George Pattison*

*As he turned he caught the feeling,*
*And he smiled as he walked down the road.*
*All my days, they are filled with meaning,*
*But I have yet to fathom the code.*
                     – Sandy Denny, 'The Optimist'

# Contents

# CONTENTS

# Preface

'A love affair is always an instructive theme regarding what it means to exist,' wrote Søren Kierkegaard, after his only love affair had ended in a broken engagement. Kierkegaard did philosophy by looking at life from the inside, and more than any other philosopher he brought his own life into his work. His romantic crisis yielded insights into human freedom and identity that earned him an enduring reputation as the 'father of existentialism'. He created a new philosophical style, rooted in the inward drama of being human. Although he was a difficult person – and perhaps dangerous as an exemplar – he was inspirational in his willingness to bear witness to the human condition. He became an expert on love and suffering, humour and anxiety, despair and courage; he made these affairs of the heart the subject matter of his philosophy, and his writing has reached the hearts of generations of readers.

When the Swedish writer Fredrika Bremer visited Copenhagen in 1849 to chronicle Denmark's cultural life, Kierkegaard had for several years been a celebrity in his home town. Bremer did not meet him – he refused her requests for an interview – though she heard plenty of gossip about his restless habits: 'During the daytime one sees him walking in the midst of the crowd, up and down the busiest streets of Copenhagen for hours at a time. At night his lonely dwelling is said to glow with light.' Perhaps unsurprisingly, she perceived him as an 'inaccessible' figure, whose gaze was 'fixed uninterruptedly on a single point'. 'He places his microscope over this point,' wrote Bremer, 'carefully investigating the tiniest atoms, the most fleeting motions, the innermost alterations. And it is about this that he speaks and writes endless folios. For him, everything is to be found at this point. But this point is – the human heart.' She noted that his works were especially admired by female readers: 'The philosophy of the heart must be important to them.' It has proved to be important to men, too, as we see from a glance at successive generations of Kierkegaard's readers, among them some of the most influential thinkers and artists of the last century.

Of course, Kierkegaard was not the first to strive to make sense of being human. He grappled with Europe's awesome intellectual tradition, absorbing ancient Greek metaphysics, the Old and New Testaments, the Church Fathers and medieval monastics, Luther and Lutheran pietism, the serially path-breaking philosophies of Descartes, Spinoza, Leibniz, Kant, Schelling and Hegel, and Romantic literature. During three fertile, tumultuous decades of the nineteenth century he channelled these currents of thought into his own existence, and felt their tensions and paradoxes move through him. And at the same time his heart was pierced, filled, stretched and bruised by a series of intense loves, each one of them – perhaps excepting the first – deeply ambivalent: his mother Anne, his father Michael Pedersen, his fiancée Regine; his city, his literary work, his God.

We will soon meet Kierkegaard as he returns to Copenhagen from Berlin in May 1843, travelling by train, stagecoach and steamship. We will see at once that he is a writer – now, in his thirtieth year, embarking on the authorship that made him famous. He wrote with extraordinary fluidity, transposing his soul into his beloved Danish language, and even in translation we can feel the rhythm of his prose, the poetry of his thinking. What Kierkegaard later called his 'activity as an author' filled up most of his life, and consumed his energies and his money. To say that he was a writer is not just to point out that he produced great books at an astonishing rate and filled numerous journals and notebooks. Writing became the fabric of Kierkegaard's existence, the most vibrant love of his life – for all his other loves flowed into it, and it swelled like the ocean that crashed restlessly against his native land. This was a compelling, consuming love: as a young man he found it difficult to start writing, but once he began he could hardly stop. He was preoccupied with questions of authorship and authority, perpetually torn between the joys of writing and the agonies of publication, fascinated by literary genre, fastidious about typography and bookbinding.

He wrote as both a philosopher and a spiritual seeker. In the parable of the cave in Plato's *Republic*, a solitary figure escapes the ordinary, deluded world in pursuit of truth, then returns to share his knowledge with the uncomprehending crowds – and this archetype of the philosopher defines Kierkegaard's relation to his nineteenth-century world. Likewise, in the Old Testament story of Abraham's arduous journey up and down Mount Moriah, Kierkegaard discerned the religious movements – the deep longing for God, the anxious struggle to understand his vocation, the search for an authentic spiritual path – that shaped his own inner life. His religion repeatedly defied convention, though his beliefs were not unorthodox.

This book travels alongside Kierkegaard as he pursues the 'question of existence' that both animated and troubled him, held him back and propelled him forwards: how to be a human being in the world? He criticized the abstractions of modern philosophy, insisting that we must work out who we are, and how to live, right in the middle of life itself, with an open future ahead of us. Just as we cannot step off the train while it is moving, so we cannot step away from life to reflect on its meaning. Similarly, this biography does not consider Kierkegaard's life from a remote, knowing perspective, but joins him on his journey and confronts its uncertainties with him.

When I first talked to my editor about my plan to write this book, he suggested that I was envisaging a Kierkegaardian biography of Kierkegaard. He was right, and his remark has guided and perplexed me through these pages. Often I wasn't sure how to go about it; looking back, I see that it meant following the blurry, fluid lines between Kierkegaard's life and writing, and allowing philosophical and spiritual questions to animate the events, decisions and encounters that constitute the facts of a life. The book takes its shape from the Kierkegaardian question about how to be a human being in the world. At the beginning of Part One, 'Return Journey', we meet Kierkegaard in the middle of writing *Fear and Trembling*, where he gives a hopeful – and rather beautiful – answer to this question. In Part Two, 'Life Understood Backwards', we find him in 1848, five years later, looking back at his life and his authorship, and answering his question of existence differently. Kierkegaard was always hyper-conscious of his mortality, but his expectation of imminent death shifted in those five years: in 1843 it was the ultimate writing deadline, giving urgency to his work as he raced to bring his books out into the world, but by 1848 he saw dying as a deed that would fulfil his authorship. In Part Three, 'Life Lived Forwards', we follow Kierkegaard into the battle with the world that will end, one way or another, with his death.

Writing a Kierkegaardian biography also meant looking beyond a conventional chronological narrative, and letting Kierkegaard's distinctive analysis of three interlocking concepts—subjectivity, truth, and time—influence the shape of the book. In constructing a 'cradle to grave' narrative, a biographer must assume a fixed position some distance from her subject in order to observe him moving through time, rather as one might sit and watch a distant figure walking across a landscape. Kierkegaard criticized this 'objective' (or objectifying) way of thinking about human beings, arguing that the deepest truth of our lives lies in our 'subjectivity' or 'inwardness'. Time is the element of subjectivity, the substance of our inner being. Our past and future are vibrant inside us. We do not experience time as an external framework or a linear sequence, like a train track on which our lives run. While we move inexorably forward, breath by breath and heartbeat by heartbeat, we circle back in recollection and race ahead of ourselves in hopes, fears, and plans. By these looping, stretching movements we shape our souls, make sense of our lives—and this is precisely what I found Kierkegaard doing in his journals. Telling this inward story required a literary form that could convey his philosophical insights about subjectivity as well as his own complex acts of soul-shaping and sense-making. This book shows Kierkegaard continually moving forward: first through a couple of days in May 1843, then through several months in 1848, and finally through the last few years of his life. Yet throughout this motion the shifting story of his past unfurls like a sail behind him, propelling him into his future and filling each moment with meaning.

Kierkegaard is not an easy travelling companion, though he was by many accounts charming, funny and compassionate as well as endlessly interesting. 'This evening I had a conversation with Magister Søren Kierkegaard,' an acquaintance wrote in his diary on 1 September 1843, 'and despite the fact that he is not exactly the person with whom one finds tranquillity, it just so happened – as often happens – that his words made clear to me precisely what I have recently been thinking about.' Kierkegaard's parents gave him a name that means 'severe', and he became more and more true to this name as he grew older. In *Concluding Unscientific Postscript*, written in his thirty-third year, Kierkegaard argued that to become religious a person must 'grasp the secret of suffering as the form of the highest life, higher than all good fortune . . . For this is the severity of the religious, that it begins by making everything more severe.' A few pages later, however, he described a religious person enjoying an excursion to Copenhagen's Deer Park – 'because the humblest expression of the God-relationship is to admit one's humanity, and because it is human to enjoy oneself'. Real joy, he argued, always lies on the far side of suffering.

It is certainly true that the joy of being human never came easily to Kierkegaard. At the beginning of the 1840s he was a wealthy, gifted, sociable young man, loved passionately by a beautiful, intelligent woman – yet he made life exceptionally difficult for himself. This deep and mysterious fact of Kierkegaard's psychology was inseparable from his philosophical stance towards the world. He was perhaps the first great philosopher to attend to the experience of living in a recognizably modern world of newspapers, trains, window-shopping, amusement parks, and great stores of knowledge and information. Although life was becoming materially easier and more comfortable for affluent people like himself, it also provoked new anxieties about who to be and how to appear. Exposed to public view not only in his published works but on the streets of Copenhagen, through the windows of the fashionable cafés on Strøget, and in the pages of his city's newspapers, Kierkegaard felt other people's eyes upon him – and he agonized about what they saw.

In *Concluding Unscientific Postscript* he described a philosopher in his early thirties – a figure very much like himself – sitting outside the café in Frederiksberg Gardens, smoking a cigar and reflecting on his place in the world: 'You are getting on, I said to myself, and becoming an old man without being anything . . . Wherever you look about you on the other hand, in literature or in life, you see the names and figures of the celebrities, the prized and acclaimed making their appearances or being talked about, the many benefactors of the age who know how to make life more and more easy, some with railways, others with omnibuses and steamships, others with the telegraph, others through easily grasped surveys and brief reports on everything worth knowing.'

Spiritual life was also being made easier, he mused, by philosophers whose systems explained Christian faith and demonstrated its truth, its reasonableness, and its moral value to society. 'And what are you doing?' he asked himself. 'Here my soliloquy was interrupted, for my cigar was finished and a new one had to be lit. So I smoked again, and then suddenly this thought flashed through my mind: You must do something, but since with your limited abilities it will be impossible to make anything easier than it has become, you must, with the same humanitarian enthusiasm as the others, take it upon yourself to make something more difficult. This notion pleased me immensely, and at the same time it flattered me to think that I would be loved and esteemed for this effort by the whole community.'

These light-hearted words are heavy with irony: by the time Kierkegaard wrote them, he was deeply disappointed by his peers' reluctance to appreciate his work. His commitment to accentuate and deepen the difficulty of being human resulted in an endlessly elusive, ambiguous series of writings, stubbornly resistant to summary and paraphrase, since so much is compressed between their lines. Within many of these texts, different narrative voices perform conflicts between life-views, with no clear resolution; they exhibit errors and misunderstandings as often as they elucidate truths. One can grapple for decades – as I have done – with their literary and philosophical complexities, and still not get to the bottom of them. For Kierkegaard, the work of philosophy was not a swift trade in ready-to-wear ideas, but the production of deep spiritual effects that he hoped would penetrate his readers' hearts, and change them. Many of his contemporaries were unsettled by this, or simply baffled; though they glimpsed his genius, it was easier to mock his personal flaws and idiosyncrasies than to understand his books.

Of course, Kierkegaard's hopes for recognition and anxieties about his public image were grounded in a sense of being exposed, seen and judged that is intrinsic to the experience of being human in the world. And we can hardly help judging other people: we weigh them up as soon as we meet them, and continually adjust our measurements as they reveal themselves. While living in uncomfortably close proximity to Kierkegaard, I have sometimes found myself disliking him – a painful feeling, similar to the pain of finding fault with a loved one. His books give his readers high expectations; his lyrical religious discourses describe exquisite ideals, like how a pure human heart reflects God's goodness as truly as a calm, still sea reflects the heavens. Yet in his journals he rehearsed his petty fixations, his jealousy of his rivals' success, his bitter fury at those who slighted him, his debilitating pride. He often felt sorry for himself, justified himself, blamed others for his disappointments.

Does this make him a hypocrite who preached something he did not practise or experience? On the contrary: Kierkegaard's remarkable ability to invoke the goodness, purity and peace for which he longed was inseparable from the storms that raged and twisted in his soul – connected by precisely this longing for what he knew he lacked. His philosophy is well known for its paradoxes, and Kierkegaard's restless desire for rest, peace, stillness, was a paradox – and a truth – that he lived daily. And like every human being, his life was a mixture of elements both petty and profound, which could exert equally powerful claims upon him; he struggled to synthesize them, though they frequently collided in flashes of comic or tragic absurdity. As a 'poet of the religious' he laboured with immense effort to keep spiritual ideals free from the compromises and corruptions that creep in, as he knew first-hand, whenever anyone tries to live up to them.

Reflecting on my disapproving reactions to Kierkegaard's all too human thoughts and feelings has led me to reflect also upon the fact that a biographer might be expected to evaluate her subject's life – to assess its success, its authenticity, its goodness. As a Kierkegaardian biographer I want to resist the urge to impose or invite these judgements. This is not because Kierkegaard was particularly non-judgemental, although he was rarely moralizing or self-righteous. It is not even because as a disciple of Socrates he valued self-knowledge more highly than any other kind of philosophy, and encouraged his readers to turn their judgements on themselves. Rather, it is because he understood that there is a freedom to be found in letting go of familiar, worldly ways of measuring a human life.

Kierkegaard had no wife to talk to at the end of the day, and instead he wrote out his anger and self-pity in lucid, finely detailed prose. This was unusual, but his feelings were not: when we read his journals we recognize his ignoble sentiments because we already know them intimately. In his philosophy Kierkegaard interrogated the human habit of judging, so deeply rooted in our private thinking and collective culture that it is very nearly inevitable, and he called this 'the ethical sphere', or simply 'the world', because (like Plato's cave) it surrounds and encloses us. But though the judgements of others are as difficult to avoid as our own, Kierkegaard believed that none of these human judgements is absolute or final. It is always possible, he suggested, to occupy a different place – for each individual belongs to a sphere of infinite depth, which he called 'inwardness', 'the God-relationship', 'eternity', 'the religious sphere', or simply 'silence'. His writing opens up this sphere, right at the heart of life, and beckons the reader into it.

# The Life of Søren Kierkegaard: Key Events and Major Publications

| | |
|---|---|
| 1813 | May 5: Søren Aabye Kierkegaard born in Copenhagen at 2 Nytorv |
| 1828 | S.K. confirmed by J. P. Mynster in the Church of the Trinity |
| 1830 | S.K. enters the University of Copenhagen |
| 1834 | death of Anne Sørensdatter Kierkegaard, S.K.'s mother |
| 1837 | S.K. meets Regine Olsen |
| 1838 | August: death of Michael Pedersen Kierkegaard, S.K.'s father |
| | September: *From the Papers of One Still Living* |
| 1840 | June: S.K. completes his theology degree |
| | September: engagement to Regine Olsen |
| | October: S.K. enrolls in the Royal Pastoral Seminary |
| 1841 | September: S.K. gains magister degree for his dissertation on irony |
| | October: S.K. breaks engagement to Regine Olsen and travels to Berlin |
| 1842 | February: S.K. returns to Copenhagen from Berlin |
| 1843 | February: *Either/Or* |
| | May: *Two Upbuilding Discourses* |
| | October: *Fear and Trembling, Repetition, Three Upbuilding Discourses* |
| | December: *Four Upbuilding Discourses* |
| 1844 | March: *Two Upbuilding Discourses* |
| | June: *The Concept of Anxiety, Prefaces, Philosophical Fragments, Three Upbuilding Discourses* |
| | August: *Four Upbuilding Discourses* |
| 1845 | April: *Three Discourses on Imagined Occasions, Stages on Life's Way* |
| 1846 | January–February: a series of satirical cartoons and sketches about S.K. appear in *The Corsair* |
| | February: *Concluding Unscientific Postscript* |
| | March: *Two Ages: A Literary Review* |

1847    March: *Upbuilding Discourses in Various Spirits*
July and August: S.K. preaches in the Church of Our Lady
September: *Works of Love*
November: Regine Olsen marries Johan Frederik Schlegel

1848    March: revolution in Denmark
April: S.K. leaves 2 Nytorv; *Christian Discourses*
July: 'The Crisis and a Crisis in the Life of an Actress' in
*The Fatherland*
September: S.K. preaches in the Church of Our Lady
October–November: S.K. writes *The Point of View for My Work
as an Author*

1849    May: *Three Godly Discourses, Either/Or* (second edition)
July: *The Sickness unto Death*

1850    September: *Practice in Christianity*

1851    August: *Two Discourses at the Communion on Fridays*
September: *For Self-Examination*

1854    January: death of Bishop Mynster
December: H. L. Martensen becomes Bishop of Zealand; S.K.
publishes two articles in *The Fatherland*

1855    January: three articles in *The Fatherland*
March: Regine Schlegel leaves Denmark; S.K. publishes seven
articles in *The Fatherland*
April–May: S.K. publishes eight articles in *The Fatherland*
May: S.K. launches *The Moment*, published fortnightly May
through September
November 11: death of S.K.

# PART ONE
# May 1843: Return Journey

*To be able to fall down in such a way that the same moment it looks as if one were standing and walking, to transform the leap of life into a walk – that only the knight of faith can do.*

# I

# Living the Question of Existence

Never before has he moved so quickly! And yet he is sitting quite still, not uncomfortably – resting, even – in a 'marvellous armchair'. The fields are flying past, still the brightest green of springtime. There's no divine wind in his sails hastening his journey. This is a new kind of miracle: an alchemical fusion of steam and steel, ingenuity and ambition, is putting railways straight through Christendom. And this new kind of motion gives a man like him time for repose. The first-class carriage is quiet, and as usual he is travelling alone. The gliding landscape makes him think of the time that has passed, all the things that have changed. He recollects the intensity of the last few weeks, the crises of the past months, and before that too many years stagnating in the university. Perhaps now there is a chance of freedom from all that? Speeding away from Berlin towards the Baltic Sea at forty miles an hour, anything seems possible. In less than two days Søren Kierkegaard will be back in Copenhagen.

It is late May 1843, and Kierkegaard has just turned thirty. Three months ago he published *Either/Or*, a huge, eccentric work of philosophy which quickly caused a sensation. He wrote much of that book in Berlin during the winter of 1841, the most productive period of his life so far. And this month he returned to Berlin for a shorter visit, hoping to do the same thing again – and, sure enough, he boarded the train today with two manuscripts in his bag. He has finished *Repetition*, the story of a man who, like Kierkegaard, gets engaged to a young woman but changes his mind and breaks it off. It is narrated by another character who – also like Kierkegaard – travels to Berlin a second time, returns to his old lodgings on Gendarmenmarkt, sees the same play in the same theatre. Part novella and part manifesto, this strange little book will propose a new kind of philosophy, in which the truth cannot be known, yet must somehow be lived.

The other book, still unfinished, is *Fear and Trembling*. It is about the story of Abraham and Isaac told in Chapter 22 of the Book of Genesis. God commanded Abraham to sacrifice Isaac, so father and son walked for three days to Mount Moriah, where Abraham bound Isaac's hands and feet and raised his knife to sacrifice him – but then an angel appeared, telling him to kill a ram instead. Abraham and Isaac walked home again, three more days. What would the old man tell his wife, Sarah, when she asked him where they had been? What was he *thinking*? We will never know: the biblical narrative says nothing about Abraham's thoughts, his feelings, his intentions, which can only be imagined. As he writes this book, Kierkegaard is creatively reconstructing Abraham's inner life.

Some will claim that this kind of poetic thinking has no place in philosophy, but Kierkegaard draws great philosophical lessons from the journey to Moriah. And he is fascinated by the dark mystery of Abraham; perhaps he even enjoys the thought that his own life holds a similar mystery, which others may one day imagine, interpret, reconstruct: 'He who explains the riddle of Abraham has explained my life – but who of my contemporaries has understood this?' He hopes that *Fear and Trembling* will guarantee his fame as a writer, that it will be translated into different languages, studied by generations of scholars.

'I have never worked so hard as now,' he wrote from Berlin to Emil Boesen, his closest friend, just before he began this journey home. 'In the morning I go out for a while, then come home and sit in my room without interruption until about three o'clock. My eyes can hardly see. Then I sneak off with my walking-cane to the restaurant, but am so weak that if anyone called out my name I think I would keel over and die. Then I go home and begin again.' Despite his physical condition, he warned his friend that 'you will find me happier than ever before'; even if he is entering 'a new crisis' he is glad to be putting his past into words. 'These last months I had in my indolence pumped up a proper shower-bath and now I have pulled the string and the ideas are cascading down upon me: healthy, happy, thriving, cheerful, blessed children, born with ease and yet all of them share the birthmark of my personality.'

Berlin's railway station in 1843

Working like this in Berlin, fuelled and frayed by sugary coffee, Kierkegaard felt most himself – yet animated by a force not entirely of his making. He submitted to a cycle of despair and exuberance which he understood as a spiritual education. In his journal he described the wretched phase of the cycle, when he was 'put down in a dark pit where I crawl about in agony and pain, see nothing, no way out'. This suffering seemed essential to what followed, like the labour pains of a woman giving birth: 'Then suddenly a thought stirs in my mind, a thought so vivid, as though I had never had it before even though it is not unfamiliar to me . . . When it has then taken hold in me I am pampered a bit, I am taken by the arms, and then I, who had been shrivelled up like a grasshopper, grow up again, sound, thriving, happy, warm, and lively as a new-born child. Then it's as though I must give my word that I shall follow this thought to the uttermost; I pledge my life and now I am buckled in the harness. I cannot stop and my powers hold out. Then I finish, and it starts all over again.' His creativity may be a blessing or a curse, but it feels inescapable, either way. The ideas flow through him, with a life of their own.

Like most homeward-bound travellers, Kierkegaard is not quite the same person as he was when he began his trip. Even in these early

5

days of 'railway mania' he cannot be the first human being to sit alone on a train, reflecting on the life he is leaving behind and imagining the destination ahead. Hypochondria and superstition have conspired to persuade him that he will die within four years, but his brief future is lit more brightly than before by the manuscripts in his bag. He sees them now, bound in thick blue paper in Reitzel's bookshop, throwing sparks into the dry pews of Christendom. He may feel freer, strengthened within himself, but he is also apprehensive as he thinks about what – and who – awaits him at home.

The first time he visited Berlin he was leaving Regine Olsen behind: twenty-eight years old and a newly qualified Magister of Theology, he was not embarking on a brilliant academic career but fleeing the aftermath of his broken engagement. A year and a half has passed since then; Regine remains at her family home in Copenhagen, and he is still writing about 'her' in his journal. In Berlin this second time, memories of their painful separation lay in wait for him at every turn, and he came to a realization: 'If I had had faith, I would have stayed with Regine.' By now, though, Kierkegaard has set his life in a different direction. He knows that he will never marry. When he sees Regine in church or on the street – and he sees her often – he cannot speak to her. The image of her face and the echo of her final desperate words to him flood his soul with confused, conflicting feelings; all his thoughts of her are tangled with his effort to understand himself.

Nevertheless, there is a pleasure in coming home. He will stroll beneath the chestnut and lime trees on Philosopher's Walk and Cherry Lane, the footpaths along the high medieval ramparts that encircle his beloved city like a verdant crown, blossoming every spring. He is looking forward to going to the Frederiksberg Gardens on Sunday afternoon, where he will sit in the shade, smoke a cigar, and watch the serving girls enjoying their day out. It will be especially lovely there now that the air is warmer, and the girls will no longer be bundled up in their shawls.

He will return to his large apartment on Nørregade, close to the university and the Church of Our Lady. From there he sets off each morning to immerse himself in the life of the city, walking through all its neighbourhoods, up on the ramparts, out along the lakes, wearing down his boots. On these daily walks he meets acquaintances on

Frederiksberg Gardens by Peter Christian Klæstrup

every street, and many of them will walk along with him, arm in arm, to converse for a while. Kierkegaard does most of the talking, of course – and no one's conversation flows and leaps more gracefully, no man's wit is sharper. He casts an odd top-hatted shadow as he veers across the street to dodge the sunlight, but his companions put up with his awkward lopsided gait and the flamboyant gestures of his free hand, which invariably holds a walking-cane or a rolled umbrella. Passers-by catch his penetrating gaze with interest and a little fear, for he seems to measure everyone he meets, body and soul, in the glance of a bright blue eye.

And since *Either/Or* came out in February, even more people recognize him and want to talk with him. Kierkegaard is curious about other human beings, but he also needs time alone – time to write! When he returns home from his 'people baths' he carries on walking, pacing around his darkened apartment as he composes his next sentence, then returning to his tall writing desk; he goes back and forth for hours, filling pages with his thoughts.

Despite the unprecedented speed of the steam engine, there is still an hour to go before the train arrives in Angermünde. When he closes his eyes he sees Abraham, on his way home from Mount Moriah.

Who had he become, having prepared a fire, tied up his son, raised his knife? What did he say to Isaac as they walked home? If he had come closer to God on the summit of that remote mountain, how could he explain to Sarah that her child's life had seemed a price worth paying?

Of course, Kierkegaard has only been to Berlin, not so different from the urbane Danish world he left behind earlier this month. And he did not, like Abraham, need a knife on his journey – just a pen and his notebooks. Nevertheless, he feels that he has sacrificed a life with Regine, and with it his own honour and his family's good name, for the sake of something that is difficult to explain. He broke his promise to marry the young woman who loved him, broke her heart, humiliated her. Everyone in Copenhagen knows about it; they all agree he was in the wrong. And now, coming home, the notebooks in his bag are full of ideas that challenge much of what the inhabitants of his city think they know. Kierkegaard is not bringing another new philosophy back from Germany, but calling into question whether doing philosophy is the right way to seek the truth, whether baptism makes people Christians, whether being human is something to take for granted.

All philosophers ask questions, but these are questions of a peculiar kind. They are the sort of questions posed by Socrates, his favourite philosopher, designed to produce confusion rather than answers – for confusion is a fertile soil in which wisdom might grow. While everyone else in ancient Athens was 'fully assured of their humanity, sure that they knew what it is to be a human being', Socrates devoted himself to the question, *What does it mean to be human?* – and from this question flowed many others: *What is justice? What is courage? Where does our knowledge come from?* The educated men of Athens had ready answers to these questions, but Socrates's inquiries persisted until their views collapsed into incoherence or paradox. This devious philosopher, who seemed to be seeking knowledge, was just playing a trick on them! And yet Socrates *was* seeking knowledge, and his questions were as sincere as they were duplicitous: these questions led in a new direction, away from what the world recognized as wisdom, and towards a higher truth.

In Plato's *Republic* Socrates offers a parable of ascent and return, which echoes Abraham's journey up and down Mount Moriah. 'Imagine a cave,' says Socrates, where people are chained up, facing a wall; behind them, unseen, is a fire and an endless puppet show, and the puppet shadows projected onto the wall are all they know. One of these prisoners is a philosopher – a lover of wisdom – who escapes into the dazzling sunlight above the cave. He basks in this light, full of wonder, his vision transformed; then he descends again, back to where he came from.

*Plato's Allegory of the Cave* by Jan Saenredam, 1604

Socrates told this story to encourage his young philosophy students to think about the dangers of inhabiting a world once they have embarked on a critique of its deepest assumptions. The dimly lit cave where people are held captive, blind to the mechanisms producing the shadows they take to be real things, is an image of the human condition: these prisoners are like all of us, explains Socrates. The cave could be the human mind, its thoughts transfixed by a drama of insubstantial appearances. It could also be the social world, for an entire culture has evolved around this shadow play: the prisoners test each other on their knowledge of the shadows, and compete to predict their movements. But the parable shows too that our minds can expand beyond their habitual limits, and that there is something else beyond this world, just as there is an entirely different light and landscape above the cave. The philosopher's first task is to wrest himself from illusions, turn around, and see how the shadow play is produced; next, he must find a way to climb up out of the darkness, see the sun, and understand things clearly in its light. This journey is a liberation, an enlightenment, and, we might imagine, a wonderful experience. But Socrates insisted that the philosopher must return to the cramped cave, bringing his insight with him. Will he be able to change the prisoners' world? Or will they turn on him, ridicule him, refuse to let him call their way of life into question?

Socrates provoked his fellow citizens until he was eventually accused of corrupting his students and charged with the crime of 'irreverence' – failure to show proper piety towards his city's gods. At his trial he refused to change his ways, declaring that 'while I live, I shall never give up philosophy or stop exhorting you and pointing out the truth to any one of you whom I may meet, saying in my accustomed way: "Most excellent man, are you who are a citizen of Athens, the greatest of cities and the most famous for wisdom and power, not ashamed to care for the acquisition of wealth and for reputation and honour, when you neither care nor take thought for wisdom and truth and the perfection of your soul?"' His incessant questions were, Socrates explained, 'what the god demands, and I believe nothing better has befallen this city than my zeal in executing this command'. He compared himself to a gadfly, or horsefly, sent to disturb the Athenians for their own good: 'I go about arousing, and urging and reproaching each one of you, constantly alighting upon you everywhere the whole day long . . . But you, perhaps, might be angry, like people awakened from a nap, and might slap me, and easily kill me; then you would pass the rest of your lives in slumber, unless God, in his care for you, should send someone else to sting you.' After they heard Socrates's defence, a large jury of Athenian citizens condemned him to death.

Two years ago, while engaged to Regine, Kierkegaard wrote his graduate dissertation on 'the concept of irony with continual reference to Socrates'. Irony is a singularly indirect mode of communication, posing surreptitious questions and expressing what cannot be said directly. Any ironic utterance calls itself into question by conveying something beyond what it literally states, like saying something deliberately naïve or stupid to show that you are in the know. Socrates was the master of irony, and he made it a philosophical method, even a way of life. He asked questions which led his students to realize that they were living like prisoners in a cave – transfixed by insubstantial shadows, encircled by high, dark walls from which it might be possible to free themselves. Socrates's irony changed their relationship to this narrow, self-enclosed world of illusions.

In the intellectual circles Kierkegaard moves in, it has become fashionable to talk about irony. It was a clever choice for a dissertation topic in 1840, giving him a chance to quote Fichte and Hegel, to discuss Friedrich von Schlegel's *Lucinde*, to critique the modern German poets. Irony was at the heart of Schlegel's vision for '*Romantisch*' literature: Romantic irony, he explained, 'surveys everything and rises infinitely above all limitations, even above its own art, virtue or genius'. The new poetry would not represent a stable reality, but create everything anew – and the poet would bring himself into existence along with his works.

In his dissertation Kierkegaard argued that this modern irony has no anchor. We rise above the world, question its meaning, expose its contingency – for what? Irony has become a matter of style: a literary form, a sophisticated posture, a rebellious attitude. Maybe there seems to be a truthfulness to it; maybe it takes courage to renounce naïve belief in the purposes and values your culture ascribes to the world. But this irony empties *everything* out: it drains the nobility out of truth, the virtue out of courage, until there's no longer any reason to be honest or brave.

Socrates's irony was not like this, for his trickery was intensely serious. While modern, Romantic irony delights in rendering all meaning unstable, Socrates unsettled ideas and values in order to grasp them again more firmly. He called his culture into question not out of nihilism or cynicism or mere cleverness, but from deep, earnest devotion to a 'higher something'. He couldn't say what this was, because it didn't exist yet in his world. Yet he longed for it, relentlessly pursued it, let his search for it animate his whole life and even take him to his death. When Socrates practised irony, he was honouring his god.

Like other people in Athens, Socrates went to the temple and made sacrifices – but he did these things differently: without certainty, without even faith and hope, but simply from longing, in an eternally questioning spirit.

If Socrates was the master of irony, Kierkegaard has been his apprentice. In his dissertation he wrote that 'no genuinely human life is possible without irony' – for each human soul yearns restlessly for truth, longs to know the source of its life, and feels this longing as its deepest need, its joy and its pain. Now his apprenticeship is over, and it is time for him to become 'genuinely human' himself – to ask his own questions in his own world, to honour his own god. A few years ago, when he was floundering and uncertain what to do with his life, he'd wanted to find 'an Archimedean point' where he could stand and move the world, 'an idea for which I can live and die'. Of course, he was foolish to think an *idea* would save him. But now he has found something to live for – and something to write about – which is indeed becoming his centre of gravity, anchoring his life and his work. It's not an idea, but a question, a provocation, in true Socratic style: *How can I be a human being in the world?*

This question, both simple and strange, confronts him continually, and it will preoccupy him for the rest of his life. It awaits him in every book he publishes, every decision he makes, every encounter on the streets of Copenhagen. It's what Regine meant to him – what she still means to him now. Of course, it echoes Socrates's questioning of 'becoming human, or learning what it means to be human', yet it also follows a long history of Christian thinkers who questioned the world, asking whether our life in this world helps or hinders the search for God.

Kierkegaard's question about how to be human in the world is unsettling – aren't we all human beings, whether we like it or not, and surely we cannot help but be in the world? Asking how to do something that we assumed we were already doing renders it questionable for the first time, and awakens a desire to know it. And being human in the world is the most basic, most universal thing we do; to question this is to question existence itself, injecting uncertainty, insecurity, an inarticulate sense of incompleteness and wonder into every gesture, every act – *does anyone here even know what it means to be human, what it means to be in the world?* Though the question makes no claim, propounds no thesis, it can transform everything.

This question of existence is perennial, ready to strike at any moment, but it is also constantly changing. Each time it is asked, it concerns a particular person at a particular moment of his life, in a particular time and place. Kierkegaard does not live in the world that Socrates inhabited, although Copenhagen, like Athens, has a harbour, a marketplace, and buildings dedicated to worship. He lives in Christendom, a world formed by eighteen centuries of Christianity: unlike the diverse cults of ancient Greece, its religion is ascetic, self-sacrificing, scriptural – a form of life reconfigured by Martin Luther three centuries ago. In Denmark the churches are Lutheran, the bibles are Lutheran, the schools are Lutheran. Luther distrusted philosophers, but now even the philosophy is Lutheran.

*Copenhagen Harbour by Moonlight, 1846*

Kierkegaard is deeply ambivalent towards Christianity, and he deploys the term 'Christendom' disparagingly. This old-fashioned word has become his epithet for a modern delusion, which resembles the cave Socrates described in Plato's *Republic*. For most of his contemporaries, being a person in this world means being a Christian in

Christendom: they believe themselves to be Christians just as they believe themselves to be human, without giving it a thought. They do not realize that becoming a Christian is a task – a task for a whole lifetime! – just as becoming human is, as Socrates discovered, a life-long task. They have forgotten the spiritual struggles of Luther, of St Augustine, of Jesus himself. At the end of the fourth century, Augustine began his *Confessions* with a prayer about searching for God: 'Our hearts, O Lord, are restless until they find their rest in you.' Luther, who spent years as an Augustinian monk before he broke with the Roman Church, found faith to be 'a living, restless thing', yet now that Lutheran religion is no longer a disruptive force but a long-established church, its original urgency has settled into tranquil complacency, or even indifference. A Socratic gadfly is needed to provoke and arouse the hearts of Danish Christians, to make them restless once again – to awaken their need for God. Kierkegaard's questions will buzz about insistently: Where, in Christendom, is Christianity to be found? Are there any Christians in the churches? At meetings of Moravian brethren? In the Theology faculty at the University of Copenhagen?

Kierkegaard also sees that the complacency of Danish Christendom is, like the comfort of the first-class carriage, a paradoxical repose. He believes that Christianity – its customs, its concepts, its ideals – has become so familiar, is taken so entirely for granted, that it might soon disappear beneath the horizon. Meanwhile, the world is changing more quickly than ever. These railways are just one part of it, but the miraculous motion of the fields, trees, farms and church spires flying past the train's windows proclaim his century's dash into the future. The way of life his parents knew is coming to an end. Denmark's economy has been in crisis; a political revolution is on its way. Everyone in the university is talking of history, progress, decline, theorizing about how the old gives way to the new. Kierkegaard is not the only person in Copenhagen who has a sense of being caught between two ages.

# 2

# 'My Regine!'

If he sits facing backwards and draws the little curtain from the window, he sees the miles travelled recede, watches his own journey unfold. He cannot see where the train is going: the landscape only comes into view once he has passed through it. He has come to think that life itself is like this. We have some knowledge of the past, but not of the future – and as for the present, it is continually in motion, always eluding our grasp. 'It is quite true what philosophy says, that life must be understood backward. But then one forgets the other principle, that it must be *lived forward*. This principle, the more one thinks it through, ends exactly with temporal life never being able to be properly understood, precisely because I can at no moment find complete rest to adopt the position: backward.'

He is wearing the engagement ring he gave to Regine Olsen in 1840. After she returned it to him he had it refashioned, the diamonds set in a small cross, and now the ring expresses what his words strive and stretch for: the paradox of remaining true to his love. Kierkegaard changed his mind and betrayed his promise, but his love for Regine is preserved within this symbol of an eternal love that encompasses all flawed, finite loves, and promises to make them whole. Forged from a crisis, this ring is a memento of his hopes and his mistakes; it will not let him forget his fiancée's tears; it embodies his change of heart. Nevertheless it is the emblem of a single heart, which dedicated itself first to one uncertain future, then to another – to a life with Regine, and then to a life without her.

Looking back from this curious position of simultaneous motion and repose, strangely outside time, Kierkegaard's own past stretches out before him. Like his future, it is always awaiting him. From this

Kierkegaard's ring

distance the whole of his engagement to Regine comes into view: its confused beginning, its uneasy duration, its fraught ending, its humiliating aftermath.

From the start, this relationship was charged with anxieties about his relationship to the world: should he set himself apart from the world like a hermit or a monk, or plunge into it – chase success, wealth, women; lay claim to the solid ground of a profession, a home, a family? Perhaps it is now becoming clearer that working out how to live in the world is the question at the centre of his philosophy and his life. For Kierkegaard, this question is never simply intellectual or pragmatic: it will always be a spiritual task, inseparable from the question of how to live in relation to God. He already had a sense of this when he met Regine for the first time, six years ago, at the home of his friend Peter Rørdam. Peter, a fellow theology student, had three pretty sisters; Kierkegaard particularly liked Bolette, and had visited the family with the thought of seeing her. As his conversation danced and his wit sparkled, he could feel his power to captivate the Rørdam sisters and their young friend Regine Olsen. That very day he thought of Jesus's warning, in Mark's Gospel, about what it profits a man if he gains the whole world but loses his soul. That night he wrote the verse in his journal. He saw himself 'returning to the world' after being 'dethroned' in his 'inner realm': it felt like some kind of fall, though whether it was a fall from grace or from his own pride was not easy to know. Was holding himself back from the world a temptation to be resisted, or an ideal to strive for? That was May 1837, just after his twenty-fourth birthday. Regine was a young girl, not yet sixteen, not yet confirmed.

Regine Olsen in 1840

Later that year he recorded in his journal that despite his poor health – he suffered from digestive problems and stomach pains, as well as from melancholy and hypochondria – he had 'managed to get out to R—'. Loneliness, anxiety about what other people thought of him, and frustration with himself spilled onto the page. 'My God, why should these feelings awaken just now – how alone I feel! oh, curse that arrogant complacency about standing on one's own – now everyone will despise me – oh, but you, my God, do not let go of me – let me live and improve myself!' Since then he often felt this tension within himself, this vacillation, in relation to Regine. And still now, six years later, when all has been decided outwardly, his heart is unresolved. He still has these conflicting desires, still the same impossible hope. Still it seems important to be faithful to her.

After that first meeting at Peter Rørdam's house, three years passed before Kierkegaard asked Regine to marry him. In that time his father died, and he finally completed his theology degree. He was about to begin his Magister's dissertation, and coming to a clearer sense of a new philosophical project. In recent decades Kant, Schelling and Hegel had pushed rationality to its limits; theoretical thinking seemed able to go no further. Yet these limits interested Kierkegaard. Where did he encounter the limits of understanding within himself – and where could he go from there? He had learned from Plato that human beings seek the truth because they do not yet possess it; but if they lack knowledge, how do they know how to find it?

When Socrates was asked this question – how can we learn anything at all? – he explained that each person has an eternal soul, which knows eternal truths. When a soul enters a body it forgets its knowledge, and needs to be taught to recollect it. Separated from the truth, we should spend our years in the world searching deep within ourselves to rediscover what we have lost. Kierkegaard thought about this idea during the summer of 1840, not long before he proposed to Regine. That July he wrote in his journal that Plato's doctrine of recollection is 'as beautiful as it is profound and valid' – for 'how sad it would be if human beings could only find peace in what lay outside themselves.' In fact the cities of Christendom throbbed and bustled with efforts to accumulate knowledge of the world by scientific experiment, historical research and news reporting, but were these cacophonous investigations drowning out quieter, deeper voices calling for self-understanding, for inner peace?

Plato's vision of souls recalling their lost knowledge led to questions about how this recollection happens: what kind of education brings young people closer to the truth? Although Hegel's philosophy – all the rage in Denmark as well as in Germany – also aspired to uncover and articulate an already-implicit truth, Kierkegaard found its methods too theoretical, its aims too worldly: the Hegelians aspired to an encyclopaedic knowledge of global history, of natural science, of different human cultures. Plato's philosophy was 'more pious', 'even a little mystical', giving rise to 'a polemic against the world'. It sought to 'quieten knowledge of the external world in order to bring about the stillness in which these recollections become audible'.

So perhaps truth could be found by withdrawing from the world. Kierkegaard thought about seeking the silence of the monastery;

Copenhagen's Franciscan friary was dissolved by reformers in 1530, but he could at least try to renounce the idle chatter of the university, which seemed to him just another strain of gossip from the market-place, only more deluded in its lofty aspirations. Were his own philosophical efforts anything more than a display of intellectual accomplishment in pursuit of worldly status and acclaim? Would those gains in the world mean losses in his soul, as the verse from Mark's Gospel implied?

And academic ambition was just one way of grasping at what the world had to offer. At that time Kierkegaard was obsessed with Mozart's *Don Giovanni*: he saw the opera performed at the theatre many times, and Don Juan, the great seducer, captured his imagi-nation. He wrote in his journal that the opera 'seized hold of me so diabolically that I can never again forget it – it was this play that drove me out of the quiet night of the cloister.' If he wished to return to silence and solitude after all these seductions – success, music, love – it would be difficult to do so.

But in another journal entry from July 1840 he sketched out a con-trary idea, that human beings do not reach their fulfilment by leaving the world behind. What if we find ourselves in relation to God *and* in relation to the world all at once, in the same movement? Here Kierke-gaard tried out the thought that worldly circumstances, which he summed up by the word 'finitude', were the fabric of religious life: 'I become conscious in my eternal validity, my divine necessity, *and* in my contingent finitude (that I am this particular being, born in this country, at this time, under the many-faceted influence of all these changing surroundings).' A human being's 'true life', he suggested, is the 'apotheosis' of finitude. This fulfilment is a spiritual elevation, but it 'does not mean stealing out of finitude to become volatilized and evaporated on the way to heaven, but rather that the divine inhabits the finite and finds its way in it'.

This account of spiritual life was one way of interpreting Christian teachings about how human beings can move towards an eternal truth. While Kierkegaard found in Plato's philosophy a 'polemic against the world', the Christian scriptures taught him that divine truth could be embodied within the world, in a human body. According to the New Testament, Jesus was Christ, the Son of God, who revealed the deep, mysterious power of his Father by 'inhabiting finitude', living in the world.

Yet Kierkegaard inherited a religious tradition deeply ambivalent towards the world. The goodness of God's creation is a fundamental tenet of Christian faith: the Book of Genesis describes how God made the world, and saw that it was good; the New Testament proclaims the 'good news' that God's Word became flesh; the Catholic Church instilled a faith in material sacraments – bread and wine, body and blood – as transmitters of divine grace; Luther brought spirituality into ordinary life with his earthy sensualism and his reforms allowing priests to marry. Alongside this positive view of embodied life persisted a more Platonic strand, entrenched in Christian theology by Augustine, who combined it with St Paul's doctrine of sin to emphasize the world's fallenness. According to Augustine, human beings are caught in a dark, troubled time between the first glory of creation and the radiant lights of final redemption. We twist in these shadows, inclining towards evil even as we yearn obscurely for the highest good.

This ambivalence is not just theoretical, but existential: it is a matter of how to live, what to do, who to be. Kierkegaard had to grow up within a world – and within a body – shaped and coloured by conflicting interpretations. If the Christian theology of incarnation showed that the spiritual and material aspects of life belong together, how should he put this into practice? How, for example, could he tell the difference between the yearnings of temptation and vocation? Perhaps he would be able to make this judgement in retrospect, with the benefit of hindsight – but what should he do when he felt his desires calling him, and had to choose which to follow? After all, although life might be understood backwards, it must be lived forwards.

Through all these reflections pulsed the question, *How to be a human being in the world?* The personal and philosophical aspects of this question became entwined and entangled. Where did love for another person, encountered in her own finitude, fit into these movements in and out of the world, back and forth between monastic solitude and the chatter of academic debates or literary salons? Does romantic love belong to the soul, or to the world? If a divine truth really inhabits the fluctuating world of human circumstances, then this could be a false dilemma – for perhaps the soul can find true love as well as true knowledge within its finite, embodied existence. Then worldly life need not be unspiritual: perhaps the soul does not lose itself in the world, but finds itself there.

Would marrying Regine be a way for Kierkegaard to realize this religious ideal – to actually live it out? It may have seemed so, late in the summer of 1840, as he 'drew closer to her'. He had passed his university exams, travelled out to the west coast of Jutland to visit the village where his father grew up, and then returned to Copenhagen in August. A few weeks later he proposed to Regine, torn between fitful passion and self-conscious detachment:

> On 8 September I left home with the firm intention of settling the whole thing. We met on the street just outside their house. She said there was no one at home. I was rash enough to take this as the invitation I needed. I went in with her. There we stood, the two of us alone in the living room. She was a little flustered. I asked her to play something for me as she usually did. She does so but I don't manage to say anything. Then I suddenly grab the score, close it not without a certain vehemence, throw it onto the piano and say: 'Oh! What do I care for music, it's you I want, I have wanted you for two years.' She kept silent. As it happens, I had taken no steps to persuade her, I had even warned her against me, against my melancholy. And when she mentioned a relationship with Schlegel, I said: 'Let that relationship be a parenthesis for I have first priority.' She mostly kept silent. Finally I left because I was anxious in case someone should come and see the two of us, with her so flustered. I went straightaway to her father. I was terribly afraid of having come on too strongly, and also that my visit might somehow occasion a misunderstanding, even damage her reputation. Her father said neither yes nor no, but it was easy to see he was well enough disposed. I asked for an appointment and got one for the afternoon of the 10th. Not a single word did I say to persuade her – she said yes.

But Regine's 'yes' did not resolve Kierkegaard's spiritual uncertainties. In fact, it seemed to exacerbate them. Just a few days later they met by chance on the street, and Regine did not recognize her fiancé at first: he had developed a 'melancholia' so intense that his appearance was quite altered. When they spent time together following their engagement he often wept, 'beside himself with sorrow and self-accusation'. Regine's father suffered from depression, so Kierkegaard's condition was familiar to her. She hoped to help him overcome it; she listened as he described his grief over the death of his father 'whom he had loved so much', his distress at being an inadequate son.

Yet Kierkegaard's depression was mixed with – maybe even caused by – worry that the engagement was a mistake. Perhaps he brooded on past sadnesses about his father to divert himself, or Regine, or both of them, from the grief that lay ahead. Soon after he proposed to Regine he started to write his dissertation on Socratic and Romantic irony. His friend Emil Boesen, who had studied theology with him, saw that he was beginning to understand more clearly 'what he himself wanted to do and what his abilities were'.

Always intensely aware of how others perceived him, Kierkegaard knew that marrying Regine would be more than a commitment to love, honour and protect her. Marriage was a public act that required him to occupy specific social roles – husband, father, head of a family – and to take up a profession. As a theology graduate, Kierkegaard would become a pastor or an academic theologian: a conventional religious teacher, and a paid official of the State Church. His life would be understood – it would be measured and judged – according to a well-established way of being in the world, shaped by a precise configuration of duties, customs, expectations.

Kierkegaard did not disparage these things. On the contrary, he wondered whether he was capable of them, and he feared the intimacy of marriage. And as the months went by he saw another kind of life open out ahead of him: he could become a writer instead of a husband. He could live on his inheritance from his father, give himself over to the philosophical task taking shape within him, let writing fill his existence. He could stand conspicuously on the margins of society, set himself at odds with it, call its assumptions into question, and allow his persistent sense of being an outsider to express itself in the world. He could become the Socrates of Christendom! And he could not subject Regine to the consequences of all this.

They were engaged for just over a year. They saw one another often, and frequently exchanged letters. Kierkegaard would send Regine

Letter from Kierkegaard to Regine, no date, sent with a scarf

notes by a messenger, arranging to visit her at home or offering to meet her after her music lesson; he wrote longer letters, poetic and affectionate, always addressed to 'My Regine!' and signed 'Your S.K.' or 'Yours eternally, S.K.' Often these letters accompanied a small gift: a rose, a violet heliotrope, a scarf, a handkerchief. Once he sent her a bottle of lily of the valley cologne – he loved this delicate white lily, the symbol of innocence that 'conceals itself so prettily within its big leaf', and the flower of May, the month of his birth. Regine sent Kierkegaard wildflowers, an embroidered lettercase, and a decorated box that, he assured her, 'is not used for tobacco but rather serves as a sort of temple archive'. On Regine's nineteenth birthday, in January 1841, he sent her a pair of candlesticks and promised to call on her later that day with another birthday present.

Each week Kierkegaard read aloud to Regine the sermons of Bishop Mynster, Denmark's most influential preacher and churchman. She tried to cheer him up by playing the piano for him: 'Although your playing may not be perfect in the artistic sense,' he wrote to her, 'in this you will, regardless, succeed. David was able to banish Saul's black mood, and yet I have never heard that he was a particularly great artist. I imagine it was his young, joyful, fresh spirit that helped so much, and you possess yet something more – a love for which nothing is impossible.'

In one letter Kierkegaard told Regine that her love 'rescued' and 'liberated' him:

> Know that every time you repeat that you love me from the deepest recesses of your soul, it is as though I heard it for the first time, and just as a man who owned the whole world would need a lifetime to survey his splendours, so I also seem to need a lifetime to contemplate all the riches contained in your love. Know that every time you solemnly assure me that you always love me equally well, both when I am happy and when I am sad – most when I am sad – because you know that sorrow is divine nostalgia and that everything good in a man is sorrow's child – know that then you are rescuing a soul from Purgatory.

Another letter to Regine was inspired by his reading of Plato's *Symposium*, which portrayed lovers as continually, restlessly desiring their beloved. Love never says, 'Now I am safe, now I will settle down,' wrote Kierkegaard, 'but runs on forever ... And what would even heavenly bliss be without wishing?' He quoted the Romantic poet Josef von Eichendorff, Paul's Letter to the Romans, the Gospel of Matthew, and ended the letter with an extravagant – yet subjunctive – declaration: 'If I dared to wish, then I certainly know what I would wish for. And that wish is identical with my deepest convictions: that neither Death, nor Life, nor Principalities, nor Powers, nor the Present, nor that which is to come, nor the Exalted, nor the Profound, nor any other creature may tear me from you, or you from me.'

Yet Kierkegaard was tearing himself away from Regine. By the summer of 1841 he had resolved to break off their engagement; he tried in August, but she begged him to stay with her. He described this time as 'fearfully painful – having to be so cruel, and loving her as I did'. The romance became a battlefield, the lovers adversaries. As late summer darkened into autumn Kierkegaard changed his tactics, feigning indifference to push Regine to end the engagement, but 'she fought like a lioness: if I had not believed there was divine opposition to the engagement she would have won.' Then he told Regine directly that *she* should break it off, so that he could take on her humiliation; 'she would have none of it, she answered that if she could bear the rest she could probably bear that too.'

Kierkegaard's niece Henriette Lund, who was then about twelve years old, visited Regine in that summer of 1841. Henriette felt a 'sense of foreboding' when she left the Olsens' house: 'Regine was just as loving as always, but it seemed to me that I noticed clouds in the skies that had previously been so bright. When we said goodbye, she followed me through the yard out to the Slotsholm side, where the canal had not yet been filled in at that time, and I remember how surprised I was at coming out of the shade and into the bright bath of light, where the sun played on the water. Here we once again said farewell, and for a long time afterward I could see her at the same spot in the clear sunshine with her hand over her eyes, nodding a last greeting to me – how definitively it was to be "the last" we did not know then, and yet I returned home with a feeling of something sad in the air.'

On 11 October Kierkegaard finally broke off the engagement. Still he had to struggle: Regine's father asked him to reconsider, for she was 'in despair, utterly desperate'. He felt moved by the humility with which this proud man, a Councillor of State, pleaded with him for the sake of his daughter, but he refused to change his mind. He visited Regine the following day and tried again to explain himself. She 'took out a small note on which there was something written by me which she used to carry in her breast; she took it out and quietly tore it into small pieces and said: "So after all, you have played a terrible game with me."'

A few days later Henriette Lund went with her brothers to visit her uncle Søren, who was staying at the Kierkegaard family home – a grand four-storey townhouse in the centre of Copenhagen, where his brother Peter Christian then lived with his new wife. 'When we children from Gammeltorv arrived there that evening,' remembered Henriette:

Uncle Søren immediately arrived to take us in to his apartment. He appeared much moved, and instead of his usual playfulness he kissed my hair so gently that I was quite touched. After a moment he wanted to speak to us, but instead broke into a violent fit of weeping, and without really knowing what there was to cry about – at least this was the case for me – but simply carried along by his suffering, we soon were all sobbing as if burdened with a heavy sorrow. Uncle Søren quickly pulled himself together, however, and he told us that one day soon he would leave for Berlin, perhaps to stay away for quite a while. We therefore had to promise to write to him frequently, because he would be anxious to hear how each of us was doing. With many tears, we promised.

The break-up, like the engagement, soon became a public affair, and for both Kierkegaard and Regine the pain of separation was deepened by wounded pride. Regine had fallen from expectant bride to rejected lover – probably destined to be a spinster, for who would want to marry her now? Kierkegaard appeared to be either a cad who had carelessly led a young woman astray, or a feeble, irresolute fool who, though twenty-eight years old and a Master of Theology, still did not know his own mind. 'It was an insulting break,' wrote his nephew Troels Frederik Lund, 'which not only called forth curiosity and gossip but also absolutely required that every decent person take the side of the injured party . . . here at home harsh judgements were unanimously voiced against him. Disapproval, anger, and shame were as strong among those closest to him as anywhere.'

On 25 October 1841, two weeks after the engagement ended, Kierkegaard boarded a Prussian mailboat to Kiel and travelled on to Berlin – philosophy's promised land, the intellectual capital of Christendom. Hegel had held the Chair of Philosophy at the University of Berlin through the 1820s, his final decade, and now Hegel's old rival Schelling was there, lecturing to audiences from all over Europe. On that first visit Kierkegaard stayed in Berlin for nearly five months, continued his philosophical studies, nursed his battered dignity, and wrote several hundred pages of *Either/Or*.

He returned to Copenhagen in the spring of 1842 and carried on writing. The finished book is a voluminous collection of disparate texts – letters, essays, a sermon, and a lengthy 'Seducer's Diary' – attributed to at least four fictitious authors, converging on the theme of romantic love and marriage. The most scandalous voice is that of the seducer, Johannes, who chronicles in minute detail and elegant prose his pursuit of a young girl, Cordelia – not to be confused with Regine's sister Cornelia. Johannes's story begins with obsessive stalking through the streets and lanes of Copenhagen, then develops into an intricate, manipulative courtship, and closes with the ambiguous ending of the affair. 'In my attack, I am beginning to close in on her gradually, to shift into a more direct attack,' he records during the early phase of his seduction: 'If I were to indicate this change on my military map of the family, I would say: I have turned my chair so that I am now turned sideways toward her. I am involved with her more; I address her, elicit her response. Her soul has passion, intensity, and, without being brought to the point of oddity by vain and foolish reflections, she has a need for the unusual. My irony over the foolishness of people, my ridicule of their cowardliness, of their tepid torpidity, captivate her.' A little later, he reflects that 'I shall very likely manage things in such a way that it is she herself who breaks the engagement . . . To poeticize oneself into a girl is an art; to poeticize oneself out of her is a masterstroke . . . I am intoxicated with the thought that she is in my power. Pure, innocent womanliness, as transparent as the sea, and yet just as deep, with no idea of love! But now she is going to learn what a powerful force love is.' His diary includes anguished letters from the young girl, written after her heart has been broken:

> Never will I call you 'my Johannes', for I certainly realize that you have never been that, and I am punished harshly enough for having once been gladdened in my soul by this thought, and yet I do call you 'mine': my seducer, my deceiver, my enemy, my murderer, the source of my unhappiness, the tomb of my joy, the abyss of my unhappiness. I call you 'mine' and call myself 'yours', and as it once flattered your ear, proudly inclined to my adoration, so shall it now sound as a curse upon you, a curse for all eternity . . . Yours I am, yours, yours, your curse.

Kierkegaard still sees this book as, in part, a continuation of his attempt to feign callous indifference to Regine, to persuade her that she was better off without him. He cannot admit, of course, that its theatrical sequence of masks and subterfuges was assembled from the wreckage of his pride, and that the Seducer's Byronic bravado, like his bold and ingenious philosophical arguments, did more to protest his own virility than to console Regine.

In February 1843 *Either/Or* was published by Carl Andreas Reitzel, who sold books by some of Copenhagen's most notable writers – Hans Christian Andersen, Johan Ludvig Heiberg, Frederik Christian Sibbern, and the anonymous author of *A Story of Everyday Life*. Yet Kierkegaard did not place himself among these eminent authors: *Either/Or* appeared in Reitzel's bookshops bearing the name of a fictitious editor, Victor Eremita. The choice of pseudonym – 'Conquering Hermit' or 'Solitary Victor' – seemed to celebrate a return to the cloister, but Kierkegaard remains ambivalent towards the 'monastic movement' of detachment from the world. True faith, he has realized, is not simply devotion to God, but faith in the world as a gift of God. This thought has preoccupied him in Berlin during this short second visit. If he'd had *this* faith – then he would have married Regine.

During their break-up, she said 'in her agony' that she would thank him her whole life if she could stay with him and live in a little cupboard in his house. In memory of those words, he has had a tall cabinet made from rosewood to his own design, with no shelves, like an upright coffin. This cupboard does not, thankfully, contain Regine – but it contains her absence. In it he carefully keeps 'everything reminiscent of her', including two copies of *Either/Or*, specially printed on vellum – 'one for her, and one for me'.

He is summoned from his recollections as the forests north of Eberswalde give way to open land: from the window of his carriage he suddenly sees, to the east, a crown of thorns rising from a field. It is a large pond encircled by sharp, stunted, leafless trees. He leans forward; it is gone in a moment, then a lake shines in the sunlight. And now the train slows and the modest spires of Angermünde come into view. Kierkegaard must surrender his solitude to the other passengers descending here, and those waiting for them on the platform. Once more he is in the world: he becomes again this slight, lopsided figure, limping a little as he walks, his stature heightened a few inches by the crest of hair swept up above his forehead. To those who look more closely he becomes again this pale intelligent face, above all these remarkable blue eyes, 'deep and soulful', shining with 'a mixture of good nature and malice'. He puts on his hat, takes up his cane, grips his bag, and continues on his journey home.

# 3

# In Defiance of Pseudo-Philosophers

After the comfort and seclusion of the train's first-class carriage, the stagecoach is grim. And it is a long, rattling ride: Kierkegaard will be in this cramped coach all the way to the port of Stralsund, still more than a hundred miles north. On the train he had only his thoughts to contend with; now his body is putting up a fight as well.

He has analysed the ordeal of the stagecoach in *Repetition*, the finished manuscript in his bag: 'There is a difference of opinion among the learned as to which seat in a stagecoach is the most comfortable. My view is the following: they are all equally terrible.' *Repetition*'s narrator Constantin Constantius recalls that on his first journey to Berlin he had 'one of the outer seats towards the front of the vehicle (this is considered by many to be a great coup) and was for thirty-six hours, together with those near me, so violently tossed about that I nearly lost not only my mind, but also my legs. The six of us who sat in this vehicle were worked together for these thirty-six hours so that we became one body, unable to recognize which legs were our own.' When Constantin returns to Berlin for his second visit, he chooses a seat in the coupé. Nevertheless, 'everything repeated itself. The coachman blew the horn, I closed my eyes, surrendered to despair, and thought, as I am wont to do on such occasions: God knows whether you will be able to endure this, whether you will actually reach Berlin, and if so, whether you will ever be human again, able to free yourself in the singularity of isolation, or whether you will forever carry this memory that you are a limb of a huge body.'

Like *Either/Or*, *Repetition* presents a ground-breaking philosophy of human freedom and responsibility, conveyed by characters immersed in romantic struggles and wrestling with questions about fidelity and marriage. Both books ask how a human being can live with others, keep his promises, and conform to social expectations, while remaining true to himself. And both blend philosophy with autobiography: *Repetition* carries a new message for Regine, named only as 'that single individual', exposing Kierkegaard's former strategy of romantic deception and offering different reasons why he could not marry her.

Writing in the wake of his broken love affair and seeking, however indirectly, to explain his change of heart to Regine, Kierkegaard has found a new way of doing philosophy. In addressing one particular human being in a singular situation, he has tapped into something universal – for the idea that '*every* human being is the single individual' is becoming more and more powerful within his work. He is creating a philosophy anchored in experience, in those questions made vivid by life's uncertainties and decisions; his concepts and arguments arise from the compelling drama of being human that unfolds within every person. A century later, his insight into the philosophical significance of 'the single individual' will inspire an entire generation of 'existentialists' to argue that human nature is not a fixed, timeless essence, nor a biological necessity, but a creative task for each individual life.

Stuck in this crowded stagecoach, Kierkegaard imagines himself towering above his peers – like Simeon Stylites, the fifth-century Syrian saint who lived on top of a pillar, conspicuously devoted to prayer, for more than three decades. People wondered whether he did it out of humility or pride: was he looking down on them from his superior height, or had he raised himself up like Jesus on his cross, held aloft in all his fragility, willing to be mocked and scorned? Simeon Stylites, the celebrity recluse: the paradox is irresistible; perhaps this should be his next pseudonym?

Last time he travelled home from Berlin, his honour still in question following the broken engagement, and *Either/Or* only half-written, he had yet to prove himself. Now that book is out, he is on his way to literary fame, an acclaimed author, whose talents will eclipse the most esteemed writers and scholars of his home town. He is already something of a celebrity: in these last three months *Either/Or* has been reviewed, debated and gossiped about everywhere. 'The entire press, from *Dagen* to *Aftenbladet*, from *Berlingske* to *Intelligensblade*, let out a cry of amazement, said a few words about it, of course, but began and ended by saying: My goodness, what a thick book,' wrote Meïr Aron Goldschmidt in his satirical weekly *The Corsair*. Heiberg himself reviewed *Either/Or* in his journal *Intelligensblade* – he called it 'a monster of a book', mainly on account of its 838 closely printed octavo pages, but also because 'one is disgusted, one is nauseated, one is revolted' by the Seducer's Diary.

Johan Ludvig Heiberg

Johan Ludvig Heiberg – playwright, critic, editor, aesthetician, whose passion for Goethe and Hegel has elevated Copenhagen's literary scene – was for years the person Kierkegaard most wanted to impress. He still wants to impress him, of course, even though he now disdains his opinion. He knows by heart that review of *Either/Or*: Heiberg found in the book 'bolts of intellectual lightning, which suddenly clarified entire spheres of existence', but regretted that 'the author's exceptional brilliance, learning and stylistic sophistication have not been combined with an organizational ability that would allow the ideas to emerge properly formed.' For days afterwards Kierkegaard drafted and re-drafted sardonic responses. Writing as Victor Eremita, he published a contemptuous 'Thank You' note in the newspaper *The Fatherland*. 'The Lord bless thy coming in, Prof. Heiberg! I will surely see to thy going out,' he wrote in his journal.

While readers of *Either/Or* are shocked and fascinated by the seducer's immorality, few grasp the book's deeper philosophical meaning or see the point of its intricate structure. Yet it has brought Kierkegaard the attention he craved, acclaim as well as notoriety; it has given him an expectant audience – and now, returning from Berlin a second time, it is time to consolidate his place as an author. After the scandalous success of *Either/Or* he must prove that he is not merely the gifted but frivolous stylist many take him to be. The day before he left Berlin this time, Kierkegaard wrote to Emil Boesen back in Copenhagen, telling him that he had finished *Repetition* and begun another book, *Fear and Trembling*. He did not mention in his letter that these two new works are written with Regine in mind. Instead he focused on their polemical impact: 'I shall never forget to employ the passion of irony in justified defiance of non-human pseudo-philosophers who understand neither this nor that, and whose whole skill consists in scribbling German compendia and in defiling that which has a worthier origin by talking nonsense about it.'

Emil would know exactly which 'pseudo-philosophers' his friend was talking about, for he has often listened as Kierkegaard poured his inimitable scorn on Hans Lassen Martensen – and, more recently, on Heiberg. Though not quite five years older than Kierkegaard, Martensen is already Professor of Theology at the University of Copenhagen. He is from Slesvig, on the border between Denmark and Germany; in the early 1830s, after studying theology in Copenhagen and being ordained in the Danish Church, he spent time in Berlin and Munich, befriended every important intellectual he could contrive to meet, and returned to Denmark an expert on the new philosophies of Schleiermacher, Schelling and Hegel.

These German thinkers were already fashionable in Copenhagen thanks to Heiberg, who went to Berlin in the 1820s, met Hegel, and actually conversed with the great man. Stopping in Hamburg on his way home, Heiberg had the deepest spiritual insight of his life, suddenly grasping Hegel's entire philosophical system: 'With Hegel on my table and in my thoughts, I was gripped by a momentary inner vision, as if a flash of lightning had illuminated the whole region for me and awakened in me the hitherto hidden central thought. From this moment the system in its broad outline was clear to me, and I was convinced that I had grasped it in its innermost core . . . I can say, in truth, that this strange moment was just about the most important juncture in my life, for it gave me a peace, a security, a self-confidence which I had never known before.' In the years following this philosophical conversion, Heiberg gave lectures on Hegel's philosophy at the University of Copenhagen. While Martensen was on his European study tour in the mid-1830s, his own star rising, he met Heiberg in Paris and cultivated a friendship with the eminent writer and his glamorous young wife Johanne Luise, Denmark's best-known actress.

Hans Lassen Martensen

Kierkegaard engaged Martensen as a private tutor in 1834, four years into his theology degree, and they read Schleiermacher together. Three years after that, still a student, he followed Martensen's influential courses on theology and the history of philosophy. The brilliant young lecturer urged his audience to look to the modern German philosophers – Kant, Fichte and Jacobi, but most of all Hegel – to guide their understanding of Christianity.

For years now Kierkegaard has disliked Martensen, disparaged his philosophical ambitions, and resented his success. And since that patronizing review of *Either/Or* in *Intelligensblade*, Heiberg has also become an enemy. Both men gained prestige by importing German idealism into Denmark: they bask in the reflected glory of Hegel's immense accomplishments. But Kierkegaard's new books will ridicule their efforts to combat the spiritual decline of the present age with second-hand Hegelian philosophy. His own ambitions as a writer have taken shape in opposition to Martensen, and to the academic and ecclesial establishment that favours him. For Kierkegaard, this well-connected professional theologian represents not just an intellectual position but an existential posture: Martensen is an influential example of what it means to be a cultured, reflective Christian in nineteenth-century Christendom.

His vow to defy 'non-human pseudo-philosophers' with his passionate irony echoes Socrates's subversive opposition to the Sophists. Plato portrayed those paid teachers of philosophy as peddlers of clever but shallow arguments, letting them be the foil for the genius of Socrates's existential irony. For Socrates, teaching philosophy meant teaching people how to be human – and he began by calling into question what a human being is. Likewise, Kierkegaard has sought to expose Martensen as a false teacher: he wants to uncover the hollowness of his work, to eclipse his philosophical facility with his own genius, to undermine the whole institution of theology in which his rival has ascended so quickly. Yet at the same time he wants to beat Martensen at his own game.

If this second trip to Berlin has repeated Kierkegaard's first, begun days after the final break-up with Regine, that first journey repeated Martensen's philosophical reconnaissance in the 1830s – which in turn followed the trail of Heiberg, who traced the footsteps of the intrepid Danish importers of Romanticism early in the century. By the time Kierkegaard made it to Berlin in 1841, Hegel had died, but he attended Schelling's lectures. While both Heiberg and Martensen returned to Copenhagen with career-advancing knowledge of German idealism, Kierkegaard brought home from that first visit a sharpened disillusionment with academic philosophy. 'Dear Peter, Schelling talks the most insufferable nonsense,' he wrote to his brother from

Berlin in February 1842. 'I am too old to attend lectures, just as Schelling is too old to give them. His whole doctrine of potencies displays the highest degree of impotence.'

Although Schelling spoke tantalizingly of 'actuality', Kierkegaard saw the entire academic enterprise as an evasive flight from actual existence. He connected this intellectual detachment with a cynical commercialization of knowledge: professors in the modern universities traded ideas as merchants traded commodities – but more duplicitously, for their smartly packaged abstractions contained no genuine wisdom. 'What philosophers say about actuality,' he wrote in *Either/ Or*, 'is often just as disappointing as it is when one reads on a sign in a second-hand shop: Pressing Done Here. If a person were to bring his clothes to be pressed, he would be duped, for the sign is merely for sale.'

With *Repetition* and *Fear and Trembling*, Kierkegaard is not just staging a new version of his engagement drama alongside a modern adaptation of the biblical story of Abraham. He is re-staging his own authorship, setting himself – or rather his pseudonyms – opposite Heiberg and Martensen on Copenhagen's literary scene. He is showing that he is a better dramatist than Heiberg, a better theologian and preacher than Martensen, a thinker of greater philosophical originality and more profound spiritual insight than either of them. Unlike his rivals, Kierkegaard has no pulpit or congregation, no lectern or students, no theatre or audience. He writes, he likes to say, 'without authority': simply as a human being, half-anonymous, with no costume of official position or institutional status. His writing will have to generate its own authority, to stake a claim through the sheer force of its argument and style. He is taking a stand as emphatically as Martin Luther when, legend has it, the polemical monk nailed his Christian manifesto to the church door at Wittenberg – though Kierkegaard is doing it indirectly, and under cover.

Without naming Martensen, *Fear and Trembling* will cast the Hegelian theologian as a nineteenth-century Sophist profiteering from dubious pedagogical enterprises. Plying the reader with a series of commercial metaphors, this new work will begin by declaring that 'in the world of ideas, as in the world of business, our age is staging a veritable clearance sale'. This is the crisis of spiritual value that

Østergade, Copenhagen, 1860: the omnibus to Frederiksberg

Heiberg, Martensen and their followers are already talking about – but Kierkegaard sees his rivals as symptoms, not saviours, of the crisis. He compares their philosophical vehicle to Copenhagen's new omnibuses, which offer a cheap alternative to carriage travel: in 1841 the first horse-drawn buses (*hesteomnibusser*) clattered through the city's streets, operated by a local entrepreneur inspired by similar ventures in Berlin, Manchester and Paris. In *Fear and Trembling* Kierkegaard will liken the students who jump aboard the bandwagon of Hegelianism to the rabble on these public carriages; he will sarcastically bestow 'every blessing upon the System, and upon the Danish shareholders in this omnibus'. The 'System' in question is Hegel's philosophical system, and 'omnibus' invokes metaphysics as well as transportation, for in his lectures on the history of philosophy Martensen had often repeated Descartes's maxim that everything should be doubted: *De omnibus dubitandum est.*

These sneers at Martensen and Heiberg will prepare a serious intellectual assault. Kierkegaard's years of study have taught him how traditional philosophical method proceeds by making distinctions between concepts – appearance and reality, faith and knowledge, necessity and freedom – and now he has begun to twist this method, applying it to life itself. He is developing a new kind of thinking to uncover the question which usually lies concealed, unasked, within every pursuit of knowledge: *how to be a human being?* His method draws distinctions not between concepts, but between 'spheres of existence': different ways of being human in the world. Highest is the religious sphere, revolving eternally on the axis of the God-relationship, infinite in its horizons and its depth. Other spheres of existence are smaller, more limited: their boundaries constrain the spiritual possibilities of those who live within them.

This new way of carving up the philosophical terrain has a sharp critical edge. It allows him to show how people, institutions, even entire cultures, fall short of the values they claim to embody. He assigns modern philosophy in general – and Heiberg and Martensen in particular – to the lowest, most constricted sphere of existence, which he calls disparagingly the 'aesthetic' sphere. This term invokes surfaces, dissemblance, detachment. In *Either/Or* he portrayed the aesthetic sphere, personified by the clever, dissolute young author of the 'Seducer's Diary', as existentially immature: the Seducer is not yet capable of the consistency and responsibility demanded by the ethical sphere, let alone the spiritual profundity of a truly religious life. This ill-formed character resembles Martensen, as Kierkegaard sees him – he flaunts his intellectual expertise, but when it comes to being human he is scarcely a beginner.

Although *Fear and Trembling* will not refer to Martensen by name, this book will expose his philosophical enterprise as both hubris and folly – and cheap, like the public buses. Martensen claims that

Hegel's philosophy elucidates the truth of Christian teachings, and embraces Hegel's ambition to show how this truth unfolded over centuries, through the progress of history. But Kierkegaard will argue that this devalues faith, and that the most essential truth unfolds within each human heart over the course of a lifetime – for love, the essence of God and the longing of every soul, is the deepest truth of Christianity. Learning to love is a new task for each individual: 'Whatever one generation learns from another, no generation learns the genuinely human from a previous one. No generation has learned to love from another; no generation can begin at any other point than at the beginning, no later generation has a shorter task than the previous one, and if someone here is unwilling to abide with love like those previous generations but wants to go further, then that is only foolish and idle talk.'

Kierkegaard knows that his educated readers will see in this argument an attack on Martensen. Yet while Kierkegaard mocks his rival's grandiose aspiration to 'go further' than Hegel in his philosophical enquiries, he is making his own grand appeal over the heads of this generation, beyond the intellectual fashions of this provincial scene. In daring to write about Abraham, he is claiming a place in the theological tradition: his new interpretation of Genesis 22 follows a history of polemical readings of biblical texts. This history has already proved the revolutionary power of scriptural exegesis, and Kierkegaard wants to change the game again.

The title of his book on Abraham comes from Paul's First Letter to the Corinthians, who were led astray by the 'human wisdom' of philosophers. 'When I came to you,' Paul wrote to the unruly Christians of Corinth, 'I did not come with lofty words or human wisdom (*sophia*) as I proclaimed to you the mystery of God. For I decided to know nothing among you except Jesus Christ, and him crucified. And I came to you in weakness and much fear and trembling.' Paul offered his own faith, empowered by 'the spirit which is from God', as a radical alternative to the diverse philosophies followed in Corinth, and he urged the Christian community there to rest their faith 'not on human wisdom but on the power of God'.

Like Luther, who gave lectures on the Book of Genesis three centuries ago, Kierkegaard will use the story of Abraham to expose the limitations of human reason and criticize the hubris of contemporary philosophy. As Paul attacked the Greek philosophers, so Luther rejected the scholastic methods that had shaped his own intellectual development: he argued that sixteenth-century theologians relied too much on Aristotle's pagan philosophy, and that only the Word of God revealed in the scriptures was an infallible source of truth. Kierkegaard does not share Luther's biblical fundamentalism, and draws liberally on ancient Greek thought: in *Fear and Trembling* he will present himself as a lyrical writer, a philosophical poet, who re-imagines Abraham for new generations of readers – just as Plato creatively transmitted the teachings of Socrates. Yet he will echo Luther's interpretation of Abraham in arguing that Martensen, like Hegel, overestimates the power of rational thinking to comprehend the truth of Christianity.

In his lecture on Genesis 22 Luther insisted that the contradiction between God's promise to make Abraham the father of a nation and his command to kill Isaac could not be resolved intellectually. It was impossible to understand Abraham's faith, he argued – and this showed that reason should surrender before faith, recognizing its higher authority and its deeper claim on the human heart. *Fear and Trembling* will make a similar argument. But whereas Luther praised Abraham's unquestioning faith in a contradictory God, Kierkegaard's interpretation of the biblical text is much more ambivalent: 'While Abraham arouses my admiration, he appals me as well.'

Abraham was willing to murder his own son, and Kierkegaard believes that this moral scandal cannot be taken lightly or explained away. By interrogating the ethics of the biblical story, *Fear and Trembling* will respond to Immanuel Kant's reading of Genesis 22 late in the last century. Kant insisted that we fulfil our duty to God simply by fulfilling our ethical duty to respect one another: in *The Conflict of the Faculties*, published in 1797 shortly after he was released from a ban on writing about religion, he wrote that 'apart from good life-conduct, anything that a human being supposes he can do to become well-pleasing to God is mere religious delusion or counterfeit service of God.' Here Kant argued that Abraham was wrong to obey the command to kill Isaac: instead, he should have reasoned that the command was contrary to the moral law, and therefore could not really be from God, but must be either a trick of the devil or a delusion.

While Luther drew from the story of Abraham a challenge to the rationalizing tendencies of his time, Kant – writing at the end of two long centuries of religious persecution throughout post-Reformation Christendom – invoked the same story to denounce blind adherence to so-called revealed truths. Though a Lutheran, Kant believed that human dignity lay in autonomous, rational moral judgements. Like other Enlightenment thinkers, he sought to bring order and peace to an unsettled society. Catholic, Lutheran and Calvinist leaders had all invoked the will of God – interpreted according to their own theologies – to sanction violence against dissenters; Kant's meticulous arguments advanced the ethical critique of religious dogmatism that had already been launched against the churches by radical thinkers like Spinoza and Voltaire.

Half a century later, Kierkegaard is addressing a different problem: he thinks Christian society has become too settled, too complacent. Confining religion to ethical life brings new dangers, for the individual's relationship to God – the heart of Lutheran spirituality – may be reduced to something all too human, all too worldly. Against Kant, Hegel has argued that rationality is not ahistorical and unchanging, but embedded within a specific culture; the moral law is not a transcendent truth, but a civic institution. This new interpretation of ethical life, when fused with Kant's insistence that religion be confined to the sphere of rational moral conduct, suggests that Christians fulfil their task of faith by conscientiously carrying out their professional, social and familial duties. But Kierkegaard believes that modern Christendom has corrupted the radical, scandalous teachings of the New Testament by merging the God-relationship with bourgeois values.

*Fear and Trembling* will warn that once God is absorbed into the ethical sphere he will become dispensable, and eventually disappear altogether. Although the ethical theories of Kant and Hegel have sincerely accorded to God the highest place, they are implicitly secular: reducing God to moral life makes human conventions, laws and judgements supreme – and then, Kierkegaard will argue, 'the whole existence of the human race is rounded off in itself, in a perfect sphere, and the ethical is at once its limit and its completion. God becomes an invisible vanishing point, an impotent thought, his power being only in the ethical.'

Without God, human beings will be left alone in a world with no divine order, no cosmic justice. And then morality itself will collapse, and life will lose its meaning: 'If there were no eternal consciousness in a human being, if underlying everything there were only a wild, fermenting force writhing in dark passions that produced everything great and insignificant, if a bottomless, insatiable emptiness lurked beneath everything, what would life be then but despair? If there were no sacred bond that tied humankind together, if one generation after another rose like leaves in the forest, if one generation succeeded another like the singing of birds in the forest, if the human race passed through the world as a ship through the sea, as the wind through the desert, a thoughtless and futile activity, if an eternal oblivion always hungrily lay in wait for its prey and there were no power strong enough to snatch it away – then how empty and hopeless life would be!'

By accentuating the horror of Abraham's story, Kierkegaard wants to shake his readers awake, to say *Look, listen,* this is what the God-relationship involves, *this* is what faith requires – it might disrupt your whole existence, overturn your sense of right and wrong, make you a criminal in the eyes of the world – and *now* do you claim to have faith? Jesus's disciples broke with the laws of their community, brought shame upon their families, with no guarantee that following their subversive, troublemaking teacher would bring the spiritual rewards they hoped for. If, eighteen centuries later, faith now means living an upright life, doing what everyone agrees is the right thing, then ethics and religion must be prised apart again to show that there might be a breach between them – and then it once again becomes possible to ask whether anyone is prepared to cross it.

*Fear and Trembling* will put this question to its readers, addressing each one as a 'single individual'. Kierkegaard is using the story of Abraham to sum up the spiritual crisis of his century, to mark a crossroads in the history of faith and show what philosophy has accomplished thus far. Christendom is coming to an end. There are two clear paths ahead: either let faith dissolve into rational, ethical humanism, or begin the task of faith anew. Neither path can be known in advance; both require those who call themselves Christians to learn how to live in their new world. And this task calls for a new teacher, a new philosopher, a new Socrates. One way or another the world is always there, making its claims and offering its temptations, but right now it is palpably changing – and philosophy has to change too.

He is impatient to get home to his library so that he can finish *Fear and Trembling*. He must get these two new books out – then he will show Martensen and Heiberg and the rest how far he has come, and how far he can surpass them all . . .

The miles seem interminable in this godforsaken stagecoach – only an Abraham could believe it otherwise! – and Kierkegaard's fellow passengers look as wretched as he feels. But who knows, perhaps each one of them is, this very moment, giving thanks to God in silent prayer – for we can never see another person's inward labour, nor know all the joys and sorrows stirring in another soul. Kierkegaard, for his part, is stiff, sore and shattered, and prays only that the coach will soon reach Stralsund.

# 4

## Following Abraham Home

Kierkegaard's wish to reach the port was eventually granted, and after a restless night in a hotel there he is ready for the final leg of his journey home. The boats in Stralsund's harbour and the smell of the sea make the call of Denmark more vivid and insistent. He boards the steamship *Svenska Lejonet*, which will sail overnight to Copenhagen. He is exhausted, but glad to be done with the stagecoach: now the horizons feel wider, his vision clear.

In Berlin he poured his energies into *Repetition*, fashioning from his own struggle for fidelity a new philosophy of life. For centuries philosophers have treated truth as an idea to be grasped intellectually, but in *Repetition* he investigated the truth of human hearts, which is found not in knowledge but in love. Drawing on this philosophical leap, the other manuscript in his bag sums up Abraham's faith in a simple answer to a perplexing question: 'What did Abraham achieve? He remained true to his love.'

He knows as well as anyone that this truthfulness does not come easily to human beings – for to live is to change, to encounter others who are also changing, to learn how to inhabit a changing world. While we exist in this world we continually forget and rediscover who we are. Kierkegaard promised to marry Regine, yet in making this very promise he gained new insight into himself which brought his promise into question. Now he is writing about Abraham, the great and terrible father of faith – what a story to be immersed in! For years he has thought about Abraham's extraordinary faith, and now the old patriarch's journey to Moriah shows his own vacillations and doubts in sharp relief, each step up the mountain measuring how far he has fallen short of Abraham's constancy and courage. He hopes in some way to remain true to Regine despite breaking the engagement. That might seem impossible, but Abraham's faith seemed impossible too.

He sees Abraham as 'a guiding star that saves the anguished' because he showed that faith is possible, even if how he did it remains a mystery. The star of Abraham, deep and unfathomable, has drawn into its orbit all the things that most concern him now, in 1843: his relationship to God, his spiritual ideals, his break with Regine; the inadequacies of modern philosophy, the complacency of the age, the threat of nihilism that is creeping into his century.

Meditating on Genesis 22 allows Kierkegaard to explore the dilemma of his own existence: how to be faithful to God – and to his own heart – within the world. Much of his life, like everyone else's, is occupied by petty concerns and narrow thoughts, and it is tempting to think that being spiritual means deeming all these things insignificant. Yet the New Testament offers a glimpse of a God who is found in the smallest details as in the greatest events – who counts every sparrow, every hair on a man's head. 'The important thing,' he recently wrote in his journal, 'is to be able to have faith in God with respect to lesser things; otherwise one does not stand in a proper relation to him . . . it is also important to draw God into the actuality of this world, where he surely is anyway. When Paul was aboard the ship that was about to capsize, he prayed not only for his eternal salvation, but for his temporal salvation as well.'

Kierkegaard drafted a short sermon on Genesis 22 in the autumn of 1840, soon after getting engaged, while he was training at Copenhagen's Royal Pastoral Seminary. He used Abraham's journey to Moriah to unsettle his imagined congregation's over-familiarity with the task of faith: 'We all know the outcome of the story. Perhaps it does not surprise us any longer because we have known it from our earliest childhood; but then, in truth, the fault lies not in the story but in ourselves, because we are too lukewarm to really feel with Abraham, to suffer with him.' In the midst of his anxiety and distress Abraham listened to 'the divine voice from heaven in his heart', and kept his 'trust in the future'. Yet the most extraordinary thing about Abraham, he suggested, was his joyful return to normal life: 'He headed home joyously, cheerfully, with trust in God; for he had not wavered, and he had nothing for which to blame himself.' At that time, with the prospect of marriage generating new anxieties, Kierkegaard might well have envied Abraham's confidence in his future. And returning to Abraham now, two and a half years later, he is even more aware of the difference between the patriarch's single-minded faith and his own uncertainty and ambivalence, between the aged father's serenity and his own bitter rage.

*Fear and Trembling* will explore further how Abraham's relationship to God did not draw him away from the world, but anchored him within it, arguing that Abraham's faith lay less in his obedient surrender of Isaac than in receiving Isaac back after giving him up. Abraham had already received an extraordinary gift when God fulfilled his promise that Sarah, his elderly wife, would bear a son. This child represented Abraham's future, all his hopes, his claim to greatness: Isaac meant the whole world to him. Then, years later, he was asked to sacrifice the boy, and with him the entire meaning of his own existence. He did so willingly, without losing trust in God's promise for worldly happiness. And so the divine gift was renewed: Abraham 'had faith for this life', and 'received a son a second time, contrary to expectation'.

In drawing these spiritual ideals from Abraham's story, Kierkegaard is forming an answer to the question that struck him six years ago, when he met Regine at Peter Rørdam's house: how to live religiously in the world. This question pursued him through the late 1830s, as he read Plato, listened to Mozart, completed his theology degree, and visited Regine. In 1840, just before he proposed to her, he had wondered whether it was possible to express his spiritual life through worldly things, so that 'the divine inhabits the finite, and finds its way in it.' But once he was engaged, the world and his soul seemed to pull in opposite directions and he felt forced to choose between them.

Now the story of Abraham shows him, more clearly than ever, the contrast between two kinds of religious life, distinguished by very different attitudes to the world. The sacrificial part of Abraham's movement – dragged out in the arduous journey up Mount Moriah and climaxing in the unthinkable binding of Isaac, the heart-stopping flash of a knife – is perceived by some people to be the summit of the

God-relationship. Kierkegaard admires the 'monastic movement' of withdrawal from the world, rarely attempted in this modern age where religious passion is no longer valued as it used to be. He calls those who live like this 'knights of resignation', in contrast to the successful figures in Danish public life who are appointed Knights of the Order of the Dannebrog by the king. While these worldly knights enjoy secular prestige, the knights of resignation stand apart from the world, spiritually elevated and remote.

Yet something higher still lies beyond them, a paradoxical peak that can be reached only by descending. Having renounced everything for the sake of God, Abraham made a further movement, returning to the world, embracing finitude, and living contentedly with his earthly gifts. Walking down the mountain with his son Isaac beside him, he was not just a knight of resignation, but a 'knight of faith'. For Kierkegaard, Abraham exemplifies a way of being human in the world that neither withdraws like a hermit or a monk, nor conforms to conventional bourgeois values. The 'guiding star' of Abraham belongs to a paradoxical constellation: a faith that is lived in the world, yet defies worldly expectations.

Kierkegaard imagines the movements of this faith as the light, graceful leaps of a ballet dancer – repeated again and again, each time a little different, and as arduous to perform as they are delightful to watch. The soul's dance expresses its longing for God, for eternity, for an unknown infinity. Most people are 'wallflowers' who do not take part in this dance; the knights of resignation 'are dancers, and possess elevation' – but when they land, they falter, showing that they cannot be at home in the world.

A knight of faith, however, lands as easily as he leapt, 'transforming the leap of life into a walk'. He makes existence look so easy that there is nothing to tell him apart from the most unreflective, spiritless person who, immersed in everyday concerns, sees no significance in life beyond its immediate satisfactions and disappointments. The knight of faith's relationship to God is entirely inward, hidden from public view. A divine grace sustains each step of his journey through the world, but he receives this gift secretly, in silence.

In *Fear and Trembling* Kierkegaard will describe a knight of faith who looks as ordinary as a bureaucrat – like a tax collector:

I examine his figure from head to foot to see if there might not be a crack through which the infinite peeped out. No! He is solid through and through. His footing? It is sturdy, belonging entirely to finitude. No dressed up citizen going out on a Sunday afternoon to Frederiksberg treads the ground more solidly. He belongs entirely to the world; no bourgeois philistine could belong to it more. Nothing is detectable of that foreign and noble nature by which the knight of infinite resignation is recognized. He enjoys and takes part in everything, and whenever one sees him participating in something particular, it is carried out with a persistence that characterizes the worldly person whose heart is attached to such things. He goes about his work. To see him one would think he was a pen-pusher who had lost his soul in accountancy, so exact is he. He takes a holiday on Sundays. He goes to church. No heavenly look or sign of the incommensurable betrays him. If one did not know him, it would be impossible to distinguish him from the rest of the crowd.

Within this undistinguished figure is an extraordinary soul. Beneath his carefree manner he labours at the most difficult human task – just as the ballet dancer's lightness comes only after years of hard training. The knight of faith 'buys every moment he lives for the dearest price: He empties the deep sadness of existence, he has felt the pain of renouncing everything, the dearest thing he has in the world, and yet the finite tastes every bit as good to him as to someone who never knew anything higher.'

Kierkegaard's distinction between 'knights of resignation' and 'knights of faith' offers a new response to a traditional philosophical problem. For centuries theologians have struggled to explain how a loving God could have created this world, with its all-too-evident sufferings and injustices; despite every ingenious argument to resolve the contradiction between the goodness of God and the evils of his creation, this contradiction remains for many people the biggest stumbling-block to faith. Yet Kierkegaard knows as well as anyone that suffering is not merely a philosophical problem – for the task of faith is not to explain suffering, but to live with it. Our most urgent existential questions ask not *Why do we suffer?* but *How should we suffer?* Like many religious people, Kierkegaard might wonder, in times of crisis, about the reasons for his suffering, but meanwhile he has to find a way to live daily with the contradictions between his expectations and his experience, between his belief in God and his dispiriting knowledge of the world.

From the manuscript of *Fear and Trembling*

He thinks that attempts at easy religious consolation, which cut too quickly to promises of a happy ending, are like the metaphysical conjuring tricks of theologians who argue that evil has no real existence because it is only the absence of goodness. He has observed among his contemporaries this tendency to soothe away the pains of living in the world: *Fear and Trembling* will describe a drowsy congregation comforted by a sermon which reassures them that Abraham's spiritual trial turned out well in the end, so that 'they leave out the distress, the anxiety, the paradox' within faith. Privately he criticizes Bishop Mynster, leader of the Danish State Church (and a Knight of the Dannebrog), for 'giving consolation by saying that things may perhaps take a turn for the better, that happier days are coming, etc.' For Kierkegaard, Mynster's response to anxiety and distress offers 'worldly wisdom', not 'genuinely religious consolation'.

By contrast, his own interpretation of Abraham shows that 'only the one who is in anxiety finds rest, only the one who draws the knife gets Isaac.' The cost of faith is always high: look at Jesus's mother, Mary, as she is depicted at the start of Luke's Gospel, when the angel

Gabriel visits her and she conceives a divine child. History later turned her into a holy queen, yet at this moment she was just an obscure girl, unmarried and mysteriously pregnant; no one else saw the angel, and 'no one could understand her' – 'Is it not also true here that the one whom God blesses he curses in the same breath? Mary needs no worldly admiration, just as little as Abraham needs tears, for she was no heroine and he was no hero, but they both became greater than these, not by being exempt from distress and torment and the paradox, but through these things.'

Kierkegaard's imagined knights of resignation and of faith are noble figures who boldly enter the battlefield of existence and confront its trials. He does not claim to be either of these knights himself: he is writing *Fear and Trembling* in the guise of a pseudonymous author who can imagine making the movements of renunciation, but finds faith impossible. 'I have looked the frightful in the eye; I do not timidly flee from it but I know very well that even if I approach it bravely, my courage is still not the courage of faith and is nothing to be compared with that,' confesses this nineteenth-century Simeon Stylites.

Kierkegaard insists that religious faith requires 'a paradoxical and humble courage', a virtue quite different from the dubious sacrificial heroism he aspired to in relation to Regine. A connoisseur of anxiety, he knows that fear is the great enemy in the spiritual life – and that courage is required to overcome it. 'Do not be afraid,' Jesus constantly told his disciples: he saw how fear contracted their hearts, preventing them from loving or receiving love; how it made them flee from the loss that follows human love like a shadow. Courage is traditionally understood as strength of heart – like the bravery of a soldier who faces the dangers of battle – but on the battlefield of existence hearts must be open as well as strong if they are to become fully human, and this is why Mary and Abraham are among the greatest spiritual exemplars. Kierkegaard calls their open-heartedness 'humble courage', and he understands too well how difficult it is to accomplish: 'It is harder to receive love than to give it,' he will admit in *Fear and Trembling*.

During this brief second visit to Berlin, he cemented a cornerstone of his philosophy: there is something contradictory about being a human in the world. His social relationships shape his life and form his self-consciousness, but the way he appears to others never quite matches his inward truth. He is on display, seen and judged, and yet his inability to disclose himself makes him feel alone. Human existence is at once inescapably public and intensely private. And the deeper a person's inner life, the more profound this contradiction becomes. Kierkegaard doubts that anyone can comprehend, let alone judge, another person's religious life, for 'the first thing the religious does is close its door and speak in secret', as God spoke to Abraham and as the angel spoke to Mary. Of course, religious people have to live conspicuously in the world like everyone else, though they harbour a 'secret' that is not willingly concealed, but impossible to express: 'Inwardness is incommensurable with outwardness, and no person, even the most open-hearted, manages to say everything.'

Each day in his familiar Berlin lodgings overlooking Gendarmenmarkt, Kierkegaard spent time in contemplation, connecting with his own inwardness and sinking deeper into it: 'I sit and listen to the sounds in my inner being, the happy hints of music and the deep earnest of the organ. Working them into a whole is a task not for a composer but for a *human being* who, in the absence of making heavier demands upon life, confines himself to the simple task of wanting to understand *himself*.' Writing is inseparable from this effort of self-understanding: it is through words as well as through silence that he brings coherence to the motions of his soul. Yet for Kierkegaard this is always a paradoxical exercise, revealing and concealing at the same time – like telling someone you have a secret that can't be told. Writing gives his most solitary reflections a public aspect, exhibits the contradiction between his inward and outward life, brings his hiddenness into the open. He evasively offers to the world an image of himself, going to great lengths to explain that he cannot be understood.

In *Fear and Trembling* Kierkegaard will communicate something about the nature of a faith that is, he insists, incommunicable. And his journals are in this respect no less paradoxical than his published writing: he expects them to be read by others, perhaps treated as a true record of his inwardness. 'After my death,' he wrote in his journal this year, 'no one will find in my papers (this is my consolation) the least information about what has *really* filled my life, find *that* script in my innermost being that explains everything, and which often, for me, makes what the world would call trifles into events of immense importance, and which I too consider of no importance once I take away the secret note that explains it.' When Kierkegaard writes something truly private, he cuts it out of his journal with a knife and throws it on the fire.

He is consoled by the thought of remaining hidden because he has been so afraid of being seen. Perhaps it was this, above all, that made him unable to marry: sheer anxiety, compounded by high ideals. He believes that marriage requires complete openness between husband and wife; 'so many a marriage conceals little histories,' he wrote in Berlin on 17 May, 'but I didn't want that'. Here, in a long journal entry reflecting on the engagement – from which one page was excised – he partially revealed his inability to reveal himself to Regine: 'If I were to explain myself I would have had to initiate her into terrible things, my relationship to father, his melancholy, the eternal night brooding deep inside me, my going astray, my desires and excesses, which in the eyes of God are nevertheless perhaps not so glaring, since after all it was anxiety that made me go astray.'

Yet Regine, though so much younger and less educated than Kierkegaard, saw something of his soul in spite of all his evasions. Last month, before he left for Berlin, a silent encounter with her made him realize that she was not fooled by his attempts to mislead her after their engagement ended. Although he had tried to hide from her, she had seen him: 'On Easter Sunday at evensong in the Church of Our Lady (during Mynster's sermon) she nodded to me. I do not know whether pleadingly or forgivingly but in any case affectionately. I had taken a seat at a remote spot but she noticed me. Would to God she hadn't. Now a year and a half of suffering are wasted and all the enormous pains I took; she does not believe I was a deceiver, she trusts me . . . Shall I in sheer madness go ahead and become a villain just to get her to believe it – ah, but what good would that do? She will still think that I wasn't [a villain] earlier.'

So now he has given up on his plan to feign indifference, supposedly for Regine's sake: he can relinquish the role of heartless seducer, which he dramatized in *Either/Or*. Of course, being away from

Copenhagen put him at a safe distance from Regine's trusting gaze, and the two books he worked on during this second stay in Berlin still interpose the voices of fictitious pseudonyms between himself and his readers. But his writing continues to reach out to Regine, even as he takes care to keep himself out of reach.

When she reads *Fear and Trembling*, will Regine recognize her Kierkegaard in Abraham, who renounced his beloved for the sake of an inexplicable higher purpose? Will she now be consoled by the spiritual significance of her suffering? Will she feel herself inspired to become a knight of faith, who willingly surrenders the gift she was given, trusting that worldly happiness will be restored to her? Or should she see how far she has fallen short of this ideal, realize how much suffering *she* caused *him* by resisting with all her devotion, all her tears, his efforts to break the engagement?

And what about Kierkegaard – who will he be when he arrives back in Copenhagen? How will he return to his world? What will his neighbours make of him? After these three solitary weeks in Berlin, he knows very well how it feels to be a 'stranger in the world'. Once he is home, will he remain a stranger among all the people who think they know him – a knight of resignation? Or can he find a way to land gracefully, like Abraham the aged father, like Mary the expectant mother, like an accomplished ballet dancer who expresses the inward leaps of faith?

The first time he returned home from Berlin, in 1842, Copenhagen seemed small, parochial, full of familiar faces. He knows very well how narrow life can feel within its medieval walls – and how quickly gossip flies through its streets and squares. Compared to Berlin, or Paris or London, Denmark's capital is a market town. But unlike those other cities Copenhagen looks out to sea: even in Gammeltorv the salty air and clear light can evoke waves and winds, mermaids and sailors, great skies and far horizons, and up on the ramparts this wide watery world comes into view. Kierkegaard's close acquaintances include men who have sailed to Greenland, to North America, to China, to Brazil; his own father made his fortune selling goods shipped to Copenhagen from the East and West Indies. Is it surprising that a Scandinavian soul like his echoes with the sounds of the sea, senses unseen possibilities, knows the ocean's expansiveness and depths? Or that his engagement crisis made him 'descend into dark waters', brought him close to drowning – even though he could say afterwards that his soul needed this 'baptism'? 'Everything churns inside me so that it seems that my feelings, like water, will break the ice with which I have covered myself,' he wrote to Emil Boesen back then, during his first stay in Berlin.

As the sun sets over the Baltic late in the evening the vast sky turns pink and blue and gold. Kierkegaard knows that countless stars hide in this last dance of daylight, waiting for darkness to fall. The bright spring of 1843 – the brightest yet, for he has been born as an author, *Either/Or* is a success, and new books are already blossoming within him – is nearly over, and the northern nights are shortening quickly now. He should try to get some rest. The steamship will arrive in Copenhagen's harbour tomorrow morning – and then he will get back to work.

# PART TWO

# 1848–1813:
# Life Understood Backwards

*Assigned from childhood to a life of torment that perhaps few can conceive of, plunged into the deepest despondency, and from this despondency again into despair, I came to understand myself by writing.*

# 5
# Learning to be Human: Lesson One

The house is still, and he stands by the tall window looking out at Nytorv, smoke rising from his pipe. On this clear spring night the wide square is silvery and shadowy in the moonlight. Over to the left, above the rooftops, he can make out the imposing tower of the Church of Our Lady, darker than the sky. It is the end of March in 1848, and nearly five years have passed since he returned home from Berlin, a newly celebrated author, hopeful and ambitious, carrying *Repetition* and half of *Fear and Trembling* in his bag. And nearly thirty-five years have passed since he was born in this house: his parents were both peasants by birth, yet his father made enough money to acquire one of the most enviable addresses in Copenhagen. As a small boy Kierkegaard sometimes stood just here, unseen, watching the passers-by below. Then, as now, he surveyed the world from his privileged vantage point, his pride secretly laced with shame for his dubious origins.

He spent the first twenty-four years of his life in this large, elegant house on Nytorv, adjoining the city hall and courthouse. These wide rooms were home before his memories were formed, before he knew the names of things, before he began to ask questions – a prehistoric, mythical place that has shaped him in ways it may take a lifetime to fathom.

He returned to live here four years ago, in 1844: in this room he wrote much of what he now calls his 'authorship', and the tall rosewood cabinet is piled high with his own books – two copies of each, printed on vellum, 'one for her, and one for me'. During those four years he often resolved to stop writing and become a pastor in 'a forgotten remoteness in a rural parsonage', where he would be left in peace to 'sorrow over his sins'. Instead he produced one book after another: slim volumes of religious discourses, and short intense works like *Philosophical Fragments* and *The Concept of Anxiety*, then the enormous *Stages on Life's Way* and *Concluding Unscientific Postscript*. And with every book he renewed his struggle to decide whether his authorship should end; *Concluding Unscientific Postscript*, which came out in 1846, explicitly brought it to a close, and ended with a 'First and Last Declaration' acknowledging that he, S. Kierkegaard, had written the works attributed to his various pseudonyms. But his weighty *Postscript* was quickly followed by *Two Ages*, a book masquerading as a book review, and the following year by *Works of Love*, a thick volume of discourses. He still does not know whether the end of his authorship lies behind him or ahead of him; in any case, he is writing furiously.

He has spent much of his father's fortune on this authorship – not just print runs of hundreds of copies of each book, and the secretarial assistance of Israel Levin, but everything he needs to sustain his life as a writer: servants, fine food, restaurants, coffee shops, cigars, books and bookbinding, hired carriages when he has to drive out of town to clear his head. Last year, 1847, he sold the last of his inherited stocks and royal bonds, losing the income they yielded, so in December he raised more cash by selling his family home. He has remained here as a tenant through the first three months of 1848, while the long dark winter slowly thawed. Meanwhile, his servant Anders, who manages his household affairs, packed his library into wooden trunks, now lined neatly along the walls. His unpublished papers and journals are kept in tin boxes, in case of fire; these are stacked on top of the trunks, for Anders knows he must save them first if the house is burning down.

When Kierkegaard sold the house, he planned to use some of the proceeds to travel for a couple of years: he is sick of Copenhagen, where he is so well known and so little understood. He hoped that going away would finally release him from his exhausting, angst-ridden yet compulsive cycle of rapid production and publication. Then he realized that travelling would probably stimulate his creativity even more, as it did during that fraught, thrilling first visit to Berlin, when his authorship began. So he invested some of the money from the sale of 2 Nytorv in royal bonds, and at the end of January signed a lease on an expensive first-floor apartment on the corner of Rosenborggade and Tornebuskegade, just inside the northern city wall, 'which had tempted me in a quite curious way for a long time and that I had often told myself was the only one I could like'. It is a grand, modern residence: six windows of the *bel étage* face north-east, over Tornebuskegade, and four windows look south-east over Rosenborggade. He will move there in April, now just a few days away. He longs to leave the city and retreat to a quiet place – yet he believes it is his 'calling' to remain in the world, in the place God has 'assigned' to him: here in his home town, exposed to the public eye.

As Kierkegaard stands by the first-floor window of 2 Nytorv, contemplating his future and circling again and again to his past, revolutionary tides are swelling and surging through Christendom. In February *The Communist Manifesto* was published in London, and quickly distributed to other European cities; in Paris another king has been overthrown; waves of protest are now breaking across Denmark. Here in Copenhagen, crowds have gathered in theatres to hear Orla Lehmann and Meïr Aron Goldschmidt call for universal male suffrage, a free constitution, even a Danish republic. Nationalist feeling runs high, flowing through the well-worn channels of hostility to foreign neighbours, yet also taking new and unpredictable forms: as the monarchy's absolute rule is challenged, conservatives, liberals and peasants are jostling for power.

In January King Christian VIII died, afraid of communism and anxious about what the new year would bring. Kierkegaard knows this because the old King, who admired his writing, invited him to Amalienborg Palace three times last year, and on each occasion they talked mostly about politics. During his last visit he tried to reassure the King that this 'class conflict' was like a dispute between neighbouring tenants, which need not trouble their landlord, and 'the whole movement would not touch kings at all'. He added that it was 'miserable to be a genius in a market town' – perhaps King Christian was fortunate to have only an uprising on his hands.

Yet the late King's fears have been confirmed: a few days ago, on the morning of 21 March 1848, thousands gathered outside the city

King Christian VIII of Denmark in 1845

hall on Nytorv, beneath Kierkegaard's window, shouting for a change of regime. The crowds were then led by L. N. Hvidt, chairman of the city government, to Christiansborg Castle to petition the dissolute new king, Frederik VII, Christian VIII's eldest son. The people's address to the Crown, written by Orla Lehmann, demanded a free constitution; King Frederik had to agree to dismiss his ministers, and a temporary 'March Ministry' was hastily formed. Now, as the trees up on Copenhagen's grassy ramparts crown the city with pink and white blossom, the long-standing conflict between Danes and Germans over the southern border duchies of Holsten and Slesvig is erupting into war – for, Kierkegaard observes, 'the new ministry needs a war in order to stay in power, it needs all possible agitation of nationalistic sentiments'.

'Out there everything is agitated; the nationality issue occupies everyone; they're all talking about sacrificing life and blood, are perhaps also willing to do it, but are shored up by the omnipotence of public opinion,' he wrote in his journal this week, as the fighting broke out in south Jutland. 'And so I sit in a quiet room (no doubt I will soon be in bad repute for indifference to the nation's cause) – I know only one risk, the risk of religiousness.'

But no one seems to care about this, or understands it. 'Well, such is my life. Always misunderstanding. At the point where I suffer, I am misunderstood – and I am hated.' He has a trail of difficult years behind him, which are not so much receding into the past as accumulating upon his present. Under their weight, he is being drawn into intensified reflection on his own unhappiness. The devastating events of 1846 – the months of public humiliation and ridicule he suffered – have decisively changed his relationship to his city and his view of the world. At times he puts himself under such 'enormous strain', feels so physically weak, that he believes he is dying. Although his authorship is a burden, he finds relief only in writing: here at home, especially in the quiet night hours, the words run freely from his pen, fluid thoughts dance with joy across the open page, not yet printed and paper-bound, not yet revealed to the public's innumerable, unforeseeable eyes. Often he returns home from his daily walk and goes straight to his writing desk, still in his hat and coat, new sentences flowing from his hand. And he continues to walk as he writes, pacing back and forth, feeling the rhythm of his prose. There are paper, pens and ink in every room: fine writing paper, cut to quarto size, folded, and sewn into booklets by his bookbinder; modern steel pens, and pencils for crossing out; good-quality black ink. He works late into the night, his windows glowing into the deserted square.

He has spent these last weeks in Nytorv writing a new work, *The Sickness unto Death*. This is a diagnostic manual for lost souls; it sets out Kierkegaard's philosophy of human existence more lucidly and directly than any of his previous works. The opening pages declare that human beings are not just bodies and minds, but spiritual beings, related to a higher power. Yet our spiritual lives are not given to us, ready-formed if not full-grown, as our bodies are: we all face the task of becoming ourselves. This means living each moment in relation to God, constantly turning and returning to the eternal source of our being. 'There is so much talk about wasting a life, but only that person's life was wasted who went on living so deceived by life's joys or its sorrows that he never became decisively and eternally conscious as spirit, as a self – or, what amounts to the same thing, never became aware in the deepest sense that there is a God and that he, he himself, exists before this God – an infinite benefaction that is never to be gained except through despair.'

Yes: despair is a benefaction, a blessing, for it is the sign of a human being's connection to God, his highest possibility. And yet it is also a curse, for the depth of the human soul is measured by the intensity of its suffering. 'Is despair an excellence or a defect? Purely dialectically, it is both. If only the abstract idea of despair is considered, without any thought of someone actually in despair, it must be regarded as a surpassing excellence. The possibility of this sickness is man's superiority over the animal, and this superiority distinguishes him in quite another way than does his upright walk, for it indicates infinite uprightness or sublimity: that he is spirit . . . Consequently, to be able to despair is an infinite advantage, and yet to be in despair is not only the worst misfortune and misery – no, it is ruination.'

And this ambiguous spiritual disease is, Kierkegaard suggests, universal – as far as he can tell; he can only see into his own soul, though the better he knows himself the more he discerns the reflections of his own despair in others:

> Just as a physician might say that there very likely is not one single living human being who is completely healthy, so anyone who really knows mankind might say that there is not one single living human being who does not despair a little, who does not secretly harbour an unrest, an inner strife, a disharmony, an anxiety about an unknown something or something he does not even dare to try to know, an anxiety about some possibility in existence or an anxiety about himself, so that, just as a physician speaks of carrying an illness in the body, he walks around carrying a sickness of spirit that signals its presence at rare intervals in and through an anxiety he cannot explain.

To be in despair is to lose one's true self, and those who realize they suffer from this disease long for a cure. Yet most people, he has observed, lose themselves in this world without even realizing it: 'The greatest hazard of all, losing the self, can occur very quietly in the world, as if it were nothing at all. No other loss can occur so quietly; any other loss – an arm, a leg, five dollars, a wife, etc. – is sure to be noticed.' And indeed, to the world this spiritual carelessness looks like the ease of a happy, successful life: 'Just by losing himself in this way, such a man has gained an increasing capacity for going along superbly in business and social life, for making a great success in the world. Here there is no delay, no difficulty with his self and its infinite movements; he is as smooth as a rolling stone, as *courant* as a circulating coin. He is so far from being regarded as a person in despair that he is just what a human being is supposed to be.'

This worldly view is perverse, paradoxical, unwittingly ironic. However vain and conceited people may be – and however much such attitudes are encouraged in the world – by this very worldliness they belittle themselves, refusing their higher spiritual calling. Choosing a metaphor apt to his present circumstances, Kierkegaard asks his reader to:

> imagine a house with a basement, ground floor, and first floor planned so that there is supposed to be a social distinction between the occupants according to floor. Now, if what it means to be a human being is compared with such a house, then all too regrettably the sad and ludicrous truth about the majority of people is that in their own house they prefer to live in the basement. Every human being is a psychical-physical synthesis intended to be spirit; this is the building, but he prefers to live in the basement, that is, in sensual categories, merely a body. Moreover, he not only prefers to live in the basement – no, he loves it so much that he is indignant if anyone suggests that he move to the superb upper floor that stands vacant and at his disposal, for he is, after all, living in his own house.

But how does a person become 'eternally conscious as spirit' here in the world, where there is so much else to do? How can he express his spiritual nature in all these everyday places – in quiet furnished rooms, on bustling streets, in smoky cafés, at the theatre, in the marketplace, or strolling in the Frederiksberg Gardens? Only by becoming 'transparent to himself', and feeling his despair in all the complex, shifting, uncertain forms it has taken within his soul:

Very often the person in despair probably has a dim idea of his own state, although here again the nuances are myriad. To some degree, he is aware of being in despair, feels it the way a person does who walks around with a physical malady but does not want to acknowledge forthrightly the real nature of the illness. At one moment, he is almost sure that he is in despair; the next moment, his indisposition seems to have some other cause, something outside of himself, and if this were altered, he would not be in despair. Or he may try to keep himself in the dark about his state through diversions and in other ways, for example through work and busyness, yet in such a way that he does not entirely realize why he is doing it, that it is to keep himself in the dark. Or he may even realize that he is working in this way in order to sink his soul in darkness and does it with a certain keen discernment and shrewd calculation, with psychological insight; but he is not, in a deeper sense, clearly conscious of what he is doing, how despairingly he is conducting himself.

All this dwelling on despair might strike people as too extreme, and as 'a sombre and depressing point of view'. Kierkegaard believes it is none of these things: 'It is not sombre, for, on the contrary, it tries to shed light on what generally is left somewhat obscure; it is not depressing but instead is elevating, inasmuch as it views every human being under the destiny of the highest claim upon him, to be spirit.' Indeed, like Socrates, he regards these provocations as a service to his country. Instead of fighting the Germans in Slesvig-Holsten, or campaigning for popular reform, or defending the monarchy, he is battling for a spiritual cause: 'I love my native land – it is true that I have not gone to war – but I believe I have served it in another way, and I believe I am right in thinking Denmark must seek its strength in the spirit and the mind. I am proud of my mother tongue, whose secrets I know, the mother tongue that I treat more lovingly than a flautist his instrument.'

Yet his patriotism goes unappreciated, and his countrymen belittle his immense efforts. 'That enormous productivity, so intense that it seems to me as if it must move stones, single portions of which not one of my contemporaries is able to compete with, to say nothing of its totality – that literary activity is regarded as a kind of hobby in the manner of fishing and such. And I am regarded as a kind of English-man, a half-mad eccentric.'

The little boy who once stood here also felt himself to be outside the world he watched from his window. The Kierkegaards were not native to Copenhagen, nor to the bourgeois society their wealth gave them access to. Søren Kierkegaard was different from the other boys, who laughed at the odd, old-fashioned clothes his father made him wear: cropped trousers and a jacket with short tails made from rough dark tweed, and woollen stockings. Now, as he prepares to leave Nytorv for good, he feels more keenly than ever the weight of his childhood home, carried deep within him.

Deeper still is his first home, his mother Anne. Like every human soul, he came into being within the quiet, dark warmth of a woman's body, and he longs for such a sanctuary when the bright lights of the world become too harsh for him. Yet in all his writings, published and unpublished, Kierkegaard has never mentioned his mother. This is not because he has forgotten her; it is the silence owed to something sacred, which held him long before he knew how to speak.

\* \* \*

In May 1813, when Anne Sørensdatter Kierkegaard gave birth to her seventh and last baby, Søren Aabye, she had been married to Michael Pedersen Kierkegaard for sixteen years, and the family were settled in the big house on Nytorv. Anne was nearly forty-five, and her husband was fifty-six: they had already exceeded the life expectancy of Copen-hagen citizens, and were old enough to be their new son's grandparents. Many years earlier, Anne had worked as a servant in the home of Michael Pedersen and his first wife, Kirstine, who died childless in March 1796. Anne was married to Michael in April the following year, and their first daughter, Maren, was born within five months of the wedding. Anne was, in fact, a distant cousin of Michael Pedersen Kierkegaard. While her husband had become a wealthy merchant and a respected citizen, she still could not write her own name.

Anne Kierkegaard was cheerful, kindly, and enjoyed looking after her children. 'She was especially gratified when she could get them peacefully into bed, since she then wielded her sceptre with delight, cosseted them and protected them like a hen her chicks,' recalled her granddaughter Henriette Lund. 'Her plump little figure often had only to appear in the doorway of the nursery, and the cries and screams would give way to a hush; the rebellious young boy or girl soon fell sweetly asleep in her soft embrace.' Of course, such a mother was especially attentive to little Søren Aabye, her youngest child, with his sensitive nature, large bright eyes, crooked spine and thin shoulders. Even when he was fifteen years old, a girl who visited his family thought him 'a spoiled and naughty boy who hung on his mother's apron strings'.

When Kierkegaard was born, his sister Maren was fifteen; next were Nicolene, aged thirteen, and Petrea, aged eleven. His eldest brother, Peter Christian, was nearly eight; Søren Michael – known as Michael – was six; and his closest brother Niels had just turned four. Although he entered a world full of children, he now regards his childhood as a paradise already lost in infancy: 'I never had the joy of being a child, for the frightful torment I suffered disturbed the peace requisite for being a child, for being capable of diligence, etc., in order to please one's father, because the unrest within me caused me to be always, always outside myself.'

Michael Pedersen and Anne Kierkegaard

Whenever he traces the roots of this unrest, reaching back to his dimmest memories, he encounters the large, looming figure of his father, whose gloomy presence seemed to fill the house on Nytorv. 'His build was powerful, his features firm and determined, his whole bearing forceful ... To him, obedience was *the* principle.' Michael Pedersen Kierkegaard was exacting, thorough in everything he did, and prone to depression. When Kierkegaard recalls him now, it is this dark, uneasy feeling that connects him to his former self, the young boy who looked up at his stern father with fear and trembling: 'Oh, how frightful it is when for a moment I think of the dark background of my life, right from the earliest days. The anxiety with which my father filled my soul, his own frightful melancholy, the many things in this connection that I cannot even write down.'

Michael Pedersen Kierkegaard grew up on farmland in Sædding, a small parish on the western side of Jutland. His peasant father, Peder Christensen, tended the parish churchyard (*kirkegaard*) and had taken that as his name, spelled according to the local pronunciation. Michael Pedersen's early years were hard; he never forgot the day he cursed God while out herding sheep in bitter weather, hungry and cold. When still a boy he went to Copenhagen to work as an apprentice in his uncle's hosiery shop. At the age of twenty-four he became a licensed hosier in the city, and a few years later he began to import goods, such as sugar and coffee, from the Danish colonies in eastern India (known as *Dansk Østindien*) and the Caribbean. By the close of the eighteenth century he had made a substantial fortune and retired from mercantile business. In 1809, his family expanding, he bought the house on Nytorv and lived there for the rest of his life in prominent yet restrained prosperity. The financial crash of 1813 – the year Søren Aabye, his seventh child, was born – ruined many Danish families, but Michael Pedersen had invested his wealth in gold-backed bonds, and came through the crisis better off than ever.

This remarkable transformation of a God-forsaken peasant boy into one of the richest men in Copenhagen is not just a story of good fortune. Michael Pedersen Kierkegaard's career exemplifies the social changes that reconfigured Europe during his lifetime: as a new ethic of self-improvement seeped through the old feudal hierarchies, thousands of people migrated from rural areas to cities. Wealth was no longer just something fathers handed down to their sons; it could be created and grown through innovation. Men like Michael Pedersen Kierkegaard – whose own father had been a serf in bondage to his landlord – could profit from slave labour in the Danish Gold Coast of west Africa, just as the next generation are now exploiting the new railways to increase profits further. In 1792 the Danish king, Christian VII, was the first European monarch to ban the slave trade. This decree took over a decade to come into effect, and slavery itself continued in far-off colonies through the first half of the nineteenth century – long enough to secure the rise of the bourgeoisie. Meanwhile, making money by trade acquired a new dignity. For centuries Christianity encouraged people to regard worldly prosperity with suspicion; now commerce is not just respectable, but virtuous.

As if demonstrating how the new affluence gained through colonial trade supported the growth of both learning and leisure, after he retired from business in his fortieth year Michael Pedersen Kierkegaard occupied himself with intellectual pursuits. That was how Kierkegaard always knew his father: he read a great deal, usually sermons or philosophical books; he had strong opinions, and an appetite for argument. Visiting relatives found it 'very intriguing to hear the old man debate with the sons, with none of them giving in, and to see the quiet activity of the old mother, and how she would sometimes listen in admiration and sometimes interrupt to calm things down when they became too heated. They talked about heaven and earth and everything in between.' Kierkegaard's view of the world as a battlefield was formed in the parlour on Nytorv: here he learned to see men of faith as knights, and love as a dance to 'martial music'. His first adversaries were his father and his brothers; later they were his fellow students, then his fellow writers. Even Regine became his opponent – one who 'fought like a lioness' when he tried to break up with her.

Although he argued with his sons, Michael Pedersen Kierkegaard was proud of their intelligence. 'When I can't sleep, I lie down and talk with my boys, and there are no better conversations here in Copenhagen,' he used to tell Søren's schoolfriends. Though the retired Jutland hosier could work his way through philosophical systems, he did the family's daily shopping himself, and could often be seen striding home from the market, carrying a fat goose.

As Kierkegaard grew up he felt his father's strict discipline and strong character as an oppressive force that he needed to fight against. His own nature was free-spirited and independent – and one way of protecting his freedom was to conceal his inner life. Even among his schoolfriends, he 'did not reveal his character in the way that young people usually do'. Exuberant as well as melancholic, he learned 'to cloak this life with an outward existence of *joie de vivre* and merriment'. This habit of secrecy and disguise is another childhood lesson, learned in 2 Nytorv, which has remained with him into his fourth decade. It has become integral to his authorship, and to his life as a writer: he has not only published many of his works under the cover of pseudonyms, but made himself conspicuous in the streets and cafés of Copenhagen in order to conceal the long hours spent at his writing desk.

His duplicity is inseparable from the deep attitude of ambivalence that shapes his relationship to the world. He longs for the 'purity of heart' that Jesus preached to his followers, yet he finds himself continually divided in two. This, too, he traces back to his father, and the religion he embodied: 'He made my childhood an unparalleled torture, and made me, in my heart of hearts, offended by Christianity, even if out of respect for it I resolved never to say a word about it to any person and, out of love to my father, to portray Christianity as truly as possible. And yet my father was the most loving father.' He wanted to please his father, and he wanted to defy him; Michael Pedersen Kierkegaard's love for his sons was confusing, for if he was well meaning, he was also destructive. This confusion deepened Kierkegaard's unrest and ambivalence: 'I acquired such anxiety about Christianity, and yet I felt myself strongly drawn toward it.' In retrospect, this seems to be not only a paternal legacy, but, stronger still, a destiny – which, he now realizes, prevented him from marrying Regine. 'It sometimes happens that a child in the cradle becomes engaged to be married to the one who will one day be his wife or her husband; religiously I was already, in early childhood – previously engaged. Ah! I paid dearly for once misunderstanding my life and forgetting – that I was betrothed!'

Perhaps his secretive habits only pushed his father's austere, frightening relationship to Christianity deeper within him, where it grew more powerful. 'Already as a small child, I was told as solemnly as possible that "the crowd" spat on Christ, although he was the truth. I've kept this hidden deep within my heart and, in order to hide it the better, have even concealed the fact that I've hidden it deep, deep within my soul under an external appearance of just the opposite . . . I constantly come back to this as to my first idea.'

Such is his duplicity, though, that even his impulse to concealment is dogged by a contrary inclination to reveal himself, through writing. In 1842, just before he launched his authorship with *Either/Or*, he began to write a philosophical satire about a character named Johannes Climacus, a young philosopher who later became one of his pseudonyms. In that unfinished, half-autobiographical work Kierkegaard described an imaginative game Johannes used to play as a boy with his elderly father, 'a very stern man, to all appearances dry and prosaic':

> But under his 'rustic cloak' manner he concealed an ardent imagination which not even his great age could blunt. When on occasions J.C. asked permission to go out, as often as not he was refused; though once in a while the father would suggest by way of compensation that his son should take his hand and go for a walk up and down the room. At first blush this seemed a poor substitute; and yet, just as with that 'rustic cloak' manner, there was more behind it than appeared.
>
> The proposal was adopted, and J.C. was given completely free choice as to where they should go. So they walked out of the city gate to a nearby country castle, or away to the beach, or about the streets, or wherever J.C. wished, for everything was in the father's power. While they walked up and down the room the father would describe everything they saw. They greeted the passers-by; the carriages rattled by them and drowned out the father's voice; the cake-woman's wares were more inviting than ever . . . If the way was unfamiliar to J.C., the boy would add suggestions, while his father's almighty imagination was able to construct anything, using every childhood fancy as an ingredient in the drama taking place. For J.C. it was as if the world was being created as they conversed; as if his father were God, and he

God's favoured one who was permitted to interpose his poor conceits as merrily as he liked.

After giving up on his book about Johannes Climacus and his quasi-divine father, Kierkegaard contemplated writing a novella called *The Mysterious Family*, which would reproduce the 'tragedy' of his childhood. 'It would begin in a thoroughly patriarchal-idyllic fashion, so that no one would suspect anything before that word suddenly resounded, providing a terrifying explanation of everything ... the terrifying, secret explanation of the religious that was granted to me in a fearful presentiment which my imagination hammered into shape.'

He did not write this book, nor disclose the mystery of his family. His father once told him a secret about his own past: a transgression which Kierkegaard sometimes hints at in his writing, but will never disclose. 'A guilt must rest upon the entire family,' he wrote during his student years, when all but one of his siblings were dead; 'the punishment of God must be upon it: it was supposed to disappear, obliterated by the mighty hand of God, erased like a mistake.' And with no hope of a happy future, he added, 'what wonder then that in desperation I seized hold solely to the intellectual side of man, and clung onto that, so that the thought of my remarkable mental capacities was my only comfort, ideas my only joy'. By then his childhood habit of self-concealment, formed partly in defiance of his father's severe attention, had taken on another, conflicting motive: from loyalty to his father, he could not tell his secrets.

\* \* \*

He has continued to carry this conflict within him since Michael Pedersen Kierkegaard's death in 1838 – ten years ago now. As he struggles with his painful memories, he dutifully remembers his father every day in his prayers. In *Works of Love*, a collection of discourses on the Christian ideal of neighbourly love published last year, in 1847, he suggested that love for the deceased is the purest kind of love, because it expects nothing in return. Yet for the same reason it is painful to be angry with a dead father; his anger can expect no response, and has only itself to fight with.

At last he turns from the window: even if he cannot sleep, he should try to rest. There will be just a few more nights like this one, looking down at Nytorv, and up across the square to the south side of the church tower. Inside the room, the moonlight touches the steel pen on his high desk, the precious tin boxes, the packing cases full of books, the tall rosewood cabinet containing his works. Kierkegaard believes that 'learning to love' is the most important human task, and also the most difficult – and he began this lesson here, with a mother and father who died in this house. He saw death and grief close-up while still a child: when he was six years old, his brother Søren Michael died after an accident in the school playground; three years later, in 1822, his eldest sister Maren died at the age of twenty-four after years of frail health. Love has proved to be inseparable from anxiety and loss. Although he has tried countless times to flee from his anxiety, or deflect it with defensive wit, or crush it between pen and paper, he knows it is more truthful, more fully human, to let himself experience it – for learning to love means 'learning to be anxious'.

Five years ago, he wrote in *Fear and Trembling* that everyone has to undertake the task of loving anew: while scientific knowledge accumulates through generations, in love we cannot build on the progress of our forebears. Nevertheless, we first learn to love – whether trustingly or anxiously, steadfastly or inconstantly, warmly or at a distance – from our parents, and we carry their long legacies folded up inside us. When Kierkegaard was a child, his peace-making mother Anne was the antidote to his forbidding, complex father, as the New Testament God of love is said to supersede the older God of law. While his father embodied a Christianity that made him anxious and taught him to fight, his mother embodied the deep rest which he now seeks in God. He learned to love the first woman in his life passionately, tenaciously, in search of solace, longingly yet secure of his own worth, with the arrogance of a clever child. He loved the first man in his life fearfully, reverently, defiantly, jealously, with the eagerness to please of a clever child. Of course he did not understand, back then, that those first forms of loving were a formation, replete with repetition; that those childish ways cut a path he would retrace long after leaving home.

# 6

## 'Come Unto Me'

In 1848 Easter has fallen later than usual, in the fourth week of April, and as he walks home from the Church of Our Lady after the Easter Sunday service the air feels almost warm. The streets are busy and spirits are high: the crowds swarm happily from the church in all directions, released at last from their Lenten restraint, enjoying the sunshine and looking forward to dinner. When he lived on Nytorv, the Church of Our Lady was less than two minutes away; now he has moved to Rosenborggade, the walk home is a little longer – round the north side of the church, past the university, along the street to the great round tower of Trinity Church; then left into Købmager-gade, past the porcelain factory, Reitzel's bookshop, and the offices of *The Fatherland*, and up through Kultorvet.

Keeping to the shaded side of the street, Kierkegaard hurries home to write. Nowadays, the sermons he hears in church are fresh fuel for his own religious discourses. The consoling teaching of Bishop Mynster, who leads the Danish State Church from his episcopal resi-dence by the Church of Our Lady, must be countered with rigorous insistence on the difficulty of the Christian life. In his mind, a new paragraph is already dashing across its page. Having drafted a trio of discourses on 'the Lilies and the Birds' of Jesus's Sermon on the Mount, he is now at work on another book, a sequel to the still-unpublished *Sickness unto Death*. While that work diagnosed the varieties of despair from which human beings suffer – many of them unaware of their spiritual disease – this new cycle of discourses proposes a single cure: following Christ. He must show that this is a demanding ideal, if not an impossible task; that Jesus called his disciples out of their comfortable, conventional lives, and set them on a dangerous and uncertain path. In this new work, provisionally titled *Come Unto Me* (Matthew 11:28), Kierkegaard is opposing the Christian establishment more directly – represented above all by Bishop Mynster, and by the Church of Our Lady, which as Copenhagen's cathedral provides the model for Christian worship throughout Denmark.

He has lived all his life in this parish, though the Church of Our Lady itself was in ruins when he was born. It burned down when the British navy bombarded the city in 1807 during the Napoleonic Wars. So in June 1813 his parents took him to be baptized in the Church of the Holy Spirit, a few streets to the east of their ruined parish church. On that day Søren Aabye Kierkegaard became both a member of the Danish State Church and a citizen of Denmark – for Lutheran Christianity is so tightly knit into civic life that baptism into the national Church also confers citizenship. It is illegal to deny in print the existence of God, and the penalty is exile from Denmark. Kierkegaard has never come close to atheism, yet his whole authorship defies his baptism by asking, over and over again, whether anyone in this Lutheran country has yet become a Christian.

Although his new home on Rosenborggade is a little further from the Church of Our Lady, through his writing he is drawing closer to it – a characteristically ambiguous movement, as if the closeness tightens his heart, intensifies his long-standing ambivalence towards the religion he inherited not only from his father, but from his native land. Perhaps he is moving towards the Church in order to bombard it from within. His new book advances a sharpened critique of Bishop Mynster, and not only through an interpretation of Christianity that diverges more radically from the Bishop's own. Mynster's best-known book is his 1833 devotional work *Observations on Christian Teachings*, and Kierkegaard will make Mynster his explicit target by attacking the idea that a Christian should be an admiring 'observer' of Jesus. No, a Christian's task is to follow Jesus, to imitate him – and this means suffering like he did.

And he has finally decided to publish his *Christian Discourses*, a collection of twenty-eight sermons which rivals, in size at least, the weighty volume of Mynster's sermons that he used to read in 2 Nytorv when he was a boy. *Christian Discourses*, written last year, will be in Copenhagen's bookshops in three days, on 25 April 1848. It may be his last book; here, for the first time, the word *Christelige* will appear in the title of a work by S. Kierkegaard. For years, of course, his authorship has circled around Christian themes. Since 1843 he has written dozens of 'edifying discourses' on the spiritual life, taking New Testament verses as their starting point; in 1844 he published *Philosophical Fragments*, on the 'absolute paradox' of the Incarnation, as well as *The Concept of Anxiety*, a new interpretation of the doctrine of original sin. But those works were written in the guise of fictional authors who addressed religious questions as logicians or psychologists, and refused to describe themselves as Christians. Under such pseudonyms Kierkegaard could approach Christianity obliquely, tentatively, covertly. A few months ago, in the autumn of 1847, he put his own name to *Works of Love*, a series of 'Christian Deliberations' on the commandment to 'Love your neighbour as yourself.' Now he is approaching directly the figure of Christ, who has summoned him, frightened him, and mystified him from his youth.

His questions about how to be a human being are converging on the task of following this compelling, enigmatic figure. Will this narrowing path draw him further into the Church – or take him outside it? This is a new, tightened form of the question that has troubled him persistently: how can he become fully, truly human within the ready-made patterns of life the world has to offer? Is the Church part of this world, or an alternative to it – a sacred refuge, a spiritual garrison, a holy citadel? Where does he *go* when he goes to church? Does he find any more truth there than in the theatre, or the lecture hall, or the marketplace – or have churches become the least truthful places in Christendom?

In this established Lutheran nation, Kierkegaard is grappling with the legacy of Luther's own struggle. In the 1520s, while still a monk and a Roman Catholic, Luther argued that the true Church was invisible, a spiritual community formed only by faith, while all the visible buildings and bishops of Christendom were corrupt monuments to his Church's distortion of the Gospel. Yet Lutheran faith rapidly made itself equally visible – in printed pamphlets adorned with pictures of Luther, in bonfires of books and wooden saints. Converts to Luther's spiritual church wrested control of physical churches throughout northern Europe – including Copenhagen's Church of Our Lady. Three hundred years later, this church is, for Kierkegaard, an ambiguous place: is it the house of the Lord, or a house of illusions?

Drawn so powerfully to his spiritual task that he can set no limits to its weight and urgency, Kierkegaard is asking how to express his inner need for God within a Church that offers to meet this need, yet seems often to diminish or divert or falsify it. He can trace this question right back to Jesus, whose teaching broke through the customs and hierarchies of his own religious community. And it runs like a spiritual pulse throughout the Christian tradition, both animating and disrupting it from within. In the Lutheran Churches, this question drove the pietist revivals which pushed at the boundaries of official religion for two centuries after Luther's death. Pietism put devotion above dogma, spiritual awakening above orthodox belief; this was a religion of the heart, emphasizing pious feeling and conduct rather than creedal formulas. While their Church acquired political power and strengthened its position in the world, many pietists drew on monastic and mystical strands of medieval Catholicism and spoke of renouncing worldly things. For others, Jesus's teaching inspired a forward-thinking egalitarianism: these pietists were actively anti-clerical and socialist, and put their radical ideas into practice by living in separate communities, largely independent of Church and State. The pietist counter-movement to Lutheran orthodoxy intertwined with Denmark's official religion to form Kierkegaard's Christian upbringing, for his father was a member of Copenhagen's pietist congregation as well as a regular churchgoer. These religious tensions have shaped his soul, just as they have shaped Protestant Christendom: his own spiritual legacy is a miniature rendition of three centuries of Reformation history.

* * *

West Jutland, where Michael Pedersen Kierkegaard grew up, was one of the regions of Denmark where Moravian pietism took hold in the eighteenth century. After he moved to the city, Michael Pedersen remained faithful to the pietism of his Jutland family, and it suffused the Christianity he passed on to his own children. Like other pietists, the Moravians aspire to a holy life that follows the example of Christ:

they seek to imitate Jesus's deep, inward faith in God, and his pure-hearted obedience, humility and poverty. Of course, no one can live up to such a demanding ideal – and every effort to do so only makes it clearer that human beings are sinners, in need of divine forgiveness and redemption.

When Michael Pedersen arrived in Copenhagen in the 1760s, the Moravians had been established there for about three decades, and their Society of Brothers was thriving. As he became a prosperous businessman, Michael Pedersen helped to guide the Society's financial affairs: he advised on the purchase of a larger meeting hall on Storm-gade in 1816, and though he was not known to be generous with his wealth he was regarded as one of the group's most faithful members. During the years of Kierkegaard's childhood, the Copenhagen Brethren flourished under J. C. Reuss, who came to the city from Christiansfeld, an egalitarian Moravian settlement in east Jutland, planned around an unadorned church and other communal buildings. Reuss's preaching drew large congregations: on Sunday evenings hundreds of Copenhageners gathered at the meeting house on Stormgade to pray together, sing hymns, and hear 'awakening discourses'. Each week Reuss reminded the crowds of their moral frailty and deep need for God, and urged them to follow Christ: 'We know we are sinners, great is our imperfection and weakness and we err often and many times over . . . Our Saviour takes pity on us, he knows our hearts, knows our sinfulness, knows how we need help, comfort, strength and encouragement in order to live for him in humility, love, and according to his mind and heart. He is also prepared to grant us all his precious blessings, and satisfy our exhausted souls with his gifts of grace. Dear Brothers, he must find our hearts opened for him.'

Michael Pedersen took this message home to his family, and in the 1820s Søren Kierkegaard began to accompany his father and older brothers to the Moravian meeting house. But Michael Pedersen was a solid citizen and a canny merchant as well as a devout man, never likely to sacrifice his hard-won bourgeois respectability to the cause of the more radical, anti-establishment Moravians. His pietist sympathies did not compromise his commitment to the Danish State Church: he went to his parish church every Sunday morning, and to Stormgade on Sunday evenings.

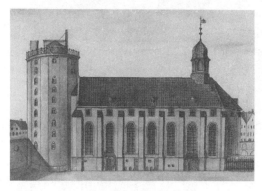

Trinity Church and the Rundetaarn (Round Tower) in 1749

While the Church of Our Lady was being rebuilt, its restoration slowed by Denmark's dire economic straits after the 1813 crash, its clergy and most of its parishioners worshipped at the nearby Church of the Trinity. This seventeenth-century church combined religion with science and learning: it housed the University Library upstairs, supported by the massive interior columns of the church below, and its adjoining Round Tower was an observatory. During the 1820s Kierkegaard's father joined the congregation at this grand university church – drawn, like many of his neighbours, by Jakob Peter Mynster, the charismatic senior pastor of Our Lady's parish. Mynster's presence 'inspired reverence': those who met him not only admired his 'warmth of heart, and dignity of character', but felt themselves uplifted by the way he embodied 'the pure loveliness of a human soul fashioned into Christ's divine pattern'. Michael Pedersen Kierkegaard went to Mynster for confession and communion, and took his family to Sunday services, where Mynster usually preached the sermon. So it was Mynster who confirmed Kierkegaard in the Church of the Trinity in April 1828, just before his fifteenth birthday, and it was Mynster who officiated at his first communion.

It was not only formally that Mynster initiated Kierkegaard into the Danish State Church: throughout his formative years this priest was his most influential Christian teacher and exemplar. He grew up on Mynster's eloquent, stirring sermons, which were frequently read in 2 Nytorv as well as heard in Trinity Church. Kierkegaard remembers how, when he was a boy, his father promised him a rix-dollar if he would read one of these sermons aloud to him, and four rix-dollars to write up the sermon Mynster had preached in church that Sunday. And he remembers how he refused, though he wanted the money, and told his father that he should not tempt him in that way. Michael Pedersen's great respect for his pastor imbued Mynster with vicarious paternal authority, which inspired in Kierkegaard the same potent mixture of sincere, overt reverence and deep, concealed defiance that he felt towards his father.

Jakob Peter Mynster by Constantin Hansen

Mynster was born in 1775, almost twenty years after Michael Pedersen Kierkegaard. He was orphaned in childhood, and the austere Christianity of his pietist stepfather injured his innate religious sensibility. Even after he became a parish priest in south Zealand, Mynster felt unsure of his vocation. But this changed in 1803, when he experienced a profound spiritual awakening, and all his doubts were assuaged by a deep trust in his own conscience, the voice of God within him. He resolved to obey this inner voice unconditionally, and in submission to it he found lasting peace. From then on, week after week, Mynster exhorted his congregations to follow their conscience, and assured them that their earnest moral efforts would be rewarded with peace and happiness. He began to publish his sermons. In 1811 he arrived in Copenhagen to take up a post at the ruined Church of Our Lady, and in the city his influence and popularity grew.

Like Kierkegaard, Mynster is a cultured, sophisticated thinker and a gifted writer as well as a remarkable preacher; he, too, struggled with his religious upbringing. Yet unlike Kierkegaard, Mynster distinguishes himself by a genius for moderation. His remarkable ability to steer a middle path has not only sustained his broad appeal, but enabled him to embody half a century of Danish Christianity while warding off its excesses. Like the Enlightenment rationalists who still dominate official theology, Mynster is optimistic about human nature: his call to conscience expresses firm faith in human judgement. Like the pietists, he is willing to venture into the emotional depths of human experience and to attend to the spiritual life. Like the Romantics, he finds harmony between God and the natural world. But he avoids the frigidity of rationalism, the fervid tendencies of pietism, the unorthodoxy of Romanticism. And Mynster's preaching is appreciated by the less as well as the more cultured among his congregation, for he combines intellectual gravitas with a taste for simple, honest faith. He is well versed in the modern German thinkers who put the idea of freedom at the centre of their philosophies – he studied Kant and Schelling before he took his first appointment as a pastor – but his instincts are conservative. He stands – moderately, of course – for order and tradition, for theological orthodoxy and absolute monarchy, arguing that these secure structures are most conducive to individual freedom.

When he gave Kierkegaard his first communion in 1828, Mynster was well into his ascent through the Danish State Church and in sight of its highest rank. During Kierkegaard's childhood, Mynster had steadily accumulated influence within the ecclesial establishment: he became a director of the Pastoral Seminary and of the Danish Bible Society, and a governor of the University of Copenhagen; he prepared a new edition of Luther's Small Catechism, used in schools throughout Denmark, and helped to revise the Danish translation of the New Testament. He married the daughter of the Bishop of Zealand, leader of the national Church. In 1826 he was appointed as a preacher to the royal court, and soon afterwards promoted to the prestigious post of chaplain at the Palace Church, 'the most fashionable place of worship in Copenhagen'. In 1834, following the death of his father-in-law, Mynster became Bishop of Zealand, and the most conspicuous representative of Denmark's visible Lutheran Church. This high office ordains a silk robe with a velvet front. And the King made him a Knight of the Order of the Dannebrog, which requires him to wear around his neck a solid gold cross, and on his left breast an even larger cross decorated with silver rays, like a star.

Mynster had left his parish for the royal court before the Church of Our Lady finally reopened in the summer of 1829. But like Mynster's preaching, the new church offered its parishioners a model of modern, enlightened Christianity rooted in biblical tradition. Its architect was Christian Frederik Hansen, renowned for his neoclassical style: he had already designed the imposing courthouse and city hall on Nytorv, next to Kierkegaard's family home. Hansen rebuilt the church's porch with six stone pillars, just like the courthouse portico. Both buildings asserted the humanist ideals of ancient Rome – now reclaimed by Protestant Christendom as the bedrock of Enlightenment rationality, the foundation for a universal morality and a stable civic life.

C. F. Hansen's Church of Our Lady

C. F. Hansen's Courthouse and City Hall, 1850
(Kierkegaard's first home, 2 Nytorv, can be seen on the far right)

Kierkegaard was sixteen years old when he entered the Church of Our Lady for the first time, on 12 June 1829, five days after the church was re-dedicated. That morning – it was a Friday – he followed his family through the great pillars into the large, light interior, and looked up at the towering statues of the apostles, six on each side of the nave. There was neither Madonna nor child in this Church of Our Lady. Bertel Thorvaldsen, Scandinavia's most celebrated sculptor, had amplified Hansen's classical theme by casting twelve muscular disciples – larger than life-sized, too large for the alcoves Hansen built for them – in the pose of Roman generals, imperiously surveying

Inside the Church of Our Lady, Copenhagen

the congregation. Yet these broad-shouldered men carried symbols of their martyrdom, reminding Kierkegaard of Jesus's terrifying warning that his followers might have to suffer and die for their faith.

And he saw, straight ahead of him, above and behind the altar, the figure of Christ himself. Thorvaldsen had made this statue massive, even bigger than the twelve apostles – yet unlike them, this Christ exuded gentleness and grace. His head was bowed, his arms were outstretched and his hands open, and he stepped forward as if to meet his followers with his vast embrace. Somehow these gestures expressed a deep stillness. His quiet power was astonishing; he drew you in, but also brought you to a halt. On the marble pedestal beneath his feet, in golden relief, were the words KOMMER TIL MIG. Kierkegaard recognized, of course, the verse from Matthew's Gospel: 'Come unto me, all you who are weary and burdened, and I will give you rest.'

Bertel Thorvaldsen's *Christus*

\* \* \*

Since that day, nearly two decades ago now, he has walked through the Church of Our Lady's grand entrance countless times. As is the custom of most church-going Danes, he attends the weekly Sunday morning service, and takes communion once or twice a year – but on a Friday, when the church is quiet and the congregation small. And each time he enters the Church of Our Lady and walks beneath the lofty gaze of those twelve disciples, as he did this Easter morning, the insistent invitation is repeated: 'Come unto me, all you who are weary and burdened, and I will give you rest.'

These words sound so sure, so definite: they give a command, and they make a promise. For Luther, it was words like these that expressed the clear certainty of salvation for all the faithful, the hallmark of his new interpretation of the Gospel. Yet for Kierkegaard they contain endless questions – that is to say, the same questions, asked over and over again. Why is mere existence wearying, and what is this heavy burden he continues to carry? Why is being human so difficult for him, when it seems to come easily to others? What kind of rest is he seeking, and why can't he find it for himself? What does it mean to follow Christ within this world, where most paths seem to lead away from what is true and conducive to peace? Why does Christ seem to be so far away, even after eighteen centuries of Christianity? Has all this preaching, prayer, refinement of doctrine, biblical commentary and ecclesial politics – in a word, the construction of Christendom – brought people closer to God, or cast them further from him? If it must be difficult to follow Christ – and look at those long-suffering apostles! – then who would choose his narrow thorny path, when there are far more comfortable ways to live?

Kierkegaard thinks that Bishop Mynster answers these questions too easily, and therefore hardly answers them at all. Over three hundred years, Luther's fiery certainty has gradually cooled into complacency: Mynster's preaching offers a 'gentle comfort' which underestimates the myriad, shifting layers of duplicity – self-evasion, self-deception, self-destruction – that shroud the human heart and turn it stubbornly away from God. 'The truth that divine governance embraces everything which happens on earth can be grasped by every human understanding and felt by every human heart,' insists Mynster. The Bishop knows that, despite the Gospel's assurances, people are naturally burdened by anxiety and doubts about God – as he was himself before his spiritual breakthrough – but he believes this burden can be eased by Christ's promise of forgiveness. Mynster's sermon on Matthew 11:28 in his thick volume of sermons from 1823, so often read in Kierkegaard's family home, explained this clearly: when Jesus says, 'Come unto me, all you who are burdened, and I will give you rest', he is offering 'certainty for the doubter, strength for the struggling, comfort for the sorrowful'. If people are honest and humble, the sermon continued, they will understand Christ's message and receive 'happiness and blessing'.

Mynster's comforting words are appealing – yet this very appeal makes them false for Kierkegaard, who has always found Christianity disturbing as well as inviting. And he certainly does not share Mynster's propensity for moderation: he is drawn to a truth that lies at two opposite extremes at once – and the truth of human experience is often like this. In a single day, even in a single hour, a human being can feel suffering and joy, despair and faith, intense anxiety and profound peace.

This is how Kierkegaard finds truth in Christianity: he does not believe that Christian teaching contains facts, which can now, in the modern age, be confirmed by historians or scientists. He sees in the example of Jesus the dual extremities of human existence that, he feels, constitute his own deepest truth. 'Though he possessed the blessing, he was like a curse for everyone who came near him . . . like an affliction for those few who loved him, so that he had to wrench them out into the most terrible decisions, so that for his mother he had to be the sword that pierced her heart, for the disciples a crucified love,' Kierkegaard wrote in one of the 'upbuilding discourses' he published last year. Jesus is a paradox: he urged his followers to be perfect, but he spent his time with sinners and tax collectors; he taught an ideal of purity of heart which demands ceaseless striving and invokes rigorous judgement, but at the same time he manifested a mercy that accepts all things with equal love. Being human is at once a blessing and a curse, Kierkegaard believes – more and more so, the closer we come to God – and Jesus exemplifies this more than anyone.

So while there is wisdom in Mynster's sermons – a grasp of human feeling, and earnestness about the spiritual life – this never goes far enough. Kierkegaard's purpose as an author is now the 'inward deepening of Christianity'. He must deepen his neighbours' need for God, so that the grace that meets this need becomes all the more powerful and profound: 'Christianity has been taken in vain, made too mild, so that people have forgotten what grace is. The more rigorous Christianity is, the more grace becomes manifest as grace and not a sort of human sympathy.' When the Bishop turns the Gospel into mere consolation, Kierkegaard believes that he renders it untrue, makes Christianity too easy, too comfortable, whereas the opposite is needed in this complacent age. In the Church of Our Lady, Thorvaldsen's welcoming Jesus echoes Mynster's theology: this serene, powerful figure bears no resemblance to the gaunt, bloody, agonized Christ of medieval devotion, adopted by the Lutheran pietists. Yet Kierkegaard hears in his words the pietist insistence on following Christ – for he does not say 'Admire me' or 'Observe me' or even 'Worship me', but 'Come unto me.'

When his *Christian Discourses* comes out, three days from now, Copenhageners will be 'awakened' from the 'soothing security' embodied in their solid cathedral church and in their Bishop's reassuring sermons. Some of the book's twenty-eight discourses are situated in the Church of Our Lady, and one considers a verse from Ecclesiastes, 'Watch your step when you go to the house of the Lord.' It begins by evoking the calm stillness embodied in Thorvaldsen's painstakingly carved statues and in the patiently embroidered velvet adorning the pulpit, before exclaiming 'How quieting, how soothing – alas, and how much danger in this security!' Religiously, we all need 'awakening', but the preaching in this church will 'lull us to sleep'. Indeed, it seems deliberately designed for 'tranquillization'. *Christian Discourses* is, by contrast, an 'attack', an assault on its reader's spiritual senses. Those who go to Christ will find rest – but first they must wake up, move, change their hearts. And who knows where the path that follows Christ will lead, before the promised rest is found?

Since 1843 Kierkegaard has regularly published collections of two, three or four sermons, though he calls them 'upbuilding discourses'. These discourses are a genre of spiritual writing partly inspired by Moravian preaching: they address each reader privately, and disavow any ecclesial authority. Yet by naming his new sermons *Christian*

*Discourses*, and setting many of them, theatrically, inside the Church of Our Lady, Kierkegaard is taking a bold step onto Bishop Mynster's territory. The last seven discourses in the book are written as if for Friday communion services in the church, when a short sermon is always preached before the bread and wine are offered. The communion discourse is becoming Kierkegaard's favourite genre: he returns to it continually, and each time he writes a new one he pushes his authorship into the heart of the church, addressing Christians as they prepare to draw close to God.

And this is not merely an imaginative act. Last summer, Kierkegaard delivered two of his Friday communion discourses in the Church of Our Lady. On the first occasion he preached on Matthew 11:28, the verse inscribed below Thorvaldsen's statue of Christ behind the altar, and as he spoke he drew his listeners' attention to this figure: 'See, he stretches out his arms and says: Come here, come here unto *me*, all you who labour and are burdened.' There were around thirty people taking communion in the church that morning, among them a retired butcher, a nightwatchman, a theology student, a sailor and his wife, an ironsmith, a state councillor, and the widow of an alehouse keeper and her daughter. The 'labour' Jesus speaks of, Kierkegaard explained to them, is the 'longing for God' that brought them into the church. Then he talked about how hard it is to suffer without being understood. This is one of the great human burdens, he said, which can only be relieved by Christ: 'I do not know what in particular troubles you, my listeners; perhaps I would not understand your sorrow either or know how to speak about it with insight. But Christ has experienced all human sorrow more grievously than any human being . . . He not only understands all your sorrow better than you understand it yourself, but he wants to take the burden from you and give you rest for your souls.'

Although that was the first time Kierkegaard had delivered one of his discourses to a church congregation, his voice was well practised: when he composes his works, he reads his sentences aloud, often many times, to sound out their rhythm and melody. He spends hours like this, 'like a flautist entertaining himself with his flute', and during these hours he falls 'in love with the sound of language – that is, when it resounds with the pregnancy of thought'. For a few minutes, those thirty Copenhageners gathered for Friday communion in the Church of Our Lady found themselves admitted into this private world. One man who heard Kierkegaard preach was struck by his 'exceedingly weak but wonderfully expressive voice'; he had never heard a voice 'so capable of modulating expression, even the most delicate nuances', and he felt that he would never forget it.

A few weeks later, in August 1847, Kierkegaard preached a second time in the Church of Our Lady. Again he spoke of the 'heartfelt longing' for God that had drawn his listeners into church; he believes that going to Mass should not abate this longing, but only deepen and intensify it. In that sermon he reflected on the practice of Friday communion, his own custom ever since he first received communion from Mynster in 1828. Friday used to be a quiet day in Copenhagen, a day of prayer, but secular routines have gradually taken over traditional religious observance, and taking communion on Fridays now goes against the flow of life on the streets, where people are working, selling and shopping as on other weekdays. These Friday services are much smaller and more intimate than the Sunday Mass, which Kierkegaard always leaves before the communion ritual begins. When he attends church on a Sunday he goes along with the crowd; on a Friday, he can go to the Church of Our Lady 'openly before everyone's eyes, and yet secretly, as a stranger, in the midst of all those many people'. And inside the church, 'the noise of the daily activity of life out there sounds almost audibly within this vaulted space, where this sacred stillness is therefore even greater.'

Kierkegaard's way of going to communion – in view of the crowd yet surreptitiously, like a secret agent – sums up his way of being a Christian. Following this half-concealed path, he struggles to preserve his 'inner need' for God from the conventional dictates of custom and obligation. Remaining a 'single individual' within the religious structures offered by the world is such a fine and complex balancing act that it sometimes seems impossible. Last year, he considered dedicating a collection of his Friday communion discourses to Bishop Mynster – 'with my father in mind I would very much like to do it' – but eventually, his attitude towards the Bishop divided between reverence and scorn, he concluded that 'my course in life is too doubtful for me to be able to dedicate my work to any living person'.

He was by then uncertain whether he would 'enjoy honour and esteem, or be insulted and persecuted' for his writing. And he has 'never been closer to stopping being an author' than now, at Easter 1848, with his *Christian Discourses*.

'Let us pay tribute to Bishop Mynster,' Kierkegaard wrote in his journal last year. 'I have admired no one, no living person, except Bishop Mynster, and it is always a joy to me to be reminded of my father. His position is such that I see the irregularities very well, more clearly than anyone who has attacked him ... There is an ambivalence in his life that cannot be avoided, because the "state Church" is an ambivalence.' Of course, there is also deep ambivalence in Kierkegaard's admiration for the Bishop, whom he associates so closely with his father.

As he finds the comfortable worldliness of the Danish Church increasingly intolerable, his question of how to live in the world is becoming more entangled with his relationship with this Church, and with Mynster. The Moravian pietists sought holiness by withdrawing from the world: they created enclaves, like Christiansfeld, that were not so different from monastic enclosures, and formed their own congregations outside the State Church – though many Danes, like Kierkegaard's father, moved easily between the Moravian meeting house and their parish church. Kierkegaard has heard pastors defend the worldly character of their Church by pointing out that Jesus himself did not enter a monastery, or go and live in the desert. But he thinks that, for Jesus, becoming a monk or a hermit was a temptation – for what a relief it would have been to leave the suspicious, uncomprehending crowds! – while being in the world was an act of renunciation. Jesus did not stay in the world 'to become a councillor of justice, a member of a knightly order, an honorary member of this or that society, but in order to suffer'.

And Kierkegaard is coming to understand his own life in this way too. Becoming a writer has in one sense set him apart from civic life: in 1841 this was, for him, the clear alternative to marrying Regine and entering a profession. Yet his writings have confronted the world and demanded its attention. He has made himself conspicuous on the streets of Copenhagen, in the local press, within the city's literary and intellectual circles, and he has subjected himself to their judgements on his life as well as on his work. Being a writer like this is no retreat from the world; this is why he has been continually tempted to stop writing, and perhaps it is also why he feels he cannot stop now. Being a recluse would be too easy, he tells himself, as he hurries home to his pen, ink and paper. Now he wonders whether he should make himself more prominent within the Church, gain greater influence there, in order to provoke it into truthfulness from within.

Just as he feels his own existence stretched between greater extremes of suffering and fulfilment, pulling him almost to breaking point, so he is trying to stretch Christianity in both these directions, in order to deepen it. Like the Moravian preachers he used to hear at the meeting house on Stormgade, he emphasizes Jesus's suffering. But he thinks less of the bloody crucifixion than of the inward torment of living among people who could not understand the extraordinary man who tried to teach them to encounter God. He feels that he, too, is suffering in a world where he is misunderstood; he wonders whether Jesus wants his followers 'to become just as wretched as he was, before the consolation comes'.

And he does believe that consolation will come – though only on the far side of pain and trial. He is convinced that faith must neither avoid suffering nor drown in it, but move through it to find joy. Even now, this bright Easter day, after everything that has happened to him, he considers himself 'an extremely unhappy man, who nevertheless, by the help of God, is indescribably blessed'.

# 7

## Aesthetic Education

Another sleepless night on Rosenborggade: now it is July, the summer solstice has passed and the nights are lengthening at last, but still it is not long until dawn. The apartment is still, the servants are sleeping; outside, the streets are silent. Inside, his thoughts are simmering, and he cannot rest. Recently there have been many nights like this one: during the day he keeps busy, out walking with friends or at home working on his book about the imitation of Christ – yet at night, when he has finished writing, his thoughts return to 'The Crisis and a Crisis in the Life of an Actress'. He wrote this article months ago – an inconsequential piece, it might seem to a casual reader – but this summer he has spent countless hours fretting about whether to make it the last act of his own literary drama.

Now it is done: today he gave the article to his friend Jens Finsen Giødvad, one of the editors of *The Fatherland*, Copenhagen's liberal daily newspaper. It will soon be published (under the pseudonym Inter et Inter, 'Between and Between') in four instalments in consecutive issues, starting on 24 July. This piece of journalism will end his authorship, giving the whole literary production a pleasing symmetry. He began in February 1843 by publishing *Either/Or*, a large 'aesthetic' book teeming with reflections on Greek tragedy, Shakespearean drama and French farce, which was followed three months later by a slim volume of religious discourses; now in 1848 his *oeuvre* is concluded with a large religious book, *Christian Discourses*, followed three months later by a short 'aesthetic' piece about an actress. The last five years of writing can now be seen, in retrospect, as a complete work of art – intricate and intense, complex and profound, yet expressing a single truth.

After weeks of anxious deliberation, there is no going back. He hoped the decision to publish 'The Crisis and a Crisis in the Life of an Actress' in *The Fatherland* would ease his mind, let him sleep. But the question of publication, alive for so long, is still vibrating within him, making him ill – 'alas, I would rather write a folio than publish a page'. And this question, to publish or not to publish, is inseparable from the question of who he is, which path he must follow through the world: to be or not to be an author?

No doubt he will be suspected as this article's author – and though its subject is not named either, she is easily recognizable as Johanne Luise Heiberg, Denmark's most celebrated actress. In reflecting on her career, Kierkegaard's article reaches back almost two decades, to the very beginning of his own life as a writer – for he was born less than half a year after Luise Heiberg, and her career has strange parallels with his own. In 1829, when she was seventeen, Luise Pätges (not yet Heiberg) starred in *Romeo and Juliet* at Copenhagen's Royal Theatre – and then last year, 1847, she played Juliet again, aged thirty-four. This symmetry mirrors the beginning and end of his authorship. Ever alive to the significance of repetitions, he has taken Mrs Heiberg's reprisal of her juvenile role as the occasion to ask how an artist should make the transition from youth to maturity; how to reconcile the frivolous and the profound elements of his work; how to express both the particularity of his experience and the shared truth of human existence – and how to live these questions onstage, beneath the bright lights of publicity.

During the years between her two Juliets, he has observed, this 'idolized' actress learned that her fame was 'empty' and her glory 'burdensome'. Now, as she reaches the height of her artistic powers, there is 'already gossip going around that she is getting older'. The public are fickle: 'The same fervid insipidity that without ceasing beat the big drum of banality in her praise and celebrated her eloquently on the cymbals, the same insipidity now becomes bored with its idolized artist; it wants to get rid of her, does not want to see her any more – she may thank God if it does not wish to have her exterminated. The same insipidity acquires a new sixteen-year-old idol, and in her honour the former idol has to experience the total disfavour of banality – because the great difficulty bound up with being an idol is that it is almost inconceivable that one can receive honour-able discharge from this appointment.' The 'banality' of public taste is particularly 'cruel' to women, who are judged by their superficial beauty: 'When it comes to the feminine, most people's art criticism has categories and thought-patterns essentially in common with every butcher's boy, national guardsman and shop assistant, who talk enthusiastically about a damned pretty and devilishly pert wench of eighteen years. On the other hand, at the point where, from the aes-thetic point of view, the interest really begins, there where the inner being beautifully and with intense meaning becomes manifest in the metamorphosis – there the crowd falls away.'

Johanne Luise Heiberg

Kierkegaard's article argues that playing Juliet a second time allowed Mrs Heiberg's true genius to shine: in the middle of her own life, she expressed Juliet's youthful vivacity in every word and ges-ture. While his own art is different – and he is certainly no idol – he is also confronting decisive questions about his creative development and his public image. Now, in 1848, he too can look back on himself at seventeen, when he stepped into a new world – and embarked on the path that led him to his life as an author.

\* \* \*

When Luise Pätges gave her first performance as Juliet in 1829, her life was undergoing a transformation. She was half-Jewish, the daughter of poor German immigrants, but her success in the theatre opened the doors to high society. In 1831 she married the well-connected writer Johan Ludvig Heiberg, who was twice her age. Not yet twenty, Madame Heiberg found herself surrounded by Copenhagen's cultural elite. Kierkegaard did not enter this world of aristocrats and artists so easily – indeed, he never made it into Heiberg's inner circle. Nevertheless, when he became a student at the University of Copenhagen in 1830, new vistas suddenly opened out before him.

He could now spend his days roaming between lecture rooms and the cafés along Strøget, the line of four busy streets running east to west through the centre of the city. Unlike the old-fashioned taverns, these modern cafés had large glass fronts: their patrons were on show to passers-by as well as to one another. Students and professors gathered in smart tea rooms with Italian names, or in Pleisch's *Konditorier*, or in Mini's, the finest coffee house in Copenhagen. They often piled into the university's Student Association, where they found a little freedom in their tightly censored city for literary readings, philosophical discourses and political debates.

Kierkegaard leapt eagerly and extravagantly into the arms of his newly unveiled city, while his father took care of the bills: he dined out, drank too much coffee, smoked expensive cigars, bought new clothes, and socialized energetically. He became a familiar figure in Reitzel's bookshop on Købmagergade, frequented by Denmark's most illustrious writers, and he took his new books, in their plain paper covers, straight to N. C. Møller's bookbindery – the best in town – to be bound in gold-embossed leather. He was already in the habit of taking long evening walks with Emil Boesen, his childhood friend, whose father was a Councillor of Justice and, like Michael Pedersen Kierkegaard, a senior figure in the Moravian community.

94

But now he found the streets of Copenhagen full of young men ready to converse with him about whatever they had just heard in their lectures or read in the newspapers. Although he confided his feelings only to Emil – and even then after imposing his own rules of censorship – he was willing to share his opinions with everyone.

The new people and ideas he encountered at the university introduced him to life-views very different from the one he knew at home on Nytorv, where his family's frugal peasant habits mixed cautiously with the mores of bourgeois respectability. Of course, by then he was already more educated than his father: at the age of eight he had followed his older brothers to the School of Civic Virtue, where he was drilled in Latin and Greek. His head teacher there, Michael Nielsen, was a strict disciplinarian, who found the youngest Kierkegaard 'extremely childish and wholly devoid of seriousness, with a taste for freedom and independence, which prevented him from entering too deeply into any subject'. But Nielsen was impressed by Søren's quick, receptive mind, his great aptitude for languages, and his lively personality, 'still open and unspoiled' at seventeen. Kierkegaard left the school having read Horace, Virgil and Cicero, Homer, Plato and Herodotus, and Xenophon's *Life of Socrates*. He could translate the Book of Genesis from the Hebrew, and the Gospel of John from the Greek.

Those years at the School of Civic Virtue prepared him well for the degree in theology he began in the autumn of 1830. Again he was following his eldest brother Peter, who by that time had graduated in theology from the University of Copenhagen placed first in his class, studied for a year in Berlin, defended his doctoral dissertation at Göttingen – where he earned a reputation as 'the demon debater from the North' – and found himself in Paris in the middle of the July Revolution. But unlike his high-flying brother, Kierkegaard was not a very diligent student of theology. Christian doctrine, biblical exegesis and Church history interested him far less than the new kinds of literature he discovered at the university.

At the turn of the nineteenth century the first generation of German Romantics in Jena and Berlin had broken the old rules of art, religion, morality, philosophy and science: in their hands, human creativity became less constrained and more highly prized than ever before. These young writers evoked a shifting, fluid world that offered itself to be transformed, not only by new aesthetic ideals but by new ways of life. Goethe, the undisputed poetic genius of the age, was held up as the highest human exemplar – but every man, the poet Novalis urged in 1798, 'should become an artist'. Unforeseen questions lay in wait for Kierkegaard as he entered this world: Could *he* become a poet? What would it feel like to live poetically? How could he make his own life into a work of art?

Ideas flowed quickly from the German cities to Copenhagen, and early in the new century Romanticism inspired a rising generation of Danish intellectuals. In 1802 Henrik Steffens returned to Copenhagen after studying geology in Germany, where he had become a disciple of the brilliant young philosopher Friedrich Wilhelm von Schelling. Hoping for a professorship in philosophy at the University of Copenhagen, Steffens gave a series of public lectures to large audiences of academics, students, and other men of culture. Modern life had become 'prosaic' and 'irreligious', he told them, and needed to be reanimated by human genius: 'that in us which is divine; that which is one with everything, our real essence'. Prose should give way to poetry – not merely a matter of versification, but the pursuit of the 'stamp of the eternal' within the finite world. 'I will open up a more significant vision of life and existence than that to which ordinary existence and daily life, confined as they are by finite needs, leads us,' Steffens promised his listeners, as he set out the controversial pantheist philosophy he had learned in Germany.

In the university town of Jena, Steffens had encountered the circle of young intellectuals gathered around two brothers, August Wilhelm and Friedrich von Schlegel – and August Wilhelm's wife Caroline, who inspired in most of these men an erotic passion that fuelled their creativity. This intimate, extraordinarily talented circle included Friedrich von Hardenberg (writing under the pseudonym Novalis), the theologian Friedrich Schleiermacher, and Schelling, who later married Caroline after she divorced August Wilhelm. They were closely acquainted with Goethe, Schiller and Fichte. The new dawn following the French Revolution still seemed bright, and the group shared high hopes for spiritual and political liberation.

In 1798 the Schlegels had started a journal, the *Athenaeum*, in which they and their friends shaped a distinctively Romantic literature, inspired by Schiller's *Letters on the Aesthetic Education of Man*, published in 1795. Here Schiller urged that 'the development of man's capacity for feeling is the most urgent need of the age', and argued that we become 'fully human beings' when we contemplate beautiful works of art, which offer an experience of 'utter repose and extreme restlessness'. The new Romantic literature, Friedrich von Schlegel explained, would draw on the vast resources of the human imagination to produce 'a feeling that is not sensual, but spiritual. Love is the source and soul of this feeling, and the spirit of love must diffuse through Romantic poetry everywhere, visibly and invisibly.' Schlegel regarded human creativity as inseparable from nature's infinitely productive powers: echoing Schelling's new philosophy of nature – which influenced scientific as well as metaphysical theories of life – he described the 'unconscious poetry that moves in the plant, that streams forth in light, that laughs out in the child, that shimmers in the bud of youth, that glows in the loving breasts of women'. This poetry was the true word of God, resounding throughout nature.

At that time Friedrich von Schlegel was living with Schleiermacher in Berlin: encouraged by his friend to write, Schleiermacher contributed dozens of fragments to the *Athenaeum*, and then published *On Religion: Talks to the Cultured among its Despisers* in 1799. This book's unconventional defence of Christianity was addressed to those who, like Schiller and Schlegel, worshipped only philosophy and art. Schleiermacher urged these readers to look inwardly into themselves as well as out at the universe, to awaken a 'feeling for that eternal and holy being which lies far on the other side of the world'. He described feelings of submission and dissolution that arise when nature is grasped intuitively, seen as an infinite but ordered whole: then one could experience 'the quiet disappearance of one's whole existence in the immeasurable'. Appealing directly to his Romantic friends, Schleiermacher deemed art 'holy', and poets 'the higher priesthood who transmit the innermost spiritual secrets, and speak from the kingdom of God'. Artists and poets, he wrote, 'strive to awaken the slumbering kernel of a better humanity, to inflame a love for higher things, to transform a common life into a higher one'.

Schleiermacher had been educated at a Moravian school and seminary; Schelling and the Schlegels were sons of Lutheran pastors; and Hardenberg's father was a strict Moravian pietist. Disenchanted with the religion of their fathers, these men had thirsted for an alternative spirituality. Yet their philosophical poetry and poetic philosophies were rooted in their shared Christian heritage, while bursting out of its constraints. Like the pietists, they turned away from the rationalizing currents of the eighteenth century, and sought spiritual 'awakening' – for themselves personally and also for society – through feeling, within the human heart. And they too returned to the medieval traditions left behind by the Enlightenment: as the pietists had revived pre-Reformation mystical and devotional literature, so these early Romantics looked back to the age of chivalry and magic, re-reading medieval tales of love and adventure. In the fantastic quests described in these courtly romances and folk tales, they found new models for the inward, spiritual journey of self-discovery and self-development that was already a well-travelled pietist path.

But while the pietists sought their true selves only in those emotions and experiences which would draw them closer to perfect holiness, the Romantics explored the whole range of human feeling, unbounded by moralism or religious orthodoxy. They were all reading Spinoza, the seventeenth-century philosopher who insisted in his masterpiece, the *Ethics*, that everything 'is in God'. They embraced Spinoza's pantheist theology, still widely condemned as heretical, and combined this doctrine with more recent ideas about art and creativity. To the Romantics, pantheism meant unprecedented freedom: if nothing is outside God, then nothing is out of bounds. While the pietists tried to cultivate humility and obedience, the Romantics worshipped the expansive power of the human imagination. Their ideal exemplar was not – or at least not only – Jesus Christ, but any artistic genius who channelled the divine power immanent in nature. Pietists held to the orthodox Christian belief that God had created the world; the Romantics believed that great artists could create new worlds, again and again.

When Henrik Steffens returned from his electrifying visit to Jena in 1802 he had his own circle of friends waiting for him in Copenhagen: J. P. Mynster, young pastor and future bishop; Adam Oehlenschläger, the finest poet of his generation; A. S. Ørsted, a jurist and legal scholar who later became Denmark's prime minister, and his brother H. C. Ørsted, then embarking on his brilliant scientific career. They often gathered at the home of the writer K. L. Rahbek and his wife Kamma, who presided over Copenhagen's leading literary salon. Like the Jena circle, this group were closely bound by family ties: Mynster's stepfather was Steffens's uncle; Oehlenschläger married Kamma Rahbek's sister; A. S. Ørsted married Oehlenschläger's sister.

Steffens's friends imbibed the new Romantic philosophy. In the summer of 1802 Oehlenschläger published a collection of poems nostalgic for 'the ancient, ancient, bygone days, when Scandinavia gleamed', blending Norse myths with Christian imagery to evoke a natural world imbued with 'mystical divinity'. Inspired by Novalis, Oehlenschläger elaborated this pantheistic vision in his 1805 lyric poem 'The Life of Jesus Christ Repeated in the Annual Cycle of Nature'. Meanwhile, H. C. Ørsted pursued research into 'the Spirit in Nature', and he eventually discovered that – as Schelling had predicted, but not proven – electricity and magnetism are two aspects of the same force. This scientific breakthrough brought into clearer view the spiritual unity which, the Romantics believed, lay hidden beneath the diverse phenomena of nature and culture.

Mynster was also influenced by Romanticism, but his religious awakening of 1803 strengthened his Christian orthodoxy. In 1805 Oehlenschläger, Kamma Rahbek and H. C. Ørsted all urged him to defend Oehlenschläger's Jesus-Nature poem, which had been denounced by Bishop Balle, then the leader of the Danish State Church. Mynster was himself troubled by the poem's pagan theology, and his cherished conscience was torn. In the end, after months of soul-searching and mounting pressure from his friends, he wrote – in verse – a sympathetic review of Oehlenschläger's poem. Steffens, meanwhile, was not offered the chair in philosophy he had hoped for, and went back to Germany.

After those early years of Denmark's cultural 'Golden Age', successive waves of Romanticism reached Copenhagen. Oehlenschläger published his second collection of poems in 1805, went on a European tour, and spent several months in Weimar with Goethe, who towered above the Romantic movement as the incarnation of divine genius. By the time Oehlenschläger returned to Denmark in 1810 to take up the chair in aesthetics at the University of Copenhagen, he had mixed with Romantic writers and thinkers in Berlin, Paris, Rome and Switzerland. When Kierkegaard entered the university in 1830, Oehlenschläger was still there, lecturing on Shakespeare and Goethe; he was recognized as the 'poetic king of Scandinavia', and in 1831 he became Rector of the university. Kierkegaard bought Oehlenschläger's books, and found in them the experimental verse, mixtures of genre, and contrasts of mood that had become familiar to readers of Romantic literature.

By the 1830s, however, Johan Ludvig Heiberg was challenging Oehlenschläger's claim to his literary throne. Heiberg was born into the elite salon that had nurtured Danish Romanticism: his parents, both talented writers, separated after his father was exiled from Denmark for political radicalism, and young Heiberg lived with the Rahbeks while his parents divorced and his mother Thomasine remarried. After he returned from his travels in Germany in 1824, newly converted to Hegelian philosophy, Heiberg wrote a series of plays that were performed at Copenhagen's Royal Theatre to great acclaim. He quickly established himself as Denmark's leading literary critic: in 1827 he founded a journal, *Copenhagen's Flying Post*, where he published his mother's stories anonymously, promoted his own aesthetic theory, and criticized Oehlenschläger's poetry. And in 1831 he married the dazzling young actress Luise Pätges.

Under Heiberg's influence, Kierkegaard's generation were taught to see Romanticism as a passing phase – even while the air was still thick with Romantic ideas about the power of poetry and philosophy to change the world. In 1833 Heiberg set out his own manifesto, *On the Significance of Philosophy for the Present Age*. There he argued that it was Hegel's philosophy, not Schelling's, which would cure the spiritual malaise diagnosed by the Romantics, whose relativistic world view had, Heiberg suggested, only hastened the decline. Hegel and Goethe were 'undoubtedly the two greatest men the modern age has produced ... their works contain the entire life of spirit of our age'; together, in their mutually complementary domains of philosophy and art, these two titans of the *Zeitgeist* would rescue European culture.

Kierkegaard's aesthetic education was also shaped by his philosophy professors Poul Møller and Frederik Christian Sibbern, both literary writers as well as scholars. Sibbern is interested in modern philosophy: as a young man, he spent two years travelling in Germany, where he met Steffens, Fichte, Schleiermacher and Goethe. When Kierkegaard first encountered him, Sibbern had recently published an epistolary novel, *Posthumous Letters of Gabriel*, modelled on Goethe's *The Sorrows of Young Werther*, and in his lectures on aesthetics – which Kierkegaard attended in 1833 – he frequently discussed Goethe. Møller, a talented poet, had adopted the Romantics' aphoristic, fragmentary style. He was a scholar of ancient Greek literature and philosophy, and an 'unforgettable' teacher who inspired Kierkegaard's love for Socrates. While other Danish intellectuals advanced their careers by travelling the familiar academic trade route to the German university towns, Møller had sailed to China and back following a romantic disappointment. He was Kierkegaard's favourite teacher.

Men like Oehlenschläger and Heiberg, Sibbern and Møller, taught Kierkegaard to speak of the modern age and contrast it with a classical past; to admire Cervantes, Shakespeare and Goethe; to see works of art as spiritually potent; to appreciate legends, myths and folk tales; to philosophize through literary criticism. They also embodied the existential possibility that he discovered during his first months at university. These men were professional poets and philosophers: they earned their living from their ideas, their imaginations, their skilled use of language; they debated, they wrote, they published; they were read, reviewed and talked about. In their writing they formed their souls, cultivated their natures, perhaps even honed their genius – and displayed these poetic selves to the world.

Gradually these exemplars entered into Kierkegaard's life; strands of their lives were woven into his own. He became well acquainted with Sibbern: they talked about philosophy while walking around Copenhagen, or sitting by the fire in Sibbern's parlour. Sibbern got to know his loquacious student well enough to see that he was 'a very inwardly complicated sort of person', 'very polemical', and 'nearly always only capable of speaking about the things with which he was engaged in his innermost self'. Yet Sibbern also noticed that 'he wanted to look after those people whom the public did not value.' During Kierkegaard's engagement to Regine, the philosophy professor spent time with the young couple, and then found himself counselling Regine after the break-up. When she confided her 'deep indignation' at how Kierkegaard had 'mistreated her soul', Sibbern told her that it would be worse if they were married, for 'his spirit was continually preoccupied with itself.'

Poul Møller became Kierkegaard's mentor; his interest in Socrates and his own unsystematic, unconventional style had an enduring influence on Kierkegaard's philosophical development. He died in 1838, in his mid-forties. But without Møller, Kierkegaard would not have written his dissertation on irony, nor aspired to be the Socrates of Christendom. Six years after Møller's death, Kierkegaard dedicated *The Concept of Anxiety* to him – 'the enthusiasm of my youth; the mighty trumpet of my awakening; the desired object of my feelings; the confidant of my beginnings; my lost friend; my sadly missed reader'.

Even Oehlenschläger, a more remote figure, has a role in his *Bildungsroman*. In letters to Regine during their engagement, he quoted from Oehlenschläger's fairy-tale drama *Aladdin*, and when he went to Berlin following the break-up he took this book with him. 'If you need me and call / I come like lightning,' he copied into his notebook while he sailed, overwrought, to Germany. He wrote to Regine of the 'genie of the ring' within him, linked to her 'with the longing of my whole soul, for did I not myself bring you the ring I obey?' As the steamship ploughed further and further away from her, he reflected that 'both you and I united together are the genie of the ring.'

And of course Heiberg, though he remained aloof, was drawn into a complex relationship with Kierkegaard. It was Heiberg who published Kierkegaard's very first article in *Copenhagen's Flying Post* in 1834; a decade later, after Heiberg reviewed *Either/Or*, Kierkegaard was spurred to polemics against his former editor and became more determined to go his own way as a writer; he is still expressing contempt for literary 'coteries'. In 1846 he repeated Heiberg's effort to set out a philosophical diagnosis of 'the present age' – in the form of a review of a novel by Heiberg's mother, Thomasine Gyllembourg. And now, in 1848, Kierkegaard has decided to end his authorship with an article about Heiberg's wife.

During those early years of the 1830s, Kierkegaard discovered a new literature, and learned to read and critique it in new ways. He also learned to read and critique himself differently: while his Christian habits of self-examination lingered – he searched his conscience, he went to confession, he pondered his vocation – he took on the poetic ideals of the Romantics and applied them to his life. Perhaps it is not surprising that he has found the energies and excesses of Romanticism magnified within his own soul. At university, his innate tendency to hyper-reflection was nourished by an intellectual culture steeped in three decades of idealist philosophy and literary irony; his experiences and feelings were wrapped in countless folds of reflection, filled with poetic significance, and suffused with existential doubts.

His memories of these student years are also suffused with grief. His two remaining sisters, Nicolene and Petrea, died in 1832 and 1834 respectively; they had married two prosperous brothers, Johan Christian Lund and Henrik Ferdinand Lund, and they each left four children. His closest brother, Niels, died alone in a hotel room in New Jersey in 1833, having sailed across the Atlantic seeking business opportunities; although Niels wanted to follow their brother Peter to university, their father told him to go into trade. And Kierkegaard's mother Anne died in 1834, leaving little record of her sixty-six years. In the raw weeks of his grief, he visited the mother of Martensen, then his philosophy tutor, who was away travelling in Europe. Mrs Martensen was struck by his profound sorrow. 'Never in her life,' she would often tell her son, 'had she seen a human being so deeply distressed as S. Kierkegaard was by the death of his mother', and she felt that he must have 'an unusually profound sensibility'. 'She was not wrong about this,' conceded Martensen. 'No one can deny him that.'

In the autumn of 1834, three months after his mother died, Kierkegaard began to write down his ideas in a journal. Following the Romantic fashion for medieval literature, he often wrote about characters from folk tales and legends, and he was drawn to figures who in some way took a stance against the world, opposing or subverting its conventions, defying its morality. 'It is remarkable,' he reflected, 'that Germany has its Faust, Italy and Spain their Don Juan, the Jews the Wandering Jew, Denmark and north Germany, Eulenspiegel.' These characters – a sceptical scholar who sells his soul to the devil; a serial seducer dedicated to sensual pleasure; a despairing outcast condemned to wander in exile; a trickster who exposes his victims' hypocrisy and folly – were anti-heroic exemplars. To a young man schooled in Civic Virtue, brought up on the sermons of Mynster and Reuss, they revealed dangerous and enticing ways of being in the world.

His first literary journal entries were on the 'master-thief': subversive characters like Eulenspiegel or Robin Hood, who were principled and good-hearted as well as cunning. By his criminal activity the master-thief consciously opposed the established order or avenged social injustice; armed with his own ethic, he chose to be an outsider. One day Kierkegaard tried out this 'youthful, romantic enthusiasm for a master-thief' in conversation with his father, and received a severe reply: 'There are some crimes that can be fought only with the constant help of God,' intoned the old man. Kierkegaard's deep-rooted fear of his own sinfulness surged up, and he ran to his room and looked at himself in the mirror. Above his bright, anxious gaze his hair was swept into a dramatic quiff, nearly six inches high: at twenty-one years old his religious melancholy had taken a visibly Romantic turn. This image of himself staring into his reflection, torn between moral anxiety and rebellion, reminded him of Friedrich von Schlegel's account of the legend of Merlin the Magician, in which a young girl becomes afraid of her own body after looking in the mirror.

Around this time, in December 1834, his first article was published in Heiberg's journal *Copenhagen's Flying Post*. This was a brittle, sarcastic response to a patronizing article by one of his university friends on the emancipation of women – 'in fashion magazines, they study the spirit of the age,' joked Kierkegaard in 'Another Defence of Woman's Great Abilities'. His writing gathered momentum in the summer of 1835 when, at his father's expense, he spent a few weeks travelling around Gilleleje. In his journal he 'poeticized' his travels through the countryside of northern Zealand in the Romantic manner: he visited ancient sites of Danish folk tales and legends, and described gloomy forests, tranquil lakes, the surging sea. 'People still do not grow weary of gadding about busily pointing out the romantic settings,' he observed.

During an excursion to Lake Esrom on 8 July the sky darkened, and Kierkegaard prepared himself for some sublime weather. 'I have seen the sea turn blue-grey and become agitated, and I have watched the gusts of wind that announced the approaching storm swirl the grass and sand upward along the coast, but I have never seen a performance in which the whole forest is set in motion by these gusts of wind (these trumpet calls that announce the judgment),' he wrote. 'But it turned out to be just rain.' Later that day, though, he found his storm, and soon he was 'soaked to the skin amid thunder and lightning and pouring rain in the heart of the Grib forest, and beside me [in the carriage] sat a boy who trembled at the lightning'. They found shelter in a peasant's house, where Kierkegaard asked for bread for his horse, and gave the peasant's wife more money than she thought she should accept – 'for I could spare it, and she needed it'.

Travelling south from Lake Esrom, past Hillerød, Kierkegaard discovered a landscape of mystical beauty: a valley of quiet beech forests and a small lake overgrown with waterlilies, resplendent in the morning light. Seen through eyes trained by pantheist poetry to discern the divine within nature, this was a spiritual place. Why did anyone need organized religion, he mused, when here 'the church bells call to prayer, but not in a temple made by human hands – and if the birds do not need to be reminded to praise God, then ought men not be moved to prayer outside of the church, in the true house of God, where heaven's arch forms the ceiling of the church, where the roar of the storm and the light breezes take the place of the organ's bass and treble, where the singing of the birds makes up the congregational hymns of praise ... where everything resolves itself in an endless antiphony –?'

Still in character as a Romantic poet, Kierkegaard took an evening walk on the northernmost cliffs of the Gilleleje coast and looked out to sea. Oceanic feelings should come naturally to a Danish soul; listening to 'the deep but quietly earnest song of the sea' and to the 'evening prayers' of the birds, he imagined himself 'empowered to perceive things differently'. He thought of his mother, of his brothers Niels and little Søren Michael, of his sisters Maren, Nicolene and

Petrea. These 'dear departed ones' rose from the grave before him, and he felt at ease in their midst: 'I rested in their embrace, and I felt as if transported out of my body and floating about with them in a higher ether.' This reverie was interrupted by a squawking seagull – so much for avian prayers – and he 'turned back with a heavy heart to mingle with the world's crowds'. Yet in such blessed moments, he wrote:

> I have often stood there and pondered my past life and the various influences that have been important to me, and the pettiness that so often creates animosity in life vanished before my eyes. When the whole, looked at in perspective this way, displayed only the larger, more vivid outlines, and I did not lose myself in the detail as I often do but saw the whole in its totality, I was empowered to perceive things differently, to understand how often I had made mistakes, and to forgive others. – As I stood there, free from the depression and despondency that would make me see myself as excluded from the men who usually surround me, or free of the pride that would make me the constituting principle of a little circle – as I stood there alone and forsaken and the brute force of the sea and the battle of the elements reminded me of my nothingness, and on the other hand the sure flight of the birds reminded me of Christ's words: 'Not a sparrow will fall to the earth without your heavenly Father's will,' I felt at one and the same time how great and insignificant I am.

It was a question, he concluded, of learning true humility. Just as Jesus retreated up a mountain when people wanted to proclaim him their king, so 'it is good for a person to withdraw from the turmoil of the world', into the heart of nature, where he can 'surrender' to a higher power. Kierkegaard resolved to take inward action, even to keep silent for three years. Of course, *that* was never a serious vow: back in Copenhagen, he resumed his sociable walks and intense coffee-shop conversations, and a few weeks into the autumn term he was addressing the Student Association on the question of free speech.

Who was that man standing 'alone and forsaken' on the Gilbjerg cliffs, contemplating his 'great and insignificant' life? How many of his thoughts arose from the swirling sea, and how many were borrowed from literary journals, volumes of poetry, or lectures on aesthetics? Which parts of him came from Nytorv, from Stormgade, from the Church of Our Lady? Had he travelled inwards on this journey to Gilleleje – or did he leave the city in order to fashion his soul according to an image he had discovered within its walls? Was he finding himself, or transforming himself, or creating himself 'out there', with the lilies and the birds? Where did his journey end and the journal begin?

By then, of course, he had learned that self-knowledge is not simply a matter of glancing in the mirror – for the person looking back at him was never a distinct, unalloyed self. 'We often deceive ourselves,' he confessed, 'by embracing as our own many an idea and observation which either springs forth vividly out of a time when we read it, or lies in the consciousness of the whole age.' If our inner lives always reflect the world, how can we know ourselves apart from that world? 'Yes, even now as I write this observation,' Kierkegaard reflected, '– this, too, perhaps, is a fruit of the experience of the age.' And within every fold of reflection there is a little space for dissemblance and deceit.

His travelogue culminated in a long passage, more like a literary essay than a diary entry, though it was headed 'Gilleleje, August 1, 1835'. Here he reflected on the scholarly life, and resolved to 'live a completely human life, and not merely one of knowledge'. This was not just a personal aspiration, but a philosophical manifesto:

> What I really need is to get clear about *what I must do*, not what I must know, except insofar as knowledge must precede every act. What matters is to find a purpose, to see what it really is that God wills *I* shall do; the crucial thing is to find a truth that is true *for me*, to find *the idea for which I am willing to live and die.* Of what use would it be to me to discover a so-called objective truth, to work through the philosophical systems so that I could, if asked, make critical judgements about them; of what use would it be to me to develop a theory of the state, getting details from various sources and combining them into a whole, and constructing a world I did not live in but merely held up for others to see; of what use would it be to me to be able to formulate the meaning of Christianity, to be able to explain many specific

points – if it had no deeper meaning *for me and for my life*? I certainly do not deny that I still accept an *imperative of knowledge* and that through it men may be influenced, but *then it must come alive in me*, and *this* is what I now recognize as the most important of all. This is what my soul thirsts for as the African deserts thirst for water. This is what I need to live, a *completely human life* and not merely one of *knowledge*, so that I could base the development of my thought not on – yes, not on something called objective – something which in any case is not my own, but upon something which is bound up with the deepest roots of my existence, through which I am, so to speak, grafted into the divine, to which I cling fast even though the whole world may collapse. *This is what I need, and this is what I strive for.* A man must first learn to know himself before knowing anything else. Not until he has inwardly understood *himself* and then sees the course he is to take does his life gain peace and meaning; only then is he free of that irksome, sinister travelling companion – that irony of life which manifests itself in the sphere of knowledge.

By this time Kierkegaard had spent five years at university, and seemed to be nowhere near completing his theology degree: when he doubted the value of theoretical knowledge, he was questioning the meaning of his own existence. Yet while he was living these questions, he was writing about them at a distance – not yet using pseudonyms, but trying out the persona of a poet.

In this journal entry, as in many others written before and after the journey to Gilleleje, Kierkegaard explored themes from the old legend of Faust, the sceptical scholar. In the 1830s everyone was talking about Faust: this medieval tale of a man who rebelled against God had captured the Romantic imagination, and Goethe finally completed the second part of his poetic drama *Faust* just before he died in 1832. According to the traditional legend Faust's life ended in damnation, but Goethe gave the story a new ending. His Faust undergoes a last-minute conversion, similar to St Paul's experience on the road to Damascus: he is suddenly blinded, cast into darkness, and then rescued from the devil by hosts of angels. In this surprising conclusion to his long-awaited *Faust*, Goethe seemed to send a parting message to the world he was leaving behind. During his lifetime the great poet had seen the German universities grow more and more professionalized, filled with men striving for enlightenment through academic study – but Faust's sudden blindness suggested that it is through its dark nights that the human soul matures, expands, deepens, and finds God within its depths.

Kierkegaard has a similar view of the spiritual life, and his soul has absorbed many dark, sleepless nights. But in the mid-1830s he disapproved of Goethe's ending, because he wanted to use the story of Faust to make his own diagnosis of the modern age. He believed that Faust personified doubt, the defining feature of this age, and that in making Faust convert before he died Goethe had betrayed his character's very essence. He, Kierkegaard, would produce a new interpretation of Faust, which – like the essays of Heiberg and Friedrich von Schlegel – would merge literary criticism, philosophy and poetry in a brilliant analysis of contemporary culture.

In 1836 the poet Nikolaus Lenau published another version of *Faust*. Lenau had recently returned to Germany, disillusioned, from Pennsylvania, where he had lived for a few months in a radical pietist commune. His *Faust* was nihilistic, for his own Romantic melancholy was shading into deep pessimism. Lenau's poem made misery for Kierkegaard too. 'Oh how unhappy I am! Martensen has published an essay on Lenau's *Faust!*' he wrote in his journal in 1837, after seeing Martensen's essay – which argued that Faust symbolized the hubristic, irreligious tendencies of modern secular knowledge – in Heiberg's new journal *Perseus*. That day, he was definitely writing in his own voice.

To his ageing father's increasing dismay, he continued to delay sitting his theology exams, and spent most of his time thinking, talking and scribbling about literature and philosophy. He made notes on humour and irony, Christianity and Romanticism, and he was often seen deep in conversation with Poul Møller, who was preoccupied with these topics. In May 1837 he turned twenty-four, and met Regine Olsen for the first time. That summer, he felt oppressed by 'the unhappy relativity in everything, the endless questions about *what I am*, about my joys and what other people see in me, and in what I do'. Yet those endless questions were at least better than unthinking contentment: he did not want to be like 'the *petit bourgeois*', who valued morality above intelligence and had 'never felt nostalgia for some unknown, remote something, never experienced the profundity of being nothing at all, of strolling out of Nørreport with four shillings in one's pocket and a slender cane in hand'.

By then, only three Kierkegaards were left in the family home on Nytorv. Søren, his brother Peter Christian – whose first wife had just died of typhoid fever after a few months of marriage – and their elderly father rattled unhappily around the big house. Until 1837 they had attended Friday communion services together twice a year; now his brother and father went separately, and he did not go at all. 'Søren these days is perhaps more than ever before weighed down by brooding, almost more than his health can stand, but it only makes him unhappy, indecisive, and is close to driving him insane,' Peter Christian wrote in his diary that August.

\* \* \*

Yes, the university years that enticed and prepared him to become an author intensified his reflection, deepened his sadness, and multiplied his anxieties. Those early disappointments still taste bitter now, more than ten years later – for this feeling, too, has been thickened by fresh layers, compacted to form a heavy pain around his heart. In 'The Crisis and a Crisis in the Life of an Actress' he has noted that the fickle cruelty which slackens 'the crowd's' admiration for Johanne Luise Heiberg as she gets older can be inflicted on authors, too – that is to say, authors who do not (like that actress's husband) flatter the shallow tastes of the public:

> If an author who neither has a considerable fund of ideas nor is very industrious were to publish at long intervals an elegant copybook that is especially ornate and is resplendently provided with so many blank pages – the crowd gazes at this elegant phenomenon with amazement and admiration and thinks that if he has been such a long time in writing it and if there is so little on the page then it really must be something extraordinary. If, on the other hand, an idea-rich author who has something else to think about than elegance and making a profit from an illusion, exerting himself with ever greater diligence, finds himself

able to work at an unusual speed, the crowd soon becomes accustomed to it and thinks: It must be slovenly stuff. The crowd, of course, cannot judge whether something is well worked out or not; it sticks to – the illusion.

He battles his disappointment daily, and defiance proves again and again to be his best defence: though *Christian Discourses* has been hardly noticed, ignored by Professor Martensen and Bishop Mynster, he is still sculpting his authorship with exquisite care. If it must end now, then it will end perfectly – exactly as he wishes it. As the grey light slowly seeps into Rosenborggade, he gives up on sleep. It is nearly five in the morning, and another dawn is breaking.

# 8

## Living without a Life-View

He says goodbye to Rasmus Nielsen on the corner of Rosenborggade and Tornebuskegade and goes inside, out of the blazing August sunshine, up the stairs to his cool, shaded rooms. In this part of town the sour stench from the tanneries along Rosenborggade overpowers the other smells of the city wafting on the breeze and rising from the open gutters – rotting fish, old meat, seaweed, sewage. The reek from the tanner's yard owned by his landlord, Mr Gram, has become unbearable in the hot weather, and his servants are instructed to close the blackened windows before he returns home from his walks. He is exhausted, but agitated; he reaches instinctively for his pen, and paces back and forth across the room. For the last few weeks, since 'The Crisis and a Crisis in the Life of an Actress' appeared in *The Fatherland*, he has agonized about it. Is this 'little aesthetic article' a fitting finale for his literary production? How will it be interpreted – or misinterpreted? Over this summer of 1848 he has filled pages of his journal answering his own doubts over whether he should have published it at all. Consumed by anxiety, and convinced he will die soon, he worries that this article will distort his entire authorship.

He does not want to be thought frivolous, or to lessen the impact of his recent religious works – but nor does he want people to think he started out as a daring aesthete, and then became a religious writer simply because he grew older. This happened to many of the early Romantics, who after their youthful pantheist rebellions returned to Christian orthodoxy in middle age – Henrik Steffens became a conservative Lutheran, and Friedrich von Schlegel converted to Catholicism – and of course Kierkegaard does not want to be regarded as a Romantic cliché. No, even the scandalous *Either/Or* aimed to deepen its reader's relationship to God; his aesthetic interests and his religious earnestness have always gone together; this late journalistic piece about Madame Heiberg is proof of that.

But *will* people see it this way? How painful it is to let himself be seen, even obliquely – to pour his energies into communicating this struggle to be human, these questions that he himself lives so deeply – and then to be misunderstood! When these anxieties about his authorship assail him, he tries to console himself with the thought of Rasmus Nielsen's friendship and loyalty. He never used to think much of Nielsen, a philosophy professor at the University of Copenhagen – indeed, he has often sneered at his mediocrity – but in recent months they have grown closer, taking weekly walks together, Nielsen full of appreciation for his work and eager to learn more about his philosophical views. Kierkegaard has begun to hope that after he dies Nielsen will defend his reputation and secure his literary legacy. This raises fresh uncertainties, though: does Nielsen understand his work sufficiently, and can he really be relied on?

> But what is the worst thing about this is that I have managed to get the matter so muddled in reflection that I scarcely know what I am doing. And therefore, even if there had been no other reason for doing so, I would have to act. Nothing exhausts me so terribly as negative decisions: to have been ready to do something, that is, to have found it entirely right, desirable, etc., and then suddenly a great many reflections drift together in a pile in which I could practically perish. It can never be right that something which in itself is insignificant could suddenly actually come to possess a dreadful reality. It is a sign that reflection has become sick. When this happens, action must be taken in order to preserve life. Then indolence will continue letting one imagine that the negative path was after all the best – but that is sheer lies. The only right thing to do is to take refuge in God – and act.

Somehow, amid all his anxiety, charged with caffeine, nicotine and thoughts of mortality – and immortality – he glimpses how these obsessive ruminations about his authorship are driven by egotism and conceit. He cares about the world's opinion much more than he thinks he should, and (because of his pride, again) more than he wants to admit. Not for the first time, he sees that he suffers because he lacks faith: 'it is reflection that wants to make me extraordinary, instead of placing my confidence in God and being the person I am.' Nevertheless this habit of reflection carries him away again and again.

And when did he become 'the person I am'? This person is inseparable from his authorship: the years before he began to write seem, now, the preparation for his literary life. Yet his authorship has had several false starts as well as false endings. Indeed his days, like some of his books, have been distended by the difficulty of making a start and the difficulty of coming to a stop.

\* \* \*

In the mid-1830s his journalistic debut in *Copenhagen's Flying Post* – the flippant dismissal of female emancipation posing as 'Another Defence of Woman's Great Abilities' – was followed by three more articles in Heiberg's journal. These pieces criticized the liberal press, a topic which allowed him to display his polemical wit against two other ambitious young writers, Orla Lehmann and Johannes Hage, who were pushing the liberal agenda. These articles were so clever and eloquent – and so close to Heiberg's style – that readers assumed Heiberg himself had written them: Kierkegaard was delighted to hear from Emil Boesen that Poul Møller thought them the best things Heiberg had written for a while. After this success, he spent several months planning his first major work, the essay on Faust, only to be beaten to it by Martensen.

Beginning again was difficult. After sulking through the summer of 1837, he moved out of Nytorv that September and rented an apartment a few streets away, on Løvstræde. His new home was at the corner of the square where Martensen lived: from his windows Kierkegaard had a clear view of his rival's house. His father gave him a generous allowance, and paid off the large debts he had accumulated from buying books, writing paper, clothes, shoes and tobacco, going to the theatre, and frequenting coffee shops and restaurants. In an effort to gain a little independence, he returned to his old school to teach Latin during that autumn term. Soon he was philosophizing about the grammar he had to explain to the boys at the School of

Civic Virtue: 'Modern philosophy is purely subjunctive,' he wrote in his journal in September; by October, he was finding the same fault in himself – 'Unfortunately my life is far too subjunctive; would to God I had some indicative power!'

After seven years as a student he felt trapped in a bubble of possibility, floating above the world, unable to enter into it. Academic study had taught him to see his own life as a symptom of a declining age, yet he still did not know how to step out into the world and make something happen. He was overflowing with ideas, but they were diverse, scattered, sketchy. Now that Faust had to be abandoned, he was casting about for a new project. One idea was to write 'a history of the human soul', which would follow 'the development of human nature' by examining what people of different ages laughed at. A week later he thought about writing a dissertation on ancient Roman satire. Another day, he contemplated 'a novella in which the main character is a man who has acquired a pair of spectacles, one lens of which reduces images as powerfully as an oxy-gas microscope, and the other magnifies on the same scale, so that he apprehends everything very relativistically'. How often he, Kierkegaard, has been like this man, and turned his distorted gaze upon himself. Meanwhile the nights drew in, the season turned: 'Why I so much prefer autumn to spring is that in the autumn one looks at heaven – in the spring at the earth.'

The following spring, 1838, he moved back home to Nytorv. In April he recorded Poul Møller's death in his journal, and resolved to pull himself together: 'Again such a long time has passed in which I have been unable to collect myself for the least thing – I must now make another little shot of it.' He started writing a review of Hans Christian Andersen's new novel *Only a Fiddler*, the story of a gifted violinist prevented by circumstances from realizing his musical genius in the world. This review gave him an opportunity to develop some of the philosophical ideas he had been discussing with Møller; he hoped it would be published, like Martensen's essay on Faust, in Heiberg's journal *Perseus*. But when Heiberg read it he disliked the heavy, convoluted prose. By August a revised version of the review was nearly finished, but that month the second – and, as it turned out, final – volume of *Perseus* appeared without it.

Poul Martin Møller at his death

On 8 August 1838 Michael Pedersen Kierkegaard died. Three days later Kierkegaard opened his journal again, and marked a page with a small black cross:

†

My father died on Wednesday, the 8th, at 2:00 a.m. I did so earnestly desire that he should live a few years more, and I regard his death as the last sacrifice his love made for me, because he has not died from me but *died for me*, so that something might still come of me. Most precious of all that I have inherited from him is his memory, his transfigured image, transfigured not by my poetic imagination (it has no need of that), but by many little individual traits I am now learning about, and this I will try to keep most secret from the world. For at this moment I feel there is *only one person* (E. Boesen) with whom I can really talk about him. He was a 'good and faithful friend'.

Emil Boesen, his confidant since childhood, might have understood why Kierkegaard saw his father as Christ-like: 'a faithful friend' – as the old pietist hymns sung of Jesus – whose death was sacrificial, and whose memory was transfigured. Among his friends, only Emil knew something of his deepest roots, had visited his family home as a boy, shared memories of the Moravian meetings on Stormgade. Emil understood what it meant to step from that earlier life into a new world of lectures, novels and newspapers; of philosophy, art and cultural criticism. Kierkegaard's brother Peter Christian knew about all this too, of course, but he preferred not to open his soul to *him*.

He soon returned to his essay on Hans Christian Andersen's new novel, and in September 1838 he published it as a short book entitled *From the Papers of One Still Living*. If he felt emboldened to put his work out into the world after the deaths of his philosophical mentor and his father, publication was still, to borrow Professor Sibbern's phrase, an 'inwardly complicated' matter. Kierkegaard's deep habit of reflection, which germinated in the inner conflict and duplicity of his childhood and was nurtured during his long student years, made him feel 'always, always outside himself' – and now that he had written something substantial, he could not be at one with it. 'One Still Living' was a kind of pseudonym, denoting a 'friend' and *'alter ego'*, and the title page indicated that he, S. Kierkegaard, had published the book against this author's will.

He wrote a preface, signed 'The Publisher', which expressed his ambivalent relationship to himself as a writer:

> Our opinions nearly always differ and we are perpetually in conflict with one another, although under it we are united by the deepest, most sacred, indissoluble ties. Yes, although often diverging in magnetic repulsion, we are still, in the strongest sense of the word, inseparable, even though our mutual friends have seldom, perhaps never, seen us together, albeit that someone or other may at times have been surprised that just as he has left one of us, he has, almost instantaneously, met the other. We are, therefore, so far from being able to rejoice as friends in the unity for which poets and orators in their repeated immortalizations have only a single expression – that it was as if one soul resided in two bodies – that with respect to us it must rather seem as if two souls resided in one body.

Like all human beings, Kierkegaard continued, the author of this review had a soul that passed through myriad phases, turning on its axis like the earth moving through the signs of the zodiac. The turbulent process of writing followed this cycle: when his soul entered 'the sign of hope and longing' he withdrew into himself and then emerged, 'half-ashamed', to struggle and strive with one of the fleeting ideas he had discovered in his 'inner sanctum'.

After many rotations of his soul – through sadness, anxiety, consternation, as well as 'moments of blessing' – the essay was finished, and then the Publisher (S. Kierkegaard), 'the medium through which he telegraphs with the world', arranged to have it printed. But the author, who suffered 'to a rather high degree from a sense of unfulfilment in the world', was recalcitrant:

> You know very well, said he, that I consider writing books to be the most ridiculous thing a person can do. One surrenders oneself entirely to the power of fate and circumstance, and how can one escape all the prejudices people bring with them to the reading of a book, which work no less disturbingly than the preconceived ideas most bring with them when they make someone's acquaintance, with the result that very few people really know what others look like? What hope can one entertain that one will fall into the hands of readers wholly *ex improviso* [without expectations]? Besides, I feel tied by the fixed form the essay has finally acquired and, in order to feel free again, will take it back into the womb once more, let it once again sink into the twilight from whence it came.

And anyway, the author added, S. Kierkegaard wished to publish his review simply because he was blinded by vanity. 'Stuff and nonsense,' the Publisher retorted: 'I will not have another word! The essay is in my power; I have the command.'

Having brought out the pathos as well as the comedy of his inner conflict, Kierkegaard's review enumerated weaknesses in the style, plot and characterization of Andersen's *Only a Fiddler*. He particularly disliked its description of genius – a subject close to his own heart – as 'an egg that needs warmth for the fertilization of good fortune . . . like the pearl in the sea it must await the diver who brings it up to the light, or cling fast to mussels and oysters, the high fellowship of patrons, in order to come into view'. Andersen, like the musician in his story, came from a poor provincial family, but he had found in Copenhagen powerful friends who helped him make his way. Kierkegaard disagreed with Andersen's depiction of genius as fragile, passive, and in need of benefaction; he thought this underestimated its power. He was thinking less of material support – which unlike Andersen he had always taken for granted – than of literary patronage. Having been spurned by Heiberg, he was defiant: 'for genius is not a rush candle that goes out in a puff of air, but a conflagration that the storm only incites'.

More fundamentally, he criticized Andersen for lacking a 'life-view'. This was something he used to talk about with Poul Møller, who had insisted that thinkers and artists should distil within their work their own experience of living. Without this experiential anchor, knowledge and erudition, and even beautiful prose, poetry and music, were insubstantial. 'A life-view is more than experience, which in itself is always fragmentary,' Kierkegaard explained: 'it is the transubstantiation of experience; it is an unshakeable certainty in oneself won from all experience.' And he contrasted a humanistic life-view, such as the philosophy of the Stoics, with a 'religious' life-view drawn from 'deeper experience': when a person has a *religious* certainty in himself – a trust, a confidence, a faith – his life gains a 'heavenly' as well as an 'earthly' orientation. He also suggested, echoing the Romantic literary theory he had imbibed, that a true poet must overcome his own mundane existence by 'transfiguring' his personality into something ideal, eternally youthful, 'an immortal spirit'. 'It is only this dead and transfigured personality that [can] produce [poetically], not the many-angled, worldly, palpable one,' he argued. It was easy to recognize the 'palpable' Andersen in his writing – and because this man had no life-view, Kierkegaard concluded, 'the same joyless battle he himself fights in life now repeats itself in his poetry'.

Hans Christian Andersen

Andersen, who was notoriously sensitive, had awaited this review anxiously. Kierkegaard met him from time to time at the Student Association or out on his walks, and soon after *Only a Fiddler* came out he told him that he admired the novel and intended to review it. Andersen received a copy of *From the Papers of One Still Living* as soon as it was published in September 1838: he found it 'difficult to read with its heavy *Hegelian* style', but its harsh judgement was clear enough. He took revenge on Kierkegaard – who still then had his funny swept-up hairstyle – by caricaturing him as a Hegelian hairdresser in his 'Vaudeville in One Act', which was performed in Copenhagen's Royal Theatre in 1840. The hairdresser spouted pretentious philosophical jargon, threw in phrases from Kierkegaard's review of *Only a Fiddler*, and declared himself 'an individual depressed by the world'.

Although Andersen was the subject of Kierkegaard's philosophical dissection, this reflected his wider critique of modern culture, which in turn mirrored his critical reflections on himself. Poul Møller used to argue that it was especially difficult to gain a religious life-view in the present age – and Kierkegaard experienced this difficulty firsthand. By writing as 'One Still Living' he suggested that he, like Andersen, was still too palpable, that he had not yet died, transfigured himself, and become immortal as a true poet should. Although his spiritual life had deepened during 1838 – one day that May he had an extraordinary experience of 'indescribable joy', and in July he resolved to 'labour to achieve a far more inward relation to Christianity' – he was still driven by his eagerness to impress others, and was not yet writing from the depths he had glimpsed.

After his father's death and the publication of *From the Papers of One Still Living*, he finally focused on finishing his theology degree. In 1840 he left Nytorv again and leased an apartment on Nørregade, a short walk away on the other side of the Church of Our Lady. That summer, nearly ten years after entering the university, he passed all his exams. He proposed to Regine in September and a few weeks later enrolled in the Royal Pastoral Seminary, where the students had to evaluate one another's sermons. Kierkegaard's preaching was judged to be thoughtful and logical, and his delivery dignified and strong – but his peers complained that he 'moved in too mystical a sphere' by reflecting on 'the blessing of silent prayer, the joyousness of contemplation, God's presence in us'.

That autumn he began to work on his doctoral dissertation, 'On the Concept of Irony with Continual Reference to Socrates'. This was his first sustained piece of philosophical writing, and an important phase in his intellectual development. Like *From the Papers of One Still Living*, it bore the influence of Poul Møller: it criticized the sweeping nihilism of Romantic irony and argued that Socratic irony was more discerning as it called into question the values of the world. He focused his critique of Romanticism on Friedrich von Schlegel's experimental novel *Lucinde*, which celebrated free, passionate love and depicted marriage as an instrument of bourgeois morality that reduces natural desires to a contractual obligation.

Was it a coincidence that he was working on this material during his engagement to Regine? Did his own romantic situation shape his philosophical analysis of *Lucinde* – or was it the other way around? It was difficult to know how experience and reflection came to mirror one another; indeed, this very question about the connection between 'ideality' and 'actuality', theory and practice, preoccupied him. How was truth to be discerned within the ideas and meanings which he, like every human being, constantly conjured out of the tangible reality of people, places, things?

In those early days he treated this as an intellectual question; now, in 1848, he regards it more as a divine mystery that has gradually revealed itself through his literary activity. God's governance, he believes, has interwoven his personal life and his philosophical labours: all this is God's way of drawing him to the questions and turning points that his soul needs to move through in order to grow, in order to become the self he is meant to be. For although human beings are not ready-made, they do not create themselves either. His life is not entirely determined by God, but he now feels that he will find his true path through the world only by submitting to divine governance.

Yet in 1841 he was more interested in control and mastery than in submission and obedience. At the end of 'On the Concept of Irony with Continual Reference to Socrates', he advocated a 'controlled' use of irony: in art, he argued, Shakespeare and Goethe – and

Heiberg – were 'masters of irony', for these great writers used the critical power of irony selectively and skilfully, in the service of a particular world view. So what would it be, he asked, to master irony in life? Here it was even more important to control irony, because irony is to existence what doubt is to science: 'Just as scientists maintain that there is no true science without doubt,' he asserted, 'so it may be maintained that no genuinely human life is possible without irony.' A disciplined, discerning scepticism is essential to scientific method, but if *everything* is doubted then science becomes impossible. Likewise, Socrates declared that the unexamined life is not worth living – but he knew better than anyone that life must be examined wisely and carefully. Kierkegaard concluded that the Romantic ideal of 'living poetically' should be reinterpreted as the mastery of irony in life, as the greatest poets mastered it in their art.

He completed his dissertation in the spring of 1841, and defended it in late September that year. It was Professor Sibbern's job to organize the committee of examiners, and they included H. C. Ørsted, now celebrated for his discovery of electro-magnetism in 1820 and spending the final years of his career as Rector of the University of Copenhagen. Kierkegaard's examiners admired his philosophical insight and originality, but thought his satirical style inappropriate. Ørsted reported that, despite its intellectual strengths, 'On the Concept of Irony with Continual Reference to Socrates' made 'a generally unpleasant impression' on him because of its 'verbosity and affectation'. Nevertheless, the dissertation was deemed acceptable for conferral of the magister degree.

Less than two weeks after he became Magister Kierkegaard, he was in disgrace. In October he made the final break from Regine, and soon left for Berlin. When he arrived there he stayed in the grand Hotel de Saxe before moving to an apartment on Gendarmenmarkt, the central market square. In the middle of Gendarmenmarkt was the Royal Theatre, built twenty years earlier in the style of a Greek temple, reclaimed by the Romantic imagination as a monument to the high culture of Prussia's most enlightened city. The theatre stood between two eighteenth-century churches, one for the German reformed congregation and the other for French Calvinists. This juxtaposition of classically inspired art and Protestant theology – the

Gendarmenmarkt, Berlin: Neue Kirk (Deutscher Dom)
and Royal Theatre

aesthetic and the religious – summed up in stone the formation of his soul, right outside his window.

By then writing was his daily habit; in Berlin it also became the only way to communicate with people at home. His long walks with Emil Boesen were replaced by long letters: he wrote to Emil every two or three weeks asking for news of Regine, confiding the turbulent motions of his soul, reporting on the progress of his writing – always urging his friend to reply, and enjoining 'the deepest secrecy'. People in Copenhagen were gossiping about him, of course; he imagined what they were saying and then responded to these criticisms, which were voiced many more times in his mind than in any parlour, café or street in town. 'The only thing I can say I miss now and then are our *colloquia*,' he wrote to Emil – 'How good it was to talk myself out once in a while but, as you know, I need a rather long time for that even though I talk quickly. Still, a letter always means a lot, especially when it is the sole means of communication.'

Unlike most people, Emil did not judge him, but Kierkegaard nevertheless wrote pages and pages justifying his decision to break up with Regine. He explained that this crisis had jolted him out of the aesthetic sphere – that this simple matter of another human being had burst the enchanting but ineffectual bubble of possibility in which he had floated for so long. 'I do not turn her into a poetic subject, I do not call her to mind, but I call myself to account,' he told Emil in November 1841: 'I think I can turn anything into a poetic subject, but when it is a question of duty, obligation, responsibility, debt, etc., I cannot and I will not turn these into poetic subjects.' He did not then feel the bitter resentment towards Regine that had grown within him by the time he returned to Berlin in 1843. If she had broken off the engagement, he remarked, she would have 'served him' – but as it was, he must serve her. 'If it were in her power to surround me with vigilant scouts who always reminded me of her, still she could not be so clearly remembered as she is now in all her righteousness, all her beauty, all her pain.'

Still, in this letter his contrition was edged with triumph – a sense that he had gained a victory over the world by refusing to conform to its demands. 'In the course of these recent events my soul has received a needed baptism, but that baptism was surely not by sprinkling, for I have descended into the waters; everything has gone black before my eyes, but now I ascend again. Nothing so develops a human being as adhering to a plan in defiance of the whole world.' He knew, of course, that he was testing Emil's patience. 'My dear Emil, if you get angry, please do not hide it from me,' he urged at the end of this letter. 'Whether my soul is too egotistical or too great to be troubled by such matters, I do not know, but it would not disturb me . . . I demand nothing of you except that you feel well, that you feel at one with your soul . . . I have lost much or robbed myself of much in this world, but I will not lose you.'

During those months in Berlin, his soul rotated not only through different moods but through the different selves summoned into being by his correspondence. In mid-December he wrote three letters on three consecutive days: to his twelve-year-old niece Henriette Lund, to Emil, and to Professor Sibbern. He sent Henriette a sweet, funny letter offering birthday congratulations on 'a special kind of paper', decorated with pictures of Berlin's grand neoclassical museum, theatre and opera house. The following day he resumed the role of omnipotent Romantic poet, sending Emil an update on the 'tactics' plotted by his 'all too inventive brain' – 'that her family hates me is good. That was my plan, just as it was also my plan that she, if possible, be able to hate me' – along with dubious advice on Emil's own romantic predicament, and a blustering postscript about an attractive Viennese singer who was playing Elvira in *Don Giovanni*: she looked just like Regine. In his letter to Sibbern he became a deferential, diligent student, reporting on philosophy lectures he had attended by Steffens, Philip Marheineke, Karl Werder and Schelling.

Being Uncle Søren undoubtedly brought out the best in him. From Berlin he kept up a regular correspondence with all his nieces and nephews back in Copenhagen – the children of his deceased sisters Petrea and Nicolene – and his letters to them were thoughtful and affectionate. He sent fourteen-year-old Sophie a teasing but kindly reply to her excited letter about going to a ball. To Carl, aged eleven, he wrote about the big dogs which pulled carriages transporting milk from the countryside, the noisy squirrels racing round the Tiergarten, the 'innumerable goldfish' in the canal, while Wilhelm, aged ten, received an elegant letter commending his neat, clear handwriting and correcting a few spelling errors. In late December 1841 Kierkegaard wrote to Carl and his elder brother Michael about Christmas in Berlin, which he had spent dining with 'all the Danes' at the Belvedere: 'We especially tried to cheer ourselves up and to bring back memories of home by eating apple dumplings. We also had a Christmas tree.' He encouraged Carl, whose last letter had been laughably short, to write again – 'just write freely about whatever occurs to you, do not be shy . . . Please tell me next time what you got for Christmas and among other things what came from me . . . I suppose there has already been frost in Copenhagen for a long time, and by now you must have been out on the ice several times. All that kind of thing interests me. This you might tell me about.' After Christmas, days of 'terrible cold' gave way to 'beautiful winter weather', and in mid-January Carl and Michael received reports of ice-skating, and of coaches and carriages converted into sleighs to ride through Berlin's snowy streets. It was a 'delightful' spectacle, though Kierkegaard found it too cold to travel this way himself.

None of his relationships, none of his selves, were free of his anxiety about Regine. He knew that Professor Sibbern would be in touch with her, that his nieces and nephews visited her. After Christmas his letters to Emil became even longer, and even more riddled with conflict and confusion. He told Emil, as he told himself, that he was in control of the situation: 'I hold my life poetically in my hand . . . My life divides itself into chapters, and I can provide an exact heading for each as well as state its motto. For the present it proclaims: "She must hate me." ' Everything, he explained, was directed to this end:

> In the company of the Danes here in Berlin I am always cheerful, merry, gay, and have 'the time of my life', etc. And even though everything churns inside me so that it sometimes seems that my feelings, like water, will break the ice with which I have covered myself, and even though there is at times a groan within me, each groan is instantly transformed into something ironical, a witticism, etc., the moment anybody else is present . . . [for] my plan demands it. Here a groan might reach the ear of a Dane, he might write home about it, she might possibly hear of it, it might possibly damage the transitional process.

As the weeks went by Berlin's bitter winter became increasingly hard to bear. The east wind was freezing, he complained to Emil in February 1842, and he had been unable to get warm for several days and nights. Every adversity compounded his spiritual trial; he returned again and again to thoughts of Regine:

> Cold, some insomnia, frayed nerves, disappointed expectations of Schelling, confusion in my philosophical ideas, no diversion, no opposition to excite me – that is what I call the acid test. One learns to know oneself . . . I broke the engagement for her sake. That became my consolation. And when I suffered the most, when I was completely bereft, then I cried aloud in my soul: 'Was it not good, was it not a godsend that you managed to break the engagement? If this had continued, then you would have become a lifelong torment for her.'

Yet in the last pages of this letter he fantasized about returning to Regine. He could no longer think about her without considering the opinion of the whole town: he imagined that he would be 'hated and detested', that he would 'become a laughing stock', or even that people would say he had something decent about him after all – which, he insisted, worried him most of all. 'This winter in Berlin will always have great significance for me,' he eventually concluded. 'I have done a lot of work. I have had three or four hours of lectures every day, a daily language lesson, and have still written so much, and have read a lot, I cannot complain. And then all my suffering, all my monologues!'

At the end of February he sent Emil one last letter from his exile. His soul had entered a new phase: now he was decisive, clear, cheerful:

My dear Emil,
Schelling talks endless nonsense . . . I am leaving Berlin and hastening to Copenhagen, but not, you understand, to be bound by a new tie, oh no, for I feel more strongly than ever that I need my freedom. A person with my eccentricity should have his freedom until he meets a force in life that can bind him. I am coming to Copenhagen to complete *Either/Or*. It is my favourite idea, and in it I exist . . .

After a few false starts, his authorship began during that first visit to Berlin – and he started to become, as he now puts it, 'the person I am'. His soul was no longer merely rotating: he had leapt into a new, religious sphere of existence, propelled by the engagement crisis. It was not theology, nor philosophy, nor art, but the break with Regine that had opened up his relationship to God, and allowed him to grow into it. In dating his authorship from the publication of *Either/Or* early in 1843, he is setting aside his earlier writings, for these did not express the religious life-view, wrought from a profound personal experience, that he described in *From the Papers of One Still Living*. The author of that review could theorize about an 'unshakeable certainty in oneself', but he did not yet possess it.

\* \* \*

Just as the break with Regine was inseparable from the beginning of his work as an author, so she has become entangled in its ending. During this gruelling summer of 1848, his thoughts have returned to her again and again; his anxiety about finalizing his authorship seems to contain the huge store of anxieties he has felt about Regine for the last ten years. Beneath them all is longing, for something that continues to elude him. Just a few days ago, he took a carriage through the country lanes all the way up to Fredensborg, where he knew the Olsens were staying – 'An inexplicable presentiment took me there, I was so happy and almost sure of meeting the family there' – and sure enough he bumped into Regine's father. 'I go up to him and say: Good day Councillor Olsen, let us talk together. He took off his hat and greeted me but then brushed me aside and said: I do not wish to speak with you. Oh, there were tears in his eyes, and he spoke these words with tormented feeling. I went towards him, but he started to run so fast that, even if I had wanted to, it would have been impossible to catch up with him.'

It is impossible to catch up with the past – to grasp it, to change it, to pull it into a new shape. All he can do is recollect it, write it out, and try to discern its meaning. 'At some point,' he resolves, 'I must give a clear explanation of myself as an author, of what I say I am, of how I understand myself as having been a religious author from the start.' Pacing through his stuffy Rosenborggade apartment over these August weeks, he has understood more clearly than before how he has been 'educated' by his own writing. Ever since his student days he has been interested in character development and spiritual growth, combining the pietists' emphasis on 'upbuilding' and 'awakening' with a Romantic faith in art as a means to self-cultivation. Now he grasps how he became an author, and how he has grown religiously through his writing: 'I have been brought up and developed in the process of my work, and personally I have become committed more and more to Christianity.' And, having brought his authorship to an end with his article about Madame Heiberg and her two Juliets, he needs others to understand that his writing was religious from the start – that it was a religious crisis which prepared the way for *Either/Or*, and for his own 'beginning'. 'I began with the most profound religious impression – alas, I who, when I began, bore the entire responsibility for another human being's life and understood this as God's punishment of me . . . In a decisive sense I had experienced the pressures that turned me away from the world before I started *Either/Or*.'

Although he has exhausted himself with deliberations on his author-ship, he feels the exhilaration of fresh beginnings – fresh thoughts, fresh pages – rising within him. 'How often haven't I had happen what has just now happened to me again? Then I sink into the most profound sufferings of melancholia; one or another thought gets so tangled for me that I cannot untangle it, and because it relates to my own existence I suffer indescribably. And then, after a little time has passed, it is as if a boil has burst – and inside is the most wonderful and fruitful productivity, precisely what I have use for at the moment.' It is not yet clear whether he needs to give an account of his author-ship in order to put it to rest – one final postscript – or in order to close the chapter of the last five years of writing, so that he can open a new one.

# 9

# The Socrates of Christendom

It is 1 September 1848, and Kierkegaard is preaching for a third time at Friday communion in the Church of Our Lady. A small, frail figure standing before Thorvaldsen's massive statue of Christ, he takes as the subject of his discourse a verse from John's Gospel, 'From on high He will draw all up to Himself', and explains to the small congregation that following Christ will lift them above worldly concerns. 'If a man's life is not to be frittered away, being emptily employed with what while it lasts is vanity and when it is past is nothingness, or busily employed with what makes a noise in the moment but has no echo in eternity, then there must be something higher that draws it,' he tells them in his soft, expressive voice.

Outside the tranquil church, the streets and the newspapers are noisy with electioneering: on 5 October all men, even peasants, will vote for members of the assembly which will draw up Denmark's new constitution. But Kierkegaard's sole concern is the spiritual life of 'the single individual'. He believes this to be 'diametrically opposite to politics', since it has nothing to do with 'earthly reward, power, honour'. The louder the public clamour about these things, the more decisively he sets himself against them: all that matters religiously, he insists, is the 'inwardness' of each human being, 'not seeking to be a power in the external world'.

He grew up with stories of the Moravian missionaries who sailed bravely to Greenland, and now he sees himself as a kind of missionary, following a divine calling. Yet his peculiar mission is not in a distant Danish colony but in a Copenhagen church, where he must introduce Christianity to people who have been Christians their whole lives. 'A missionary in Christendom will always look different from a missionary in paganism. If he is addressing Christians, what then does it mean to get them to become Christians?' Through his authorship he has tried, year after year, to address his neighbours as human beings whose relationship to God is a question that remains to be answered, a task to be lived. His extraordinary literary gifts, his philosophical ingenuity, his powerful imagination, were, he believes, given to him by God – not to enable him to become an eminent professor or win the approval of reviewers, but to 'make manifest the illusion of Christendom and provide a vision of what it is to become a Christian'. All his resources must be summoned daily in the service of this religious calling.

As usual, his anxieties have been resolved by writing. Now that he has ended his authorship, this resolution is trickier than ever; his latest anxiety is about how the authorship will be interpreted, and the only way out of it is to write a book about his authorship. Reitzel, the publisher of his pseudonymous works, has been talking about printing a second edition of *Either/Or* since 1846, when the first edition of 525 copies sold out, and if the book is reissued he will have to show how its immoralism and aestheticism were always intended to serve a religious purpose. 'Now I see my way to writing a short and as earnest as possible explanation of my previous authorship': everything he has published is an 'indirect communication' of Christianity, and only now that this authorship is finished can he finally express his religious commitment directly. 'For this very reason I am now able to illuminate and interpret indirect communication. Earlier I had been continually unclear. One must always be over and beyond what one wants to interpret.'

Whether or not *The Point of View for My Work as an Author* will be published is another question – attended, of course, with fresh anxieties – but while he is writing he need not worry about that yet. He is sure to die soon; perhaps Rasmus Nielsen will help to secure his literary legacy, but it cannot be left in his hands. His works will be read by generations, and instead of letting people misunderstand his authorship, misunderstand his life, he must make his own 'report to history'. After years of literary subterfuge, he will explain his strange vocation and his peculiar methods, beginning with *Either/Or*. One day, even if he does not live to see it, it will become clear that the man who stood quietly preaching in the Church of Our Lady in 1848 did not differ, in his soul, from the man who created the 'Seducer's Diary' in Berlin in 1842 – for these men shared the same mission.

His task as an author has not been to expound a theology, teach a creed, or correct heresies. 'Christianity is not a doctrine, but an existence communication. (This is the source of all the nuisances of orthodoxy, its quarrels about one thing and another, while existence remains totally unchanged.) Christianity is an existence communication and can only be presented – by existing,' he wrote in his journal a few weeks ago. Yet he will never claim to set an example for others to follow, for he believes, like the Moravians, that 'every human being is equally near to God' – and that Jesus is the only exemplar. 'Compel a person to an opinion, a conviction, a belief – in all eternity, that I cannot do. But one thing I can do: I can compel him to become aware.'

\* \* \*

*Either/Or* was the first in a series of 'aesthetic' works, written for the kind of reader who 'thinks he is a Christian and yet is living in purely aesthetic categories'. This is the widespread 'illusion' of Christendom: in a culture so steeped in Christianity as nineteenth-century Denmark, it is possible to do all the things expected of a Christian and yet never embark on the task of faith that takes a lifetime – perhaps longer than a lifetime – to accomplish.

Before Kierkegaard began his authorship, he had learned from Socrates that 'there is nothing that requires as gentle a treatment as the removal of an illusion' – for a direct confrontation only makes people more defensive and resistant, and strengthens their self-deceptions. It is not easy to correct a mistake that concerns a person's entire existence. As a Socratic missionary, he has tried to teach his readers 'not to comprehend Christianity, but to comprehend that they cannot comprehend it'. And so he entered into their illusion in order to draw them out of it: 'One does not begin directly with what one wishes to communicate, but begins by taking the other's delusion at face value. Thus one does not begin in this way: It is Christianity that I am proclaiming, and you are living in purely aesthetic categories. No, one begins in this way: Let us talk about the aesthetic.'

This was, he now admits, a 'deception', for he entered the aesthetic sphere only 'in order to arrive at the religious'. But this deception was in the service of the highest truth, the truth of Christianity. 'One can deceive a person out of what is true, and – to recall old Socrates – one can deceive a person into what is true. Yes, only in this way can a deluded person actually be brought into what is true – by deceiving him.' A missionary in Christendom must move through the world like a secret agent, working 'under cover', for if he presents himself as religious 'the world has a thousand evasions and illusions with which they protect against him and get rid of him.'

When he began *Either/Or* in Berlin, he was reaching for a form of writing that signals its own limits, points to something that can't be captured by either philosophy or art. 'Life isn't like a romantic novel,' he wrote in the preface to *Either/Or*. The book took up the critique of Romanticism that he had set out in his dissertation on irony, but developed it in a new direction: while his dissertation examined the deficiencies of Romantic irony in a theoretical way, *Either/Or* showed what it would be like to adopt this irony as a life-view. And he now included in this 'aesthetic' life-view not just Romanticism, but the more general tendency of human beings to pursue worldly desires – for material comfort, sensual pleasure, or intellectual stimulation – while avoiding the demands of ethical life, and their own need for God.

Kierkegaard was well aware, of course, of his own aesthetic tendencies. Like the little preface to *From the Papers of One Still Living*, *Either/Or* staged a debate between two parts of his soul; this time the argument stretched over several hundred pages, and it was not about publishing a book, but about getting married. On one side of this question stood an aesthete, known only as 'A', a witty, melancholy intellectual, a literary critic and an experimental poet: he wrote essays, reviews, fragments and aphorisms, and his eclectic papers made up Part I of *Either/Or*. Among them was the 'Seducer's Diary', written by the calculating but irresistible Johannes – the character who would supposedly convince Regine that she was better off without Kierkegaard.

Like Johannes, the aesthete 'A' turned whatever he encountered into a subject for intellectual reflection or a source of poetic inspiration. He floated above everything – even his own existence – in a bubble of possibility; the world was an endless landscape arrayed before him, which he surveyed with fluctuating interest or disinterest, amusement or boredom, pleasure or irritation. He had no anchor in this world: no commitments, no investments, no moral code, no religion to tie him down. His own actions seemed to him weightless; it made no difference whether he did something, or did not do it. Easily bored, he moved from one thing – an idea, a mood, a woman – to the next. Like Friedrich von Schlegel's novel *Lucinde*, his writings scorned bourgeois morality in general, and marriage in particular: 'Marry or do not marry, you will regret it either way . . . Laugh at the stupidities of the world or weep over them, you will regret it either way . . . Trust a girl or do not trust her, you will regret it either way . . . Hang yourself or do not hang yourself, you will regret it either way. This, gentlemen, is the quintessence of all the wisdom of life.'

On the other side of the debate was Judge William, an older and more conscientious man, married with children, a model of civic virtue. He personified the ethical sphere, where a man could carve out his place within the world: build a solid home and a stable self out of meaningful decisions, enduring commitments, faithful relationships. In two letters to 'A', each one the size of a short book, he extolled the duties and the joys of married life. Judge William saw great potential in 'A', but was disturbed by his life-view: he told him that he loved him as a son, a brother, and a friend; that despite all his 'bizarre qualities' he loved his intensity, his passions, his frailties. He loved him, he wrote, 'with the fear and trembling of a religious person, because I see the aberrations'.

Although these two literary personas both had watery Scandinavian souls, they were very different: 'for you,' Judge William wrote to his younger friend, 'a turbulent sea is the symbol of life; for me it is the quiet, deep water.' William's inner being was like Peblinge Lake on a still day, and he saw his marriage as a stream flowing into this lake, gentle and constant yet full of life:

> I have often sat beside a little running stream. It is always the same, the same gentle melody, on the bottom the same green vegetation that undulates with the quiet ripples, the same tiny creatures that move down there, a little fish that slips in under the cover of the flowers,

spreads its fins against the current, hides under a stone. How uniform, and yet how rich in change! So it is with the domestic life of marriage – quiet, modest, humming. It does not have many *changements*, and yet it is like that water, running, and yet, like that water, it has melody, dear to the one who knows it, dear to him precisely because he knows it. It is not showy, and yet at times it has a sheen that nevertheless does not interrupt its usual course, just as when the moon shines on that water and displays the instrument on which it plays its melody.

The Judge urged the young aesthete to 'earnestness of spirit' – without this, he warned, 'you will miss out on the highest, on the one thing that truly gives life meaning; you may win the world and lose yourself.'

This protracted dialogue between two life-views was not just an exercise in ironic self-examination, nor was its purpose solely – or even primarily – to heal Regine's broken heart. Between the lines of this odd compendium of writings was a scathing commentary on an entire age. Martensen and Heiberg had championed Hegel's philosophy as the solution to the spiritual crisis of their century, which Romanticism had exposed and, they argued, exacerbated. But *Either/Or* obliquely portrayed Hegelian thought as equally nihilistic, belonging, like Romanticism, to the aesthetic sphere. Of course, many people lived aesthetically – they lacked an ethical or a religious lifeview – without knowing anything about Romantic literature or Hegelian philosophy. Nevertheless, Kierkegaard treated these intellectual trends as signs of the times, symptoms of spiritual vacuity.

In its poetry, science and metaphysics, Romanticism had sought a deeper unity underlying the endless diversity of the world, and Hegel's philosophy gave a logical structure to this pantheistic quest for unity. Human beings usually understand and order their world by recognizing differences between things – day and night, life and death, male and female, masters and slaves, black and white. Underlying such distinctions is an implicit logic of 'either/or': it must be either day or night; animals are either male or female; a man is either alive or dead, either a master or a slave. This logical principle had been formalized by Aristotle, providing the bedrock for philosophical reasoning for many centuries. Yet Hegel emphasized that these differences not only separate things, but join them together, for opposites depend on one another. Days are known as days in contrast to night; slaves are slaves only when they have masters, and masters are masters only when they have slaves; men become conscious of their masculinity in relation to women, and women feel feminine in relation to men. The process of living is inseparable from dying. And the differences between any two human beings are also contained inside each of them, shaping their identity from within.

Hegel's substitution of a dynamic, dialectical logic for the binary logic of common-sense thinking grounded a bold new theory of history. Writing in the wake of the long revolutionary struggle in Haiti, which ended in 1804 with the slaves in that French colony declaring their independence from Napoleon's regime, Hegel argued that categories such as master and slave, hitherto regarded as a fixed natural order, shifted through time. Oppressive social relationships could evolve into a balanced civil state based on mutual recognition and respect. This was a philosophy of progress: Hegel argued that when we look at reality from a higher, more objective point of view – as when a historian surveys the epochs of the world, or a scientist uncovers the principles of unity within nature – then we understand that day and night, life and death, male and female, masters and slaves, are moments or phases in a continuous process. The goal of this process, Hegel claimed, is spiritual freedom. As they gain ever greater knowledge, human beings would become more and more like God, who knows everything because he is outside space and time, and sees the entire universe and its history in a single glance.

By the time he wrote *Either/Or*, Kierkegaard regarded the immense ambition of Hegel's philosophical system as a symptom of the modern hubris that Martensen had discussed in his 1836 essay on Faust. Part I of *Either/Or* parodied this Promethean ideal – an ideal with which, Kierkegaard knew, his own generation was particularly burdened. In his 'Seducer's Diary' Johannes described himself looking down upon his own existence, surveying his soul as God surveys his creation, or as a Hegelian philosopher surveyed world history:

> My mind roars like a turbulent sea in the storms of passion. If someone else could see my soul in this state, it would seem to him that it, like a skiff, plunged prow-first down into the ocean, as if in its dreadful

momentum it would have to steer down into the depths of the abyss. He does not see that high on the mast a sailor is on the lookout. Roar away, you wild forces, roar away, you powers of passion; even if your waves hurl foam toward the clouds, you still are not able to pile yourselves up over my head – I am sitting as calmly as the king of the mountain. I am almost unable to find a foothold; like a water bird, I am seeking in vain to alight on the turbulent sea of my mind.

Perhaps Kierkegaard himself had lived like this before his engagement crisis – always outside himself, hovering above his world. And then he was shipwrecked on the warm-blooded, irrefutable existence of a young woman who lived a few streets away, who loved him and expected to marry him, whose eyes gazed directly into his own, whose tears he could reach out and touch. From Regine he learned that no philosophical system, no merely intellectual approach to life, helps a human being to live in the world, to make decisions, to become himself.

Beyond wrestling with his inner turmoil, he wanted to depose Hegelian philosophy – and he particularly wanted to take the wind out of Martensen's sails. Through the character of the aesthete 'A', so richly drawn because he knew his soul from the inside, he showed that the distinctive dialectical logic that shaped Hegel's thinking, and reproduced itself at every level of his encyclopaedic philosophy, becomes ridiculous when it is adopted as a life-view. The aesthete finds that his choices mean nothing, for in every decision he contemplates, the alternatives lead to the same outcome: 'Marry or do not marry; you will regret it either way.' Neither Hegel nor Martensen had intended their philosophical logic to be applied to ethical life like this – but then Kierkegaard's point was that someone who pursued a philosophy which didn't help him to live in the world was distracting himself from the most urgent questions of existence.

While *Either/Or*'s aesthetic writings parodied Martensen's Hegelianism as well as the more amorphous poetic ideals of the Romantics, Judge William's letters expressed the kind of ethical life-view taught by Bishop Mynster. In fact, Judge William's chastisement of the aesthete echoed Mynster's criticisms of Martensen's theology. Just before Kierkegaard wrote *Either/Or*, Mynster had disputed with Martensen about the merits of Hegelian philosophy: the two theologians exchanged a series of learned articles about the relationship between philosophy and faith. Other scholars lined up on both sides of their debate, and the phrase 'either/or' became a slogan for the issue that divided them. Martensen used Hegelian dialectics to show how opposing theological positions could be reconciled or 'mediated' from a philosophical perspective. For Mynster, what mattered most was personal religious commitment: he argued that each individual should affirm his faith – either 'pantheism' or 'supernaturalism', either Judaism or Christianity, either devotion to God or atheism – and then be true to it in his life.

Judge William's letters showed how the question of marriage made Bishop Mynster's position crystal clear. A man either marries or does not marry, and if he does marry he cannot have two wives at once. The Judge's attitude to women was like Mynster's attitude to Christianity: he had chosen a wife, and he remained faithful to her. In calling his book *Either/Or*, Kierkegaard signalled that he was stepping into the debate between Martensen and Mynster. Yet as well as contributing to this debate – apparently siding with Mynster – he was satirizing the whole thing; *Either/Or* was a philosophical comedy, though within the humour there was deep earnestness. By turning a polite scholarly exchange into a clash of life-views, he showed that this academic dispute posed a question of existence that cannot be answered until it is lived.

Although Judge William – like Bishop Mynster – took this existential question seriously, Kierkegaard did not let him have the last word. The Judge's two long letters to the aesthete were followed by a sermon, describing how a human being understands himself differently when he lives in relation to God. The sermon was accompanied by a note explaining that its author was an old friend of Judge William, now an obscure pastor in a little rural parish in Jutland – 'A little man with a squarely built figure, merry, light-hearted, and uncommonly jovial. Although in the depths his soul was serious, his outward life seemed gaily inconsequent.' He had, he told the Judge, found the Jutland heath to be 'an incomparable study room for a parson': 'There I go on Saturdays to prepare my sermon, and everything widens out before me. I forget every actual listener and gain an ideal one, gain complete self-forgetfulness, so that when I mount the pulpit it is as though I were still standing upon the heath where my eye discovers not a single soul, where my voice lifts itself with all its strength to outdo the violence of the storm.'

A sermon by a country parson seems an innocent thing, but in fact its inclusion in *Either/Or* was a subversive act. By assigning Martensen to the aesthetic sphere and Mynster to the ethical sphere, Kierkegaard posed a daring question: Were either of these high priests of Danish Christendom approaching life *religiously*? Was there anything truly Christian in their Christianity? And if neither the Professor of Theology nor the Bishop of Zealand had reached the religious sphere of existence, then who in Copenhagen *did* exemplify and teach a genuinely religious life? At the end of *Either/Or* Kierkegaard projected the voice of the religious sphere far beyond his city walls – as if no one within those walls knew how to live in relation to God.

Though they loomed especially large for Kierkegaard as inspirations and adversaries, Mynster and Martensen were not the only influential Christian teachers in Copenhagen in the early 1840s. Another powerful figure was Henrik Nicolai Clausen, who had taught theology at the university since 1822: he was a New Testament scholar and a rationalist of the eighteenth-century Enlightenment order. Professor Clausen trained his students – including Kierkegaard, who attended his classes throughout the 1830s – to read the Bible with a rigorous discipline. In 1825 he published *Catholicism and Protestantism: Their Church Constitutions, Doctrines and Rites*, which made the familiar Lutheran claim that while Catholics recognized the Church as the highest spiritual authority, Protestants grounded their faith upon scripture. More controversially – and certainly a departure from Luther's own teaching – Clausen argued that the divine Word should not be simply proclaimed from the pulpit: it needed to be interpreted by the light of reason, guided by historical research. This was a task for biblical scholars, like himself, who were experts in Hebrew and Greek, trained in theology and philosophy. While many of his generation were rebelling, one way or another, against rationalism, Clausen remained confident that human reason could free their faith from the superstition and ignorance which, empowered by dogma, had breached the peace of Christendom for too many dark decades.

For Clausen, professional theologians were the quiet guardians of Christian truth, the enlighteners of the Lutheran Church.

Opposed to Clausen in almost every respect was N. F. S. Grundt-vig, a firebrand priest, poet, hymnist and political agitator who hustled noisily – and effectively – at the margins of the Danish State Church. In his youth, his nationalism had found expression in a Romantic nostalgia for Norse mythology: inspired by Oehlen-schläger, Grundtvig wrote poetry that envisioned restored glory for the Scandinavian people, 'sons of the giant race'. But after a personal spiritual crisis he turned against the pagan, pantheist ideas of the Danish Romantics, attacking both Oehlenschläger and H. C. Ørsted. During the years after Kierkegaard's birth, when Denmark remained battered and bankrupted by the Napoleonic Wars, Grundtvig's na-tionalist fervour blossomed into a campaign of poetry and preaching that sought to reawaken 'the heroic spirit of Scandinavia unto Chris-tian deeds'. Like a prophet of ancient Israel he lamented his nation's spiritual corruption: self-interest had become a god, money was the soul of the state, and unbelief posed more of a threat to Denmark than any foreign army.

In the late 1820s Grundtvig turned his polemical spirit against Pro-fessor Clausen, whom he attacked so vehemently that he was sued for libel. Keen to wrest spiritual authority from the hands of biblical scholars, Grundtvig trumpeted his own 'matchless discovery' that the original source of Christianity was not the scriptures, but an oral tradition – including the Lord's prayer, words of baptism and the Apostles' Creed – that came directly from Jesus and was passed down through generations by word of mouth. Christian truth, he argued, was to be found in this 'living word' of the congregation, and not in the dead letters of learned scholars.

Grundtvig's vigorous preaching of his populist, communitarian theology drew many people of a dissenting bent – including Kierke-gaard's brother, Peter Christian – away from Copenhagen's established pietist congregation. While the Moravian pietists had practised their faith in separate communities, Grundtvig agitated to change the Danish State Church. Having travelled to England in the early 1830s, he argued for a liberal civil state that permitted religious freedom and allowed the orthodox Christian community, the bearers of the 'living word', to flourish on their own terms.

Bishop Mynster, whose zeal for moderation usually tempered his disputes – with Clausen and Martensen, among others – could not abide Grundtvig's intemperate activism. Mynster tried to thwart Grundtvig by banning him from administering the sacraments, and when this did not work – for Grundtvig was a skilled strategist, and his populist message made him powerful – he tried to contain him by appointing him pastor of Vartov, a residence for the sick and elderly. But by the 1840s Grundtvig had made Vartov Church the centre of a movement that harnessed not only the spiritual energies of pietism, but growing currents of social unrest among the peasants. He conducted these forces from the pulpit; his rousing hymns were sung to the glory of the true, living faith of the Danish people. Peter Christian Kierkegaard, by then also a pastor, was one of his closest followers.

Ever since his student days Kierkegaard has disagreed with his brother about Grundtvig: in 1835 he wrote in his journal that 'Grundtvig looks on the development of Christian understanding not as progress down a difficult road but like a steam engine running on a railway, with steam fired up by the apostles, so that Christian understanding is prepared in closed machines.' He distrusts the way Grundtvig's critique of the Christian establishment seems to go hand in hand with his political ambition: now the polemical pastor is harnessing the new democratic spirit of 1848, and standing for election to Denmark's Constitutional Assembly. And as he accentuates his own religious purpose as an author, Kierkegaard is anxious to distinguish his mission from Grundtvig's campaigning career: 'I have continually objected to a certain party of the orthodox here, that they band together in a little circle and strengthen one another in thinking that they are the only Christians.' These direct polemics might be politically effective, but they cannot succeed in the complex, delicate spiritual ministry that Christians in Christendom require: 'Every once in a while a religious enthusiast appears. He makes an assault on Christendom; he makes a big noise, denounces nearly all as not being Christians – and accomplishes nothing. He does not take into account that an illusion is not so easy to remove.'

In the years before he wrote *Either/Or*, Kierkegaard watched Grundtvig's rise at close quarters, just as he watched Martensen's rapid ascent to an influential university position. Mynster and Clausen, of course, already stood at the top of their professions. He heard these four men – his father's confessor, his theology professor, his nearest rival, and his brother's spiritual mentor – teach different versions of the truth of Christianity, empowered by their worldly positions. Even Mynster, with whom he sympathized personally, was compromised by his role as leader of a Danish Church inseparable from the political establishment. In *Either/Or* he opposed them all, showing that none of these powerful Christian figures belonged to the religious sphere.

Of course, Kierkegaard did not claim to speak directly from the religious sphere himself. Yet the sermon at the end of *Either/Or* drew on his own experience of being dragged into the harsh light of the ethical sphere, where he was judged by human eyes and confronted with his own moral failure. Through this anxiety-inducing experience, he suggested, a human being comes to know his need for God.

His sermon began with a prayer, that 'the restless mind, the fearful heart may find rest'. And then he described the anxieties and doubts that came with the kind of ethical religion preached by Mynster, who exhorts his congregations to do their best, to act as honourably as possible, while acknowledging that human beings 'are weak and imperfect creatures'. This way of thinking, the sermon suggested, leads an earnest person to interminable calculations about to what extent he is in the right, and to what extent in the wrong. And of course everyone makes these judgements about others at least as readily as they make them of themselves: in the ethical sphere, people measure their deeds against the conduct of their neighbours, compare their relative imperfections, and claim their share of righteousness. Explaining that respite from this endless, anxious judging can be found only in God, before whom everyone has equal certainty of being a sinner in need of forgiveness, the sermon beckoned the readers of *Either/Or* beyond the ethical sphere.

It ended with a direct appeal to the pastor's rural parishioners – and an indirect appeal to Kierkegaard's urban readers:

Perhaps my voice does not possess enough strength and heartiness to penetrate to your inmost thought – O, but ask yourself, ask with the solemn uncertainty with which you would address a man who was able, you knew, by a single word to decide your happiness in life, ask yourself still more seriously, for truly it is a question of salvation. Do not check your soul's flight, do not grieve the better promptings within you, do not dull your spirit with half wishes and half thoughts, ask yourself, and continue to ask until you find the answer; for one may have known a thing many times and acknowledged it, one may have willed a thing many times and attempted it, and yet it is only by the deep inward movements, only by the indescribable emotions of the heart, that for the first time you are convinced that what you have known belongs to you, that no power can take it from you; for only the truth which edifies is truth for you.

Kierkegaard completed *Either/Or* in Copenhagen through the spring, summer and autumn of 1842; he asked his friend Jens Finsen Giødvad, who worked at *The Fatherland*, to help him publish it pseudonymously. Then as now, he trusted Giødvad to keep the secret of his authorship. Proofreading the manuscript was a tremendous task, and he was impatient: each day he brought a new pile of pages to the *Fatherland* office on Købmagergade. He often spent the whole morning there, along with other friends of Giødvad who treated the office as 'a kind of club'. This irritated the newspaper's chief editor, Carl Ploug – and Kierkegaard was especially distracting: 'One must imagine what it is like to have to have a newspaper ready at a definite time – and in those days it was early in the afternoon, because the police inspector had to look at the issue before it was distributed – and to have an impractical and very self-absorbed man sitting in the office, ceaselessly lecturing and talking without the least awareness of the inconvenience he is causing. However captivating Ploug found him, and however often he might have felt an urge to sit and listen, he nonetheless had to carry out his . . . daily task, while Giødvad sat reverently listening at the master's feet.'

*Either/Or* was finally published in February 1843 bearing the name Victor Eremita, who had supposedly edited the book after finding the loose papers of the aesthete 'A', along with Judge William's letters, in a secret drawer in a second-hand writing desk. Despite Giødvad's discretion, the identity of the real author quickly became common knowledge. 'Recently a book was published here, with the title *Either/Or*!' wrote Henriette Wulff to her friend Hans Christian Andersen that February. 'It is supposed to be quite strange, the first part full of Don Juanism, scepticism, etc., and the second part toned down and conciliating, ending with a sermon that is said to be quite excellent. The whole book has attracted much attention. It is actually supposed to be by a Kierkegaard who has adopted a pseudonym: do you know him?'

A few weeks later Andersen was informed by another friend, Signe Læssøe, that she was reading '*Either/Or* by Søren Kierkegaard'. She found it 'demonic' but compelling. 'You have no idea what a sensation it has caused,' she wrote to Andersen:

> I think that no book has caused such a stir with the reading public since Rousseau placed his *Confessions* on the altar. After one has read it one feels disgust for the author, but one profoundly recognizes his intelligence and his talent. We women have to be especially angry with him: like the Mohammedans, he assigns us to the realm of finitude, and he values us only because we give birth to, amuse, and *save* menfolk. In the first part (this is a work of 864 octavo pages) he is aesthetic, that is, evil. In the second part he is ethical, that is, a little less evil. Everyone praises the second part because it is his *alter ego*, the better half, which speaks. The second part only makes me angrier with him – it is *there* that he ties women to finitude. In fact I only understand a fraction of the book; it is altogether too philosophical. For example, he says, 'There is no bliss except in despair; hurry up and despair, you will find no happiness until you do.' At another point he says, 'One's happiness can consist only in choosing oneself.' What does that mean?

Poor Andersen, still smarting from *The Papers of One Still Living*, sensed that his reviewer had become his literary rival. 'What you have sent me about Kierkegaard's book does not exactly excite my curiosity,' he wrote to Signe. 'It is so easy to seem ingenious when one disregards all considerations and tears to pieces one's own soul and all holy feelings!'

Kierkegaard, meanwhile, was no less sensitive than Andersen about the opinions of his peers. However often he turned inward, in search of God, away from the world, he could not escape his own anxieties about what other people thought of him. Indeed, the scandal of *Either/Or*, though published in the name of a hermit, exposed him to unprecedented publicity. The ethical sphere – still ringing with the judgements that had shamed and wounded him after his broken engagement – expanded, became more populous, and its attentions intensified.

\* \* \*

Here in the Church of Our Lady this Friday morning, he receives a different kind of attention. Let the crowds outside shout for Grundtvig; here, a few human beings are gathered quietly, preparing to receive communion, and his task is to help draw them inward, away from the world. He does this by offering his own inwardness, turning his soul inside out. If he has anything to offer his neighbours, it comes from his long struggle to tear himself from his worldly cares – his disappointed expectations, shattered hopes, bitter recollections.

'If from on high Christ is able to draw the Christian to himself,' he tells the little congregation:

> there is much that must be forgotten, much that must be disregarded, much that must be died away from. How can this be done? Oh, if you have ever been concerned, perhaps concerned about your future, your success in life, have truly wished to be able to forget something – a disappointed expectation, a shattered hope, a bitter and embittering recollection; or if, alas, out of concern for the salvation of your soul, you have quite fervently wished to be able to forget something – an anxiety of sin that continually confronted you, a terrifying thought that would not leave you – then you yourself have no doubt experienced how empty is the advice the world gives when it says, 'try to forget it!' For when you anxiously ask 'how shall I go about forgetting?' and the reply is 'you must try to forget', this is only an empty mockery, if it is anything at all. No, if there is something you want to forget, try to find something else to remember, then you will certainly succeed.

They are gathered in the church to remember Christ: to hear again the words Jesus spoke the night before his arrest, and to take bread and wine, as he instructed, 'in memory of me'.

'He will draw all to himself; *draw* them to himself, for he will *entice* no one to himself.' Jesus did not entice his followers with easy consolation, or with promises of 'power and honour and glory'. The truth that Jesus lived 'was insulted, mocked, and as the scripture says, spat upon' – yet it is not right to dwell only on these things, either. Christians should love Christ in his weakness and misery and humiliation, *and* in his glory, 'for melancholy is no closer to Christianity than frivolity; they are both equally worldliness, equally far away from the truth, equally as much in need of conversion.' There are, indeed, many ways to go to Christ, yet they all converge at one place – the consciousness of sin – and every human being must pass through this place within his own heart:

> My listener, you, to whom my discourse is addressed! Today he is indeed with you as if he were closer to the earth, as if he were, so to speak, touching the earth; he is present at the altar where you seek him; he is present there – but only in order once again from on high to draw you to himself ... Oh, and is it not true, just today and just because you feel yourself drawn today, just for that reason you would no doubt be willing today to confess to yourself and to him how much is still left, how far it is from being true that he has entirely drawn you to himself – from on high, away from everything base and worldly that would hold you back. Oh, my listener, it is certainly not me nor any other human being who says or will say or dares say this to you; no, every human being will have enough with saying it to himself – and should have praise for God if he is ever sufficiently moved to say it to himself. My listener, I do not know where you are, how far he has perhaps already drawn you to himself, how far more advanced in being a Christian you may be than I, and so many others, but God grant this day, wherever you are and whoever you are, you who have come here today in order to participate in the sacred meal of the Lord's Supper, that this day may truly be blessed for you.

# IO

# Repetition:
# A New Philosophy of Life

The season has turned, control of the country has changed hands, and he looks out from new windows, but the night sky is unchanged. And he can imagine the sea, close by, resting on this quiet night. He tries to open his soul to this sea, deep and transparent beneath the stars; it is possible, for a few moments, to let himself 'rest transparently in God', as he has described the experience of faith in *The Sickness unto Death*. This is one of his favourite thoughts. 'When the sea exerts all its might, then it is precisely impossible for it to reflect the image of the heavens, and even the smallest movement means that the reflection is not quite pure; but when it becomes still and deep, then heaven's image sinks down into its nothingness,' he wrote in 1844. 'Just as the sea, when it is still, deep and transparent longs for the heavens above, so too does the heart that has become pure long for the good. And as the sea reflects the vault of heaven in its pure depths, so too does the heart that has become still and deeply transparent reflect the heavenly sublimity of the good in its pure depths,' he wrote last year, 1847. There is always longing in this stillness – a longing that touches what it longs for, and desires it all the more. When he lets his longing for God fill and expand his soul, everything else is silenced.

It is October, and earlier this month he changed addresses for the second time in 1848. Unable to bear the smell of the tanner's yard below, he leased another 'fine and expensive' apartment on the same street, Rosenborggade. Copenhageners move house only on the 'Flitting Day' that falls every April and October, 'when all the furniture of the town is exchanging quarters, and the streets are full of straw, feathers, dust, and every abomination'. In a sense, this practical

disruption has done him good, for it forced him to write less strenu-
ously: 'Here, too, Governance came to my assistance and turned my
mistake into a good. If anything helps me to be less productive and
diminish my momentum and generally limit me, it is finite anxieties
and inconveniences.' He has also been worried about money. The
bonds he bought with the cash from the sale of 2 Nytorv were quickly
devalued as the political situation in Denmark became unstable, and
he has lost hundreds of rix-dollars. 'It was no doubt good,' he has
reflected, 'that I became thoroughly aware of it in time. It also helps
to burn away whatever selfishness there is in me and my work.'

Despite these upheavals and distractions, he worked on *The Point
of View for My Work as an Author* as the October elections came
and went. Having explained the spiritual origins of *Either/Or*, he has
now turned to consider the very different work that followed it in the
spring of 1843 – a slender pamphlet containing two sermons. 'What
is most important often seems so insignificant': his first two discourses were 'a little flower under the cover of the great forest', and
they received little attention. Although he was never on better terms
with 'the public' than in the second or third month after *Either/Or*
was published, what he produced during those weeks seemed to be of
little consequence to readers who had excitedly devoured the 'Seducer's Diary'. Yet those quiet, unassuming pages introduced his crucial
philosophical 'category', *that single individual*, in which 'a whole
life-view and world view is concentrated' – and at that very moment
he 'made a break with the public'. This is not a new category, but an
ancient one: he borrowed it from Socrates, 'the most eccentric of
men'. But in 1848 it has become more important than ever, for 'if the
crowd is the evil, if it is chaos that threatens, there is rescue in one
thing only, in becoming the single individual.'

* * *

It was just before he took his second trip to Berlin in May 1843 that
he arranged for his two sermons to be published by P. G. Philipsen,
who ran a fairly new bookshop and publishing house on Købmager-
gade specializing in works of popular science. One sermon was on
'The Expectancy of Faith', which also became the central theme of

REPETITION: A NEW PHILOSOPHY OF LIFE

*Fear and Trembling*; the other was on his favourite New Testament text, from the Letter of James: 'Every good and every perfect gift is from above and comes down from the Father of lights, in whom there is no change or shadow of variation.' *Two Upbuilding Discourses* was the first of several slim volumes of literary sermons on biblical texts, and he has continued to keep his religious discourses, signed in his own name, separate from the pseudonymous works published by Reitzel.

Although he dedicated *Two Upbuilding Discourses* to his late father, he gave it a brief preface – dated 5 May 1843, his thirtieth birthday – addressed to '*my* reader'. Here he explained that his discourses could not be called sermons because he was not ordained, and had no authority to preach. He described his little book setting out on its journey to meet 'that single individual whom with joy and gratitude I call *my* reader, that single individual it is seeking, to whom, so to speak, it stretches out its arms'.

And it was during that fertile time that Kierkegaard drew the deepest philosophical lessons from his personal experience, beginning with his first appeal to the 'single individual' on his birthday, and continuing in his writing in Berlin that May. Yet he has not disclosed – neither in 1843, nor now in 1848 – that when he wrote his preface to *Two Upbuilding Discourses* he was thinking particularly of Regine: '*my* reader, because this book contained a little hint to her'. With Regine in mind, he wrote with an affectionate intimacy, laced with longing, to a 'single individual' – but he quickly realized that he could also address many unknown readers in this way. In late April 1843 he had a surprising encounter with the typesetter of his manuscript:

Quite strange, really. I had decided to change that little preface to the 'Two Sermons', since it occurred to me that it harboured a certain hidden spiritual eroticism . . . I rush up to the printer's. What happens? The typesetter begs me to keep the preface. Although I laughed a little at him, to myself I was thinking: Well let *him* be the 'single individual'! It was my delight at this that at first made me decide to have only two copies printed and to present one of them to the compositor. It was really wonderful to see his emotion. A typesetter – who you would have thought must be just as tired of the manuscript as an author!

Exhilarated by this new thought about how his writing might affect countless single individuals, he set off for Berlin, hoping to repeat the amazing productivity of his first visit to the city. When he got there, though, he was drawn back to the original 'single individual'. Familiar sights and sounds evoked memories of his arrival in 1841, when he was still reeling from the break with Regine, and summoned old emotions: loss and grief, guilt and shame, self-doubt and anxiety, the sense of exile from ordinary life – and then the habitual lapses into self-pity and defiant self-justification. 'The day after my arrival I was in a very bad way, on the brink of collapse,' he wrote to Emil Boesen on 10 May 1843. Already in Stralsund, where he arrived by steamship from Copenhagen, he had 'almost gone mad hearing a young girl play on the piano Weber's last waltz' – for when he came to Berlin before, this was the first piece he heard in the Tiergarten, 'played by a blind man on a harp'.

The whole city conspired to remind him of his younger, freshly wounded self. As before, he spent his first couple of nights at the luxurious Hotel de Saxe on the bank of the River Spree: 'I have a room looking out on the water where the boats lie. Heavens, how it reminds

View of the Spree and the Lustgarten from the Hotel de Saxe in Berlin

me of the past. In the background I have the church – and when it sounds the hours the chimes go right to the marrow of my bones.' He then returned to the house on a corner of Gendarmenmarkt, where he had lived during his first visit. Then he had occupied the second floor – 'But the owner has married and therefore I am living like a hermit in one room, where even my bed stands,' he wrote to Emil.

Former habits were immediately revived, as if the city had stored them safely for him, ready for his return. He resumed his daily walks along Unter den Linden; it seemed 'as if everything were designed just to bring back memories', for even those things that had changed since his previous trip evoked feelings from the past. His newly married landlord, 'a confirmed bachelor' less than two years earlier, explained his change of heart: 'One lives only once, one must have someone to whom one can make oneself understood. How much there is in that; especially when said with absolutely no pretension. Then it hits really hard.'

A year and a half after leaving Regine, he was still trying to make sense of his own change of heart. Having proposed to her and then confronted his deep conviction that he could not marry, he had to break the engagement to remain true to himself – true to his emerging sense of who he was, and what his life should be. And yet his thoughts kept returning to Regine; he wore her engagement ring, refashioned into a diamond cross. Since they parted he had prayed for her every day, often twice a day. And so this second trip to Berlin brought to life a philosophical problem, entwined with the question of fidelity that preoccupied him: Who was he, Søren Kierkegaard, and how did he endure through time? Were the threads of memory connecting him to the past strong enough to secure his identity amid the constant flow of experiences and encounters? Did an eternal soul rest within him as he moved through changing landscapes? Could he find himself only by going backwards, and recollecting who he used to be? Should he be thus tethered to the past, when life must be lived forwards?

As his past life assailed him in the Tiergarten, on Gendarmenmarkt, beneath the blossoming trees along Unter den Linden, he thought about how he might find constancy through repetition. A faithful husband returns to his wife every night; a faithful Christian returns to God every day in prayer, every Sunday in church; a mother's thoughts return continually to her child. Through such repetitions people keep their promises, and endure through time. They return to themselves, but by stepping forwards, not by thinking back – and this is how human beings remain true to their loves. With each step he took on his long journey to Moriah, Abraham repeated his leap of faith; with each step on the way home, he rejoiced again in the gift of Isaac. In every little movement he renewed his trust in God.

Yet the more Kierkegaard contemplated repetition, the more it puzzled him. Strictly speaking, it is impossible to repeat anything, for what was new the first time becomes familiar the second time, and so altered; the third time will strengthen memories or habits from the second time. The very act of repetition produces these differences – as if repetition continually thwarts itself! Repeating his previous experience in Berlin connected him to his former self, yet also made him conscious of the time that had passed, and how he had changed in the intervening months. Returning to this familiar place put him directly in touch with the deep paradox of constancy and change, sameness and difference, that makes repetition so elusive.

Inspired by his philosophical discoveries, Kierkegaard spent those spring days in Berlin writing furiously. Each morning he returned to the café he had frequented during his first visit to the city, which had 'better coffee than in Copenhagen, more newspapers, excellent service'. Then he set to work. Once he had recovered from the long journey – the overnight steamship, the dreadful stagecoach and the miraculous train – he found that the change of scene did him good. 'When one does not have any particular business in life, as I do not,' he wrote to Emil Boesen on 15 May, 'it is necessary to have an interruption like this now and then. Once more the machinery within me is fully at work, the feelings are sound, harmonious, etc.' That was less than a week after his arrival in Berlin, but he could tell his friend that 'I have already achieved what I might wish for ... now I am climbing.'

He rapidly transmuted his experiences of repetition and recollection into a philosophical text, filling two notebooks with a draft of *Repetition*. As he relived his memories, he set out an original critique

Sketch of Kierkegaard reading in a café, 1843

of Plato's doctrine of recollection, drawing on notes he had taken with him to Berlin. During the first months of 1843 he had gained a deeper understanding of Plato by studying the Greek philosophers who came before and after him: he read about the Eleatics, the Sceptics, the Cynics, the Stoics and Aristotle. He used a notebook, labelled 'Philosophica', to record details of the Greeks' metaphysical theories, cribbed from a German textbook on the history of philosophy. This notebook also contained a series of unanswered questions, each one written at the top of a blank page: What do I learn from experience? What is the universally human, and is there anything universally human? What is the self that remains behind when a person has lost the whole world and yet has not lost himself?

That last question echoed the one from Mark's Gospel which he wrote in his journal on the day he first met Regine in 1837: 'What does it profit a man if he gains the whole world, but loses his own soul?' Six years later, this question was reversed: one world, at least, had been lost – but where was the self he had hoped to gain? He realized that these deep philosophical questions replayed within his own soul the debates among the ancient Greeks, who contemplated the cosmos as they contemplated themselves, trying to discover the secrets of existence.

First there was Heraclitus, who taught that everything is in motion. The whole of nature flows like a river, blazes like a fire, substanceless, essenceless, and this was the only truth he knew, for he could experience it. Turning his attention inwards, Heraclitus felt sensations flowing, emotions blazing. But Parmenides found timeless truths in mathematics: he believed these fixed relations to be truly real, and all the shifting things which appeared to his senses – the winds, the seas, the stars – mere illusions. His followers the Eleatics, among them Zeno with his famous paradoxes, argued that motion and change were logically impossible. How could anything new come into being? Either there is nothing, or there is something; and where is the time for becoming in between these contrary states of absence and presence? Plato's pupil Aristotle tried to solve this paradox by defining change as a movement from potential existence to actual existence: the new qualities that emerge as a tree grows to maturity – branches, leaves, fruit – were already potentially present, though not yet actualized, in the seed. And as a tree stretches its branches, leaves seeking the light, it shows a human being his own nature. 'The secret of all existence: movement,' Kierkegaard wrote in his notebook.

Those studies of ancient Greek philosophy helped him to see how Plato's doctrine that knowledge is recollection responded to an ancient question about the connection between movement and truth. Plato taught that human lives are stretched between time and eternity: between Heraclitus' world of change and becoming, and Parmenides' ideal, timeless truths. Plato agreed with Parmenides that truth is unchanging – yet our embodied lives begin, unfold and end within this changing world. *This* is our place of learning, our academy: on its return journey to eternity, each soul travels through the world of becoming, which offers reminders of timeless truths. At the sight of a beautiful woman, the soul recollects an immortal, incorruptible beauty; when it is touched by the partial, relative goodness of a human act, it recollects the immaculate Idea of the Good, impartial and absolute. Plato argued that knowledge concerns what is unchanging – but he also emphasized that knowing is itself a movement, a pursuit, in the direction of eternity. Inspired by Socrates, he taught that living a truly human life means making this movement of recollection.

Armed with these insights into the dawn of European philosophy, Kierkegaard began *Repetition* with an elliptical critique of the whole tradition, from the ancient Greeks to the modern Germans – for Hegel had also analysed the movement of knowledge, showing how one concept emerges logically from another in a dialectical pattern that leads progressively towards an absolute truth. In *Repetition* Kierkegaard turned Plato's term 'recollection' into an epithet for the process of thinking which converts life into ideas, in an attempt to understand it. Recollection produces truth in the form of knowledge, but when a human being asks how he himself can *be true* – true to another person, or true to God, or true to himself – he is concerned not with a truth to be known, but with a truth to be lived. This truth is a matter of fidelity, constancy, integrity, authenticity. Conscious of the fluctuations in his soul, and still mostly in the dark about who he was and who he might become, Kierkegaard wondered how he could promise to be faithful to others, knowing that his mind might change. And how can any human being, whose existence is continually in motion, accomplish constancy in relation to God?

The answer to all these questions, which he wrote out in his small, slanting hand in that single room on Gendarmenmarkt, is repetition. A relationship – whether to another person, to God, or to oneself – is never a fixed, solid thing. If it is to endure through time, it must be repeatedly renewed. And each human self is made up of such relationships. The 'new category' of repetition would, Kierkegaard argued, finally allow philosophy to say something meaningful about the truth of life.

Meanwhile, he was struggling to reconstruct the truth of his own life – for *Repetition* was the revised story of his engagement crisis as well as a manifesto for existentialism. He embedded his metaphysical reflections within an experimental psychological narrative, dividing himself, once again, between two characters: an amateur philosopher called Constantin Constantius who travelled twice to Berlin, and his

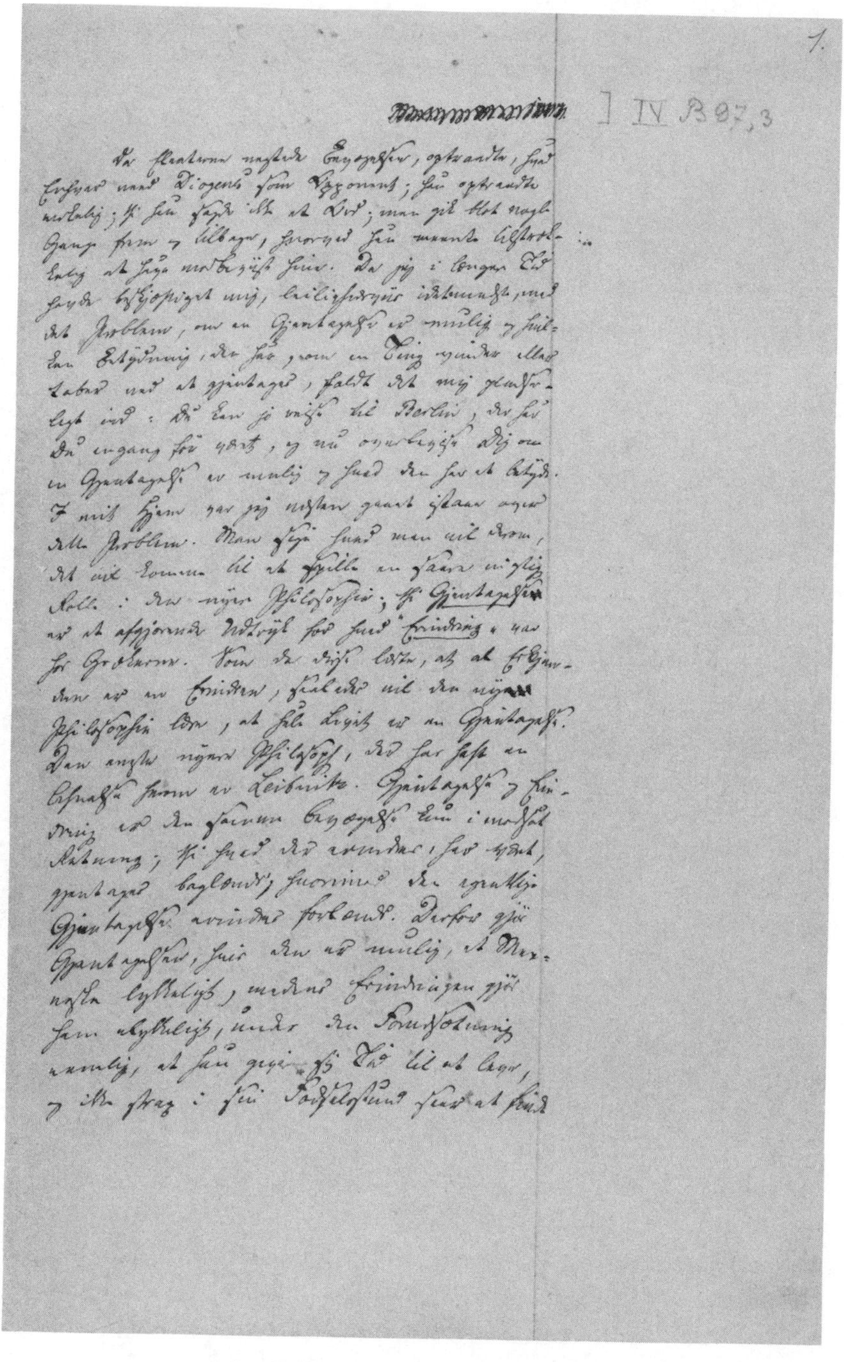

Manuscript of *Repetition*: first page

friend, a young man who wanted to break up with his fiancée and become a writer. Both these men were foolish, though in different ways. They played out a story composed from episodes in Kierkegaard's life, loosely following the model of Goethe's early epistolary novel *The Sorrows of Young Werther*, a founding text of Romantic literature, which had already inspired F. C. Sibbern, Kierkegaard's former philosophy professor, to write a similar kind of novel.

*Repetition*'s narrator, Constantin Constantius, proposes a new theory of truth, but despite his erudition he does not fully understand his own theory. Writing in the voice of this character allowed Kierkegaard to stake his claim as a philosopher while pointing out the limits of a purely intellectual approach to questions of existence. 'The question of repetition will play a very important role in modern philosophy,' announces Constantin boldly, after dropping an insouciant reference to Leibniz's metaphysics, 'for *repetition* is a crucial expression for what "recollection" was to the Greeks. Just as they taught that all knowing is a recollecting, so modern philosophy will teach that all life is a repetition ... Repetition is the new category that will be discovered!'

Having sketched out his theory of repetition in a few cryptic paragraphs, Constantin Constantius decides to test it by returning to Berlin, a city he has visited once before. While other well-off Danes travel abroad to see notable sights or to ride on a train – or, if in London, to take a carriage through the new tunnel under the Thames – Constantin likes to travel with no particular purpose except to observe people and philosophize. His 'investigative journey' will be an experiment in 'the possibility and meaning of repetition'.

In Berlin, Constantin returns to his former lodgings on Gendarmenmarkt, in order to discover 'whether a repetition is possible'. He has fond memories of this place:

> Gendarmenmarkt is certainly the most beautiful square in Berlin; *das Schauspielhaus* [the theatre] and the two churches are superb, especially when viewed from a window by moonlight. The recollection of these things was an important reason for taking my journey. One climbs the stairs to the first floor in a gas-lit building, opens a little door, and stands in the hallway. To the left is a glass door leading to a

small room. Straight ahead is an anteroom. Beyond are two entirely identical rooms, identically furnished, so that one sees the room double in the mirror. The inner room is tastefully illuminated. A candelabra stands on a writing table; a gracefully designed armchair upholstered in red velvet stands before the desk. The first room is not illuminated. Here the pale light of the moon blends with the strong light from the inner room. Sitting in a chair by the window, one looks out on the great square, sees the shadows of passers-by hurrying along the walls; everything is transformed into a stage setting. A dream world glimmers in the background of the soul. One feels a desire to toss on a cape, to steal softly along the wall with a searching gaze, aware of every sound. One does not do this but merely sees a rejuvenated self doing it. Having smoked a cigar, one goes back to the inner room and begins to work. It is past midnight. One extinguishes the candles and lights a little night candle. Undiluted, the light of the moon reigns supreme. A single shadow appears even blacker; a single footstep takes a long time to disappear. The cloudless arch of heaven has a sad and pensive look as if the end of the world had already come and heaven, unperturbed, were occupied with itself. Once again one goes out into the hallway, into that little room, and – if one is among the fortunate who are able to sleep – goes to sleep.

Alas, reality does not match Constantin's dreamy recollection of his Berlin residence – part theatre, part Platonic cave, part writing retreat – with its secluded view on the world. Since his previous visit, the owner of the house has married, and only one room is available for rent. More disappointments quickly follow. Constantin goes to the Königstädter Theatre to see the same actors play in the same farce he enjoyed last time: he remembers sitting in the quiet theatre, alone in a box, and abandoning himself to laughter – but on this second visit the theatre is busy, none of the boxes are empty, he cannot get comfortable, and the play does not amuse him; after half an hour he gives up and leaves. He returns to his room, where the splendour of the red velvet chair seems to mock his cramped living quarters. The lighting is all wrong. He sleeps badly that night.

The next morning, as he tries to work, thoughts of the past prevent him from philosophizing:

My mind was sterile, my troubled imagination constantly conjured up tantalizingly attractive recollections of how the ideas had presented themselves the last time, and the tares of these recollections choked out every thought at birth. I went out to the café where I had gone every day the previous time to enjoy the beverage that, according to the poet's precept, when it is 'pure and hot and strong and not misused', can always stand alongside that to which the poet compares it, namely, friendship. At any rate, I am a coffee-lover. Perhaps the coffee was just as good as last time; one would almost expect it to be, but it was not to my liking. The sun through the café windows was hot and glaring; the room was just about as humid as the air in a saucepan, practically cooking.

Every attempt to relive his recollections is frustrated, and Constantin becomes 'weary of repetition'. 'My discovery was not significant, yet it was curious,' he reports, 'for I had discovered that there is simply no repetition, and had verified it by having it repeated in every possible way.'

Meanwhile, Constantin's friend is caught in a different kind of recollection. This young man, whose 'handsome appearance, large glowing eyes, and flippant air' appeal to Constantin, is 'deeply and fervently and beautifully and humbly in love'. But he is melancholy: his love for his fiancée has quickly turned into longing, even mourning, and he has begun to 'recollect his love'. Having turned her into a fixed idea, which he can summon and sigh over at will, he no longer relates to her as a living person. Constantin observes that his friend is 'essentially through with the entire relationship', though he does not yet know this himself: 'It was obvious that he was going to be unhappy; that the girl would also become unhappy was no less obvious, although it was not so immediately possible to predict how it would happen ... Nothing could draw him out of the melancholy longing by which he was not so much coming closer to his beloved as forsaking her. His mistake was incurable, and his mistake was this: that he stood at the end instead of at the beginning.'

The young man gradually realizes that there has been 'a misunderstanding' between himself and his fiancée, and as she becomes 'almost a burden to him' Constantin sees 'a remarkable change' in his friend:

'A poetic creativity awakened in him on a scale I had never believed possible. Now I easily grasped the whole situation. The young girl was not his beloved: she was the occasion that awakened the poetic in him and made him a poet. That was why he could love only her, never forget her, never want to love another, and yet continually only long for her. She was drawn into his whole being; the memory of her was forever alive. She had meant so much to him; she had made him a poet – and in doing this she had signed her own death sentence.'

When Regine read this, she would find a new explanation for Kierkegaard's behaviour: while *Either/Or* perpetuated the deception that he had callously used her, *Repetition* suggested that he loved her exclusively, in the only way he was capable of loving any woman. This book also exposed his previous strategy of subterfuge. 'Transform yourself into a contemptible person,' Constantin advises his friend – this will allow his fiancée to become 'the victor', for then 'she is absolutely right and you are absolutely wrong.'

Kierkegaard's resentment and indignation towards Regine gleamed through these thoughts of self-sacrifice. 'I cannot deny that I gradually came to regard the young man's beloved with a prejudiced eye,' admits Constantin: 'That she should notice nothing whatever, that she had no suspicion of his suffering and of the reason for it, that if she suspected it she did nothing, made no effort to save him by giving him the one thing he needed and which she alone could give him, namely, his freedom.' He believes that feminine love should be sacrificial, that a woman becomes masculine if she has enough 'egotism' to imagine that 'she proves the fidelity of her love by clinging to her beloved instead of giving him up.' Such a woman, he contends bitterly, 'has a very easy task in life, which permits her to enjoy not only the reputation and consciousness of being faithful, but also the most finely distilled sentiment of love ... God preserve a man from such fidelity!' And in any case, Constantin didn't find this woman particularly special; he is amazed that she had such significance for his friend, 'for there was no trace of anything really stirring, enrapturing, creative. With him it was as is usually the case with melancholy people – they trap themselves. He idealized her, and now he believes that she was that ... What traps him is not the girl's lovableness at all but his regret at having wronged her by upsetting her life.'

These pages of *Repetition* echoed a journal entry written in Berlin on 17 May 1843, where idealistic love and romantic regret battled with angry, self-justifying complaints about Regine's 'pride' and 'arrogance'. During and after the break-up, Kierkegaard tried to play the hero by playing the villain, feigning indifference and cruelty, and sacrificing his reputation to make her feel happier about losing him. He resented this role, and he resented Regine too for not letting him go more easily, for making him feel – and look – so guilty. As usual, the sensitivity which makes him so compassionate to others also distorted his sense of injury; defensiveness stifled his generosity, and he reacted harshly. 'Humanly speaking I have been fair to her,' he protested. 'In a chivalrous sense, I loved her far better than she loved me, for otherwise she would neither have shown me pride nor alarmed me later with her shrieking . . . I have behaved most magnanimously towards her in not letting her suspect my pain.'

While Constantin criticizes the fictional version of Regine, the young hero of *Repetition* cannot let her go. Kierkegaard's inner conflict and confusion were refracted through the ambivalent relationship between these two characters: Constantin finds his friend 'quite irritable, like any melancholic, and despite this irritability as well as because of it, in a continual state of self-contradiction. He wants me to be his confidant, and yet he does not want it.' The young man is appalled by Constantin's cool, detached attitude to his situation. He leaves town, and writes letters to Constantin: he reports that he is sinking in recollections of his beloved; that he has read the Old Testament story of Job, who protested his righteousness when God took everything from him; that he is 'nauseated by life'; that he agonizes over his guilt about breaking the engagement; that, in spite of all appearances, he is in the right.

'I am at the end of my tether,' begins one letter:

My whole being screams in self-contradiction. How did it happen that I became guilty? Or am I not guilty? Could I anticipate that my whole existence would undergo a change, that I would become another person? Can it be that something darkly hidden in my soul suddenly burst forth? But if it lay darkly hidden, how could I anticipate it? But if I could not anticipate it, then certainly I am innocent. Am I unfaithful? If she were to go on loving me and never loved anyone else, she would then certainly be faithful to me. If I go on wanting to love her, am I then unfaithful? Why should she be in the right and I in the wrong? Even if the whole world rose up against me, even if all the scholastics argued with me, even if it were a matter of life and death – I am still in the right. No one shall take that away from me, even if there is no language in which I can say it. I have acted rightly. My love cannot find expression in a marriage. If I do that, she is crushed. Perhaps the possibility appeared tempting to her. I cannot help it; it was that to me also.

As he reads the young man's tormented, passionate letters, Constantin understands that repetition is 'a religious movement'. He realizes that he was foolish to seek repetition in external things – a theatre, a coffee shop, a writing desk and a velvet chair – for true repetition is an inward, spiritual movement wherein a human being receives himself anew. Job obtained repetition when everything he had lost was restored to him, even more plentifully than before; Abraham obtained it when God renewed his gift of Isaac, and he 'received a son a second time'. Constantin also sees that he cannot accomplish such a repetition: 'I am unable to make a religious movement, it is contrary to my nature.'

The young man, meanwhile, hopes for an inward repetition that will restore the freedom he lost when he became romantically ensnared. Perhaps he can regain this freedom if he stops claiming to be in the right, and asks forgiveness for his mistakes – but this seems to be contrary to *his* nature. Instead, inspired by the Book of Job, he demands a divine miracle: 'Make me fit to be a husband, shatter my whole personality, render me almost unrecognizable to myself.' As he waits for grace to strike, he tries to change himself – to become a man who can be true to his love: 'I sit and clip myself, take away everything that is incommensurable in order to become commensurable. Every morning I discard all the impatience and infinite striving of my soul – but it does not help, for the next morning it is there again. Every morning I shave off the beard of all my ludicrousness – but it does not help, for the next morning my beard is just as long again.'

By the end of *Repetition* the fiancé is desperate, as convinced of his righteousness as Job, yet incapable of repetition. Eventually, despairing of reform, despairing of release, he follows the example of Goethe's romantic hero Werther, who has already inspired many sensitive young men to suicide. Seeing no way forward, all hope exhausted, Kierkegaard's *alter ego* takes a pistol and shoots himself in the head.

Boarding the train in Berlin at the end of May 1843, he hardly knew how a mess of scribbled ideas and a dark tangle of feelings, some of them generations old, had been condensed into this little manuscript. It was barely coherent: its strangeness and obscurity were perhaps inevitable effects of his effort to bring together philosophy and experience, to draw out the universal significance of questions that both shaped and fractured his own life.

Had he solved the problem of how a human being can remain true to his love? He had shown that recollection preserves love only by displaying it like an exhibit behind glass, or keeping it like a lock of hair inside a reliquary – at the cost of denying it life, of closing down the future. He had also suggested that philosophical thinking, which treats truth as an idea to be grasped, is similarly sterile when it comes to making sense of human existence. And he had hinted that this kind of theoretical truth needs to give way to a religious movement – to the 'good and perfect gifts' repeatedly given from above to anyone willing to receive them – if human beings are to be true to themselves from moment to moment, through all the minute shifts and momentous upheavals of their lives.

By then, his effort to be true to himself had eclipsed the ideal of being true to Regine in any worldly sense. That year he noted in his journal Socrates's 'very fine' remark in the *Cratylus* that 'to be deceived by oneself is the worst thing of all, for how could it not be terrible when the deceiver never disappears, even for an instant, but is always ready at hand?' Of course, being honest with himself was not exactly comfortable either. Burdened with this absurd ego slumped like a fragile giant upon his shoulders, confronted by his own faults at every turn, still filling pages with his rancour at the young woman who loved him, he reached the conclusion that 'the main thing is that one is truly forthright with God – that one does not attempt to escape from anything, but pushes on until he himself provides the explanation. Whether or not this will be what one might wish it to be, it is still the best.'

\* \* \*

Now, in the autumn of 1848, in his new apartment, he is still 'pushing on', still seeking 'the explanation' for what happened with Regine, for his authorship, for the man he has become. He can only bare his soul to God at times like this – at home in quiet hours, in solitude. Ancient spiritual teachers taught that 'to pray is to breathe', and thus it makes no sense to ask why one should pray: 'Because I would otherwise die – so it is with praying. Nor by breathing do I intend to reshape the world, but merely to refresh my vitality and *be renewed* – that is how it is to pray in relation to God.' He spends most of his time pursuing 'the explanation' in another way: in his journals, now in *The Point of View for My Work as an Author*. But when he holds his beloved pen, thoughts of the reader – whether this is Regine, or Bishop Mynster, or Professor Martensen, or an unknown reader in the distant future, far beyond his death – interpose their folds of reflection between himself and God. Quick and gossamer thin as insects' wings, barely discernible, these fluttering thoughts pull his gaze in myriad directions. Then his soul, like the sea in a breeze or a misty night sky, loses its transparency. All his thoughts, all his journal notes, 'are too wordy for me, and yet they do not exhaust everything I carry in my inner self, where I understand myself much more easily in the presence of God, for there I can bring everything together at once, and yet in the end understand myself best by leaving everything to him'.

# 11

# How to be Anxious

'I am still very exhausted, but I have almost reached my goal,' he writes in his journal in November 1848, as he completes *The Point of View for My Work as an Author.* 'Recently I have been only a writer. My mind and spirit are strong enough, but regrettably all too strong for my body. In one sense it is my mind and spirit that help me to endure such poor health; in another sense it is my mind and spirit that overwhelm my body.' His ideas are so abundant that he could write incessantly day and night, though if he did this he would soon collapse. 'After becoming an author, I actually have never once experienced what I hear others lament over – the lack of thoughts, or that they would not present themselves. If that were to happen to me, I very likely would almost be happy that at last I had a day off.'

He is concluding *The Point of View for My Work as an Author* with a chapter on 'Governance's Part in my Authorship'. There he describes how he has 'continuously needed God's assistance day after day, year after year', in order to write. When he starts to work he feels agitation, restless passion, 'a poet impatience' in his soul; he picks up his pen, but cannot move it. Then he seems to hear a voice telling him, like a teacher speaking to a boy, to write his assignment: 'Then I become completely calm; then there is time to write every letter, almost meticulously, with my slower pen. Then I can do it, then I dare not do anything else, then I write each word, each line, almost unaware of the next word and the next line. Then, when I read it through later, I find an entirely different satisfaction in it. Even though some glowing expressions did perhaps elude me, what has been produced is something else – it is not the work of the poet passion or of the thinker passion, but of devotion to God, and for me a divine worship.'

With this account of his authorship, Kierkegaard is setting himself decisively, defiantly apart from the world, showing his disdain for worldly success. He has come to believe that 'the world, if it is not evil, is mediocre.' Nevertheless, the lure of this world is powerful, and as a writer he has had to struggle to avoid falling into 'the untruth that, as it always does, would have secured for me money, honour, esteem, approval, etc., the untruth that what I had to say was "the demand of the times", that it was submitted to the lenient judgement of a highly esteemed public, moreover, that it was owing to the approval and support and acclamation of my contemporaries that it prospered'. No, he has channelled his efforts into expressing the truth that his entire life makes indubitable for him: 'that there is a God'. He has sought to understand 'what it means to be a human being' by inquiring philosophically, spiritually, religiously into 'this *human-ness*' belonging to every single individual. Yet this lonely, narrow path has cut through the middle of his city, kept him in full view of the crowds.

After his break with Regine, he had wanted to retreat. If he was destined to be a strange, solitary figure standing on the edge of the world, perhaps it would be better to slip over the horizon and disappear from view. Just as he imagines that Jesus was tempted to go out into the desert, to become a hermit, so withdrawing to a remote place in the countryside is his own continual temptation. 'It was my plan as soon as *Either/Or* was published to seek a call in a rural parish and sorrow over my sins. I could not suppress my creativity, I followed it – naturally it moved into the religious.'

For these seven years since leaving Regine, it has been his self-imposed 'penance' to remain in Copenhagen and, by being an author, work as a Christian missionary in the heart of Danish Christendom. Having been cast out of the ethical sphere through his own failings, he has come to see the world as a place of suffering and sacrifice – and he has resolved to live in this world, exposed to the public eye. Though his thoughts have often returned to the idea of retreat, in the end he has always renewed this resolution and stayed in Copenhagen: 'I understood that my task was to do penance by serving the truth in such a way that it virtually became burdensome, humanly speaking, a thankless labour of sacrificing everything.' He knows that God does not want people to punish themselves, that there is no merit in it – but he has felt 'such a driving need' for penance that he could not do otherwise, and hopes this will be forgiven. And for all its difficulty, there is joy to be found on this path: following it seems the only way to be truthful, faithful, obedient to his deepest self, who is seen and known only by God. Now, as this turbulent year draws near its close, he is adamant that 'this is how I serve Christianity – in all my wretchedness happy in the thought of the indescribable good God has done for me, far beyond my expectations'.

These words echo what he wrote about Abraham five years ago, in *Fear and Trembling*. Abraham received great gifts from God, contrary to all his expectations, but he became a 'knight of faith' – resumed his place in the world as a father, husband and householder – only after the most agonizing ordeal which required him to relinquish everything. Then, Kierkegaard contrasted this religious movement with the mere 'resignation' of someone who withdraws to a monastery, or remains in the world but never expects to feel at home there. He felt that the faith of Abraham was beyond his reach – and yet if all things were possible for God, as the Gospels taught, he had to believe that God could grant him fulfilment and peace. In truth, during the years since then his daily life has oscillated between retreat – not to a monastery or a rural parish, but to quiet hours of devotional reading and prayer, and to tranquil days in the woodlands of north Zealand – and blistering immersion in the world.

\* \* \*

During the summer of 1843, soon after he finished writing *Fear and Trembling*, he heard that Regine was engaged to Johan Frederik Schlegel, a government official, formerly her music tutor, who had admired her since her youth. 'I showed the girl my confidence in her by believing all the great things it pleased her to tell me concerning herself,' he wrote scathingly in his journal, adding that 'it is in fact curious – that a girl can be so great in her own eyes; that she honoured me with her love (or rather, with being engaged) – that it should shake me like this.' Later he covered these lines with dense loops of ink to make them unreadable. But he left unaltered a cooler entry, in which he imagined a chance encounter with Regine: 'An individual with a sense of humour meets a girl who had once assured him that she would die if he left her. When he now meets her she is engaged.' He makes the girl 'speechless with rage' by offering her a few coins – 'to show my appreciation', he tells her.

He returned to his draft of *Repetition*, and changed the ending. Instead of killing himself in despair of becoming a suitable husband, the book's young hero learns that his beloved is engaged to someone else; this unexpected news liberates him from his crisis of identity, and he thanks God for granting him his freedom – here, at last, is the 'repetition' he has longed for. Once again his future lies open before him; he has another chance to choose his path in life.

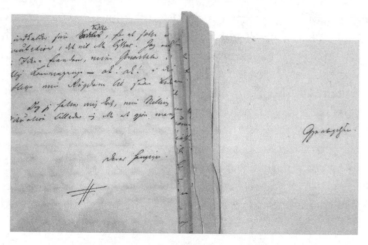

The manuscript of *Repetition*,
where Kierkegaard cut out the young man's suicide

*Repetition* and *Fear and Trembling* were published on the same day – under different pseudonyms, of course – in October 1843, along with *Three Upbuilding Discourses* by S. Kierkegaard. *Four Upbuilding Discourses* followed in December 1843, and *Two Upbuilding Discourses* in March 1844. Like Kierkegaard's first collection of discourses, which introduced the category of 'the single individual', these slim volumes were dedicated to his father. And despite Regine's changed situation, he gave them similar prefaces alluding to her, the 'single individual' whom he called 'my reader'. From a practical point of view, the possibility of marrying her had slipped into the past, but this possibility remained a fact of his soul; it continued to shape his understanding of himself. Becoming an author was inseparable from leaving Regine, yet through his writing he expressed his continuing faithfulness to her – in a sense that perhaps he alone could understand.

Now an established author, he lived submerged in writing. His work gave the rhythm to his days and nights: back and forth between his apartment on Nørregade and the streets of Copenhagen, back and forth between creative exhilaration and physical exhaustion. While he was at home his blackened windows were kept closed to shut out the sun; when he went out, his servants opened the windows to freshen the air, laid a fire in the stove, and made sure the room was the right temperature – for he was as exacting as his father in household matters, and would check the thermometer when he returned. He employed Israel Levin, an accomplished linguist, as a secretary and proofreader. Levin sometimes spent whole days at his home, helping him to work through the corrections to his manuscripts – 'an enormous amount of work'. On these days they dined together on strong soup, fish, melon and fine sherry, followed by ruinous coffee served in silver pots, which Kierkegaard drank with cream and nearly a cupful of sugar. 'It amused him every day to see the sugar melt. This really delighted him,' observed Levin, but 'the coffee was so extremely strong that he destroyed himself with it.'

This intensive work was relieved by walks with friends almost every day: often with Peter Johannes Spang, pastor at the Church of the Holy Spirit, or with Hans Brøchner, a young philosopher who admired Kierkegaard immensely and found him 'very kind'. They walked through the city, along the lakes, up on the ramparts, or out to Frederiksberg. When he wanted companionship at home he invited Emil Boesen to dine with him, but received few other visitors. For a while he took up horse riding to improve his digestion – but Kierkegaard 'did not cut a particularly good figure on a horse', for he sat stiffly and looked as though he were constantly recalling the riding master's instructions. Occasionally he hired a carriage in the morning, and ordered the coachman to drive as fast as possible to the countryside, where he walked through the forest and then had lunch at an inn and talked volubly with the locals, before speeding back to Copenhagen and beginning work again, refreshed by his 'air bath'.

Early in 1844 he was finishing *The Concept of Anxiety*, beginning *Philosophical Fragments*, planning a humorous book called *Prefaces*, and drafting another collection of religious discourses. Yet he remained unsure of his vocation, and ambivalent about being an author. It seemed virtually impossible to publish his works without being assailed by unending worries about how they would be received; his pride bristled at these anxieties over esteem, success, status, to which he longed to be indifferent – if only he could confine his profound sensitivity to profound things! He was still contemplating retreat to a rural parish, and in February 1844 he preached a qualifying sermon at the Church of the Trinity, where he had been confirmed by Bishop Mynster in his youth. This made him eligible for an appointment in the Danish State Church. The text for that sermon was from the second chapter of Paul's First Letter to the Corinthians, the same text that had inspired the title of *Fear and Trembling*. Christian wisdom, Paul explains here, is not 'human wisdom', not 'a wisdom of this age or of the rulers of this age', but 'God's wisdom, secret and hidden'. In drawing this contrast between divine wisdom and the false wisdom of the world, Paul argued that serving God and pursuing worldly things – including esteem, success, status – are two diverging paths through life: an either/or.

This New Testament view of the world as a place of untruth and corruption that leads people away from God echoes distinctly, if now more faintly, through centuries of Christian history. During 1844 Kierkegaard's devotional reading included *True Christianity* by Johann Arndt, the Lutheran theologian whose literary work sowed the seeds of pietism, and then nourished its growth. In the first years of the seventeenth century Arndt published new editions of medieval books, including Thomas à Kempis's *Imitation of Christ* and the sermons of Johannes Tauler. *True Christianity*, his own guide to the holy life, went through more than a hundred editions between 1605 and 1740. Inspired by the mystical insights and ascetic practices of his Catholic forebears, who had themselves studied, lived and elaborated St Paul's theology within their monasteries, Arndt urged generations

Johann Arndt (1555–1621) and an illustration from an eighteenth-century
edition of his *True Christianity*, similar to the one Kierkegaard owned.
Above the woman holding a dagger is the motto 'I kill myself daily.'

of Protestant Christians to purify their souls by practising self-denial
and 'dying to the world'. In *True Christianity* Kierkegaard found a
spiritual teaching which deepened his own ambivalence towards the
world. 'A Christian is truly in the world but not of the world,' he read
in this old devotional book. 'He lives indeed in the world but he does
not love it. The world's pomp, honour, pretence, glory, lust of the
eyes, lust of the flesh, pride of life, is for a Christian a dead thing, a
shadow to which he pays no attention.'

What would Johann Arndt, or his medieval sources – or even Paul
himself – have made of Kierkegaard's world? Within his lifetime
Copenhagen has acquired the features of urban life that have already,
he reads in the press, transformed the capitals of France and England,
cities he likens to Sodom and Gomorrah. The nineteenth-century
metropolis does not just gratify the perennial desires of the flesh, but
offers a new and distinctly modern temptation: to put oneself on display, and to become a spectator of the lives of others. Copenhagen is
becoming more and more like a machine that constantly produces
images of itself. Its newspapers present ephemeral patchworks of city
life, hastily tacking together snatches of gossip from different corners

of the town – every edition new and enticing, but stale and boring a few days later. Heiberg's Danish vaudevilles have accustomed theatre audiences to enjoy satirical plays about themselves. The grander shops on Østergade, where the sewerage gutters are boarded over, have introduced Copenhageners to the modern art of window-dressing: like the attire of fashionable young ladies, their displays change frequently to draw the attention of passers-by. Along Østergade parade there are 'a variety of black silk capes or mantillas, white bonnets, trimmed with flowers and feathers' amid the carts, sailors and tradeswomen.

By 1844 these everyday spectacles had been joined by something more exotic: Tivoli-Vauxhall, an amusement park named after similar ventures in Paris and London. It was opened in the summer of 1843 by newspaper-owner Georg Carstensen, and hundreds of thousands of people poured through its gates during the first full season in 1844. Carstensen's Tivoli is a world within a world, bringing cosmopolitan culture to the inhabitants of a market town: visitors can shop in an oriental-style bazaar and marvel at the latest recreational technologies – a panorama (displaying a tableau from the Tivoli in Hamburg), a diorama, fireworks, a steam-powered carousel, a daguerreotype studio, mechanical waxworks enacting scenes from the life of Christ – alongside more traditional entertainments like peep shows, pantomimes and concerts. Here bourgeois families enjoy pursuits formerly reserved for aristocratic young men: they can be tourists, theatre-goers, restaurant diners. Tivoli offers Copenhageners not only new images of the world, but also new images of themselves – even if they cannot afford to have their daguerreotype taken.

Like Heiberg, who has long scorned Carstensen as a purveyor of low-brow entertainment, Kierkegaard disdains the attractions on offer at Tivoli. But he does not need to visit the new amusement park to join in the culture of spectatorship that is pervading his city: sitting in one of the modern cafés on Strøget feels rather like being exhibited in a shop window, or in a diorama. And for someone as self-conscious as Kierkegaard, walking through town is always a public performance. Now, as he completes *The Point of View for My Work as an Author*, he recalls how he played the role of *flâneur* on the streets of Copenhagen in the early days of his authorship; his books have been advertised and reviewed in the press to catch the eye of readers for whom perusing a journal is a little like window shopping. And ever since his literary debut in *Copenhagen's Flying Post* in 1834, he has continued to publish occasional newspaper articles; some of his contemporaries regard him as 'nothing other than a very talented and well-read feuilleton writer'. Even when he writes his journals, he knows he is exhibiting his inner life to posterity. So he has found himself confronted daily with the question of *how* to be seen: Who should he be in this new-fashioned, glass-fronted world? Which mask should he wear, what image should he display? And what images will other people make of him?

Perhaps these questions are particularly urgent for Kierkegaard because of his intensely reflective character, because *Either/Or* made him a local celebrity, and because since his father's death his choices have been remarkably unconstrained by circumstance: he does not need to earn a living, and he does not have to be a son, a husband, or a father. But the city itself seems to pose such questions to its inhabitants: he has discovered that living in a modern metropolis intensifies an experience of anxiety that he recognizes as universally human. Ever since Adam, he believes, human beings have felt anxious – and now, caught in the city's myriad reflections, their anxieties multiply as they become uneasy spectators of their own lives.

'No Grand Inquisitor has such dreadful torments in readiness as anxiety has,' he wrote in 1844 in *The Concept of Anxiety*, 'and no secret agent knows as cunningly as anxiety how to attack his suspect in his weakest moment or to make alluring the trap in which he will be caught, and no discerning judge knows how to interrogate and examine the accused as does anxiety, which never lets the accused escape, neither through amusement, nor by noise, nor during work, neither by day nor by night.'

Like *The Concept of Irony*, *The Concept of Anxiety* was an intricate and demanding academic treatise. It engaged with recent German philosophy, including the Hegelian Karl Rosenkranz's philosophical psychology and the fragmentary works of Johann Georg Hamann, admirer of Socrates and critic of the Enlightenment. But Kierkegaard also drew on his own life-experience, which he contrasted with the 'scientific' method frequently extolled by contemporary philosophers and theologians. 'And this is the wonderful thing about life,' he wrote, 'that every human being who gives attention to himself knows what no science knows, since he knows who he himself is.'

Anxiety arises within a person when he becomes conscious of his freedom. This is why Hamann called anxiety a 'holy hypochondria': it is a spiritual awareness unknown to animals, which are merely physical creatures. But human beings are not angels, either. We live in the world anchored by gravity, feet on the ground, rooted in actuality – our mortal bodies, our circumstances, the facts of our lives. And yet we breathe the air of possibility, and the force of gravity is seldom so strong that we cannot lift a foot into this air and take a step, one way or another. We all long to claim our freedom, and when actuality becomes a swamp we gasp desperately for air. Yet this same freedom, with its dizzying proliferation of possibilities, fills us with anxiety the moment we experience it. An open future is, like the nothingness of death, an unknown abyss. Glancing down, afraid of falling, we anxiously grasp and cling onto anything solid we can find – possessions, money, food, drink, other people – in an effort to steady ourselves. Thus we live, clutching at things in the world, whether or not it is for our good, or theirs. But we can learn to be anxious only by letting go, and finding out what happens when we fall. 'This is an adventure that every human being must go through – to learn to be anxious so that he may not perish either by never having been in anxiety, or by succumbing in anxiety. For whoever has learned to be anxious in the right way has learned the ultimate.'

Kierkegaard connected this psychological analysis of anxiety with the Christian doctrine of original sin, which awkwardly holds together inherited sinfulness and individual responsibility. Augustine, still the orthodox voice on this question, taught that after Adam and Eve sinned in the Garden of Eden they transmitted their sinfulness – and its consequent suffering and mortality – biologically to the whole human race. Kierkegaard disagrees with that explanation: he interprets the biblical story of Adam's lapse into sin as dramatizing a fall that happens again and again throughout each person's life, every time a moment of freedom arises. Nevertheless, he shares Augustine's view that human beings are constitutionally restless: never completely at ease in the world, and able to find real rest only in God. People sin, thought Augustine, when they seek relief or satisfaction in something other than God – in some finite thing, some sensual distraction, some transitory experience. Although his language was sometimes moralizing, Augustine regarded sin more as spiritual disorientation than as moral failure.

Kierkegaard developed this idea in *The Concept of Anxiety*. Although pietism taught him from his earliest years to attend to his own sinfulness, he does not, like most pietists, preach the cultivation of moral purity. Instead he tries to confront his anxieties with clear-sighted courage, to let them move through him and experience all their power and subtlety. He sees anxiety as a blessing as well as a curse, a privilege as well as an affliction, a mark of spiritual nobility; after all, Jesus prayed anxiously in the garden at Gethsemane before he faced his death, and Socrates, condemned to die by drinking hemlock, raised his poisoned cup as if toasting his own anxiety. 'The more profoundly a human being is in anxiety, the greater he is', for anxiety 'consumes all finite ends and discovers their deceptiveness'. When a human being 'passes through the anxiety of the possible' – an indeterminate horror of existence that finds no worldly foothold, since it senses an infinite nothingness beneath every step – he will be 'educated to have no anxiety, not because he can escape the terrible things of life but because these always become weak by comparison with those of possibility'. Kierkegaard imagined such a man saying, as a patient might say to his surgeon when a painful operation is about to begin: Now I am ready. 'Then anxiety enters into his soul and searches out everything and anxiously torments everything finite and petty out of him.'

'One should certainly not be in anxiety about men and about finitudes,' he declared in 1844. Nevertheless, he is frequently troubled by such things. Slights or criticisms lodge painfully in his heart for days, weeks, months, like thorns in his flesh; events that seem insignificant to others take on magnificent proportions in the mirror of his egotism. Without a wife to confide in at the end of each day, he pours his injuries and indignations onto the pages of his journal. But paper is less absorbent than a sympathetic listener, and ink more tenacious than a voice: once written down, his cares stare starkly back at him, fixed into refrains that echo through his mind. His close friends, like Emil Boesen and Hans Brøchner, understand this: 'With K. it frequently happened that when he reflected on some minor matter, he could make it into a little piece of world history. His sense of reality did not always keep pace with his expertise at reflection, and so he came to view facts oddly displaced or transformed to abnormal dimensions.'

Early in 1844, while Kierkegaard was at work on *The Concept of Anxiety*, Brøchner played a character called Søren Kirk in *Gjenboerne*, a comedy performed at the Student Association. The playwright, Jens Christian Hostrup, did not intend this as a personal attack – Søren Kirk was a young theology student intoxicated by Part I of *Either/Or*, and he parodied the sort of philosophical pretensions which the book itself satirized – but Kierkegaard was deeply distressed by *Gjenboerne*. With Brøchner and Hostrup, of course, he pretended not to care about it.

By the summer of 1844 he had finished three books and a new collection of discourses. While preparing the final manuscripts of *The Concept of Anxiety* and *Philosophical Fragments*, he deleted his own name from the title pages and gave each book a pseudonym. For the treatise on anxiety he chose Vigilius Haufniensis, 'the watchman of Copenhagen': a wakeful, observant figure in a city of slumbering spirits. He had conceived *Philosophical Fragments* as the first in a series of pamphlets, but in the end he presented it as a self-contained book by Johannes Climacus, the young hero of the satire on Hegelian philosophy he had left unfinished two years earlier. This pseudonym had echoes of *Either/Or*'s Victor Eremita, for the original Johannes Climacus was a seventh-century monk who left his monastery on Sinai to live as a hermit.

The third book was *Prefaces*, a satire on Copenhagen's literary industry. Its pseudonymous author was Nicolas Notabene, a married man whose wife considers writing books to be a kind of infidelity. 'You are in a cocoon of thoughtfulness from morning til night,' Mrs Notabene complains: 'at the dinner table you sit and stare into space like a ghost.' As a compromise, she allows Nicolas to write only the prefaces to his books, and this volume was a collection of eight such prefaces. More than one of these vented Kierkegaard's fresh annoyance at Heiberg, who at the end of 1843 had published a decorative yearbook, designed to be purchased as a smart New Year gift, which included a brief critical review of *Repetition*. 'What a pleasure it is indeed to have written a book!' Nicolas Notabene's first preface begins – 'a book that does not owe its origin to an inexplicable inner need and is therefore ignorant of whether it fits into the world, indeed, is bashful and ashamed like an ambivalent witness to a secret love affair – no, a book that is the fruit of a marriage of convenience between publisher and public.' Affecting a high-minded vacuity, he ridicules Heiberg's interest in astronomy; he also attacks low-brow journalism, comparing the writing in newspapers to a wastewater drain, 'for it would indeed be too bad if the public's gossip were to go to waste'. He writes prefaces to a scholarly book, to a collection of sermons, to the first issue of a new philosophical journal. Another preface lampoons Copenhagen's new Temperance and Abstinence Union: in January 1844 Kierkegaard had read with scorn an article in *The Fatherland* publicizing the Union's 'lofty endeavour to restore lost souls to society and the family, to God and to virtue'.

Over the course of a few days in June 1844, Nicolas Notabene, Vigilius Haufniensis, Johannes Climacus and S. Kierkegaard – author of *Three Upbuilding Discourses* – were sent into the world. Emissaries of Kierkegaard's inner life, these four authors were as artful in deceit as they were lyrical in their exposition of his soul. Each one bore some aspect of their creator. But they were his 'ideality', magnificently indifferent to the world: none of them had to walk the streets, or listen to the opinions of other people. They did not feel any secret longing for success, or leaden aches of disappointment; they need not endure countless trivial humiliations; they never entered the storms of self-pity, or wrestled with rage when things did not go their way. They did not worry about how they looked. Even 'S. Kierkegaard' was a disembodied being who dwelt in the cloistered ambiance of old devotional books: humble and serene, he meditated on scripture, contemplated himself, and wrote with assured clarity about the human heart and its yearning for God. 'To be an author in Denmark is almost as troublesome as having to live in public view, just about as problematic as concealing oneself on a plate,' Nicolas Notabene wrote in *Prefaces*. Kierkegaard's pseudonyms did not conceal his identity, but they helped to mask his desire for recognition.

After those June books came out, he decided to stop writing upbuilding discourses. Instead he would write discourses for imagined occasions: weddings, funerals, confession, communion. First, though, he completed a final collection of *Four Upbuilding Discourses*, which he published at the end of August. These discourses were especially profound, compassionate and severe; they echoed Arndt's *True Christianity* in their emphasis on suffering and human frailty. Arndt insisted that 'without misery God does not appear to man, and without the knowledge of his misery man does not find God's grace.' In his discourse 'To Need God is a Human Being's Highest Perfection', Kierkegaard acknowledged that a deep spiritual need 'makes life more difficult', but explained that a person becomes conscious of God through the 'piecemeal experience' of his own anxiety, confusion, despair – and 'in this difficulty his life also acquires ever deeper and deeper meaning'. As he comes to feel his need of God, the suffering person learns more and more 'to die to the world, to esteem less and less the external, what life gives and takes, what he himself is permitted to achieve in the external world, but to be all the more concerned about the internal, about an understanding with God'.

\* \* \*

Reading Arndt has clarified and deepened the conviction already expressed in *Fear and Trembling*: that joy lies on the far side of suffering, that struggle must precede consolation, that 'only the one who was in anxiety finds rest.' Kierkegaard believes, now as then, that experiences of suffering and doubt are a crucial training in becoming fully human. And he communicates his own intimate acquaintance with suffering not only in his writing, but also in his friendships – for his is not the only anguished soul in Copenhagen, and he is sensitive to others who are in distress. When he knows that Emil Boesen is overwrought, he writes offering his sympathy, observing that 'you gather everything together all at once and surround yourself with it, and then you succumb beneath its weight. But existence demands to be understood bit by bit.'

Last year, 1847, he wrote long letters to his brother's wife Henriette, who suffers from severe depression. '*See to it that you love yourself*,' he urged his sister-in-law. 'When one is suffering and unable to do much for others, it is easy to fall prey to the melancholy thought that one is superfluous in this world, as others perhaps sometimes give one to understand. Then one must remember that *before God every person is equally important, without reservation equally important*; indeed, if there were any distinction, then one who suffers the most must be the closest object of God's care.' After his friend Pastor Spang died, he frequently visited his widow to comfort her in her grief. 'He understood as few do,' Hans Brøchner will recall, 'and he comforted not by covering up sorrow but by first making one genuinely aware of it, by bringing it to complete clarity.' Kierkegaard's work of soul-searching, exploring his own anxiety and suffering, has deepened his understanding of being human, giving his philosophy a power to affect others. He lives this philosophy inwardly, often painfully, and expresses it in his relationships to those closest to him.

# 12

# Life's Labyrinth

At the end of the year, deep in mid-winter, night falls early in Copenhagen. Along Rosenborggade, lamplight and firelight and candlelight fill the upper windows by four o'clock. Passers-by who brave the cold streets glimpse Christmas trees in glowing rooms, hear snatches of songs and children's laughter. Kierkegaard's rooms are quiet, and he is alone. '1848 has raised me to another level,' he writes in his journal: 'it has shattered me religiously; God has run me ragged.'

All year long he has thought about endings – the end of his authorship, the end of his life – and veered between calm acceptance of death and intense anxiety about his literary legacy. Here on Rosenborggade he has produced 'some of the best things' he has ever written: the new manuscripts stored carefully in their tin box are, he feels, the 'fulfilment' of his life. And yet:

> Conditions are so wretched here in Denmark that if I were now to publish, all at once, everything that God has permitted me to finish, I would be positively laughed out of court and accosted by every bully on the street. Merciful God, was it something wicked I had done, then? That once again, in the year just past, I had been so diligent? That God granted me these abilities? Was that a crime, then? And that I should deny God out of fear of the people in this market town! Show me an author who has suffered on this scale in any other country! If you can show me him, so much the better – then I will have someone with whom I can commiserate.

*The Point of View for My Work as an Author* is now in the metal box: it is finished – but he does not know whether he should publish it. Perhaps God is urging him to bring his long-concealed inner life out into the open, to drag himself through the deep thicket of thorns surrounding him, and show himself to the world. This disclosure would be excruciating. 'And yet,' he reflects:

> it is perhaps my duty to God, and the hiddenness of my interior life may be something God has permitted until I've grown strong enough to speak about it: My unhappy childhood, my abysmal melancholia, the misery of my personal life before I became an author; all this has contributed to my hidden interiority. Until now God has permitted it, but, in one respect, it has been a form of coddling. God has been so good to me, so loving, that I can truly say that my association with him has been my only trusting relationship; and he, in all my misery, has permitted me to find the strength to endure it all, yes, to find salvation in it.

The moments of 'salvation' he has found in these intense, difficult months of 1848 remind him of his first love – a gentle, comforting maternal embrace. Now, in his mid-thirties, he is finding his earliest childhood restored to him: he lives each day 'in relation to God as a child to a father (mother)'. At times his painful memories are accompanied by a new understanding of the past, and what seemed for so long to be a curse can be accepted as a blessing. His perpetual unrest during the early years on Nytorv gave him a deep longing for peace – and this very longing, he believes, brings human beings closer to God. Despite all his anxiety and ambivalence about Christianity, so deeply entangled with his relationship to his father, he sometimes feels that 'nearly all my life has been so terribly wasted in order that I might experience it all the more truly a second time, in relation to God.'

Yet the question of Regine remains unresolved. Over these last few months, as he revised the story of his life and his authorship, he has thought often about her, and her 'situation'. She has just celebrated her first wedding anniversary, for she finally married Johan Frederik Schlegel in November 1847, in Our Saviour's Church. Kierkegaard was sitting in that church on the Sunday when the marriage banns were read for her; on her wedding day he hired a carriage and drove out of town. 'The keystone of her marriage is and will continue to be that I am a villain, or at least someone who wanted to be important in the world,' he recently wrote in his journal. 'She would be completely unhinged if she found out the truth of the matter.' He believes that his relationship with Regine will outlive the circumstances that drew them apart: 'The moment I die (which I have constantly expected will happen soon) she will of course have what is rightfully hers. In that respect everything is ready. Her name will be a part of my work as an author, remembered for as long as I am remembered.'

Whatever the future holds, the past has not yet given way. Each time he recalls the broken engagement, he rediscovers his own sins. 'What a constant torment it has been to me that she should be humiliated for my sake,' he wrote in the autumn of 1848, seven years after he had returned her engagement ring, and several months into her marriage to Schlegel. He still feels that she was too proud of her relationship to him, that she should have let him go more easily, but he is also convinced that 'it remains my guilt nevertheless, for my guilt in relation to her is so great that it swallows up her guilt in relation to me.' He wronged Regine because he did not understand himself – did not understand that he was 'already betrothed' to Christianity, with all the complexity this entails. When he asked her to marry him in 1840, he could not see clearly that his own nature prevented him from being a husband, a father, a bourgeois citizen. And he had not yet grasped who he could be in the world.

This Christmas, as families gathered in their homes, he recalled his engagement and felt his solitude. He complained to his journal that 'the Christmas festival as it is now celebrated in so-called Christendom is pure paganism, mythology. Its idea or thought is thus as follows: a child is what saves, or to become a father and mother is life for a second time, something that purifies, ennobles. Life's earnestness truly begins when one leaves a new generation after oneself and only then comes in a deeper sense to live in love for one's offspring, with responsibility for their upbringing, etc.' Danish Christmases have become festivals of nostalgia for childhood, 'which is understood to be dancing around the Christmas tree, wanting to play board games and eat pfeffernusse'. This is not how he sees it: 'No, the Christ child is related to the spiritual category of becoming a human being, and thus is not related to marriage, father, mother, child, but to every individual human being as spirit.'

And now, in the very last days of 1848, he returns to the thought that if he had married Regine she would have been unhappy – 'There is an infinite difference between her and myself. She wished to shine in the world – and I with my melancholia, and my melancholy view of suffering, and of having to suffer. For a while she would probably have been pleased with her relationship with me, which perhaps at first would have satisfied her with respect to shining. But then, when it was to become earnest, either by my withdrawal into insignificance or by my navigating out into actual, Christian suffering, where no honour and respect are to be won: then she would quickly have lost her good humour. And I – well, I would never have become myself.'

The engagement remains a fork in the road: he took the path that led away from Regine, and he has not turned back, cannot retrace his steps – and yet the lonely path he has chosen keeps circling back to her. Looking back, the September day in 1840 when he proposed to Regine seems to lead inexorably to the events of 1846, when his relationship to the world shifted once again – and from there to this very moment, at the end of a year of reckoning, on the brink of a new beginning.

\* \* \*

In the summer of 1844, after he published *The Concept of Anxiety*, *Philosophical Fragments* and *Prefaces* – books which were not directly connected to Regine – his writing returned to the question of marriage that dominated *Either/Or* and *Repetition*. He was then drafting two separate books on women, love, engagement, marriage. This was a complex literary project: in the first work, divided into an aesthetic and an ethical part, he assembled characters from his 1843 books; the second work reprised the story of a broken engagement, but used a new pseudonym, Frater Taciturnus, to push it in a more religious direction than in *Repetition*. In 1845 he would publish the two works as a single volume, *Stages on Life's Way*, under an editor-pseudonym called Hilarius Bookbinder. At over five hundred pages this was his longest book since *Either/Or*.

'I am constantly re-writing parts of it, but it does not satisfy me,' he reported in his journal at the end of August 1844. 'At present the productivity has miscarried and makes me constantly write more than I want to.' For a long time he had expected to die in 1846, when he reached the age of thirty-three – that was now less than two years away, and he wanted to finish these books and write something 'more important'. He had no time to waste: 'I cannot write it here in the city; so I must take a journey,' he concluded.

That day he drove out to Lyngby, about ten miles north of Copenhagen. He did not leave Denmark until May the following year, but all through the summer and early autumn of 1844 he took frequent carriage rides to the countryside, most often to Nyholte, a couple of miles past Lyngby, and once or twice all the way to Fredensborg on the far side of Lake Esrom.

Andreas Juuel, *Summer Day at Geel's Hill near Holte* (1856)

Those days in the countryside – driving through open vistas, walking in the peaceful woods – nourished his imagination and made his writing even more lyrical, as if lightened by clear air. Each part of *Stages on Life's Way* has a rural setting. The book begins 'in the solitude of the forest', where a shadowy pseudonym called William Afham recollects a late-night drinking party, modelled on Plato's *Symposium*. At this gathering were Victor Eremita and Johannes the Seducer from *Either/Or*, Constantin Constantius from *Repetition*, a fashion designer, and a nameless, inexperienced young man. They took turns to deliver speeches in praise of women, William Afham recalls, as he sits meditating among the trees.

'By now I have learned not to need nighttime in order to find stillness,' he explains, 'for here it is always still, always beautiful, but it seems most beautiful to me now when the autumn sun is having its mid-afternoon repast and the sky becomes a languorous blue, when creation takes a deep breath after the heat, when the cooling starts and the meadow grass shivers voluptuously as the forest waves, when the sun is thinking of sinking into the ocean at eventide, when the earth is getting ready for rest and is thinking of giving thanks, when just before they leave they have an understanding with one another in that tender melting together that darkens the forest and makes the meadow greener.' In these golden hours, he adds, 'an overstrained person who has suffered much can seek solace, for there is nothing more gentle and more peaceful and more calming than the waning radiance of the afternoon light.' This was the refuge from anxiety, from judging eyes, from noisy grubby streets, that Kierkegaard had dreamed of ever since his break with Regine – a place where he could retreat and sorrow over his sins.

The first part of *Stages on Life's Way* closes with the symposium of pseudonyms taking a carriage to the countryside at dawn, after staying up all night drinking and discoursing about women. Walking through the fields, they glimpse Judge William conversing affectionately with his wife in the garden of their country house – and while the couple enjoy their morning tea, Victor Eremita sneaks into the Judge's study and discovers a new essay on marriage on his desk.

This essay compares marriage to the monastic life; it praises the humble beauty of maternal love, the deepening beauty of an ageing woman. Like Nicolas Notabene, Judge William has found a way to be both a husband and a writer. His essay ends when he hears his wife walk quietly by his study in the evening:

Just one minute, my beloved, just one moment – my soul is so rich, I am so eloquent at this moment that I want to write it down on paper, a eulogy on you, my lovely better half, and thus convince the whole world of the validity of marriage. And yet in due time, tomorrow, the day after tomorrow, in a week, I shall throw you away, you wretched pen – my choice is made, and I follow the beckoning and the invitation. Let a wretched author sit trembling when a thought presents itself in a lucky moment, shivering lest someone disturb him – I am afraid of nothing, but I also know what is better than the most felicitous idea in a man's mind and better than the most felicitous expression on paper of the most felicitous idea, and what is infinitely more precious than any secret a poor author can have with his pen.

After this touching garden scene and uxorious paean to domesticity comes 'Guilty?/Not Guilty?', a series of highly wrought diary entries recounting a broken engagement, followed by a long reflection on religious existence. All this is attributed to a monkish pseudonym called Frater Taciturnus, who explains that during a trip to the northern Gilleleje coast he found a sealed wooden casket sunk in Søborg Lake. Inside the casket was the diary, wrapped in oilcloth, as well as 'a plain gold ring with an engraved date, a necklace consisting of a diamond cross fastened to a light blue silk ribbon, a page torn from the New Testament, and a withered rose in a little box with silver overlay'. But Frater Taciturnus later admits that he composed the diary himself as an 'imaginative construction', a thought experiment.

This 'Story of Suffering' was the most autobiographical part of *Stages on Life's Way*: here Kierkegaard seemed to dive deep into the lake of his soul in order to recover its secrets. He also reproduced word for word the note he sent to Regine when he returned her engagement ring in 1841: 'Above all, forget the one who writes this; forgive a man who, even if he was capable of something, was nevertheless incapable of making a girl happy.' He acknowledged his guilt, yet he sensed the divine direction of 'Governance' in the whole affair; his life contains an 'error' – perhaps his whole life is an error! – and yet this error nevertheless expresses a truth:

> June 18th. *Midnight.* Am I guilty, then? Yes. How? By my having begun what I could not carry out. How do you understand it now? Now I understand more clearly why it was impossible for me. What then is my guilt? That I did not understand it sooner ... What can serve as your excuse? That my total individuality predisposed me to something in which I have been corroborated on all sides, which, if I had sought a

confidant, I would find confirmed – namely, that a depressed person should not torment his wife with his sufferings but like a man should enclose them within himself. What is your consolation? That I, in acknowledging this guilt, also sense a Governance in it all ... What is your hope? That it can be forgiven, if not here then nevertheless in an eternity.

During another brief, sleepless summer night, this diarist resolves 'with all my power to remain faithful to my spiritual experience'. It would have been better, he admits, if he 'could have remained faithful to her; it would have been greater if my spiritual existence had countenanced everyday use in a marriage, and I would have understood life more surely and easily.' Yet he knows that the past cannot be erased or rewritten. His life is like 'a book that was printed once and could not be reprinted and in it there was no place to make corrections'. However, a writer can add to his book a list of printing errors, which might even include 'a reading that was much more expressive than what stood in the same place in the text – then it would have to be satisfied to remain standing among the printing errors but nevertheless with its fullness of meaning'.

Kierkegaard knew that, without Regine, he would not have become himself. But *who* had he become, apart from lines of ink on a page? This question never seemed to find an answer: even the hundreds of pages in *Stages on Life's Way* – several thousand pages, when *Either/ Or, Repetition, Fear and Trembling, Prefaces, Philosophical Fragments* and *The Concept of Anxiety* are counted too – did not express everything he was. Perhaps the answer was unending; perhaps he came closest to himself in the deep wordless moments he sometimes fell into amid his strenuous days and restless nights.

In *Stages on Life's Way*, as in his productions of February 1843, October 1843 and June 1844, he gathered a little troop of imagined selves and sent them off in different directions through the world. This time there were eight of them: William Afham, Victor Eremita, Johannes the Seducer, Constantin Constantius, a fashion designer, an innocent young man, Judge William and Frater Taciturnus. None of these men are Søren Kierkegaard: they are paths which converge at the question of his own existence.

Is he the source of these paths, or their destination? There is a place in Gribs Forest, off the road to Fredensborg, called the Nook of the Eight Paths. His soul resembles this elusive place: 'Only the one who seeks worthily finds it, for no map indicates it. Indeed, the name itself seems to contain a contradiction, for how can the meeting of eight paths create a nook, how can the beaten and frequented be reconciled with the out-of-the-way and the hidden? And yet it is so: there actually are eight paths, but nevertheless it is very solitary out there . . . No one travels this road except the wind, about which it is unknown whence it comes or whither it goes.' If all those trails, all those pseudonyms, all those books convey a single truth, it is that human beings can discern no clear path through life while they are walking. Inside the forest, a man never sees far ahead. And *Stages on Life's Way* itself is not a simple journey like the drive out to Fredensborg, passing through Lyngby, Holte, Hørsholm. The book is labyrinthine, disorientating. Kierkegaard knew it would be difficult to understand.

In October 1844 he moved out of his apartment on Nørregade, back down the road to 2 Nytorv, his family home, where he occupied the first-floor apartment. His servant Anders arranged everything, put his library back in order; 'He is, in truth, my body,' Kierkegaard joked to Hans Brøchner. As for the rest of him – soul, spirit, pen – he just carried on writing. The drafts of *Stages on Life's Way* became even more voluminous, and dense with alterations. Israel Levin had to spend every day at 2 Nytorv for weeks on end to help prepare the manuscripts for publication.

*Stages on Life's Way* came out at the end of April 1845, along with *Three Discourses on Imagined Occasions* by S. Kierkegaard. On 6 May, the day after his thirty-second birthday, an anonymous review of both books appeared in *Berling's Times* – and there, for the first time in print, he was named as the author of his pseudonymous works. The reviewer praised his 'authentic poetic genius' and astonishing productivity: 'One would think that Magister Kierkegaard possessed a kind of magic wand by which he instantaneously conjures up his books, so incredible has his literary activity been in recent years . . . Each of these works is remarkable for a depth of thought that pursues its object to its most minute thread and unfolds a rare beauty and elegance of language, and particularly a fluency that surpasses that of any contemporary Danish writer.' If he had any negative criticism of these 'fine books', added the unknown reviewer, it was that 'the author takes almost too much time elaborating his reflections, so that they sometimes become rather prolix'.

Despite this extravagant praise, Kierkegaard was furious that his authorship had been made public. He responded three days later with an article in *The Fatherland* protesting against the 'unauthorized' claim that he had written the pseudonymous works – for only an author himself is entitled to make such a declaration. Furthermore, this reviewer did not have the authority even to commend his work. His frustration that his books received scant attention from more influential readers seeped through his disdain: 'When it is the legitimate leader in Danish literature, Professor Heiberg, for example, who speaks, when it is that masterful, most reverend writer under the pseudonym Kts' (this was Bishop Mynster) 'who speaks – well, then a beckoning has a meaning, then an encouraging word has validity, then a kind literary greeting is a joy.'

Less than a week later he went to Berlin for a few days. He was by then immersed in his new book, *Concluding Unscientific Postscript*, a sequel to *Philosophical Fragments*. This was a ground-breaking treatise on 'the task of becoming a Christian' by Johannes Climacus, his most dialectical pseudonym. Although not a Christian himself, Climacus brilliantly addressed the philosophical problems arising from Christianity; he debated with Lessing and Jacobi, dealt more blows to Hegel's system, and proposed a new method of philosophy to tackle 'the subjective individual's relationship to Christianity'. Kierkegaard had decided that this 'Postscript' would be his last book, so it had to secure his reputation. And, wresting control of his authorship from the *Berling's Times* reviewer, he ended it with a 'First and Last Declaration' which acknowledged that he was behind all his pseudonyms.

Back in Denmark that summer the storm clouds gathered. His work received more praise in the press – not from Heiberg or Mynster, as he wished, but from the disreputable *Corsair*, Copenhagen's bestselling weekly newspaper. In July *The Corsair* expressed admiration for Hilarius Bookbinder, editor of *Stages on Life's Way*, and in November the paper paid tribute to *Either/Or* by declaring that 'Victor Eremita will never die!' These slight remarks pricked Kierkegaard's sensitivity, and sowed the seeds for his collision with the men behind the newspaper.

*The Corsair* was edited covertly by a subversive young writer, Meïr Aron Goldschmidt, who founded the paper in 1840 when he was just twenty years old. Inspired by the republican and socialist satirical press in Paris, *The Corsair* mocked the Danish establishment, criticized the King and spread malicious gossip. Goldschmidt was fascinated by the Greek myth of Nemesis, the goddess who punished hubristic mortals: it was Nemesis who lured Narcissus to the pool where he fell in love with his reflection and died by the water's edge, unable to tear himself away from his beloved image. *The Corsair* used a different method of retribution, punishing Copenhagen's celebrities by laughter, and its cartoonist Peter Klæstrup made decidedly unlovely images of these modern mortals. By 1845 Goldschmidt had been found out, imprisoned, fined and censored by Copenhagen's government – but *The Corsair* continued. That year Goldschmidt published his first novel, *A Jew*, drawing on his experience of Danish anti-Semitism.

Goldschmidt admired Kierkegaard's writing, and they had been on friendly terms since their student years. But another ambitious writer, Peder Ludvig Møller, helped Goldschmidt to edit *The Corsair* – and Kierkegaard's relationship with him was much less cordial. Møller, a minor poet and notorious womanizer, would not have been out of place in Part I of *Either/Or*: he cultivated a virile Byronic image, rather like Johannes the Seducer. He aspired to succeed Oehlenschläger to the Chair of Aesthetics at the University of Copenhagen, and he worked incognito at *The Corsair* to protect his career prospects.

In December 1845, as *Concluding Unscientific Postscript* was on its way to the printer, Møller published his literary yearbook *Gæa 1846*, which included a review of *Stages on Life's Way*. Referring to Kierkegaard as 'the philosopher with the many names', Møller praised his more aesthetic qualities, acknowledging his 'remarkable gifts', philosophical 'genius', 'brilliant wit', 'amazing abundance of thought and feeling', and 'richness and eloquence of writing one rarely finds equalled'. But Møller was irritated by Kierkegaard's tendency to 'expose his whole inner development to the public eye', which was particularly pronounced in Frater Taciturnus's conclusion

The editors of *The Corsair*:
P. L. Møller (left) and M. A. Goldschmidt (right)

to *Stages on Life's Way*: 'Every time one feels able to surrender to pure literary enjoyment the author gets in the way with his own personal ethical and religious development, which no one is actually asking about.'

Nevertheless, Møller turned out to be interested in these 'personal' issues, as his review drifted from literary criticism to psychological appraisal to character assassination. With the swagger of a true corsair, he suggested that Kierkegaard's productivity was the effect of a sickly nature – unwholesome, unnatural and unmanly. 'Writing and producing seem to have become a physical need for him, or he uses it as medicine, just as in certain illnesses one uses bloodletting, cupping, steam baths, emetics, and the like. Just as a healthy person rests by sleeping, he seems to rest by letting his pen run; instead of eating and drinking, he satiates himself by writing; instead of reproducing himself with a baby a year like an ordinary human being, he seems to have a fish nature and spawns.' Møller accused him of mistreating women in his writing and also, he hinted, in his life: 'the feminine nature placed on the experimental rack turns into dialectic in the book and vanishes, but in actual life she inevitably must go mad or into Peblinge Lake.'

'If you regard life as a dissecting laboratory and yourself as a cadaver, then go ahead, lacerate yourself as much as you want to,' Møller continued, sharpening his attack with a direct address. 'But to spin another creature into your spider web, dissect it alive or torture the soul out of it drop by drop by means of experimentation – that is not allowed, except with insects, and is there not something horrible and revolting to the healthy human mind even in this idea?' By questioning his moral integrity and his virility, Møller's claws sank into the deep sensitivities Kierkegaard had made such strenuous and complex efforts to protect ever since breaking with Regine and beginning his authorship.

'To me,' Møller opined, this perverse author's reflections 'are like daguerreotypes in which not only the most important and characteristic features are depicted, as in regular painting, but everything possible is caught so that the whole thing becomes a tangle and a trackless labyrinth. Despite all his intelligence, reflection for him has become a severe sickness; his religiousness, which renounces the whole world in order to be occupied with itself, appears to me to be a pusillanimity at which our Lord and his angels must laugh ... If he had lived under conditions that forced him to concern himself with something other than his own whims, he no doubt would have developed his talents to a higher degree.'

As he read Møller's review, these excoriating words flew at his soul, inscribed themselves in his memory, moulded his thoughts, pierced his heart. And the sharp grains of truth were like salt in his wounds. He retaliated at once, publishing a long article in *The Fatherland* signed by Frater Taciturnus, who dismissed Møller imperiously: 'Such persons are not part of my environment, and no matter how obtrusive and rude they are, it makes no difference; this does not disturb my joy over the little world that constitutes my surroundings.' He ended with a provocation – half-sarcastic, half-serious – that exposed Møller's connection to *The Corsair*: 'Would that I might only get into *The Corsair* soon! It is really hard for a poor author to be so singled out in Danish literature that he (assuming that we pseudonyms are one) is the only one who is not abused there.'

Soon afterwards he met Goldschmidt on the street, and they discussed these literary hostilities as though neither of them were personally involved. Goldschmidt remarked that Frater Taciturnus had broken a literary rule of honour in naming Møller in connection with *The Corsair*; Kierkegaard replied that Frater Taciturnus's 'right' must be seen from 'a higher point of view'. Goldschmidt disagreed, and then they spoke of other things.

On 2 January 1846 *The Corsair* responded to Kierkegaard's battle cry by printing a satirical story about Frater Taciturnus – 'a great and famous recluse and philosopher, who has another name, under which he strolls the streets every day, but it would be indiscreet to mention it' – colluding with *The Fatherland* to disclose the identity of *The Corsair*'s editor. 'I am as happy as I would be if Heiberg had got one of my books stuck in his throat,' exclaims Frater Taciturnus once the deed is done, and proposes to celebrate by doing something for the poor: 'I shall imagine the thought-experiment that I have given a rix-dollar to a poor woman with five small children. Imagine her joy! Imagine those innocent children seeing a rix-dollar!' The following week the paper ran a sketch featuring 'Søren Kierkegaard', accompanied by a cartoon accentuating his curved spine.

Through January and February *The Corsair* continued to lampoon him every week, mocking his philosophical pretensions and his thin legs – one a little longer than the other – in their uneven trousers. Klæstrup's drawings depicted Kierkegaard on horseback, Kierkegaard fighting a duel, Kierkegaard sitting outside the office of *The Corsair* waiting to be let in. The 'artificial experiment with a young girl' from *Stages on Life's Way* was likened to horse-training; the illustration accompanying this piece had Kierkegaard riding on a lady's shoulders, reviving Møller's accusation that he had exploited Regine in his pursuit of literary fame.

When *Concluding Unscientific Postscript* came out at the end of February – another huge volume, even thicker than *Stages on Life's Way* – *The Corsair* mocked his arrogance in refusing praise for his books:

It is really strange that a man does not have control of the book he buys and pays for with 3 rix-dollars and 64 shillings. If Magister Kierkegaard has a book printed for private circulation among his friends and gives it away, then he can request first of all: Do you acknowledge this book to be perfect, so pure and sensitive that the mere breath of human judgement defiles it? But when someone has honestly and uprightly paid his 3 rix-dollars and 64 shillings and then is told: Read it as you read the Bible; if you do not understand it, then read it over again; if you do not understand it the second time, you may just as well blow your brains out – then a strange feeling comes over him. There is a moment when his mind is confused and it seems to him that Nicolaus Copernicus was a fool when he insisted that the earth revolves around the sun; on the contrary, the heavens, the sun, the planets, the earth, Europe and Copenhagen itself revolve around Søren Kierkegaard, who stands silent in the middle and does not once take off his hat in recognition of the honour shown to him.

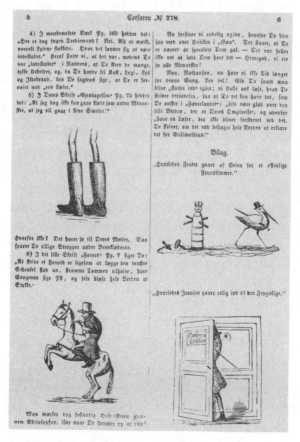

From *The Corsair*, no. 278, 16 January 1846

From *The Corsair*, no. 278, 16 January 1846

Next time he encountered *The Corsair*'s editor during his daily walk he did not greet him, but met his eyes with a look that was 'intense, very bitter'. Goldschmidt suppressed his urge to laugh: 'In the bitterness of that glance, just as in Kierkegaard's entire personal appearance and manner, there was something that verged on the comic.' Yet suddenly amusement gave way to 'the loftiness, the ideality that were also present in his personality' – for Goldschmidt saw 'something in that intense, wild glance that drew the curtain, as it were, away from the higher right that Kierkegaard had asserted earlier and that I had not been able, or rather was unwilling, to understand, though I did suspect it. It accused and depressed me.' That very day Goldschmidt decided to quit *The Corsair*. He sold the paper a few months later, then travelled to the Continent for a year; when he came home he founded *North and South*, a political and literary journal which, Møller jibed, was respectable enough to be quoted by Bishop Mynster. Møller himself left Denmark at the end of 1847, and did not return.

From *The Corsair*, no. 285, 6 March 1846

Back in 1843, Kierkegaard had described Copenhagen as 'my beloved capital city and place of residence'. Despite his adversaries' retreat from the battlefield, it became a different place for him after *The Corsair*'s attack, which spread from the pages of the newspaper through the city's streets. Now when he went on his daily walks he was laughed at by strangers, heckled by children. 'Every kitchen boy feels justified in almost insulting me in accordance with *The Corsair*'s orders; young students titter and grin and are happy to see a prominent person trampled on; professors are jealous and secretly sympathize with the attacks, and spread them, too, with the appendage, of course, that it is a shame. The slightest thing I do, if it is merely to pay a visit, is twisted and distorted into lies and told everywhere; if *The Corsair* finds out it is printed and read by everybody . . . What pains me most is not the vulgarity of the rabble but the secret participation in it by the better people,' he wrote in his journal in the spring of 1846. He felt betrayed by friends who re-assured him that *The Corsair*'s campaign was insignificant, a trifle, instead of taking a stand in his defence. And he wished that Bishop Mynster, in particular, would speak up for him – for hadn't he been attacked for an authorship produced in devotion to Christianity? 'God in heaven, who could endure this if there were not an interior place in a man where it can all be forgotten in communion with you!' he wrote, adding that he was grateful that his activity as an author was already finished, that 'it has been granted me to conclude it myself, to understand myself when it ought to stop, and next to pub-lishing *Either/Or* I thank God for that.' He once more resolved to become a pastor in the countryside, and imagined himself doing a little writing in his free time: 'Out there in quiet activity, I shall breathe easier, however much my present life has gratified me.'

He saw *The Corsair*'s attack as more than a personal ordeal: beyond his own devastated pride and bitter fury, it had political sig-nificance. The press is the mirror of the modern city, the murky pool in which a vain populace stares at its reflection – and *The Corsair* was, he believed, a symptom of Denmark's degeneracy. Being at the centre of this arena was humiliating, yet he remained defiant, deem-ing himself 'as correctly situated in literature as possible, and also in such a way that to be an author becomes a deed' – for now he was 'advancing polemically against the age'.

Having declared an end to his authorship, he decided to allow him-self to write book reviews – 'in this way I can still avoid becoming an author.' In March 1846, as *The Corsair* continued to lampoon him, he published 'a little review' of *Two Ages*, the new novel by the anonymous author of *A Story of Everyday Life*, which he had praised in *From the Papers of One Still Living*. Both novels bore the name of J. L. Heiberg as editor, and it was not difficult to guess that their author was Thomasine Gyllembourg, Heiberg's mother. Her new novel was set in contemporary Copenhagen, opening in the summer of 1844, when its hero Charles Lusard returns to the city after thirty years abroad and finds it much changed. Lusard is struck by the bright lights, loud music and great crowds in the newly opened Tivoli Gardens, taking the sight of 'so many people of different classes who gather there' as a sign of the great progress made in his century: 'one cannot but marvel when one thinks of the discoveries in science, the inventions that make life easier and more agreeable. Who in past times dreamed of steamships, of railways, that seem to compensate man for his lack of wings?' Yet other characters in *Two Ages* lament 'the dreadful vanity' of those who go out in town 'in order to be seen', and 'the craving for entertainment that, like an epidemic, is ever more rife among us, destroying the integrity of the family'.

Kierkegaard used his review of *Two Ages* to develop his own critique of the present age. He drew on Heiberg's 1842 essay 'People and Public', which warned of 'the people's dissolution into a public', of 'the public itself being transformed from an organic, representative body to an atomized crowd that represents nothing'. But his own analysis of modern life emphasized the pernicious influence of the press. In the preface to his review – which had expanded to over a hundred pages, and had to be published as a book – he insisted that it was intended 'not for aesthetic and critical readers of newspapers but for rational creatures'. Envy, he believed, had motivated the attacks on him by Møller and *The Corsair*, and his review identified envy as the 'unifying principle' of his 'passionless', 'indolent' and 'reflective' age; he castigated scurrilous journalism as a 'nasty dog' which the public keeps for its amusement. When this dog attacks its 'superior' victim, he wrote, 'the public is unrepentant, for after all it was not the public – in fact, it was the dog; and the public is unrepentant, because after all it was not really slander – it was just a bit of fun.'

Yet if someone should think this tragic, and feel pity for the man who has been attacked, he continued:

> I cannot agree with that at all, for the person who desires assistance in reaching what is highest benefits from experiencing such a thing and should rather desire it, even if others may be disturbed on his behalf. No, the terrible thing is something else, the thought of the many human lives that are squandered or may easily be squandered. I will not even mention those who are lost or led astray to their downfall, who play the role of the dog for money, but of the many rootless ones, the

superficial ones, the sensuous, those who in snobbish indolence get no deeper impression of life than this foolish grinning, all the second-raters who are led into new temptation because in their limitation they even derive self-importance from having sympathy for the victims of the attack, without grasping that in such a situation the victims are always the strongest, without grasping that here it is dreadfully and yet ironically appropriate to say: Weep not for him, but weep for yourselves.

In early May 1846 he took his customary trip to Berlin: he liked to be away for his birthday. Soon after he returned to Copenhagen he became immersed in the case of Adolph Peter Adler, a pastor who had been dismissed from his office by Bishop Mynster the previous year. Kierkegaard had known Adler for more than two decades: they were classmates at the School of Civic Virtue, and then fellow theology students at the university; Adler became a 'zealous Hegelian' during those years, and published his lectures on Hegel's logic in 1842. Then one night Pastor Adler received a revelation: Jesus appeared to him, dictated a new doctrine of the fall – in which Adam sinned because he lost himself in thought – and then commanded him to burn his works and 'keep to the Bible'. Week after week he announced this revelation from his pulpit; after he had published these inspired sermons in 1843, he visited Kierkegaard and read one of them aloud, partly in a strange whisper, and suggested that Kierkegaard was like John the Baptist in relation to himself, the living vessel of God's word.

In June 1846, a few months after his dismissal from the Church, Adler published four books. Kierkegaard bought them all, and through that autumn and winter worked on a lengthy essay which stretched his commitment to write only literary reviews. His *Book on Adler* was subtitled 'The Religious Confusion of the Present Age, Illustrated by Magister Adler as a Phenomenon'. Adler's situation raised questions about who has authority to judge what comes from God, and what is mere delusion, and about how the world – and the Church – should respond to someone who receives a divine revelation.

There were echoes of Abraham in the case of Adler, and Kierkegaard saw strange inverse symmetries between himself and this other controversial, preternaturally prolific Christian author. He always disclaimed authority for his writing, while Adler claimed the highest spiritual authority as a witness to Christ; he was still considering seeking an appointment as a pastor, while Adler had lost his clerical living. He thought Adler was confused, but he felt inclined to support him: 'We need dynamic personalities, unselfish people who are not immersed and exhausted in endless considerations for job, wife, and children,' he wrote in his journal last year, in the summer of 1847. He spent much of that year revising his book on Adler, and he has considered publishing it under a variety of possible pseudonyms – but he is afraid the book will harm Adler, and the manuscript remains in a tin box in his study.

Instead he published *Works of Love*, which looks like previous editions of religious discourses by S. Kierkegaard, though much larger. But like his review of *Two Ages*, *Works of Love* bears the scars of the *Corsair* battle: it is a polemical book that questions whether 'people really know what love is', and seeks to 'turn their convenient ways of thought upside down'. One of the discourses contrasts the worldly understanding of love's selflessness with true Christian love: '*The merely human idea of self-denial* is this: give up your self-loving desires, cravings, and plans – then you will be esteemed and honoured and loved as righteous and wise. *The Christian idea of self-denial* is: give up your self-loving desires and cravings, give up your self-seeking plans and purposes so that you truly work unselfishly for the good – and then, for that very reason, put up with being abominated almost as a criminal, insulted and ridiculed.'

\* \* \*

Since the *Corsair* affair, his ambivalent suspicion of the world has hardened into a wholehearted, militant opposition. As 1848 draws to an end, his neighbours gather round their Christmas trees, eat apple dumplings, and chatter about all the changes this year has brought: a revolution, an election, plans for a Danish constitution, new laws on freedom of speech, debates about dividing Church from State, the abolition of slavery in Danish colonies. For Kierkegaard, these long dark evenings offer plenty of time to recall his 'persecution by the mob, the people, the public, in short the scum that the daily press is able to dredge up'. He now regards newspapers as 'a form of evil', and angrily pronounces *The Corsair* a symptom of Denmark's 'demoralization', 'disintegration', 'envy, caprice, pettiness'. In a different mood, he can insist that 'I feel no bitterness at all at the thought of all the indignities I have suffered and all the times I have been betrayed; I never think of escaping all of this all at once, so to speak, by death. If there is time and place for jest in eternity, I am sure that the thought of my thin legs and my ridiculed trousers will be a source of salutary amusement to me.' But in this life his trousers have received too much attention, and his authorship too little. His work has been ignored by those qualified to evaluate it – by Heiberg, Martensen, and Mynster most of all – because 'they are envious'. His brother Peter is his closest kin, and it is difficult to work up much festive cheer for him; instead, he recalls how Peter responded to him a year or so ago when he joked that 'I think I will entirely give up being an author and go in for horse-riding or things of that sort', and Peter 'replied (in all seriousness), "That would be the best thing." That is how pointless my endeavours look to him.'

As Professor Sibbern observed during Kierkegaard's student days, he is polemical by nature, and his extraordinary fluency and wit make him a formidable combatant in the literary field. He is still contemplating retreat; since publishing *Concluding Unscientific Postscript*, he has not added to the pseudonymous authorship – apart from that *Fatherland* article about Madame Heiberg which caused him such agonies this summer. Yet the events of 1846 showed him that he himself, in his suffering, can be an indictment of his city, of his age, of the world. 'They must be permitted to trample me down – but they are caught, and I am the stronger,' he writes now. 'In physical terms no individual can triumph over the masses. But if the single individual is the one who is truly justified, he is infinitely the stronger. Ah, with a certainty that nothing, nothing can shake, I sense how I am thus infinitely the stronger; all the mistreatment merely increases my certainty of this.' Of course, his ordeal is nothing compared to what Jesus suffered; he has not been hung on a cross for all to see, and *The Corsair*'s teeth drew no real blood. Nevertheless he has been ridiculed and scorned and made a public spectacle – and he has tasted the subversive power of martyrdom.

In spite of everything, he can see the funny side. He has offered to his city an authorship posing the deepest existential questions, probing the furthest reaches of the human heart; he has searched and exposed his own soul, stretched his poetic powers and his philosophical ingenuity, spent his money, exhausted his body in this immense effort to revive Christendom, to bring spirituality to life again – and people are jeering at his spindly legs. He imagines his future readers, 'who will be able to sit in peace and quiet and enjoy, purely intellectually, the infinitely comic drama that, by existing here, I have had the whole of Copenhagen perform'. Only it has been going on for so long now, every single day, year after year. This would be no fun for the audience, and it is worse for him, cast in the leading role. 'From the poetic point of view, it must be abridged. And that is how it will be for my reader. On the other hand, the religious begins in and with the daily routine, and that is how I understand my life: for me, this infinitely comic drama is a martyrdom.' If he did not consider it his duty to remain in Copenhagen, then he would travel to some isolated place, look back at his tiny city in the distance, 'and laugh and laugh'.

'Dying is the only thing that can clear the air,' he declared in his journal earlier this year. His existence is troublesome to everyone; when he dies his profound, funny, intricate, eloquent authorship will float free, no longer tethered to the stumbling block of his personality. 'At that very instant I will be in my ideality, because the problem is that I am too ideally developed to live in a market town . . . Every day I live, I simply become more of a burden to the envy of the market town.' He tells himself he has been 'truly unselfish, by renouncing all worldly advantages': marriage to a beautiful woman, fatherhood, a family of his own to spend Christmas with; and a career to rival Heiberg's, Martensen's, or even Mynster's, had he been more willing to submit to public approval. Yet he knows too well the exertions of egotism, and he longs for rest. The gentleness that would release his spirit, calm his body, has never come easily to him – and there is no one else to call him softly from his thoughts, to tell him he has done enough for the day and, like Judge William's patient wife, beckon him gently into bed. He still strains at the leash of self-assertion: it will not loosen, but twists into self-sacrifice.

# PART THREE

# 1849–1855:
# Life Lived Forwards

*How many times have I said that a warship doesn't receive its orders until it's out on the deep? And therefore it might be entirely in order for me to go further as an author than I had originally intended.*

# 13

## At Odds with the World

'The question is: When should all the latest works be published!'
Through the winter and spring of 1849 this question pursued Kierkegaard, pinned him down, and paralysed him. The pile of manuscripts
he produced during 1848 lay ready, but he had cornered himself into
a dilemma about his future: either continue to be an author, or seek
an appointment in the Church. The temptation to withdraw from
the world to a quiet rural pastorate was now quickened by fear that
otherwise his money would run out. His financial situation was
not so pressing, however, that it outweighed existential concerns:
'Humanly speaking, there is something pleasant about having secure
employment, comfort; there is something agreeable about working
for a living. – And then there are only two classes of people who come
together in the opposite kind of life. Wrecked selves, fallen persons –
and those who seriously and truly live for an idea. Ah, and in the eyes
of the world, it's all too easy to confuse the two.'

Kierkegaard was well qualified to be a parish priest, or to teach
in the pastoral seminary he had attended in 1840: he was an expert
theologian, a gifted preacher, and a sensitive counsellor with 'a special ability to talk with ordinary people'. But would he be offered a
clerical appointment if he asked for one? Would publishing the 1848
works damage his prospects? And how could he continue his subversive authorship – which had been produced undercover, without
authority – if he held an official position in the Church?

Regine deepened his dilemma further. Whenever he saw her in church
or passed her on the street, her presence flooded his soul; he was
intensely aware of her slightest movements, and sometimes he felt
her eyes on him. They never spoke or exchanged letters, and in this

silence every small gesture became a step in a private, infinitely expressive dance. Through her he had become an author and she was inextricable from his writings, yet the professional life he now envisaged was the one that, back in 1840, went hand in hand with marrying her. Seeking an appointment felt like returning to that abandoned path, and was linked obscurely with his wish for a reconciliation with Regine – for forgiveness, if not friendship, though he imagined a brotherly relationship with her, like the spiritual love between a monk and a nun.

He still felt compelled to write. His sense that divine governance directed his authorship was difficult to distinguish from his need to write to assuage his deep anxiety. And however earnestly he assumed the role of suffering Christian – in relation to Regine, a sinner and penitent; in relation to *The Corsair*, a martyr who endured persecution to banish the evil forces of the present age – the fact remained that writing gave him great pleasure. 'It is certainly true that I have been unspeakably unhappy ever since I was a child, but nonetheless I must confess that the avenue of escape God provided for me by permitting me to become an author has been rich, rich in enjoyment. So I have surely been sacrificed, but my work as an author is not a sacrifice – it is indeed what I would absolutely most like to continue doing.' And of course there was also his pride: 'It is difficult to decide whether it is more humiliating to straightforwardly declare that I can no longer afford to be an author and then take on the burden of finite matters, or to expose myself to everything that might follow if I publish something.' He did not want to be extraordinary, notorious, misunderstood, and his authorship seemed to demand this of him. As he wrestled with his dilemma he prayed for guidance, and searched for signs of God's response. He resolved to go, like Abraham, wherever God commanded him: 'How many times have I said that a warship doesn't receive its orders until it's out on the deep? And therefore it might be entirely in order for me to go further as an author than I had originally intended.'

He inhabited the question of publication like a lonely room, its walls plastered with possibilities. In that room he spent days, weeks, months pacing back and forth, miserably shuffling his manuscripts and tinkering at their margins – deleting a word here, altering a phrase there – and debating with himself in his journal. Could he publish *The Point of View for My Work as an Author* now, or let it wait until after his death? What should he do with *The Book on Adler*? For a while he considered publishing *The Sickness unto Death* and its two-part sequel (*Come to Me* and *Blessed Is He Who Is Not Offended*) together with a new essay, *Armed Neutrality*, in one volume titled *Collected Works of Fulfilment*. Then he amended this to *Collected Works of Consummation* – for if these works ful-filled his vocation 'to introduce Christianity into Christendom', they had also consumed him. He was exhausted, while his prose danced with the agile, fluent energy of his life-force. He composed for this possible collection a brief preface: 'Just as a cabinet minister steps down and becomes a private citizen, so I cease to be an author and lay down my pen – I actually have had a portfolio. Just one word more, but no, no more words now, for now I have laid down my pen.'

Yet he found temporary relief from these anxious ruminations by producing something new. He returned to three exquisite sermons on the lily of the field and the bird of the air he had drafted in the early spring of 1848, and reworked them to accompany the second edition of *Either/Or*, which Reitzel published in May 1849. He saw these 'Godly Discourses' as a repetition of his very first 'Upbuilding Dis-courses', which had followed *Either/Or* in 1843: like those, they bore a preface dated 5 May, his birthday. As well as balancing the 'Se-ducer's Diary' with spiritual teachings drawn from Jesus's Sermon on the Mount, these lyrical meditations on nature's exemplars of care-free devotion worked through Kierkegaard's worries for his future.

They opened with a petitionary prayer: 'Father in heaven! Would that we might learn what it is to be a human being.' Kierkegaard took Jesus's instruction to 'Consider the lily' as an invitation to consider the human condition in contrast with the rest of nature, which expresses God's goodness spontaneously, in the present moment, without questions or thoughts for tomorrow. From the lily and the bird, he suggested, a human being can learn silence, obedience and joy. And these qualities need to be learned and practised, because human life always strains in the opposite direction. We are pulled away from silence by the constant chatter around us and by our own incessant thoughts, and we are constitutionally disobedient: even the most earnest religious people are divided between doing God's will and following their own inclinations. Knowing nothing of this ambivalence, the lily and the bird remain obediently 'in the place assigned' to them, Kierkegaard wrote, echoing the words he used in his journal in 1848 when he reflected that being an author in Copenhagen, exposed to the public eye, was 'the place assigned' to him. And finally he wrote of joy: other living beings take joy in their nature, while we feel anxious and dissatisfied – and yet we share the same gifts as the lily and the bird, and much more besides. 'That you came into existence, that you exist, that today you receive the necessities of existence, that you became a human being, that you can see – consider this: that you can see, that you can hear, that you have a sense of smell, that you have a sense of taste, that you can feel; that the sun shines for you, and for your sake, that when it becomes weary, the moon begins to shine and the stars are lit; that it becomes winter, that all of nature disguises itself, pretends to be a stranger – and does so in order to delight you; that spring comes, that birds come in large flocks – and do so in order to bring you joy; that green plants spring forth, that the forest grows into beauty.'

Nevertheless, no one knew better than Kierkegaard that being human is never a simple matter of opening one's petals or spreading one's wings. As he explained in *The Sickness unto Death*, another of his still unpublished manuscripts, all human beings have to become themselves, and can hardly avoid falling into despair. Some despair from too many possibilities, others from too few: when overwhelmed by thoughts of what might have been and what may come, 'the self runs away from itself', 'tires itself out with floundering in the possible', and is unable to move – yet without possibility 'a man cannot draw breath.' Only God is the one 'for whom all things are possible', and praying to this God keeps a human soul alive, for 'to pray is to breathe.' Determinists and fatalists cannot pray; they are in despair, having lost God along with all their possibilities. *The Sickness unto Death* also distinguished between a despair of weakness and a despair of defiance: some people cannot face their existential task, succumb to melancholy, do not want to be themselves, while others despair through rebellious self-assertion, refusing to acknowledge their need for God.

Kierkegaard had constructed this taxonomy of spiritual disease within the laboratory of his own soul, and as he agonized over his future he felt himself prone to every kind of despair. For a while the decision not to publish anything more than the second edition of *Either/Or* and *Three Godly Discourses* had the upper hand. He prayed for success in securing a position at the pastoral seminary – and for reconciliation with Regine. But on 5 May 1849, his thirty-sixth birthday, he repented the 'melancholia' and 'hypochondriacal evasion' that caused him to flee from his authorship. His daily devotional reading had drawn him towards a new decision: Luther's sermons prepared him to stand against the world; Thomas à Kempis counselled that peace came from following God's will rather than his own; Fénelon warned against doing anything less than God expected of him. 'I wanted to be so terribly clever – rather than relying on faith and prayer,' Kierkegaard confessed in his journal:

> I wanted to secure a comfortable future . . . I wanted to play lord, decide for myself . . . Because of the fear of danger, my hypochondria, and a lack of trust in God, I've wanted to regard myself as inferior to the gifts I've been given, as if taking ownership of those gifts would defraud the truth, and as if viewing myself as inferior weren't in fact an act of defrauding God and the truth . . . Humanly speaking, there's certainly nothing fun or pleasant about being the extraordinary one in these petty circumstances we have in Denmark; it's becoming painful. But God has overwhelmed me with kindness, granted me so much more than I expected; and he (both by means of the abundance he has granted me during the past year – and its sufferings) has led me to understand my destiny – true enough, it's different from what I had originally imagined . . . I had to get that close to the thought of stopping before I picked up the momentum again.

Despite the inspiration of the lily and the bird, this was only a tentative resolution: spring passed into summer, and Kierkegaard remained unsure about publishing his *Collected Works of Consummation*. 'What makes my life so difficult,' he reflected, 'is that I'm tuned an octave higher than other people are; where I am, what preoccupies me, is not the particular but a principle or idea. Most people think – at most – about whom they ought to marry. I have to think about marriage itself. And so it goes with everything. That's fundamentally my situation now. Most people think – at most – about what job they ought to apply for, while my fortune is to be deeply involved in a struggle, the battle of ideas, the question of principle about whether so-called Christian professional offices are appropriate in Christianity.'

Meanwhile, at a lower octave, the foundations of Danish Christendom were being dismantled and rebuilt following the revolution that took place in spring 1848, during Kierkegaard's final weeks in 2 Nytorv. On 5 June 1849 King Frederik VII signed the Constitution of the Kingdom of Denmark, which granted freedom of religion to all citizens: their civic rights no longer depended on membership of the Lutheran Church. The Danish State Church became the Danish People's Church. But the Constitutional Assembly had not acceded to Grundtvig's demands to separate the Church from the State, and the establishment of the *Danske Folkekirke* was enshrined in civil law.

Later in June, Kierkegaard visited Bishop Mynster at his episcopal residence opposite the Church of Our Lady, and asked about an appointment in the pastoral seminary. Privately he now believed Mynster to be 'allied with worldliness as much as anyone', and denounced him in his journal for 'transforming Christianity into such serene tenderness'. Mynster was in his seventies: 'He will soon be on his way – to be judged. And what harm he's done to Christianity by conjuring up a false appearance.' For years Kierkegaard had charged this man with his own anxieties about his relationship to the Church, his place in the world, the reception of his authorship, his loyalty to his late father; now the Bishop loomed larger than ever in his imagination, vibrating with his own existential angst, and after months of inward turmoil about seeking employment Kierkegaard was agitated when he entered Mynster's house. The Bishop dealt with him kindly, smoothly, efficiently: 'Good day, dear friend, dear friend – and then he said he didn't have time to speak with me . . . And then he repeated this "Dear friend" six or seven times, slapped my back and patted me – i.e. he's frightened to speak with me because he's frightened about getting too involved with me.' He told Kierkegaard to come 'another time' – but it wouldn't be any time soon, because Mynster was about to leave Copenhagen to visit his other Zealand parishes. Kierkegaard complied with Mynster's deft evasion, and

Bishop Mynster in his later years

left the episcopal residence with his questions unanswered – and with his resolve to resume his campaign against Christendom renewed.

Three days later he wrote to Bianco Luno, the printer, to ask him to print *The Sickness unto Death*. Luno agreed to receive the manuscript the following day, 29 June. That evening Kierkegaard learned that Regine's father had died. His resolution once more shattered into possibilities: if he had known about Councillor Olsen's death sooner, perhaps he would have taken this as a sign that it was time to approach Regine, and held off writing to the printer. He spent a restless night, unable to order his thoughts, trying to grasp and follow the long, tangled threads that connected Regine to his authorship. He lay in the dark for hours, his mind splitting itself in two: he seemed to be in dialogue with another person, but he could not tell which voice belonged to him. 'Look, now he wills his own destruction . . . You could certainly wait a week or so . . . Who does he think he is?'

By sunrise he was worn out and utterly confused. It seemed so foolish to spend months wrestling with the question of publication, finally reach a decision, make an agreement with Luno – and then change his mind the next day. Yet he felt that something was warning him off: was this a divine signal, or merely his own cowardice? Kierkegaard knew there was always terror in sending his books out into the world; now, at the dawn of a new battle, was God urging him to pause, perhaps to retreat, or summoning his courage for the fight? His decisive thought was this: 'The fact that God frightens a person does not always mean that this is something he should refrain from doing, but that it is the very thing he should do; but he must be terrified in order that he learn to do it in fear and trembling.' So he sent *The Sickness unto Death* to the printer, and prayed to God for guidance about how far he should go.

'I've been willing to ask God to free me from this terrifying business, and I'm still willing,' Kierkegaard wrote in his journal later that summer, when things seemed clearer. 'Moreover, I'm a human being myself and, humanly speaking, would love to live happily here on earth. But because of the Christian state, Christendom, which is evident throughout Europe, I've decided to call attention to the price of becoming a Christian, beginning here in Denmark, in such a way that the whole concept – State Church, official posts, salaries – is blown apart. For a few years now I've borne the treachery and ingratitude of a tiny country, the envy of respectable people and the mockery of the mob, in such a way that – for want of someone better – I am perhaps qualified to proclaim Christianity. Let Bishop Mynster keep the velvet coat and the grand cross.'

Perhaps Kierkegaard had a right to proclaim Christianity – but perhaps not. This had become the question of his authorship, inseparable from the question of his own existence. If he was to publish *The Sickness unto Death* and its sequel, now a single work titled *Practice in Christianity*, he had to settle it somehow. The answer eventually came in the form of a new pseudonym: Anti-Climacus, 'a Christian to an extraordinary degree', in contrast to Johannes Climacus, author of *Philosophical Fragments* and *Concluding Unscientific Postscript*, who philosophized about Christianity while claiming not to be a Christian. Although Kierkegaard placed himself, allegedly a 'perfectly simple Christian', in between these two pseudonyms, the relationship was more complicated than that – for his pseudonyms

AT ODDS WITH THE WORLD

expressed the conflict within his soul. In one draft preface to *The Sickness unto Death*, Anti-Climacus explained that he and Johannes Climacus were brothers, exactly the same age, with everything in common, and yet utterly different: 'We are not twins, we are opposites. Between us there is a deep, fundamental relationship, but despite the most desperate efforts on both sides we never get any further, any closer, than a *repelling contact*. There is a point and a moment at which we touch, but at the same moment we fly from each other at infinite speed. Like two eagles plunging from a mountain top to the same point, or like one eagle plunging down from the top of a cliff and a predatory fish shooting from the ocean's depth to the surface with the same speed, we two both seek the same point; there is a contact, and at the same moment we rush from each other, each to his extremity.' This image of a divided self, split between inseparable antagonists, echoed Kierkegaard's dialogical preface to his very first book, *From the Papers of One Still Living*.

During the winter and spring of 1849, while Kierkegaard was pacing round his Rosenborggade apartment torn between two possible futures – and two possible selves – Fredrika Bremer was paying visits to Copenhagen's best-known writers and intellectuals. Bremer, a Swedish author and feminist reformer, was researching a series of articles on 'Life in Scandinavia': while in Denmark, she interviewed Bishop Mynster, Grundtvig, Oehlenschläger, Heiberg, Carsten Hauch, Hans Christian Andersen, H. C. Ørsted, F. C. Sibbern and Martensen. Kierkegaard refused to see her, so she asked her other interviewees about him – especially Martensen, who invited her to his home several times. In August 1849 Kierkegaard picked up a newspaper and saw his name next to Martensen's:

> Whereas from his central standpoint the brilliant Martensen sheds light upon the entire sphere of existence and upon all the phenomena of life, *Søren Kierkegaard* stands on his isolated pillar like a Simon Stylites, his gaze fixed uninterruptedly on a single point. He places his microscope over this point, carefully investigating the tiniest atoms, the most fleeting motions, the innermost alterations. And it is about this that he speaks and writes endless folios. For him, everything is to be found at this point. But this point is – the human heart.

And – because he unceasingly has this changeable heart reflect itself in the Eternal and Unchangeable that 'became flesh and dwelt among us', because in the course of his exhausting dialectical wanderings he says divine things – he has gained a not inconsiderable audience in happy, pleasant Copenhagen, particularly among ladies. The philosophy of the heart must be important to them.

'Concerning the philosopher who writes on these matters,' Bremer's article continued:

> people speak well and ill – and strangely. He who writes for 'that single individual' lives alone, inaccessible and, when all is said and done, known by no one. During the daytime one sees him walking in the midst of the crowd, up and down the busiest streets of Copenhagen for hours at a time. At night his lonely dwelling is said to glow with light. The cause of this behaviour seems to be less his wealth and independence than a sickly and irritable nature, which finds occasion to be displeased with the sun itself when its rays shine in a direction other than what he wishes.

Bremer's remark about his 'sickly' nature echoed P. L. Møller's spiteful review of *Stages on Life's Way*, which had triggered the *Corsair* affair. Kierkegaard had long believed that Martensen, envious of his talent, passively colluded in *The Corsair*'s attack, and Bremer's article pushed that thorn a little deeper. Martensen, the Professor of Theology, Court Preacher, Knight of the Dannebrog – that exemplar of Christianity! Kierkegaard could not bear to think of his hypocrisy and self-satisfaction, but he thought about it anyway. Through the summer and autumn of 1849 he wrote long, bitter journal entries on Martensen's success.

He also spent weeks drafting letters to Regine. He asked for forgiveness, offered explanations, thanked her for her 'lovable simplicity' and her 'passionate despair', expressed his wish to talk with her now and then, and assured her that 'neither I nor history will forget you.' The letter he finally settled on, in November, was brief:

> Cruel I was, that is true. Why? Indeed, *you* do not know that.
> Silent I have been, that is certain. Only God knows what I have suffered – may God grant that I do not, even now, speak too soon after all!

Marry I could not. Even if you were still free, I could not.

However, you have loved me, as I have you. I owe you much – and now you are married. All right, I offer you for the second time what I can and dare and ought to offer you: reconciliation.

I do this in writing in order not to surprise or overwhelm you. Perhaps my personality did once have too strong an effect; that must not happen again. But for the sake of God in heaven, please give serious consideration to whether you dare become involved in this, and if so, whether you prefer to speak with me at once or would rather exchange some letters first.

If your answer is 'No' – would you then please remember for the sake of a better world that I took this step as well.

In any case, as in the beginning
so until now, sincerely and completely
devotedly, your S.K.

He sealed this letter and enclosed it in another letter, to Regine's husband Johan Frederik Schlegel, requesting that he decide whether to give it to his wife. It was returned unopened, accompanied by a 'moralizing and indignant epistle' from Schlegel. Kierkegaard stubbornly recorded in his journal 'One last step concerning "Her" – It is my unalterable will that my writings, after my death, be dedicated to her and to my late father. She must belong to history.'

The following month Kierkegaard read another newspaper article comparing him with Martensen. This one was written by his brother: in a speech at the Roskilde Convention, printed in the *Danish Church Times*, Peter Christian Kierkegaard had remarked that Professor Martensen was 'sober-minded' while Søren Kierkegaard was 'ecstatic'. Although Kierkegaard's writings addressed 'the single individual', his brother's discourse continued, he was acquiring imitators and adherents: men like Rasmus Nielsen, who expounded his philosophy in academic treatises.

That winter Kierkegaard raged against all these worldly priests of Christendom. He sent his brother – who was elected to the upper house of parliament in the last days of 1849 – a polite but indignant letter, suggesting that if Peter wanted to compare him with Martensen he should indicate the 'essential difference' between them:

'that I have been sacrificed to an extraordinary extent and that [Martensen] has profited to an extraordinary extent'. He celebrated the end of the year with a journal entry headed 'Protest against Bishop Mynster': 'He has cravenly evaded actuality, has arranged a sort of private world consisting of circles of the elite in which – as he himself knows, by the way – Christianity has not exactly been the dominant factor: and that is where he has lived,' he wrote sourly. Mynster enjoyed 'a life of glory, honour, esteem, abundance, pleasure, distinction' – but from a Christian point of view that life was 'a lie'. Kierkegaard was sick of Copenhagen; it was 'a little, cooped-up place, the homeland of nonsense, a provincial market town', and its air was polluted by the daily press, 'the government's filth machine'. Should he try harder to turn the other cheek? St Augustine, he noted, pointed out that even Jesus did not always keep that commandment.

He found ammunition in Luther's sermons, which he continued to read regularly along with various mystical writers – Johann Arndt; the eighteenth-century poet and lay preacher Gerhard Tersteegen; and medieval monks like Hugh and Richard of St Victor, whose texts he discovered in a German anthology of Christian mysticism. As he traced a dialectic between medieval Catholic spirituality and Luther's turn away from monastic life, he began to discern his own task more clearly: just as Luther had corrected the corruptions and excesses of his sixteenth-century Church, so he must correct the worldliness of nineteenth-century Lutheranism. And Luther had wrestled with the same questions about how to be a Christian in the world. In one of his model sermons for reforming preachers, the former monk argued that 'it is the great, unreasonable fool who runs out of the world into a desert or a wild forest . . . No, you must be in whatever station and arrangements you are in – for after all, you must be in one place the entire time you live on the earth – so God has not cast you *away from* people, but *among* them . . . Nor should you shroud yourself in a cowl and creep into a corner or hide yourself in a desert. For in so doing you do not avoid the devil and sin – they will find you as well in the desert in a grey cowl as they would in the marketplace in a red coat.' Yet Luther also insisted that spiritual fulfilment has nothing to do with worldly success: the Christian must 'regard this life on earth as a pilgrim regards the land through which he makes his journey and the inn at which he spends the night; for he does not think of remaining here; here he expects to become neither a citizen nor a mayor.' Luther's words now consolidated Kierkegaard's view of his own position in the world.

Spring finally arrived, and each day the sun rose a little higher in the sky. His old friend Emil Boesen, who had recently left Copenhagen to take up a pastorate in Jutland, married Louise Holtermann in the Church of Our Lady. Emil was keen for him to visit Louise, but he was reluctant. One cool, sunny Thursday beneath the blossoming trees on the ramparts, he quarrelled with Rasmus Nielsen during their weekly walk: in 1849 the philosophy professor had published a big book, which Kierkegaard regarded as 'a slavish imitation' that 'plundered' his writings and conversations, 'battled mediocrity with borrowed weapons', and 'spoiled the whole thing with all that scholarly apparatus'. Having brooded on this for nearly a year, he decided that Thursday to reprove Nielsen for plagiarizing his work and turning it 'into a doctrine', which it was never supposed to be. Nielsen was angry, and a few days later sent a letter 'renouncing' their walks. Then the second edition of Martensen's weighty *Christian Dogmatics* came out, with a new preface casting shade on Kierkegaard: 'Each of us possesses the faith only to a certain limited degree, and we must certainly guard against making our own individual, perhaps rather one-sided, perhaps even rather sickly life of faith into a rule for all believers.'

In April 1850 Kierkegaard moved to a cheaper apartment on Nørregade. On Rosenborggade he had lived in six rooms – there was also a kitchen, maid's room and garret – and paid two hundred rix-dollars per half year; in the Nørregade apartment he had five rooms and the rent was one hundred and forty rix-dollars. His new home came with fresh irritations. 'In the afternoons I suffer so much from reflected sunlight that I feared at first that I might go blind,' he wrote in his journal a few weeks after moving in. And the tenant upstairs had a dog which was at home all day long: 'it lies by an open window and takes an interest in everything. If a man walks past and sneezes unusually loudly, the dog barks and can go on barking for a long time. If a coachman drives past and cracks his whip, it barks; if another dog barks, it also barks. Thus there is not the least little incident in the street that I do not receive in a second edition, thanks to this dog.' At odds with the world – and its dog – Kierkegaard found solace in Seneca's letters, Pascal's *Pensées*, Montaigne's essays, Rousseau's *Émile*.

# 14

## 'This is How it is with Me'

The weeks between 9 August, the anniversary of his father's death, and 10 September, the day of his engagement to Regine, were always the most difficult time of the year. Most Danes 'longed and prayed for summer', but Kierkegaard did not like the relentless Scandinavian summer days, when the sun was too strong for him. He stayed indoors in his darkened rooms, and as he waited for autumn – his favourite season, bittersweet with longing and recollection – he remembered how an old man's 'noble wisdom' and a young girl's 'loveable foolishness' had educated him to become an author. Between them, his father and Regine had shaped his soul into 'a unity of age and youth', of severity and mildness. Now he knew, though, that this combination of extremes was already deep within him, always his 'possibility'.

In 1850 he spent this period reading through *Practice in Christianity* one last time before sending it to the printer: it would be published in late September under his new pseudonym, Anti-Climacus, and 'S. Kierkegaard' would be named on the title page as its editor. Day after day autumn's gentle, melancholy dusk descended on Copenhagen's streets like an incoming tide, each wave of darkness a little more forgiving than the last. With his heart in his mouth, Kierkegaard sent Bishop Mynster a copy of his new book, printed with a personal dedication. *Practice in Christianity* deployed bolder, more aggressive tactics than *The Sickness unto Death*, making significant moves against Mynster as well as against Martensen. The question of this book was how to follow Christ, and it explored the difference between rigorous and lenient Christianity, between asceticism and worldliness, between imitating Jesus in his suffering and admiring him from a safe distance. Mynster, well known as the author of *Observations on Christian*

*Teachings*, was implicitly but unmistakably cast in the role of a lenient, worldly 'observer' of Christ, and his familiar style of preaching was parodied and denounced as un-Christian: 'The Christian sermon today has become mainly "observations": *Let us in this hour consider*; *I invite my listeners to observations on*; *the subject for our consideration is*, etc. But "to observe" can mean in one sense to come very close to something; in another sense, it signifies keeping very distant, infinitely distant – that is, personally . . . Christian truth cannot really be the object of "observations".'

For pages and pages Anti-Climacus went on like this, evidently with the approval of his editor, S. Kierkegaard. Mynster was like an artist – perhaps like Thorvaldsen – who chiselled or painted the figure of Christ, then stepped back to survey his work. This aestheticization of Christianity was an evasion, a lie, self-indulgence, sheer hypocrisy. 'I do not comprehend this calmness of the artist,' Anti-Climacus declared, 'this artistic indifference that is indeed like a callousness toward the religious impression of the religious . . . And yet the artist admired himself, and everybody admired the artist. The point of view of the religious is completely dislocated; the beholder looked at the picture in the role of an art expert: whether it is a success, whether it is a masterpiece, whether the play of colours is right, and the shadows, whether blood looks like that, whether the suffering expression is artistically true – but the invitation to imitation he did not find. The artist was admired, and what was actual suffering, the artist has somehow turned into money and admiration.' The person who merely admires Christ from a distance, he argued, 'will make no sacrifices, renounce nothing, give up nothing earthly, will not transform his life, will not *be* what is admired, will not let his life express it . . . Only the imitator is the true Christian.'

Kierkegaard himself was caught between these two versions of Christianity, unable to live with either of them. 'Ah, a person can certainly proclaim leniency. One spares oneself, one is loved by people, receives their gratitude, their devotion; one can look out with self-satisfaction, or at any rate with tranquillity, upon the many happy and smiling people who find repose in what one proclaims,' he wrote in his journal just before *Practice in Christianity* was published. But such a teacher was not imitating Jesus, who 'could not reassure a single one of [his disciples] with the joy of a secure life'. Proclaiming a properly rigorous Christian teaching, on the other hand, was 'sheer spiritual trial: whether you can endure it yourself; whether you ought not to spare yourself; whether it might not end with corrupting instead of benefiting, tearing down instead of building up. Sheer unrest and worry and fear and trembling for the sake of others about whether you are not demanding too much of them. And then this dismal sight, to see their anger and bitterness – to have no one's gratitude, but to have everyone eager to get away from you.'

One day in October, Kierkegaard heard from Just Paulli, a priest and theologian who was married to Mynster's eldest daughter, that the Bishop was 'very angry' about *Practice in Christianity*. 'These were his words, the minute he came into the living room he said: "The book has provoked me intensely; it makes profane sport of the holy." And when Paulli most obligingly asked him if he might say so to me, since he would presumably speak to me, Mynster answered, "Yes and he will no doubt come to see me sometime and I will tell him myself."' The following morning Kierkegaard visited Mynster, full of anxiety. 'Pastor Paulli told me yesterday that you intend as soon as you see me to reprimand me for my latest book. I would ask you to regard it as a fresh expression of the respect I have always shown to you that I come to see you immediately upon hearing of this,' he began. The Bishop was as diplomatic and affable as ever. 'He answered: "No, indeed I have no right to give a reprimand. As I have said to you before, I have nothing at all against each bird singing its own song." Then he added: "Indeed people can say what they like about me." He said this mildly and with a smile but the added remark made me fear a little sarcasm nonetheless, and I immediately sought to rescue the situation. I answered that this was not my intention, and I would beg him to say if I had in any way distressed him by publishing such a book. Then he replied: "Well, it's true I do not believe it will do any good."'

Mynster's disapproval seemed to channel the judgement of his father from beyond the grave, but he was even more afraid of God's judgement, now and in eternity. Although Jesus offered his followers grace and love, promised to ease their burdens and give them rest, they were first 'rent asunder in terror and fear' – and Kierkegaard felt the ripples of this terror in his own soul. Sometimes Jesus appeared to him a fearsome figure: 'You became a sword through the heart of your mother, a scandal to your disciples,' he wrote. 'Oh, why did you not lower the price? When I have doubts about myself, and it seems to me as if I must first and foremost cut the price for my own sake, and when it seems to me as if I owe it to others to cut the price – now it can cause me anxiety to think of you, as if you would become angry, you, who never cut the price yet nonetheless were love.' He felt 'infinitely far' from the Christian ideal that he now believed to be the only true one, and which he finally dared to write of directly – though still in the voice of a pseudonym. He, Kierkegaard, shuddered at the thought of dying to the world, dying to ordinary human life: 'For my part, I love being a human being; I do not have the courage entirely to be spirit in that way. I still so much love to see the purely human delight that others take in life – something for which I have a better than ordinary eye, because I have a poet's eye for it.'

More and more, though, he thought that the situation in Christendom called for a renewed emphasis on the ideal of dying to the world that Arndt and Tersteegen – who gave away his inheritance and lived as a hermit on bread, milk and water – and their medieval forebears impressed upon him. Modern Christianity leaned too far towards worldliness, and Kierkegaard countered this by leaning further in the opposite direction. He continued to study Luther's sermons, and in his journal he analysed Luther's religious innovations and their effects on later generations of Christians.

As a young man, Luther was tormented by the question of his salvation; in an effort to earn God's grace, he entered a strict Augustinian monastic order, pushed his ascetic practices to extremes, spent his days in penance, slept in the snow. Then this same religious passion – and not its abating – drove him out into the world. Only after posting his ninety-five theses and refusing to recant at the Diet of Worms did Luther finally leave his monastery and – in defiance of his Church, in defiance of public opinion – marry a former nun, Katherine von Bora, who bore him six children. Yet Luther's reforms coupled worldliness and religion in ways that suited the secular mentality already creeping into Europe: 'Luther certainly possessed the inner truth to dare to venture doing opposite things and yet be quite free in doing them:

married and yet as if not married, within worldliness and yet as if alien to it despite partaking of everything, etc. Ah, but it was dangerous simply to teach this in a straightforward manner, because it made things altogether too easy for the whole of worldliness.'

During the autumn and winter of 1850 these reflections brought Kierkegaard back to the question of marriage, which ten years earlier had been his life's turning point, and occupied his longest books. Now that the principle of religious freedom was enshrined in the Danish constitution, marriage was a political question as well as a personal one. Several influential voices in Copenhagen were calling for the introduction of civil marriage, some citing Luther's own example in support of their cause. 'Shall we continue to force all members of the People's Church to undergo church wedding ceremonies, of which the Gospels know nothing, and which Martin Luther openly disdained when he himself entered into a civil marriage that – as a marriage between a monk and a nun – broke with all the notions of churchly marriage in his day?' asked Grundtvig. In the strange new world of post-1848 Denmark, ardent Christians who sought to protect their Church from the influence of the state, and freethinkers campaigning to liberate civic life from ecclesial control, made different arguments for the same reform.

The defence of the traditional position was led, of course, by Bishop Mynster, who argued that Luther's marriage to Katherine von Bora was a Christian union, not merely a civil contract. Kierkegaard, however, saw this marriage as significant not because it belonged inside or outside the Church, but because it was a subversive, scandalous religious act that echoed the 'divine scandal' of original Christianity. He argued that Luther could just as well have married a kitchen maid, or a doorpost (despite the six children) – for his sole aim was 'defying Satan, the pope, the whole world'. This marriage had nothing in common with the conventional family life enjoyed by nineteenth-century Danish clergy. When Kierkegaard compared Bishop Mynster to Luther, he saw 'a clever and prudent man, who shrinks from nothing, nothing, as much as he shrinks from scandal'. He did not go quite so far as to argue that it was now more Lutheran to abstain from marriage – especially in a way that scandalized public opinion, like his own decision not to marry.

In January 1851 Kierkegaard published an article in *The Father-land* in response to Andreas Rudelbach, a theologian and Church historian who argued on Lutheran grounds for civil marriage. 'Surely the deepest and highest interest of the Church in our day is to become emancipated particularly from what is rightly called *habitual* and *state Christianity*,' Rudelbach urged in his book *On Civil Marriage*, before adding that 'this is the same point that one of our outstanding contemporary writers, Søren Kierkegaard, has sought to inculcate, to impress, and, as Luther says, to drive home to all those who will listen'. In his *Fatherland* article Kierkegaard protested that he had never, in all his authorship, called for reform: 'Simply because I have from the beginning understood Christianity to be inwardness and my task to be the inward deepening of Christianity, I have scrupulously seen to it that not a passage, not a sentence, not a line, not a word, not a letter has slipped in suggesting a proposal for external change.' Individual Christians might feel called by conscience to agitate for social, political or ecclesial reform, but '*essentially* Christianity is inwardness'. Kierkegaard felt that he and Dr Rudelbach – whom he knew personally, and respected as a scholar – would never under-stand one another religiously: 'For him it has long since been settled that he is a Christian. And now he busies himself with the history and the external forms of the Church. He has never felt the unrest of the question, every single day, about whether he is in fact a Christian. Never, no, because the person who has felt it one time, one day, one hour will not let it go for his whole life, or it will never let go of him.'

Early in May he paid another visit to Bishop Mynster. Again he was agitated when he entered the episcopal residence, but this time he trembled more from anger than from fear. Mynster's recent book on religious freedom and civil marriage mentioned Kierkegaard along-side Meïr Aron Goldschmidt, whose journalism – as P. L. Møller had predicted back in 1847 – the Bishop now cited approvingly. Gold-schmidt, Mynster remarked, was 'one of our most talented authors'; Kierkegaard was 'the gifted author' who rightly opposed 'the disas-trous confusion of politics and Christianity'. This juxtaposition was enough to enrage Kierkegaard; for several weeks before his visit, he had rehearsed and elaborated his fury by drafting numerous polem-ical responses to Mynster.

When he saw the Bishop he was too proud to tell him that he was hurt by his endorsement of Goldschmidt, still deeply hurt that five years ago Mynster had not defended him against *The Corsair*'s attack. Instead he harangued Mynster with concern for *his* reputation: 'I repeated again and again that what concerned me was whether his reputation might not have suffered too much by presenting Goldschmidt in this way. I pointed out to him that he ought to have required a retraction [of the *Corsair* writings] on Goldschmidt's part . . . that it was impossible for me to defend this conduct of his.' Mynster was evasive: in order to demand a retraction, he said, he would have to read through all Goldschmidt's writings – 'So, can M. really be ignorant of the fact that there existed a journal called *The Corsair*, that G. had edited it for six years, and can M. be supposed not to understand that this was what I was referring to!' Again Kierkegaard repeated his objections: '"I want to have it said, and quite clearly, I want my conscience to be clear, it must be noted that I have said that I cannot approve of it" (and in saying this I leaned across the table and wrote it in my hand, as it were) . . . Every time I said this, I saw to it that he replied and indicated that he had heard it.'

Towards the end of the summer he was back on Mynster's doorstep, a few days after sending him two new publications: *On My Work as an Author* – a short version of *The Point of View for My Work as an Author* – and *Two Discourses at Friday Communion*. (He also sent copies to J. L. Heiberg: the discourses for him, and the essay on his authorship for his wife Luise.) He was anxious to hear Mynster's opinion of these little books, but the Bishop had only looked at one of them. Kierkegaard returned to the subject of Goldschmidt, and then 'there were a few words about the pastoral seminary, but he tried to evade this and was of the opinion that the best thing would be for me to start founding a pastoral seminary myself.' The Bishop dismissed him gracefully with a 'Farewell, dear friend.'

Between these troubling visits to Mynster, Kierkegaard preached a Sunday sermon on 'The Unchangingness of God' at the Citadel Church inside the garrison by the entrance to Copenhagen's harbour. That Sunday morning he prayed to God 'that something new might be born in me' – for he felt that this church service was his 'confirmation'. The sermon was on his favourite biblical passage, from the Letter of James: 'Every good and perfect gift is from above and comes down from the Father of Lights, in whom there is no change or shadow of variation.' He had planned his sermon 'with the thought of "her"': unable to talk to Regine directly, he felt that it might please her to hear him preach, and unusually he allowed his name to be listed as preacher when the service was announced. 'Beforehand I suffered greatly from every sort of strain, as is always the case when I have to use my physical person.'

Though not yet forty years old, Kierkegaard stood before his listeners a frail figure: more stooped and slender than ever, his hair thin, his face tired. He addressed the congregation in such a weak voice that they had to strain to hear him, but his words were full of feeling. He spoke at length of the 'sheer fear and trembling' which the thought of God's changelessness causes 'for us light-minded and unstable human beings'.

> And now the eternal Changeless One – and this human heart! Ah, this human heart, what do you not hide in your secret inclosures, unknown to others – that would not be the worst – but at times almost unknown to the person himself! It is almost, as soon as a person is a few years old, it is almost like a grave, this human heart! There lie buried, buried in forgetfulness, the promises, the intentions, the resolutions, complete plans and fragments of plans, and God knows what – yes, that is how we human beings talk, for we seldom think about what we say; we say: There lies God knows what. And we say this half light-mindedly, half in weariness of life – and then it is so frightfully true that God knows what. He knows down to the least detail what you have forgotten, knows what has changed in your remembering; he knows it unchanged . . . an Omniscient One, and an eternally change-less memory from which you cannot escape, least of all in eternity – frightful!

He spoke like this for fifteen minutes – 'It is almost as though it were far, far beyond human powers to have to be involved with a change-lessness such as that; indeed, it seems as if this thought must plunge a person into anxiety and unrest to the point of despair.' Then he paused; and yet, he said, *there is also reassurance and blessedness in this thought*. It is really so that when you, weary from all this human, all this temporal and earthly changefulness and alteration, weary of your own instability, could wish for a place where you could rest your weary head, your weary thoughts, your weary mind, in order to rest, to have a good rest – ah, in God's changelessness there is rest!'

The whole church was silent, full of faces turned towards him, and it was as though their hearts were turned too. 'Be like the child,' he told them, 'who really profoundly senses that it is in the position of being face-to-face with a will where only one thing helps, to obey. That the thought of God's changelessness is blessed, indeed, who doubts that; just see to it that you become like that so that you can blessedly rest in this changelessness! Ah, such a person speaks as someone who has a happy home: My home is eternally safeguarded; I rest in God's changelessness. No one but you yourself can disturb this rest.' And there will be, paradoxically, freedom in this submission: 'If you could become completely obedient in unchanged obedience, you would at every moment freely rest in God with the same necessity as a heavy body sinks to the earth, or with the same necessity as something that is light rises toward heaven.' Of course, such constancy is so difficult, probably impossible, for human beings to accomplish, even though they long for God as the thirsty man in the desert longs for a cool spring. And yet, Kierkegaard concluded, another paradox of God's changeless omnipresence is that it is not inert, but continually, actively seeks those who long for him:

No one, either in life or in death, travels so far away that you, O God, are not to be found, that you are not there; you are indeed, everywhere – this is not the way springs are on this earth, springs are only in special places. Moreover – what overwhelming security! – you do not remain on the spot like a spring; you travel along. No one strays so far away that he cannot find his way back to you, you who are not only like a spring that lets itself be found – what a poor description of your being! – you who are like a spring that even searches for the thirsting, the straying, something unheard of about any spring. Thus you are unchanged and everywhere to be found. And whenever a person comes to you, at whatever age, at whatever time of day, in whatever condition – if he comes honestly, he will always find (like the spring's unchanged coolness) your love just as warm, you Changeless One! Amen.

That Sunday sermon was a turning point in Kierkegaard's authorship. 'When I went home,' he later wrote in his journal, 'I felt well, animated . . . On Monday I was so weak and exhausted that it was frightful . . . I became weaker and weaker . . . Then I became really sick. The lamentable, tormenting pain that constitutes the limit of my person began to rear up in fearsome fashion, something that had not happened to me in a long, long time. For a moment, I understood this as a punishment for having failed to act quickly enough.' Nevertheless, he felt that his prayers were answered: he had received his 'confirmation'. 'Something new has been born within me,' he wrote, 'for I understand my task as an author differently; it is now dedicated in a quite different way to straightforwardly advancing religion. And I have also been confirmed in this: this is how it is with me.'

That week he received letters from two unknown women who, having read his books, had gone to the Citadel Church to hear him preach. One letter was from a young woman who ventured to address him because, she explained, 'I have been told that you are gracious and kind to the young and lenient to those who have gone astray.' Kierkegaard's writing, she continued, had helped her to a spiritual awakening:

In the frivolous, or perhaps, as you remark somewhere, the melancholy spirit of the times, I long ignored God and my relation to him, but this was an unhappy state of affairs, as I soon realized. I sought comfort in prayer, but I felt that God would not hear me; I went to church, but my scattered thoughts would not follow those of the preacher; I tried, in the philosophy books that I could understand, to find rest for my lost soul, and I found some. I had read *Either/Or* with profound admiration, and I tried to obtain some of your works by borrowing them since I could not afford to buy them. I received the *Christian Discourses* of 1848, which were not what I had wanted, but I read them – and how can I ever thank you enough? In them I found the source of life that has not failed me since. When I was troubled, I sought refuge there and found comfort; when need or chance brought me to church and I walked away downcast, conscious of one more sin for having been in the House of the Lord without reverence or humility, then I would read your discourses and find comfort. In everything that happened to me, in sorrow or in joy, this small portion of the riches you have bequeathed to the world became the constant source from which I drew comfort and sustenance.

Last Sunday you were listed as the preacher in the Citadel. What could I do but walk out there, and I was not disappointed. This was not one of those sermons I have heard so often and forgotten before it was concluded. No, from the rich, warm heart the speech poured forth, terrifying, yet upbuilding and soothing at the same time; it penetrated the heart so as never to be forgotten.

'If only you would preach more often, but please, always with your name posted,' begged the author of the other letter, who also spoke of her heart as she reflected on Kierkegaard's sermon. 'From the very outset when you began to publish your pseudonymous works,' she wrote:

I have pricked up my ears and listened lest I should miss any sound, even the faintest, of these magnificent harmonies, for everything resounded in my heart. This was what needed to be said – here I found answers to all my questions; nothing was omitted of that which inter-ested me most profoundly . . . I doubt that there is a single string in the human heart that you do not know how to pluck, any recess that you have not penetrated. I thought I knew what it meant to laugh, before 1843 as well, but no, it was not until I read *Either/Or* that I had any idea what it meant to laugh from the depths of my heart; and it is with my heart that I have come to an overall understanding of everything you have said. Many a time I have been almost embarrassed to hear clever people say that they did not understand S. Kierkegaard, for I always thought that I understood him. I am never lonely, even when I am by myself for long periods of time, provided only that I have the company of these books, for they are, of all books, those that most closely resemble the company of a living person. But please do not think that these books have only taught me to laugh; oh no, please believe that again and again I have been roused by them to see myself more clearly and to understand my duty, to feel myself ever more closely tied to 'the truth, the way, the life'; I have become infinitely liberated by musing on them – but – also infinitely tempted to give up all that gregarious society in which one lives, which is so far from

knowing what it really means to live that, if anything, it mostly resembles a parody on it. Yet it is not by fleeing that one shows one's
strength.

Since Sunday this woman had been talking about Kierkegaard's sermon to everyone she met; he had expressed eternal truths, yet 'nobody
has proclaimed those truths to *me* before as you did so in such a way
that I could hear them, that is, with the ears of my soul.' Now,
although she knew he would not permit it, she needed to thank him
personally. 'Were I a man and therefore someone who could think
and write coherently,' she added, 'surely it would then be a different
matter, for I could publish something about you and would have no
need to trouble you privately.'

In the early autumn of 1851 Emil Boesen visited Copenhagen for
a few days. Kierkegaard gave his old friend a copy of *For Self-
Examination: Recommended to the Present Age*, which he had just
published. Here he imagined Luther returning to test the faith of
nineteenth-century Danish Lutherans: 'You know that faith is a restless thing,' says Luther. 'To what end has faith, which you say you
have, made you restless, where have you witnessed for the truth,
where against untruth, what sacrifices have you made, what persecu-
tions have you suffered for your Christianity, and at home in your
domestic life where have your self-denial and renunciation been
noticeable?' This book contained three discourses, on the New Testament texts assigned by the Church to the fifth Sunday after Easter,
to Ascension Day, and to Pentecost. It offered a rigorous interpretation of Christianity as a hard, narrow path that followed Jesus into
suffering. Jesus was born in poverty and wretchedness, and he knew
his fate from the very beginning – 'And this way, which is Christ, this
narrow way, as it goes on, becomes narrower and narrower to the end,
to death.' The Holy Spirit would, Jesus promised, bring gentle comfort, new life, faith, love – but these blessings came only to those who
had first died to themselves, died to the world.

By then Kierkegaard was living, for the first time in his life, outside
the city walls, on the second floor of a newly built villa in Østerbro.
It was a tranquil place at the end of Sortedam Lake, surrounded by
private gardens. When Emil called on him there they talked late into

Emil Boesen

the night, and Kierkegaard asked him to return the next evening, and again the next. He had few opportunities, these days, to 'talk himself out' as he used to.

When he lived at his previous address on Nørregade, he had often seen Regine during his daily walks – sometimes 'every blessed day' for weeks at a time. Soon after he moved out to Østerbro he began to encounter Regine at around ten o'clock each morning on his way back home from town. On 1 January 1852 he resolved to change his route, anxious to avoid any appearance of impropriety, and now took the lakeside path. One morning he saw Regine there, and changed his route again. But then he began to meet her at eight o'clock in the morning by Østerport, the city's eastern gate, or a little later on the ramparts, as he walked to town. 'Perhaps it was coincidence, perhaps. I could not understand what she was doing on that route at that hour,' he wrote in his journal. He also continued to see her in church on Sundays.

'Then came my birthday. As a rule, I am always away on my birthday, but I was not feeling quite well. So I stayed at home; as usual, I walked into town to talk with the doctor because I had considered celebrating my birthday with something new, something I had never tasted before, castor oil. Right outside my door, on the pavement in front of the avenue, she meets me. As so often happens of late, I cannot keep from smiling when I see her – ah, how much she has come to mean to me! – she smiled in return and nodded. I took a step past her, then raised my hat and walked on.' After years of the most indirect communication, this meeting of glances, smiles and silent greetings lightened Kierkegaard's heart. Perhaps reconciliation and friendship were not impossible after all. It was as if a window had suddenly opened to let the spring breeze flow into an airless room, bringing with it a blessing on his birthday.

The following Sunday, Regine was there in church, sitting near the place where he always stood. Pastor Paulli, Bishop Mynster's son-in-law, gave the sermon – and like Kierkegaard's own life-changing sermon at the Citadel Church the year before, the text was his favourite passage from the Letter of James, 'Every good and perfect gift is from above.' 'She turns her head to the side and looks at me, very fervently. I look straight ahead, at nothing in particular.' Then Paulli began his sermon in a manner so out of character that Kierkegaard found it 'inexplicable': these sacred words about God's good gifts were, said the pastor, 'implanted in our hearts – yes, my listener, if these words should be torn from your heart, would not life have lost all its value for you?'

Regine must have felt overwhelmed by this, he reflected afterwards. 'I have never exchanged a word with her, have gone my way, not hers – but here it was as though a higher power said to her what I have been unable to say.' As for his own feeling – 'It was as if I were standing on glowing coals.'

# 15

## The Last Battle

One autumn night in 1853 Kierkegaard opens his journal and writes a heading at the top of the page: 'New "Fear and Trembling" '.

He imagines Abraham, on the way to Mount Moriah, telling Isaac that God wants him to be the sacrifice; when they reach the mountain Abraham cuts the wood, binds Isaac, lights the fire – and plunges the knife into his son. Jehovah appears, and asks Abraham if he did not hear his command to stop, to kill a ram in Isaac's place – No, replies Abraham, I did not hear it. Jehovah brings Isaac back to life, but this is not the same Isaac who followed his father trustingly to Moriah: having understood that he was 'chosen by God as a sacrifice', the carefree boy has become like an old man. Abraham sorrows over his lost son; Jehovah promises that they will be united in eternity, where all joy will be restored to them. 'Had you heard my voice, had you held back – then you would have had Isaac for this life,' explains Abraham's God, 'but what concerns eternity would not have been clarified for you. You went too far, you ruined everything – yet I am making it even better than if you had not gone too far: there is an eternity.' In this retelling of Genesis 22, Abraham does not stop until he has carried out his awful task, going even further than God had intended. All is lost, and relief lies only beyond this world.

Kierkegaard looks up: through his window he sees, in the moonlight, the tower of the Church of Our Lady against the night sky. A year ago, in October 1852, he moved house again, leaving his peaceful villa by the lake for a cheap lodging at the top of a house in the centre of Copenhagen, a few steps from the church and Bishop Mynster's episcopal residence. These low-ceilinged rooms, usually rented by students, are all he can now afford. His morning walks begin at the cathedral of Danish Christendom – this church in which he has spent countless hours since his youth, sitting with his family beneath the towering apostles, listening to Mynster's sermons; where he so often stood yards from Regine and felt her gaze upon him; where he three times preached at Friday communion in the hard years following *The Corsair*'s attack.

In his cramped rooms on Klædeboderne, he surveys the enemy and prepares for battle. He broods on Mynster – his worldliness, his hypocrisy, his approving remark about Goldschmidt – as he sharpens his polemic against Christendom, and contemplates his own relationship to God. In 1843, when he began *Fear and Trembling* in Berlin, Kierkegaard admired Abraham as a 'knight of faith' who joyfully returns to the world he had left behind, and receives his beloved son a second time after giving him up. He even longed for this remarkable faith of Abraham's, which would – had it been possible – have allowed him to live out his relationship to God within the world, inconspicuous, to all appearances an ordinary man. In *Fear and Trembling* he compared Abraham to Mary, Jesus's mother, as she appears at the beginning of Luke's Gospel: young, unmarried and suddenly pregnant, summoned by God to bear an illegitimate, holy child. Both Abraham and Mary went willingly to their divine tasks, misunderstood by their families and friends, and faced the loss of their sons.

But now, ten years later, Kierkegaard regards Abraham's trial as a 'child's category' compared to the suffering required by true Christianity: 'Abraham draws the knife – then he gets Isaac back again; it wasn't serious. The most serious thing was the trial, but then it once more became enjoyment of this life.' It was different in the New Testament, where 'the sword . . . actually came to pierce Mary's heart, to penetrate her heart – but then she got a referral to eternity; Abraham did not get that.' For Kierkegaard, Christian faith now means 'quite literally letting go and giving up, losing the earthly, and sheer suffering, and dying away [from the world]'.

His journal entry on Abraham is not a plan for another book – but if he were to write a 'New "Fear and Trembling"' in 1853, he would explain that the sword through Mary's soul, which the prophet Simeon foresees in Jesus's infancy, is even more than a mother's pain at seeing her son crucified. It is also her doubt 'whether it was not all a fantasy, a deception, the whole affair of Gabriel being sent by God to announce to her that she was the chosen one. As Christ cries: My God, my God, why have you forsaken me – so must the Virgin Mary suffer the human analogue of this.' In 1843 Kierkegaard made his literary persona Johannes de silentio marvel at Abraham's faith, which did not long for the hereafter but expected joy in this life. Now he believes that 'Christianity is suffering to the end – it is consciousness of eternity.' There is no more need for the dialectical leaps of his pseudonyms, for his own existence has composed a simple theological formula: 'The closer to God, the more suffering.'

For two years he has published nothing, and written little. As a consequence, he notes in his journal, 'an enormous productivity has, as it were, accumulated in my head and in my thoughts – indeed, I believe that at this moment a rich assortment of professors and poets could be made out of me.' Since moving back to the city he has lived more spartanly than before, denying himself various material comforts – even, for short periods, renouncing his writing – 'all in order to see what I can bear'. In this autumn of 1853, however, he reflects that 'asceticism is sophistry', for these finite renunciations put him in a calculating frame of mind, weighing every abstinence, as if renunciation were an end in itself. 'And so I come once again to grace,' he wrote on another October night. What matters is his stance towards the world; all that should concern him is the question of how far he needs to go to fulfil his divinely appointed task. 'You went too far, you ruined everything,' he now imagines God saying to an Abraham who has blood on his hands – are these words intended for himself? He is considering 'breaking with everything' in order to proclaim an austere, terrifying Christianity, but 'one thing' gives him pause: Regine. 'She has no inkling of that sort of Christianity. If I seize hold of it, if I follow through, then there is a religious difference between us.' This autumn Kierkegaard has felt himself coming under greater and greater strain. Writing is making him weary; it seems 'almost like foolishness'.

He renounces his journal for a month, then opens it again one cold November night to write a couple of pages about Bishop Mynster – and also, of course, about himself. Until 1848, he records, he remained loyal to 'the established order'. In spite of his ambivalence towards

Mynster, he has respected him more than any other churchman, and, until *Practice in Christianity*, spared him his polemics. The *Corsair* affair, and then Mynster's refusal to condemn Goldschmidt, were decisive turning points. As Kierkegaard's interpretation of Christianity has leaned further towards ideals of sacrifice, suffering and martyrdom, becoming more and more uncompromising in rejecting 'the world', he has come to believe that Mynster himself is 'without character': not a true religious teacher but merely an orator, a rhetorician – in short, 'a journalist'. He knows that his 'defence' of true Christianity is 'something like a plague to Bishop M. – for the truth and such matters do not concern him'. No doubt the Bishop is sleeping soundly in his comfortable residence around the corner. Kierkegaard, the vigilant night-watchman, cannot sleep. He closes his journal, and writes nothing more for three months.

\* \* \*

'Now he is dead,' he began again on 1 March 1854, under the heading 'Bishop Mynster'. 'If he could have been moved to end his life by confessing that what he represented was not really Christianity but a lenient version of it, it would have been extremely desirable, for he carried an entire age.' Kierkegaard believed that 'deep down' Mynster had conceded to him 'with respect to matters of the spirit', but refused to acknowledge this openly. The preface to *Practice in Christianity* had called for 'admission and confession concerning oneself' – and if Mynster had admitted that even he, the Bishop of Zealand, fell short of the highest Christian ideals, then Kierkegaard's task as an author would have been fulfilled. But he had waited in vain for this confession. Now, he concluded, 'everything is changed: now the only thing left is that Mynster preached Christianity firmly into an illusion.' He condemned the Bishop not for failing to follow the most radical teachings of Jesus and the apostles – for of course he too failed in this – but for passing off the false for the true.

Bishop Mynster had died at the end of January, four weeks before Kierkegaard returned to his journal to write this entry. Mynster gave his last sermon on 26 December 1853; for once, Kierkegaard did not go to hear him preach, and in retrospect he took this as a sign from

God: 'Now it must happen. You must break with your father's tradition.' In early February, two days before Mynster's funeral, Martensen included a eulogy to the late Bishop in his Sunday sermon,
exhorting his congregation to 'imitate his faith'. 'From the man whose
precious memory fills our hearts,' declared Martensen, 'our thoughts
are led back to the whole succession of truth-witnesses that like a
holy chain stretches through the ages from the days of the Apostles to
our own day.' Bishop Mynster was, he continued, a link in this holy
chain, an 'authentic truth-witness'.

Within days Kierkegaard drafted a scathing attack on Martensen's
memorial discourse. 'Bishop Mynster a truth-witness!' – when this
meant someone who 'unconditionally suffers for the doctrine', whose
faith leads him 'into spiritual trials, into anxieties of soul, into torments of spirit'. To prove Martensen's error in linking Mynster to the
apostles, Kierkegaard cited the First Letter to the Corinthians, where
Paul was particularly blunt in contrasting worldly power and arrogance with the humiliations of Christian discipleship. 'You are held
in honour, but we in disrepute,' Paul wrote to the Greeks in Corinth,
'we are hungry and thirsty, we are poorly clothed and beaten and
homeless . . . We have become like the rubbish of the world.' Kierkegaard accused Martensen of playing at Christianity 'entirely in the
same sense as the child plays at being a soldier' – by removing all the
dangers.

Through the spring of 1854 he drafted more polemical articles contrasting contemporary Christendom with New Testament teachings,
but he did not publish them. He upset his relatives by denouncing
Bishop Mynster at the dinner table. Meanwhile, he elaborated his
critique of worldliness in his journal, insisting on the most radical
demands of original Christianity. This was a religion that asked its
adherents to let go of the 'egotistical trivia' with which most human
beings filled their lives: 'commerce, marriage, begetting children,
amounting to something in the world' – the cornerstones of the
respectable society that now passed itself off as a Christian community. He blamed women for imposing on men 'all the nonsense of
finitude', and deplored the 'aggressive egotism' of the wife and mother
who loves herself 'by loving those who are her own'. Women were
naturally inclined to family life, which drew men away from their

spiritual concerns – for this reason, Kierkegaard added, nuns deserved to be esteemed above monks, 'for when she renounces this life, and marriage, the woman gives up much more than does the man'.

He found some support for these views in Schopenhauer's essays, which articulated an otherworldly (and misogynistic) pessimism in beautifully lucid German prose. He appreciated Schopenhauer's polemical bent – his critiques of Hegel, of academic philosophy, of Christian theology – as well as his emphasis on asceticism, suffering and compassion, drawn from ancient Indian spirituality as well as from Jesus's teachings. But he complained that Schopenhauer's reclusive way of life showed that he had no ethical character:

> He leads a withdrawn existence, occasionally emitting a thunderstorm of epithets – which are ignored. No. Approach the matter differently. Go to Berlin. Move the stage for these scoundrels out into the street. Endure being the most notorious person of all, recognized by everyone . . . This, you see, undermines the vileness of ignoring. That is what I have practised – on a smaller scale, of course – here in Copenhagen: they became fools with their ignoring. And then I have even dared to do one additional thing – precisely because I have been placed under religious command – I have voluntarily dared to expose myself to being caricatured and ridiculed by the whole mob, from the simple people to the aristocrats, all in order to explode the illusions.

More than a decade after *Fear and Trembling*, Kierkegaard's own existence was still caught in a dialectic between worldly achievement and ascetic renunciation. He still believed that neither of these alternatives, though both great temptations for him, were the highest way of being human, that neither were true Christianity. In 1843 he had been inspired by Abraham to envisage a return to the world, an embrace of finite life, which was empowered by divine grace; he had compared the old father's journey up and down Mount Moriah to a balletic leap, animated by an invisible inward movement that sacrificed the world and then received it back again as a gift. Now the same dialectic pushed Kierkegaard into a different way of being in the world: collision with the established order, disdain for political life, conspicuous suffering, a 'martyrdom of laughter'.

Nevertheless, he held back from publishing his articles attacking

Christendom. At first he did so to maintain a lofty distance from the debate about Bishop Mynster's successor: Martensen was the preferred candidate of the conservatives, led by the prime minister A. S. Ørsted, while H. N. Clausen, who had taught Kierkegaard biblical exegesis at university, was supported by the National Liberal Party and by the King. But even after Martensen was appointed Bishop of Zealand, head of the Danish People's Church, in April 1854, Kierkegaard still held fire. For there was also Regine. He could sacrifice many things, but his connection with her – their frequent passings, his sense of responsibility and of a deep, unspoken reconciliation between them – was a kind of anchor in the world. His concern for her soul, his reluctance to denounce the religion by which she lived, made him pause before charging into battle.

Through the summer and the autumn of 1854 he waited. Then in December he sent his first article protesting against Martensen's eulogy on Mynster to his friend Giødvad, editor of *The Fatherland*, to be published in the newspaper. By then Regine's husband Johan Frederik Schlegel had been promoted from Head of the Colonial Office to Governor of the West Indian Islands. In 1855 Schlegel would take up this post – and Regine would leave Denmark.

Bishop Mynster had been loved in life, and virtually 'canonized' in death, yet Kierkegaard's article denounced him as a fraud. Mynster's preaching, he argued, 'veiled, suppressed, omitted some of what is decisively Christian, what is too inconvenient for us human beings, what would make our lives strenuous, prevent us from enjoying life', and Mynster's existence fell even further short of true Christianity – 'he was not in character, not even in the character of his preaching'. An authentic Christian truth-witness, Kierkegaard insisted, 'is a person who in poverty witnesses for the truth, is so unappreciated, hated, detested, so mocked, insulted, laughed to scorn'. Martensen's memorial discourse was, he added, self-serving – 'a worthy monument to Prof. Martensen himself', which 'called to mind Prof. Martensen for the vacant bishopric'. The article concluded that by calling Mynster a truth-witness, Martensen replaced the danger and risk of Christianity 'with power (to be a danger to others), goods, advantages, abundant enjoyment of even the most select refinements', and thus 'played a game' with holiness and truth: 'Truly, there is something that is more against Christianity than any heresy, any schism, more against it than all heresies and schisms together, and it is this: to play at Christianity.'

Kierkegaard's article appeared in *The Fatherland* a week before Christmas, and eight days before Martensen was consecrated as Bishop in the Church of Our Lady. Before the year was out Bishop Martensen published a lengthy, supercilious response in *Berling's Times*, defending Mynster – and himself – and predicting that Kierkegaard would justify his 'slovenly' attack by 'some other, higher morality of genius, perhaps even by some other, higher religious requirement that . . . gives him a criterion for his conduct far elevated above the ordinary'. Kierkegaard read Martensen's article, then tore it into little pieces to be swept away by the woman who cleaned his rooms. Two days later he published a second piece in *The Fatherland*, repeating his objections to the claim that Mynster was a truth-witness, and adding disdainfully that Martensen's criticism of his conduct 'makes no impression on me at all': it was based on a misunderstanding, and in any case 'Martensen is too subaltern a personality to be able to be impressive.' He continued his barrage of *Fatherland* articles against Martensen's 'blasphemy' into the new year, 1855, but at the end of January he ceased fire. His attack provoked much indignation: several pastors stepped forward to defend their new Bishop – who made no further response himself – while Rasmus Nielsen wrote in defence of Kierkegaard in *The Fatherland*.

One morning in mid-March, Kierkegaard encountered Regine on the street near his home. She walked purposefully towards him and passed him close enough to quietly say, 'God bless you – may all go well with you.' At the sound of Regine's voice, unheard for fourteen years, he stopped, almost took a step backwards, then greeted her before she hurried away. Thus in a moment, a glance of an eye, their long silence was broken. Later that day Regine and her husband set sail, crossing the North Sea to Southampton and then journeying on across the Atlantic Ocean. Kierkegaard would never see her again. He had lost his anchor in the world.

A day or two after Regine's departure he sent Jens Giødvad another article. Instead of focusing on the idea of a truth-witness, this one declared 'aloud and publicly' what Kierkegaard had said privately to

Bishop Mynster: that 'official Christianity is not in any sense the Christianity of the New Testament.' He had wanted Mynster to confess this disparity between his own teaching and that of Jesus and the apostles, he explained; without this confession, the Church's proclamation was – perhaps 'unconsciously or well-intentionedly' – an illusion. For the rest of March, Kierkegaard 'kept up a brisk fire against official Christianity', publishing seven articles in less than a fortnight. This renewed, intensified attack, cut loose from his concern for its effect on Regine's faith, encompassed the whole of Danish Christendom. He railed against Denmark's 'silk-and-velvet pastors, who in steadily increasing numbers were ready for service when it appeared that the profit was on the side of Christianity!' His tenth article, 'A Thesis – Just One Single One', was figuratively nailed to the door of the Church of Our Lady: here Kierkegaard stated that while Luther's ninety-five theses were 'terrible' enough, now 'the matter is far more terrible – there is only one thesis. The Christianity of the New Testament does not exist at all.'

Although Kierkegaard had left Abraham behind in his pursuit of a truly religious life, he remained as close as ever to Socrates, the gadfly of Athens. 'The whole of my existence is really the most profound irony,' he wrote in his journal in December 1854, just before he began his attack on official Christianity – and Socrates showed what it means to say that irony is a profound way of life:

> In what did Socratic irony consist? In felicitous turns of phrase and the like? No. Such virtuosity in ironic banter and verbal niceties does not constitute a Socrates. No, the whole of his existence was irony. While every womanizer and businessman, etc. of his time – in short, these thousands – were fully assured of their humanity, and were sure that they knew what it is to be a human being, Socrates lagged behind (ironically) and busied himself with the problem of what it is to be a human being . . . Socrates doubted that a person is human at birth – one does not slip into being human or gain knowledge of what it is to be human so easily.

Kierkegaard owed his first philosophical awakening to this eccentric teacher, who had introduced him to the deepest questions of existence and taught him how to expose the illusions of an entire age.

Socrates did not add another voice to the hubbub of teachings in the Athenian marketplace, but moved among these voices in a way that called them all into question. While at university Kierkegaard had learned from Socrates to ask whether wisdom could be found in any lecture theatre, in any philosophical treatise, in any logical argument; now he asked whether Christianity could be found in any church in Europe. His single thesis – that Christianity no longer existed – was as subversive as any Socratic provocation, for it challenged the assumption underlying his whole culture. And, following Socrates, he found a way to pose his questions in the midst of the crowd. Just as Socrates philosophized in the market square – a place that embodied the values of his age – so Kierkegaard launched his attack on nineteenth-century Christendom in a daily newspaper.

In late May 1855 Kierkegaard sent his twenty-first article to *The Fatherland*, berating Martensen for failing to respond to his critique of official Christianity, despite this being 'much more earnest' than the tussle over Bishop Mynster's reputation at the beginning of the year. And as this final newspaper article appeared Kierkegaard began a fresh assault, publishing the first in a series of polemical pamphlets collectively titled *The Moment*. Once again he summoned his literary and philosophical forces, beginning the first issue with an elegant preface which, recalling Plato's remark that the only people fit to govern are those who have no wish to do so, expressed his reluctance to enter into battle – 'to work in the moment'. He loved writing, he explained, and his 'polemical nature' made him inclined to 'contend with people', but he had also wished 'to satisfy the passion that is in my soul, disdain'. Now, though, his urgent task required him to give up the 'beloved distance' from which he disdained the world. He must also relinquish the leisure of his earlier authorship, in which there was 'always plenty of time to wait for hours, days, weeks to find the expression exactly as I wanted it'. That summer, Kierkegaard cast aside his doubts and poured his energies into a literary activity, devoted now to his single thesis, that echoed the intense productions of the 1840s.

Through June, July, August he published nine issues of *The Moment*, each pamphlet a collection of articles seeking to dispel the 'enormous illusion' of contemporary Christianity. 'All religion in which there is any truth aims at a person's total transformation,' he argued, which meant not just inward change but a new relationship to the world, breaking with all attachments to family, possessions, and professional success. The apostle Paul, he pointed out, was not married, had no official position, earned no money from his spiritual labour. Yet instead of teaching this hard, narrow path, the pastors of Christendom offered 'to glue families together more and more egotistically and to arrange beautiful, glorious family festivities – for example, baptism and confirmation, which compared with, for example, picnics and other family delights, have their own special charm – that they are "also" religious'. And pastors were no more inclined than anyone else to follow the path of renunciation: 'One cannot live on nothing. One hears this so often, especially from pastors. And the pastors are the very ones who perform this feat: Christianity does not exist at all – and yet they live on it.' Kierkegaard called on his readers to stop going to church; he no longer went himself, and was often seen in the Athenaeum, a private library, on Sunday mornings.

These explosive pamphlets 'aroused a great sensation', provoking outrage, enthusiasm, and plenty of gossip. Many students were inspired by the radical message of The Moment, while the older generation tended to be sceptical and indignant. 'I am in complete agreement with your judgement of Kierkegaard's behaviour,' wrote the eminent poet Carsten Hauch to his friend Bernhard Severin Ingemann, who had complained of 'the impudence and shamelessness' of the polemic against the Church. 'All reverence is to be uprooted from the heart,' Hauch lamented: 'if nothing on earth be respected, nothing in heaven need be respected either. How unfortunate is the younger generation, which is educated and grows up under these auspices.' Professor Sibbern, now approaching his seventies, still saw the good in his former student, but he regretted that Kierkegaard's 'onesidedness' now dominated his philosophy – and Sibbern regarded 'the anger he has stirred up against himself as a good testimony to the Danish people's sense of truth, justice and gratitude [to Bishop Mynster]'.

Others, though – and not just rebellious theology students – were sympathetic to Kierkegaard's cause and took his provocations seriously. One of his acquaintances, Pastor Birkedal, felt 'the strong words cast a profound shadow' over him as he read *The Moment*: 'I couldn't shake off these questions, but had to subject my entire spiritual posture to renewed testing.' Magdalene Hansen, a follower of Grundtvig and wife of the artist Constantin Hansen, told a friend that 'it has been a continuing source of sorrow to me to hear people tear S.K. apart and, so to speak, diligently deafen themselves to the truth in his conduct in order to discern his human weakness all the more distinctly – as if the question were, What sort of a person is S.K.? and not, Am I a Christian?'

Those who encountered Kierkegaard on the streets of Copenhagen in the midst of his full-blown attack on Christendom found him 'quite his usual self in conversation, even though his voice was weaker and his glance sadder'. When Hans Brøchner met him out walking one summer evening, he was surprised by the great 'clarity and calmness' with which he discussed *The Moment*. Although Brøchner knew many people who were 'in profound sympathy' with Kierkegaard's polemic, he saw how thoroughly this 'ferocious battle' had disrupted his friend's life and consumed his energies – and yet Kierkegaard still showed 'his usual equanimity of mind and cheerfulness', and also his sparkling sense of humour.

In September 1855 his former friend and old adversary M. A. Goldschmidt assessed the 'Kierkegaardian dispute' with his usual perceptiveness in his journal *North and South*. 'Until now it has not been clear whether or not K. was a noble character,' wrote Goldschmidt. 'He lived in the world without participating in the business of the world. He took no actions, he was free of visible flaws but also of the temptations of the world, because he didn't concern himself with them, he didn't struggle. On the contrary, he was viewed as a noble thinker. Yet . . . it can be said – truly, without any bitterness, perhaps bluntly (but he himself has served as an exemplar of bluntness) – that he is an unhappy thinker. Many of the outbursts issuing from him testify to sufferings that his pride will not confess.'

By then Kierkegaard was writing the tenth issue of *The Moment*. He was exhausted, and had a painful cough. One evening he collapsed at a gathering at Giødvad's house; the next day he fell again, and struggled to his feet with 'a feeling of utter weakness'. He began to feel numbness and piercing pains in his legs. Still he pressed on, preparing the next pamphlet for publication. It included an article titled 'My Task'. 'The only analogy I have before me is Socrates,' Kierkegaard declared here: 'my task is a Socratic task, to sound out the definition of what it is to be a Christian – I do not call myself a Christian (keeping the ideal free), but I can make it manifest that the others are that even less. You, antiquity's noble simple soul, you, the only *human being* I admiringly acknowledge as a thinker – how I long to be able to speak with you for only half an hour, far away from these battalions of thinkers that "Christendom" places in the field under the name of Christian teachers! "Christendom" lies in an abyss of sophistry that is much, much worse than when the Sophists flourished in Greece. Those legions of pastors and Christian assistant professors are all sophists, supporting themselves by making those who understand nothing believe something, and then making this human number the authority for what the truth is, what Christianity is.'

He had completed this issue of *The Moment*, though not yet sent it to the printer, when on 2 October he collapsed in the street. A carriage took him home, where he managed to take off his hat to his landlady 'with a charming look', and then drove on to Frederiks Hospital. He was admitted to a private room with a view of the hospital gardens. He described his condition to a doctor, who diligently took notes: 'The patient cannot offer any specific reason for his present sickness. However, he does associate it with drinking cold seltzer water last summer, with a dark dwelling, together with the exhausting intellectual work that he believes is too taxing for his frail physique. He considers the sickness fatal. His death is necessary for the cause which he has devoted all his intellectual strength to resolving, for which he has worked alone, and for which alone he believes that he has been intended; hence the penetrating thought in conjunction with so frail a physique. If he goes on living, he must continue his religious battle; but in that case it will peter out, while, on the contrary, by his death it will maintain its strength and, he believes, its victory.'

Kierkegaard's nephews Michael and Henrik Lund were both physicians at the hospital, and they visited him every day. His niece Henriette Lund also visited, and sensed that 'a feeling of victory was mixed in with the pain and sadness', for his face 'glowed' and 'his eyes shone like stars'. His brother Peter Christian came to the hospital, but Kierkegaard refused to see him. He knew, however, that sooner or later Peter Christian would go to his modest lodgings on Klædeboderne and find locked in his desk a sealed document addressed to him and marked 'To be opened after my death' – and that Peter Christian would open it, and read:

*Dear Brother,*

*It is of course my will that my former fiancée, Mrs. Regine Schlegel, inherit without condition whatever little I may leave. If she herself will not accept it, she is to be asked if she would be willing to administer it for distribution to the poor.*

*What I wish to give expression to is that to me an engagement was and is just as binding as a marriage, and that therefore my estate is her due, exactly as if I had been married to her.*

*Your brother*
*S. Kierkegaard.*

Kierkegaard also expected Peter Christian to find in his desk a second sealed document, dated August 1851, containing his literary testament: 'The unidentified one whose name shall one day be identified – to whom all my activity as an author is dedicated – is my erstwhile fiancée, Mrs. Regine Schlegel.'

When Emil Boesen heard of his friend's illness, he made the long journey from his Jutland home to Copenhagen. After two weeks in the hospital Kierkegaard's lower body was paralysed, and he felt that death was near; Emil found him 'gentle and at peace'. 'It seemed as though he wanted me to come so that he could say something,' Emil wrote to his wife Louise back in Jutland. 'How strange it is now, when he is perhaps going to die, that I, who was his confidant for so many years and was then separated from him, have come here almost to be his father confessor . . . Much of what he talks about I may not report.'

Kierkegaard spoke to his old friend about his 'thorn in the flesh', a secret suffering which prevented him from having ordinary relationships. 'I therefore concluded that it was my task to be extraordinary, which I sought to carry out as best I could,' he told Emil. 'I was a plaything of Governance . . . And that was also what was wrong with

Frederiks Hospital, Copenhagen

my relationship to Regine. I had thought it could be changed, but it couldn't, so I dissolved the relationship.' In recent years he had alluded to this 'thorn in the flesh' several times in his journals, but he was determined to hide its nature from posterity.

'I am financially ruined,' Kierkegaard went on, 'and now I have nothing, only enough to pay the expenses of my burial. I began with a little, twenty-some thousand, and I saw that this amount could last for a certain length of time – ten to twenty years. It has now been seventeen years, that was a great thing.' The doctors did not understand his illness, he said: 'It is psychical, and now they want to treat it in the usual medical fashion. It's bad. Pray for me that it will soon be over . . . What matters is to get as close to God as possible.'

By Emil's third visit, on 18 October, Kierkegaard was very weak. He slept badly at night and dozed a little in the daytime. His head hung down on his chest and his hands trembled. Emil asked him if there was anything he still wanted to say. 'No. Yes, greet everyone for me, I have liked them all very much, and tell them that my life is

PHILOSOPHER OF THE HEART

a great suffering, unknown and inexplicable to other people. Everything looked like pride and vanity, but it wasn't. I am absolutely no better than other people, and I have said so and have never said anything else.' Could he pray in peace? 'Yes, I can do that. So I pray first for the forgiveness of sins, that everything might be forgiven; then I pray that I might be free of despair at the time of my death, and I am often struck by the saying that death must be pleasing to God. And then I pray for something I very much want, that is, that I might be aware a bit in advance of when death will come.'

Emil visited him every day for a fortnight. There were always fresh flowers by his bed, brought by Ilia Marie Fibiger, a writer who served as a hospital attendant – 'At night she is the supervisor of the hospital. In the daytime she supervises me,' Kierkegaard joked. Emil was troubled by his refusal to take Holy Communion from a pastor – no, not even from his lifelong friend – though he would accept it from a layman. That would be difficult to arrange, Emil said. 'Then I will die without it.' A few days later they talked about his attack on the Church, on which they could not agree. Kierkegaard had used his last few hundred rix-dollars to publish *The Moment*; how strange, remarked Emil kindly, that his resources had just sufficed. 'Yes,' he replied, 'and I am very happy about it, and very sad, because I cannot share my joy with anyone.'

Soon after this visit the conversation that for four decades had flowed so abundantly from his lips dwindled to a few sentences, a few words, until he was almost incapable of speaking. Emil returned to his wife. Day by day, as the dry leaves fell outside his window, Kierkegaard's paralysis worsened and his strength declined. He drifted into unconsciousness, and died after sunset on 11 November: the feast of St Martin, and the last day of autumn. After the light left his eyes, the diamond ring Regine had once worn shone on his hand in the moonlight.

# Kierkegaard's Afterlife

Throughout his life Kierkegaard wrestled with the question of exis tence: how to be a human being in the world? For him, as for most of his contemporaries – and for many of us now – another question of existence hovered behind, above, below this one, inextricably linked to it but also pointing in another direction. What happens to human beings after they die? Is this life a stage on our journey to eternity? Does it bear the traces of countless past lives, and sow seeds for the soul's next incarnation? Or does life end with death, and nothing more?

Hegel's lectures on the philosophy of religion, which were published posthumously in 1832, prompted a fierce debate about the Christian doctrine of immortality. Ludwig Feuerbach ended his academic career by arguing that people endure after death only as collective historical memories, while Friedrich Richter suggested that our eternal life consists in our descendants and our works. In Denmark this theological controversy was restrained by censorship laws prohibiting, on penalty of exile, any publication denying the immortality of the soul. But in 1837 Kierkegaard's philosophy teacher Poul Martin Møller published a long essay titled 'Thoughts on the Possibility of Proofs of Immortality', where he argued that Hegelian philosophy was too abstract to deal with this question. In 1841 J. L. Heiberg wrote 'The Soul after Death', an apocalyptic poem, which Martensen reviewed in *The Fatherland*.

Kierkegaard followed these debates, of course, but he did not contribute to them until 1844, in *The Concept of Anxiety*, where he claimed that recent 'metaphysical and logical efforts' to prove personal immortality were self-defeating: 'strangely enough, while this is taking place, certitude declines'. When he analysed Christian faith in *Concluding Unscientific Postscript*, he declared that 'immortality is the subjective individual's most passionate interest', and argued that the power of a person's faith in his eternal destiny lay in this passion, not in any logical demonstration. When these thoughts were published Kierkegaard was almost thirty-three years old – and, he believed, close to death; for many years he had expected to die before his thirty-fourth birthday.

In 1847, surprised to be still alive, he returned to the question of immortality in one of his *Christian Discourses*, published in the spring of 1848. His sermon 'There Will Be the Resurrection of the Dead, of the Righteous – and of the Unrighteous' was intended, he proclaimed, to 'violate security' and to 'disturb peace of mind'. Every proof of immortality treated the soul's fate as a universal question, but Kierkegaard argued that this question always concerns a single individual: 'in *my* view it pertains to *me* most of all, just as in *your* view it pertains to *you* most of all.' And no one, he continued, should be so sure of his own salvation that he begins to speculate on another's eschatological prospects: 'Save me, O God, from ever being completely sure; keep me unsure to the end so that then, if I receive eternal blessedness, I might be completely sure that I have it by grace!'

In his 1849 *Godly Discourses* on the lily and the bird he took a more mystical, panentheist direction, suggesting that the Christian doctrine of eternal life means 'abiding in God' in this life as well as beyond it. 'If you abide in God, then whether you live or you die, whether things go well or badly for you while you are alive; whether you die today or only after seventy years; and whether you find your death at the bottom of the sea, at its greatest depth, or you are exploded in the air: you still do not come to be outside of God, you *abide* – thus you remain present to yourself in God.'

As on so many issues, Kierkegaard rose above the scholarly debate on immortality among his peers and showed why the entire discussion was misguided. Yet his public pronouncements on the afterlife were not merely polemical. His trusted servant, Anders Westergaard, once asked him, as a learned man, to give assurance of the immortality of the soul – this would comfort him a great deal, Anders said. No, replied Kierkegaard: we are all equally ignorant on this question.

Each person must choose between the one possibility and the other, and conviction will follow in accordance with his choice.

Kierkegaard chose eternal life, along with the deep anxiety and deep peace this belief brought him. Whatever the fate of his soul, his afterlife in this world has been extraordinary. I write this concluding chapter in April 2017 at the Søren Kierkegaard Research Centre at the University of Copenhagen, which this year moved from the centre of the city to a vast new campus in Amagerbro, south of the medieval ramparts. Parts of the site are still under construction, and on the newly laid lawns you can see joins between the slabs of turf. On the day I arrived at the campus it was difficult to find the right building, and once inside it – one of several cavernous, light-filled blocks of glass and creamy concrete – I couldn't find the Søren Kierkegaard Research Centre. I asked a passing law student: she wasn't sure, but then she exclaimed 'Oh – there he is!' and pointed to the large bust of Kierkegaard outside the entrance to the Centre. She had recognized him as easily as his acquaintances on the streets of nineteenth-century Copenhagen.

Outside the Søren Kierkegaard Research Centre

The research centre houses offices for about a dozen Kierkegaard scholars employed by the university, and desks for graduate students. Ettore Rocca, an Italian professor, has kindly let me lodge in his office while he is away: one wall is filled with works on Kierkegaard in several languages, and there are nine shelves of Kierkegaard's Danish writings. The offices open onto a library stocked with translations of his books: I try to decipher the titles, and find *Repetition* in Russian, *Fear and Trembling* in Icelandic, *Either/Or* in Slovenian, *Philosophical Fragments* in Portuguese, *The Concept of Anxiety* in Korean, *The Book on Adler* in Japanese, *The Concept of Irony* in Polish, *The Sickness unto Death* in Lithuanian, 'Diary of a Seducer' in Turkish, *From the Papers of One Still Living* in Hungarian, and *Works of Love* in Chinese.

Here I can consult entire scholarly volumes about Kierkegaard's reception in Northern, Western, Southern, Eastern and Central Europe, the Near East, Asia, Australia and the Americas. There must be tens of thousands of monographs, chapters and articles on every conceivable aspect of his work – his philosophy, his theology, his politics; his views on Shakespeare, punctuation, and pietist hymns; his influence on French existentialists, Italian Catholics and Latin American liberation theologians in the twentieth century. There are also books about men like J. P. Mynster, H. L. Martensen, J. L. Heiberg and F. C. Sibbern, once Copenhagen's most illustrious figures, now remembered chiefly for their relation to the poetic gadfly they tried to keep at arm's length. I can read an English catalogue of Kierkegaard's library, consisting of more than two thousand books, which were sold by auction a few months after his death.

Back in the centre of the city, most visitors to the Copenhagen Museum want to see the permanent Søren A. Kierkegaard Collection, which includes his tall writing desk, the key to 2 Nytorv, a lock of his hair, his pipe, his reading glasses, some coffee cups, a silver pen holder, and the engagement ring he gave to Regine and later wore on his own finger. His manuscripts, journals and other literary remains are archived in the Royal Danish Library – although when in 1856 his relatives offered the library four of his books with handwritten annotations, the head librarian refused 'for fear that too many people would want to have a look at them'.

Kierkegaard's papers, which filled a desk and two large chests of drawers in his rooms on Klædeboderne, ended up in his brother's house. In 1859 Peter Christian Kierkegaard, by then Bishop of Aalborg, arranged for *The Point of View for My Work as an Author* to be published. Peter Christian was not sure what to do with the rest of the papers, and for years they lay piled up in the provincial bishop's residence. Eventually he appointed a former newspaper editor, H. P. Barfod, to 'examine and register, etc. Søren's papers'. Barfod soon came across a journal entry from 1846 about Kierkegaard's father: 'The frightful story of the man – who as a little boy watching sheep on the heath of Jutland, in great suffering, in hunger and cold, once stood on a hilltop and cursed God – and the man was unable to forget this when he was 82 years old.' He showed it to Peter Christian, who wept and said, 'That is my father's story, and *ours, too*.'

The first volume of *Søren Kierkegaard's Posthumous Papers* appeared in 1869, and was met with such strong criticism that Barfod, having spent years inhabiting Kierkegaard's consciousness, wrote a preface to the second volume defending his efforts to reveal 'the colossal and clandestine workshop of the soul [of] this thinker, this melancholy hermit, in his daily sufferings'. Despite the controversy that continued to follow Kierkegaard's writings two decades after his death, the Royal Danish Library agreed to receive his manuscripts and journals in 1875. Since 1918 a statue of Kierkegaard has reclined, in a very Danish manner, on a chair in the library's garden.

The entrance to the Royal Danish Library is now on Søren Kierkegaard Plads, which leads along Christians Brygge to Børsgade, the wide street where Regine lived as a girl. During my days in the library's reading room I leafed, heart racing, through boxes of Kierkegaard's letters to Regine and notebooks containing *Repetition*, *Fear and Trembling*, *The Sickness unto Death* and *Practice in Christianity*, breaking for lunch at the café in the library's glassy modern extension, named after Kierkegaard's final polemics: *The Moment* or, more literally, *The Glance of an Eye*. I sat by Café Øieblikket's huge window overlooking the water and watched pedestrians, cyclists and kayakers pass by. Next door to the café is Søren K, a smart minimalist restaurant.

Kierkegaard in the Royal Danish Library's garden

Yesterday, a Sunday, I walked up through Nørrebro to Assistens Cemetery, where Kierkegaard was buried. His grave is in the oldest part of the cemetery, shared with his parents, his eldest sister Maren, and his brother Søren Michael, who died in childhood, though the family plot is dominated by the tombstone for Michael Pedersen Kierkegaard's first wife, Kirstine. During the 1840s Kierkegaard wrote instructions for repairs to the burial plot, and for a new stone to include his own name, which now marks his grave. Beneath 'Søren Aabye' is engraved, as he requested, a verse from an eighteenth-century hymn by Brorson, whose hymns he sang with his father at the Moravian meeting house:

In yet a little while
I shall have won;
Then the whole fight
Will all at once be done.
Then I may rest
In bowers of roses
And perpetually
And perpetually
Speak with my Jesus.

Kierkegaard also instructed that 'the whole burial plot be levelled and seeded with a fine species of low grass, but a tiny spot of bare soil should show in the four corners, and in each of these corners should be planted a little bush of Turkish roses, as I believe they are called, some very tiny ones, dark red'. Though peaceful, the grave is not a lonely place: during the hour I was there, about twelve visitors strolled by in the April sun, pausing to read the words Kierkegaard chose to mark his departure from the world. Daffodils bloomed in the little plot, as well as the red flowers in each corner.

At the graveside, April 2017;
Kierkegaard's tombstone is on the left.

Kierkegaard's funeral in the first week of winter, 1855, was not so tranquil. Ironically, it was his old enemy M. A. Goldschmidt who confirmed in print Kierkegaard's own hope about the significance of his death: 'The most dangerous part of his actions against the clergy and the official Church is now only just beginning, because his fate undeniably has something of the martyr about it: the sincerity of his passion helped hasten the course of his illness and bring about his death,' Goldschmidt wrote in his journal *North and South* a few days after Kierkegaard died. Meanwhile, Kierkegaard's most respectable relatives – Peter Christian Kierkegaard, his brother-in-law Johan Christian Lund, and his nephews Carl Ferdinand Lund and Henrik Ferdinand Lund – decided to hold the funeral service in the Church of Our Lady.

'The crowd in the aisles was large,' reported Hans Christian Andersen to the ballet dancer August Bournonville; although women unrelated to the deceased were not supposed to attend funerals, 'ladies in red and blue hats were coming and going'. Bishop Martensen did not attend, but he kept a close eye on the proceedings: 'Today, after a large service at the Church of Our Lady, Kierkegaard was buried; there was a large cortège of mourners (in grand style, how ironic!),' he wrote to his friend Pastor Gude on 18 November 1855. 'We have scarcely seen the equal of the *tactlessness* shown by the family in having him buried on a *Sunday*, between two religious services, from the nation's *most important church* . . . The newspapers will soon be running a spate of burial stories. I understand the cortège was composed primarily of young people and a large number of obscure personages. There were no dignitaries, unless one wishes to include R. Nielsen in this category,' the Bishop sneered.

One of the obscure young people in Vor Frue Kirke that day was Frantz Sodemann, a theology student, who eagerly wrote to his fiancée's father with news of the 'scandal' he had just witnessed:

There was an enormous crowd present. Church was full to bursting; it was all I could do to get a spot upstairs by one of the columns at the back, from which I could see the coffin. Rumour has it that the clergy had refused to speak, some say at the suggestion of Bishop Martensen . . . No clergy wearing vestments were present other than

Archdeacon Tryde and Dr. [Peter Christian] Kierkegaard, who gave the eulogy . . . First he explained the family relationships, how their father, who had once herded sheep on the moors of Jutland, had loved the children most intensely; that gradually all but the two of them had departed this life . . . Next he said that this was not the time or the place to discuss Søren's actions; that we neither dared to nor could accept much of what Søren had said . . . ; that [Søren] himself had not been conscious of how far he had gone; and that he had gone too far . . . Then the body was carried away.

The author of this letter regretted not following the crowds to the cemetery, where 'things really came to a head'. After a handful of earth was cast on the small coffin, Kierkegaard's nephew Henrik Sigvard Lund, who worked at Frederiks Hospital and spent time with his uncle until the very end of his life, stepped forward to protest against the proceedings. Archdeacon Tryde attempted to stop him, for only ordained clergy were allowed to speak at the graveside – but the crowd urged Henrik on with shouts of 'Bravo! Bravo!' and the young man continued his speech: 'He, my deceased friend, stands and falls with his writings. But I have not heard them mentioned in a single word!'

Henrik read aloud from the Book of Revelation and quoted an issue of *The Moment*. 'Is what we are all witnessing today – namely, that this poor man, despite all his energetic protests in thought, word and deed, in life and death, is being buried by "the Official Church" as a beloved member – is this in accordance with his words?' he asked the gathered mourners. Brandishing his Bible and his uncle's pamphlets, he declared that Kierkegaard had been 'violated' by a Church that resembled 'the great whore of Babylon, with whom all the kings of the earth have fornicated'.

Four days later, Jens Giødvad printed Henrik Lund's graveside speech in *The Fatherland*. 'To me, the entire affair is a distorted picture of Søren K.; I don't understand it!' wrote Hans Christian Andersen in another letter. Bishop Martensen made sure Lund was prosecuted, and the young man had to make a public apology and pay a fine of one hundred rix-dollars. Poor Martensen: even now his massive head, cast in bronze and mounted alongside Mynster next to the Church of Our Lady, looks nervous, as though at any moment he expects Kierkegaard to come round the corner, waving his walking-cane.

Bishop Martensen outside Vor Frue Kirke

\* \* \*

As if Kierkegaard's persistent attacks and his troublesome funeral were not punishment enough for Martensen's sins, on Sunday 5 May 2013 another service was held for Kierkegaard in the Church of Our Lady: the commemoration of his two-hundredth birthday. From the church's polished pulpit the velvet-clad Bishop of Copenhagen preached to a congregation that included Queen Margrethe II and several cabinet ministers. Scholars of Kierkegaard from all over the world were present – and on them, at least, the irony of the great state occasion was not lost. From the Church of Our Lady the most illustrious dignitaries moved on to the University of Copenhagen's ceremonial hall, where a new fifty-five-volume critical edition of Kierkegaard's writings, in preparation for years under the visionary direction of Niels Jørgen Cappelørn, stood complete. Cappelørn, a Lutheran pastor and

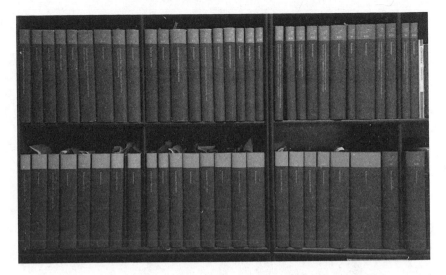

Søren Kierkegaards Skrifter, 2013: texts and commentaries

theologian, founded the Søren Kierkegaard Research Centre in 1994 and made it his life's work to allow Kierkegaard's journals and notebooks to be read alongside the published works: he wrote 41,512 of the 72,628 explanatory notes contained in the new edition. After this blue-bound monument of scholarship was formally presented to the university, the birthday festivities continued into the evening with a premiere of *Promenade Abyss*, a one-act opera with lyrics inspired by *The Sickness unto Death*.

Kierkegaard's birthday was commemorated in many other cities around the world; in London, the celebration took place one week early at St Katharine's, the Danish Lutheran Church next to Regent's Park. Kierkegaard's favourite New Testament passage from the Letter of James was one of the texts for the Sunday morning service, and the sermon recalled his life and his works. It was a beautiful service: I loved the simple grace of the bare white church, and was touched by the openness with which the pastor invited everyone to take communion. After a lunch of rye bread, herrings and Danish cheese, there were lectures by three academics: Joakim Garff, Kierkegaard's biographer from Copenhagen; George Pattison, then a professor at Oxford; and me. I gave a talk about Mary, Jesus's mother, whose faith and courage Kierkegaard admired throughout his authorship, though I began by remembering Anne Kierkegaard, the middle-aged peasant who gave birth to Denmark's greatest philosopher.

Joakim Garff, whose rich, sophisticated biography *SAK* is almost as long as *Either/Or*, spoke about the peculiar task of writing the life of Kierkegaard. Though writing was a kind of therapy for him, it was also true, said Garff, that 'Kierkegaard in his journals did not talk only to reveal but also to conceal', writing and editing his own papers 'as if future readers stood and looked over his shoulder', and 'planning his own posthumous rebirth'. While the journals return again and again to Regine, to Mynster and to 'Myself', they skip across an extraordinary range of subjects, from fishwives to the Incarnation, and 'not even the biographical culmination points are straightforwardly accessible'. For example, Kierkegaard represented Regine only in a fragmentary way during their engagement, and readers 'must go all the way to the end of August 1849 before he presents posterity with his "Relationship to Her"' – in an entry that is marked 'Something Poetic'. Garff described how he tried 'to coax the narrative elements forth' from the 'monstrous material' while allowing Kierkegaard to remain an ambiguous, open-ended figure.

George Pattison's lecture explored Kierkegaard's love of the theatre, and he had written for the occasion a stage adaptation of *Repetition*, which was performed in the church that evening by a small cast of Oxford students. The play brought Kierkegaard to life in a way I could not have imagined possible. As his *alter ego* Constantin Constantius paced across the stage, I marvelled at this echo, in a Camden church, of questions pursued two centuries ago by a small, hunched, bright-eyed figure in odd trousers – pursued from Copenhagen to Berlin, and back across the Baltic Sea, through a series of apartments on Nørregade, Nytorv, Rosenborggade, Østerbrogade and Klædeboderne, in his city's theatres, churches, newspapers, through the pages of countless books, to and fro across the vast stretches of his soul. I found myself in tears.

Without George Pattison I would not have been in the Danish Church that day, nor written a PhD thesis on Kierkegaard – and it would never have occurred to me to write this book. I met George over twenty years ago, when he taught me metaphysics during my first year at university. An Anglican priest as well as a scholar, he was then Dean of Chapel at King's College, Cambridge, and a lecturer in the Faculty of Divinity. He occupied these roles with a combination of lightness and depth, earnestness and irony, which now strikes me as distinctly Kierkegaardian. There is something paradoxical about a Kierkegaard expert holding an official position in the University and the Church: this situation naturally poses a question of existence, and George somehow seemed to find a way to live that question well. When I finished my philosophy degree he agreed to supervise my PhD. Though I was not a very diligent graduate student, George remained generous and patient; he advised me to attend conferences, which I dreaded, and he arranged my Danish lessons, which I neglected. He told me to consider publishing my thesis, but I felt more inclined to burn it – I would invite my friends, and we'd dance round the fire. Staying in Cambridge and doing a PhD was my path of least resistance: it was a way of deferring the question of what to do with my life. I was more interested in travelling and falling in love than in pursuing a career. I had no intention or aspiration to become a Kierkegaard scholar, or a lecturer in philosophy, or any kind of academic.

I became those things anyway, and Kierkegaard remains endlessly interesting to me. This is because he spoke of, and to, a deep need for God within the human heart – a need for love, for wisdom, for peace – and he did so with a rare and passionate urgency. Though he relentlessly pursued 'the task of becoming a Christian', he did not see this as a question of religious identity or affiliation. Perhaps he had too much disdain for institutional religion, but by looking elsewhere he appealed to people who, like the woman who wrote timidly to thank him for his sermon in the Citadel Church, felt uninspired by more conventional Christianity. Through his authorship, which lasted barely more than ten years, he communicated infinite things from his own very human heart – in sparkling prose, with exceptional sensitivity and nuance, and with little trace of dogmatism or moralism.

It is difficult to say what caused my tears as I watched *Repetition* in the Danish Church in 2013, but it had something to do with casting a sideways glance at my life as a whole, and seeing meaning there. Over the years I had often doubted the value of intellectual work, doubted whether the studies of philosophy I had drifted into were what I should be doing, doubted that I had much to offer my students. Sitting in that white church with all the other people who cared enough about Kierkegaard to spend a day celebrating his birthday, I felt a new confidence in whatever it was that brought me there. And in recent weeks, as I have come close to the end of this book, I have been moved in a similar way, though not so much in relation to my own life. Following Kierkegaard through his final months to his last days in Frederiks Hospital, I sensed the mysterious weight of a human life, glimpsed in its entirety. It is elusive and intimate, slight and immense, fragile and astonishing.

# Prayer*

Father in heaven! That which we in the company of other people, especially in the throng of humanity, have such difficulty learning, and which, if we have learned it elsewhere, is so easily forgotten in the company of other people – what it is to be a human being and what, from a godly standpoint, is the requirement for being a human being – would that we might learn it, or, if it has been forgotten, that we might learn it anew from the lily and the bird; would that we might learn it, if not all at once, then learn at least something of it, little by little – would that on this occasion we might from the lily and the bird learn silence, obedience, joy!

* From the beginning of Kierkegaard's *The Lily of the Field and the Bird of the Air: Three Godly Discourses* (1849), translated by Bruce H. Kirmmse.

# Notes

## PREFACE

p. xi     '*A love affair*': S. Kierkegaard, *Concluding Unscientific Postscript to the Philosophical Crumbs*, ed. and trans. Alastair Hannay (Cambridge University Press, 2009), p. 222.

p. xi     '*During the daytime one sees him walking*': *Kierkegaard's Journals and Notebooks, Volume 6: Journals NB11–NB14*, ed. and trans. Niels Jørgen Cappelørn, Alastair Hannay, David Kangas, Bruce H. Kirmmse, George Pattison, Joel D. S. Rasmussen, Vanessa Rumble and K. Brian Söderquist (Princeton University Press, 2013), p. 550.

p. xiv     '*This evening I had a conversation with Magister Søren Kierkegaard*': *Encounters with Kierkegaard*, ed. Bruce Kirmmse, trans. Bruce Kirmmse and Virginia Laursen (Princeton University Press, 1998), p. 59.

p. xv     '*grasp the secret of suffering*': *Concluding Unscientific Postscript*, p. 372.

p. xv     '*because the humblest expression*': ibid, p. 413.

p. xv     '*You are getting on, I said to myself*': ibid, pp. 156–7.

p. xviii     '*silence*': See Niels Jørgen Cappelørn's 'Postscript' to Søren Kierkegaard, *The Lily of the Field and the Bird of the Air: Three Godly Discourses*, trans. Bruce Kirmmse and illustrated by Maja Lisa Engelhardt (New York: Elizabeth Harris Gallery, 2013), pp. 69–72. See also S. Kierkegaard, *The Book on Adler*, ed. trans. Howard V. Hong and Edna H. Hong (Princeton University Press, 1998), p. 280.

## PART ONE

p. 1     '*To be able to fall down in such a way*': S. Kierkegaard, *Fear and Trembling*, ed. C. Stephen Evans and Sylvia Walsh, trans. Sylvia Walsh (Cambridge University Press, 2006), p. 34.

NOTES

CHAPTER I

p. 3    *a 'marvellous armchair'*: S. Kierkegaard, *Letters and Documents*, ed. and trans. Henrik Rosenmeier (Princeton University Press, 2009), p. 152 – letter from S. Kierkegaard to A. F. Krieger, May 1843.

p. 3    *railways straight through Christendom*: the first Prussian railway opened in 1838, from Berlin to Potsdam. The Berlin–Stettin line, which Kierkegaard travelled on in 1843, opened in the early 1840s; the first Danish railway opened in 1844. In 1850 Kierkegaard wrote in his journal: 'The railroad mania is altogether an attempt a la Babel. It is also connected with the end of a cultural era, it is the final dash. Unfortunately, something new began at almost the same moment: 1848. Railroads are related to the idea of intensification of centralization.' *Kierkegaard's Journals and Notebooks, Volume 7: Journals NB15–NB20*, ed. and trans. Niels Jørgen Cappelørn, Alastair Hannay, Bruce H. Kirmmse, David D. Possen, Joel D. S. Rasmussen, Vanessa Rumble and K. Brian Söderquist (Princeton University Press, 2014), p. 112.

p. 3    *Søren Kierkegaard will be back in Copenhagen*: on the details of Kierkegaard's journey home – by train, stagecoach and steamship – see *Kierkegaard's Journals and Notebooks, Volume 2: Journals EE–KK*, ed. and trans. Niels Jørgen Cappelørn, Alastair Hannay, David Kangas, Bruce H. Kirmmse, George Pattison, Vanessa Rumble and K. Brian Söderquist (Princeton University Press, 2008), p. 491.

p. 4    *'He who explains the riddle of Abraham'*: ibid, pp. 154–5: JJ 87 (1843).

p. 4    *'In the morning I go out for a while'*: S. Kierkegaard, *Letters and Documents*, ed. and trans. Henrik Rosenmeier (Princeton University Press, 2009), p. 154 – letter to Emil Boesen, 25 May 1843.

p. 5    *'Then suddenly a thought stirs'*: *Kierkegaard's Journals and Notebooks 2*, pp. 158–9: JJ 99 (1843).

p. 6.    *'If I had had faith, I would have stayed with Regine'*: ibid, p. 164: JJ 115 (17 May 1843).

p. 6    *the high medieval ramparts*: see Niels Thulstrup, *The Copenhagen of Kierkegaard*, ed. Marie Mikulová Thulstrup, trans. Ruth Mach-Zagal (Reitzel, 1986), pp. 24–6. Kierkegaard's favourite philosophy teacher, Poul Møller, wrote a poem about the ramparts, which begins:

The hedge of spring is verdant,
The cloak is cast away,
Maidens sun themselves upon the ramparts.
The air is so lovely,
Their sighs of longing
Known by their silk dresses.

p. 8    *Socrates devoted himself to the question*: for Kierkegaard's clear-
est exposition of Socrates's devotion to 'the problem of what it is
to be a human being', see *Kierkegaard's Journals and Notebooks,
Volume 10: Journals NB31–NB36*, ed. and trans. Niels Jørgen
Cappelørn, Alastair Hannay, Bruce H. Kirmmse, David D. Possen, Joel D. S. Rasmussen and Vanessa Rumble (Princeton
University Press, 2018), p. 371: NB35 2 (December 1854).

p. 9    *'Imagine a cave,' says Socrates*: my reading of Plato's cave is in-
debted to Jonathan Lear: see 'Allegory and Myth in Plato's
*Republic*' and 'The Psychic Efficacy of Plato's Cave', in Jonathan
Lear, *Wisdom Won from Illness: Essays in Philosophy and
Psychoanalysis* (Harvard University Press, 2017), pp. 206–43.

p. 10   *'While I live, I shall never give up philosophy'*: Plato, *Apology*,
29d–31a.

p. 11   *Any ironic utterance calls itself into question*: as Kierkegaard put
it in his dissertation, 'the quality that pervades all irony [is] that
the phenomenon is not the essence but the opposite of the essence':
in other words, the surface meaning is the opposite of the true
meaning. See S. Kierkegaard, *The Concept of Irony with Continual Reference to Socrates*, trans. Howard V. Hong and Edna
H. Hong (Princeton University Press, 1992), p. 247.

p. 11   *'surveys everything and rises infinitely above'*: Friedrich von
Schlegel, *Schlegel's Lucinde and the Fragments*, trans. Peter Fir-
chow (University of Minnesota Press, 1971), p. 148. On Kierkegaard's
response to Romantic irony, see Joel Rasmussen's excellent *Between
Irony and Witness* (T&T Clark, 2005).

p. 12   *'no genuinely human life is possible without irony'*: *The Concept
of Irony*, p. 326. My grasp of Kierkegaard's conception of irony is
deeply indebted to Jonathan Lear's *A Case for Irony* (Harvard University Press, 2014).

p. 14   *'a living, restless thing'*: cited by Roland Bainton in *Here I Stand:
A Life of Martin Luther* (Abingdon-Cokesbury Press, 1951), p.
331, and by S. Kierkegaard in *For Self-Examination / Judge For*

NOTES

*Yourself!*, ed. and trans. Howard V. Hong and Edna H. Hong (Princeton University Press, 1991), pp. 17–18. In his lectures on Romans (1515–16) Luther emphasized that faith is a continuous inward movement. Commenting on Romans 12:2, for example, Luther notes that Paul 'is addressing those who have begun to be Christians, whose life is not at rest [*in quiescere*] but in movement [*in moveri*] from good to better'; that the different phases of spiritual growth in a human being are 'always in motion'; that the Christian must always 'press on' in prayer, so that praying is 'a continuous violent action of the spirit,' like 'a ship going against the stream'. Commenting on Romans 4:7, he argues that when 'people are confident that they are already justified, they come to ruin by their own sense of security'.

CHAPTER 2

p. 15  *'It is quite true what philosophy says'*: Kierkegaard's Journals and Notebooks, Volume 2: Journals EE–KK, ed. and trans. Niels Jørgen Cappelørn, Alastair Hannay, David Kangas, Bruce H. Kirmmse, George Pattison, Vanessa Rumble and K. Brian Söderquist (Princeton University Press, 2008), p. 179: JJ 167 (1843). In his 1838 essay on Hans Christian Andersen, Kierkegaard cited the German theologian Carl Daub, who, according to Kierkegaard, observed that 'life is understood backward through the idea': see *From the Papers of One Still Living*, in S. Kierkegaard, *Early Polemical Writings*, ed. and trans. Julia Watkin (Princeton University Press, 2009), pp. 78, 255.

p. 17  *'managed to get out to R'*: Kierkegaard's Journals and Notebooks, Volume 1: Journals AA–DD, ed. and trans. Niels Jørgen Cappelørn, Alastair Hannay, David Kangas, Bruce H. Kirmmse, George Pattison, Vanessa Rumble and K. Brian Söderquist (Princeton University Press, 2007), p. 47: AA, 54 (1837). 'R—' might mean Regine, or the Rørdams; if the latter, it may indicate that at this time Kierkegaard was most interested in Bolette Rørdam – or that he was by then visiting the Rørdams with the hope of seeing Regine there. In another entry in this journal, Kierkegaard mentions 'going out to Rørdam's to talk to Bolette': see p. 47: AA 53. In 1849 he acknowledged that he felt a certain 'responsibility' to Bolette: they had made an 'impression' on one another, though this attraction was 'in all innocence' and 'purely

268

intellectual': see *Kierkegaard's Journals and Notebooks, Volume 3: Notebooks 1–15*, ed. and trans. Niels Jørgen Cappelørn, Alastair Hannay, David Kangas, Bruce H. Kirmmse, George Pattison, Vanessa Rumble and K. Brian Söderquist (Princeton University Press, 2010), p. 431: Notebook 15, 4 (August to November 1849).

p. 17    *'My God, why should these feelings awaken'*: *Kierkegaard's Journals and Notebooks, Volume 1: Journals AA–DD*, p. 47: AA54 (1837).

p. 18    *When Socrates was asked this question*: see Plato's *Meno*.

p. 18    *'how sad it would be if human beings could only find peace in what lay outside themselves'*: *Søren Kierkegaard's Journals and Papers*, eds. Howard V. Hong and Edna H. Hong (Bloomington: Indiana University Press, 1970), p. 528: Pap. III A 5 (July 10, 1840).

p. 19    *Kierkegaard was obsessed with Mozart's* Don Giovanni: on Kierkegaard's interest in Don Giovanni and his discussion of Don Juan in his writings, see Jacobo Zabalo, 'Don Juan (Don Giovanni): Seduction and its Absolute Medium in Music', in Katalin Nun and Jon Stewart (eds.), *Kierkegaard's Literary Figures and Motifs, Tome I: Agamemnon to Guadalquivir* (Ashgate, 2014), pp. 141–57.

p. 19    *A human being's 'true life'*: *Søren Kierkegaard's Journals and Papers*, pp. 213–14: Pap. III A 1 (July 4 1840).

p. 21    *travelled out to the west coast of Jutland*: Kierkegaard kept a journal during this trip; see *Kierkegaard's Journals and Notebooks, Volume 3: Notebooks 1–15*, pp. 187–98; pp. 567–73. One entry in this Jutland journal, marked with a small cross, reads as follows: 'To you, O God, we turn for *peace* ... but give us also the blessed assurance that nothing could take this peace from us, *not we ourselves*, not our poor, earthly wishes, my wild desires, not the restless craving of my heart!' – p. 189: NB6, 6 (July to August 1840).

p. 21    *'On 8 September I left home'*: see ibid, pp. 431–2: NB15, 4 (August to November, 1849). In the margin by this entry Kierkegaard wrote: 'It must have been on the 10th that she first mentioned Schlegel, for she said not a word on the 8th.'

p. 22    *'beside himself with sorrow'*: *Encounters with Kierkegaard*, ed. Bruce Kirmmse, trans. Bruce Kirmmse and Virginia Laursen (Princeton University Press, 1998), p. 36 – from Regine Schlegel's account of her relationship with Kierkegaard, told to Hanne

Mourier in 1896 following her husband's death that year, subsequently published in Hjalmar Helweg, *Søren Kierkegaard: En psykiatrisk-psykologisk Studie* (H. Hagerups Forlag, 1933), pp. 385–92.

p. 22    *'whom he had loved so much'*: Encounters with Kierkegaard, p. 40.

p. 22    *'what he himself wanted to do'*: ibid, p. 29 – from a letter from Emil Boesen to H. P. Barfod, May 22 1868.

p. 23    *lily of the valley cologne*: see S. Kierkegaard, *Letters and Documents*, ed. and trans. Henrik Rosenmeier (Princeton University Press, 2009), p. 64. Kierkegaard owned a German book on the 'language' or symbolism of flowers, *Die neueste Blumensprache*, published in 1838; see Niels Jørgen Cappelørn, Gert Posselt and Bent Rohde, *Tekstspejle: Om Søren Kierkegaard som bogtilrettelægger, boggiver og bogsamler* (Rosendahls Forlag, 2002), p. 155.

p. 23    *'is not used for tobacco'*: Letters and Documents, p. 74 – letter to Regine Olsen, 30 December 1840.

p. 23    *Each week Kierkegaard read aloud to Regine*: see *Kierkegaard's Journals and Notebooks, Volume 2: Journals EE–KK*, p. 174: JJ 145 (1843).

p. 23    *'Although your playing may not be perfect'*: Letters and Documents, pp. 78–9 – letter to Regine Olsen, undated.

p. 24    *'Know that every time you repeat that you love me'*: ibid, p. 65 – letter to Regine Olsen, undated.

p. 24    *'Now I am safe, now I will settle down'*: ibid, pp. 67–8 – letter to Regine Olsen, undated.

p. 24    *'she fought like a lioness'*: see *Kierkegaard's Journals and Notebooks, Volume 3: Notebooks 1–15*, p. 434: NB15, 4 (August to November 1849)

p. 25    *a 'sense of foreboding'*: Encounters with Kierkegaard, p. 162 – from Henriette Lund, *Eringringer Fra Hjemmet* (Gyldendal, 1909).

p. 25    *'So after all, you have played a terrible game with me'*: see *Kierkegaard's Journals and Notebooks, Volume 3: Notebooks 1–15*, p. 434: NB15, 4 (August to November 1849).

p. 25    *'Uncle Søren immediately arrived'*: Encounters with Kierkegaard, pp. 162–3 – from Henriette Lund, *Eringringer Fra Hjemmet* (Gyldendal, 1909).

p. 26    *'It was an insulting break'*: ibid, pp. 177–8 – from Troels Frederik Troels-Lund, *Et Liv. Barndom og Ungdom* (H. Hagerups Forlag,

1924). Troels-Lund, born in 1840, was an infant at the time of the break-up, so his account was based on family legend.

p. 27     '*In my attack I am beginning to close in on her gradually*': S. Kierkegaard, *Either/Or*, Part I, ed. and trans. Howard V. Hong and Edna H. Hong (Princeton University Press, 1988), pp. 355–6.

p. 27     '*I shall very likely manage things*': ibid, pp. 367–8, 377.

p. 27     '*Never will I call you "my Johannes", for I certainly realize that you have never been that*': ibid, p. 312.

p. 28     *he has had a tall cabinet made from rosewood*: see *Kierkegaard's Journals and Notebooks, Volume 3: Notebooks 1–15*, p. 438: NB15, 6 (August to November 1849).

p. 28     '*one for her, and one for me*': ibid.

p. 28     *a crown of thorns rising from a field*: I saw this 'crown of thorns' when I took a train from Berlin to Angermünde in the spring of 2016, following Kierkegaard's journey in May 1843.

p. 28     *remarkable blue eyes, 'deep and soulful'*: see *Encounters with Kierkegaard*, p. 111. Here Tycho Spang, the son of Kierkegaard's friend Peter Johannes Spang, pastor of Copenhagen's Church of the Holy Spirit, recalls Kierkegaard's visits to his childhood home: 'He prepared food with my sister, tasted the children's food, and was so happy and merry that one could be tempted to think that he was a very happy person with easygoing, hilarious spirits. Then, during this happy, delighted laughter his head could sink way down between his shoulders while he leaned back in his chair and rubbed his hands so that the diamond in his ring would sparkle so much that it rivalled his deep, soulful eyes, which were blue and gentle . . . We *all* liked him, and an old aunt often said to us, "My, but isn't that S.K. a truly nice person!"' Similarly, Otto Wroblewski, who worked in Reitzel's bookshop during the 1840s, recalled Kierkegaard's 'deep blue, melancholy eyes': see *Encounters with Kierkegaard*, p. 110.

p. 28     '*a mixture of good nature and malice*': from Meïr Aron Goldschmidt's autobiography: see *Encounters with Kierkegaard*, p. 65; see also ibid, pp. 111, 116.

## CHAPTER 3

p. 29     '*There is a difference of opinion among the learned as to which seat in a stagecoach is the most comfortable*': S. Kierkegaard, *Fear and Trembling / Repetition*, ed. and trans. Howard V. Hong and Edna H. Hong (Princeton University Press, 1983), pp. 150–51.

p. 30    *Simeon Stylites, the celebrity recluse*: on the title page of the manuscript of *Fear and Trembling*, Kierkegaard wrote 'Simon Stylites, Solo Dancer and Private Individual', but crossed this out and replaced it with the pseudonym 'Johannes de silentio'.

p. 31    *'My goodness, what a thick book'*: Corsaren [*The Corsiar*], 10 March 1843. *The Corsair* was published weekly in Copenhagen between 1840 and 1846.

p. 31    *Johan Ludvig Heiberg*: for a summary of Kierkegaard's relationship to J. L. Heiberg, see Jon Stewart, 'Johan Ludvig Heiberg: Kierkegaard's Criticism of Hegel's Danish Apologist', in *Kierkegaard and His Danish Contemporaries, Tome I: Philosophy, Politics and Social Theory*, ed. Jon Stewart (Ashgate, 2009), pp. 35–76.

p. 31    *'bolts of intellectual lightning'*: see J. L. Heiberg, 'Litterær Vintersæd', *Intelligensblade* 24 (1 March 1843), pp. 285–92.

p. 32    *'The Lord bless thy coming in'*: see S. Kierkegaard, *Either/Or*, Part II, ed. and trans. Howard V. Hong and Edna H. Hong (Princeton University Press, 1988), p. 407.

p. 32    *'I shall never forget to employ the passion of irony'*: S. Kierkegaard, *Letters and Documents*, ed. and trans. Henrik Rosenmeier (Princeton University Press, 2009), p. 155 – letter to Emil Boesen, 25 May 1843.

p. 32    *'With Hegel on my table and in my thoughts'*: this autobiographical account was first published in an 1840 article entitled 'Johan Ludvig Heiberg', by Christian Molbech, in *Dansk poetisk Anthologie*, edited by Molbech. See Jon Stewart (ed.), *Johan Ludvig Heiberg: Philosopher, Littérateur, Dramaturge, and Political Thinker* (Museum Tusculanum Press, 2008), pp. 222–3.

p. 33    *He followed Martensen's influential courses on theology and the history of philosophy*: see George Pattison, 'How Kierkegaard Became "Kierkegaard": The Importance of the Year 1838', *Revista Portuguesa de Filosofia*, 64 (2008), pp. 741–61. We do not know for sure how conscientiously Kierkegaard attended Martensen's lectures on philosophy and theology in 1837–8 and 1838–9, for although he owned notes taken from these lectures, the notes may have been copied or borrowed from another student.

p. 34    *'Dear Peter, Schelling talks the most insufferable nonsense'*: *Letters and Documents*, p. 141 – letter to P. C. Kierkegaard, February 1842.

p. 35    *'What philosophers say about actuality'*: S. Kierkegaard, *Either/Or*, Part I, ed. and trans. Howard V. Hong and Edna H. Hong (Princeton University Press, 1988), p. 32.

p. 35     *'in the world of ideas'*: S. Kierkegaard, *Fear and Trembling*, ed. C. Stephen Evans and Sylvia Walsh, trans. Sylvia Walsh (Cambridge University Press, 2006), p. 3.

p. 37     *'every blessing upon the System'*: ibid, p. 6.

p. 37     *De omnibus dubitandum est*: Kierkegaard took this Latin phrase as the title of a semi-fictional treatise attacking Martensen, and the phrase also featured in his satirical play *The Battle of the Old and New Soap-Cellars*, which he wrote five years earlier. *Johannes Climacus, or De Omnibus Dubitandum Est* was begun in 1842 but left unfinished in 1843. The phrase 'de omnibus dubitandum est' appears in Scenes 2 and 3 of *The Battle of the Old and New Soap-Cellars*. This play's character Herr von Springgaassen, 'a philosopher', is a caricature of Martensen; his name has been translated as 'Jumping Jack', and one of Kierkegaard's journal entries from 1837 describes Martensen as 'leap-frogging' over his philosophical predecessors: see *Kierkegaard's Journals and Notebooks, Volume 1, Journals AA–DD*, ed. and trans. Niels Jørgen Cappelørn, Alastair Hannay, David Kangas, Bruce H. Kirmmse, George Pattison, Vanessa Rumble and K. Brian Söderquist (Princeton University Press, 207) p. 189, and Pattison, 'How Kierkegaard Became "Kierkegaard"', p. 760.

p. 38     *'Whatever one generation learns from another'*: *Fear and Trembling*, p. 107.

p. 38     *'I did not come with lofty words or human wisdom'*: 1 Corinthians 2:1–5.

p. 39     *'While Abraham arouses my admiration'*: *Fear and Trembling*, p. 53.

p. 39     *Fear and Trembling will respond to Immanuel Kant's reading of Genesis 22*: the extent of Kierkegaard's reading of Kant is debated by scholars; the most forceful case in favour of his serious engagement with Kant's works, and particularly *The Conflict of the Faculties*, is made by Ronald M. Green in *Kierkegaard and Kant: The Hidden Debt* (State University of New York Press, 1992), and summarized in Green's essay 'Kant: A Debt Both Obscure and Enormous', in *Kierkegaard and His German Contemporaries, Tome I: Philosophy*, ed. Jon Stewart (Ashgate, 2007), pp. 179–210.

p. 40     *the ethical critique of religious dogmatism*: see Dominic Erdozain, *The Soul of Doubt: The Religious Roots of Unbelief from Luther to Marx* (Oxford University Press, 2016), pp. 69–172.

p. 40     *'the whole existence of the human race'*: *Fear and Trembling*, p. 59.

p. 41     *Without God, human beings will be left alone in a world with no divine order, no cosmic justice*: at the end of the nineteenth century Friedrich Nietzsche announced the 'death of God', declaring himself the prophet of a new nihilistic age – but Kierkegaard saw it coming four decades earlier.

p. 41     *'If there were no eternal consciousness in a human being'*: Fear and Trembling, p. 12.

## CHAPTER 4

p. 43     *'What did Abraham achieve?'*: S. Kierkegaard, *Fear and Trembling*, ed. C. Stephen Evans and Sylvia Walsh, trans. Sylvia Walsh (Cambridge University Press, 2006), p. 106.

p. 44     *Abraham's faith seemed impossible*: see Fear and Trembling, p. 13: 'No one who was great in the world will be forgotten, but each became great in proportion to his *expectation*. One became great by expecting the impossible, another by expecting the eternal, but the one who expected the impossible became greater than all.'

p. 44     *'a guiding star'*: ibid. p. 18.

p. 44     *'The important thing is to be able to have faith in God with respect to lesser things'*: Kierkegaard's Journals and Notebooks, Volume 2: Journals EE–KK, ed. and trans. Niels Jørgen Cappelørn, Alastair Hannay, David Kangas, Bruce H. Kirmmse, George Pattison, Vanessa Rumble and K. Brian Söderquist (Princeton University Press, 2008), p. 168: JJ 124 (1843).

p. 44     *'He headed home joyously, cheerfully, with trust in God'*: ibid, pp. 121–2: HH8 (1840).

p. 45     *Abraham 'had faith for this life'*: Fear and Trembling, pp. 7, 17.

p. 46     *he receives this gift secretly, in silence*: Kierkegaard returned to this account of an incognito person of faith, contrasted with the person who withdraws to a monastery, in Concluding Unscientific Postscript (1846): see S. Kierkegaard, Concluding Unscientific Postscript to the Philosphical Crumbs, ed. and trans. Alastair Hannay (Cambridge University Press, 2009), e.g. pp. 344–5, 396–8, 413, 419–20.

p. 47     *'I examine his figure from head to foot'*: Fear and Trembling, p. 32

p. 48     *'worldly wisdom'*, not *'genuinely religious consolation'*: Kierkegaard's Journals and Notebooks, Volume 2: Journals EE–KK, p. 153: JJ 82 (1843).

p. 49     *'Is it not also true here that the one whom God blesses he curses in the same breath?'*: Fear and Trembling, p. 57.

p. 49   'I have looked the frightful in the eye': Fear and Trembling, p. 28.
p. 49   'It is harder to receive love than to give it': ibid, p. 91.
p. 50   'the first thing the religious does is close its door and speak in secret': Kierkegaard's Journals and Notebooks, Volume 2: Journals
EE–KK, p. 158: JJ 96 (1843).
p. 50   'Inwardness is incommensurable with outwardness': ibid, p. 158:
JJ 96 (1843).
p. 50   'I sit and listen to the sounds in my inner being': ibid, pp. 159–60:
JJ 103 (1843).
p. 50   'After my death, no one will find in my papers': ibid, p. 157: JJ 95 (1843).
p. 51   'so many a marriage conceals little histories': ibid, p. 165: JJ 115
(17 May 1843).
p. 51   'On Easter Sunday at evensong': ibid, p. 161: JJ 107 (April 1843).
p. 52   sailed to Greenland, to North America, to China, to Brazil: as a
child, Kierkegaard heard stories about Danish missionaries in
Greenland; in 1841 he wrote to Emil Boesen, who was suffering
from his love for a woman, 'Get into your kayak (surely you know
those Greenland boats), put on your swimming suit, and be off with
you to the ocean of the world. But that is certainly no idyll. If you
cannot forget her, cannot write poetry about her, all right then, set
all sails' (S. Kierkegaard, Letters and Documents, ed. and trans.
Henrik Rosenmeier (Princeton University Press, 2009), p. 103). Poul
Møller, Kierkegaard's favourite philosophy teacher at the University
of Copenhagen, sailed to China after a romantic disappointment.
Peter Wilhelm Lund, the brother of Kierkegaard's two brothers-in-
law, went to Brazil to study meteorology, biology and zoology: see
Kierkegaard's Journals and Notebooks, Volume 1: Journals AA–
DD, ed. and trans. Niels Jørgen Cappelørn, Alastair Hannay, David
Kangas, Bruce H. Kirmmse, George Pattison, Vanessa Rumble and
K. Brian Söderquist (Princeton University Press, 2007), p. 319.
p. 53   'descend into dark waters': Letters and Documents, p. 93 – letter
to Emil Boesen from Berlin, 16 November 1841.
p. 53   'Everything churns inside me': ibid, p. 122 – letter to Emil Boesen
from Berlin, 16 January 1842.

## PART TWO

p. 55   'Assigned from childhood to a life of torment': S. Kierkegaard,
The Point of View, trans. Howard V. Hong and Edna H. Hong
(Princeton University Press, 2009), p. 162.

## CHAPTER 5

p. 57     'one for her, and one for me': see Kierkegaard's Journals and Notebooks, Volume 3: Notebooks 1–15, ed. and trans. Niels Jørgen Cappelørn, Alastair Hannay, David Kangas, Bruce H. Kirmmse, George Pattison, Vanessa Rumble and K. Brian Söderquist (Princeton University Press, 2010), p. 438: NB15, 6 (August to November 1849).

p. 57     'a forgotten remoteness in a rural parsonage': see S. Kierkegaard, The Point of View, trans. Howard V. Hong and Edna H. Hong (Princeton University Press, 2009), p. 157 (journal entry, 1847).

p. 58     He has remained here as a tenant: Kierkegaard and his brother Peter Christian Kierkegaard inherited the house, 2 Nytorv, when their father died in 1838, and in 1843 Kierkegaard bought his brother's share.

p. 59     'which had tempted me in a quite curious way': Kierkegaard's Journals and Notebooks, Volume 5: Journals NB6–NB10, ed. and trans. Niels Jørgen Cappelørn, Alastair Hannay, David Kangas, Bruce H. Kirmmse, George Pattison, Joel D. S. Rasmussen, Vanessa Rumble and K. Brian Söderquist (Princeton University Press, 2012), p. 144: NB7, 114 (1848). In 1849 Kierkegaard reflected in his journal that 'My home has been my consolation, having a pleasant home has been my greatest earthly encouragement': see Kierkegaard's Journals and Notebooks, Volume 6: Journals NB11–NB14, ed. and trans. Niels Jørgen Cappelørn, Alastair Hannay, David Kangas, Bruce H. Kirmmse, George Pattison, Joel D. S. Rasmussen, Vanessa Rumble and K. Brian Söderquist (Princeton University Press, 2013), p. 234: NB12, 143 (July to September 1849).

p. 59     'the whole movement would not touch kings at all': Kierkegaard's Journals and Notebooks, Volume 5: Journals NB6–NB10, p. 230: NB9, 42 (1849).

p. 59     'miserable to be a genius in a market town': ibid, p. 228: NB9, 41 (1849)

p. 59     on the morning of 21 March 1848, thousands gathered: this summary of Denmark's peaceful (and lasting) 'revolution' is drawn from the longer accounts in Bruce H. Kirmmse, Kierkegaard in Golden Age Denmark (Indiana University Press, 1990), pp. 64–8, and Joakim Garff, Søren Kierkegaard: A Biography, trans. Bruce Kirmmse (Princeton University Press, 2005), pp. 493–5.

p. 60     'the new ministry needs a war in order to stay in power': Kierkegaard's Journals and Notebooks, Volume 4: Journals NB–NB5, ed. and trans. Niels Jørgen Cappelørn, Alastair Hannay, David Kangas, Bruce H. Kirmmse, George Pattison, Vanessa Rumble and K. Brian Söderquist (Princeton University Press, 2011), p. 348: NB4, 123 (1848).

p. 60   *'Out there everything is agitated'*: Kierkegaard's Journals and Notebooks, Volume 4: Journals NB–NB5, pp. 347–8: NB4, 118 (27 March, 1848).

p. 61   *There are paper, pens and ink in every room*: See Niels Jørgen Cappelørn, Joakim Garff and Johnny Kondrup, *Written Images: Søren Kierkegaard's Journals, Notebooks, Booklets, Sheets, Scraps, and Slips of Paper*, trans. Bruce H. Kirmmse (Princeton University Press, 2003), pp. 159–72; *Encounters with Kierkegaard*, ed. Bruce Kirmmse, trans. Bruce Kirmmse and Virginia Laursen (Princeton University Press, 1998), p. 112: here Tycho Spang recalls Kierkegaard's 'large elegant apartment with a series of furnished rooms which in winter were heated and illuminated, and in which he did a good deal of pacing back and forth. As best I can remember, in each room there was ink, pen, and paper, which he used during his wanderings to fix an idea by means of a few quick words or a symbol.'

p. 61   *'There is so much talk about wasting a life'*: S. Kierkegaard, *The Sickness unto Death*, ed. and trans. Howard V. Hong and Edna H. Hong (Princeton University Press, 1983), pp. 26–7.

p. 62   *'Is despair an excellence or a defect?'*: ibid, pp. 14–15.

p. 62   *'Just as a physician might say'*: ibid, p. 22.

p. 63   *'The greatest hazard of all, losing the self'*: ibid, pp. 32–4.

p. 63   *'imagine a house'*: ibid, p. 43.

p. 64   *'Very often the person in despair probably has a dim idea of his own state'*: ibid, p. 48.

p. 64   *'I love my native land'*: Kierkegaard's Journals and Notebooks, Volume 5: Journals NB6–NB10, p. 101: NB7, 41 (1848).

p. 64   *'That enormous productivity, so intense that it seems to me as if it must move stones'*: ibid, p. 95: NB7, 31 (1848).

p. 65   *'She was especially gratified when she could get them peacefully into bed'*: Encounters with Kierkegaard, p. 153.

p. 66   *'a spoiled and naughty boy'*: ibid, p. 228. This remark was reportedly made by a cousin of Hans Brøchner, who was a friend of Kierkegaard from his student days.

p. 66   *'I never had the joy of being a child'*: Kierkegaard's Journals and Notebooks, Volume 5: Journals NB6–NB10, p. 211: NB9, 8 (January or February 1849).

p. 67    'His build was powerful': see Encounters with Kierkegaard, p. 151: this is from Henriette Lund's account of Michael Pedersen Kierkegaard. See also descriptions by Peter Brun (ibid, p. 6) and Frederik Welding (ibid, p. 7).

p. 67    'Oh, how frightful it is when for a moment I think of the dark background of my life': Kierkegaard's Journals and Notebooks, Volume 5: Journals NB6–NB10, p. 166: NB8, 36 (November or December 1848).

p. 67    tended the parish churchyard (kirkegaard): See Thorkild Andersen, 'Kierkegaard – Slægten og Sædding', Hardsyssels Aarbog, 27 (1933), p. 26; cited in English in Christopher B. Barnett, Kierkegaard, Pietism and Holiness (Ashgate, 2011), pp. 47–8.

p. 67    By the close of the eighteenth century he had made a substantial fortune: see Kierkegaard's Journals and Notebooks, Volume 1: Journals AA–DD, ed. and trans. Niels Jørgen Cappelørn, Alastair Hannay, David Kangas, Bruce H. Kirmmse, George Pattison, Vanessa Rumble and K. Brian Söderquist (Princeton University Press, 2007), p. 533.

p. 68    That was how Kierkegaard always knew his father: see Encounters with Kierkegaard, p. 3 – from Frederik Hammerich's (b. 1809) autobiography Et Levnedsløb, vol. I (Forlagsbureaet i Kjøbenhavn, 1882), pp. 58–9.

p. 68    'very intriguing to hear the old man debate with the sons': see Encounters with Kierkegaard, p. 137 – from the account of Eline Heramb Boisen, who visited the Kierkegaard household several times in the winter of 1833–4.

p. 68    Kierkegaard's view of the world as a battlefield: on 'martial music', see S. Kierkegaard, Letters and Documents, ed. and trans. Henrik Rosenmeier (Princeton University Press, 2009), p. 124 – letter to Emil Boesen, 16 January 1842; S. Kierkegaard, Either/Or, Part 1, trans. Howard V. Hong and Edna H. Hong (Princeton University Press, 1988), p. 349.

p. 68    'When I can't sleep, I lie down and talk with my boys': see Encounters with Kierkegaard, p. 6. This account comes second- or third-hand from Peter Munthe Brun (b. 1813).

p. 69    he did the family's daily shopping himself: ibid, p. 3 – from Frederik Hammerich's autobiography.

p. 69    His own nature was free-spirited: see Letters and Documents, pp. 4–5 – Kierkegaard's school report, written by his headmaster Michael Nielsen.

p. 69     he 'did not reveal his character in the way that young people usually do': see *Encounters with Kierkegaard*, p. 7 – from a letter written by Frederik Welding (b. 1811) to H. P. Barfod in 1869. On the clothes Kierkegaard wore as a boy, see *Kierkegaard's Journals and Notebooks Volume 5: Journals NB6–NB10*, p. 344: NB10, 153 (spring 1849).

p. 69     'to cloak this life with an outward existence of joie de vivre': *Kierkegaard's Journals and Notebooks, Volume 5: Journals NB6–NB10*, p. 259: NB9, 78 (1849); p. 166: NB8, 36 (winter 1848); pp. 368–9: NB10, 191 (spring 1849).

p. 69     'He made my childhood an unparalleled torture': *Kierkegaard's Journals and Notebooks, Volume 4: Journals NB–NB5*, pp. 401–2: NB5, 68 (May to July 1848).

p. 69     'I acquired such an anxiety about Christianity': *Kierkegaard's Journals and Notebooks, Volume 5: Journals NB6–NB10*, p. 166: NB8, 36 (winter 1848); p. 259: NB9, 78 (1849); pp. 368–9: NB10, 191 (spring 1849).

p. 70     'But under his "rustic cloak" manner he concealed an ardent imagination': S. Kierkegaard, *Philosophical Fragments / Johannes Climacus, or De omnibus dubitandum est*, ed. and trans. Howard V. Hong and Edna H. Hong (Princeton University Press, 1985), p. 120f. In this passage from *Johannes Climacus*, the Danish phrase *en enkelt Gang* – here translated 'once in a while' – can also mean 'on one occasion'. The virtual excursion with his father almost certainly occurred in Kierkegaard's childhood at least once, since he refers to an imagined trip to Frederiksberg in an 1844 letter to his brother Peter Christian's wife Henriette: see *Letters and Documents*, p. 174: 'Often in my childhood I was not permitted by my father to walk out to Frederiksberg, but I walked hand in hand with him up and down the floor – to Frederiksberg.' In an 1847 letter to Peter Christian, Kierkegaard wrote that 'a curious thing about Father was that what he had most of, what one least expected, was imagination, albeit a melancholy imagination . . . However little I otherwise agreed with Father, in a few singular ideas we had an essential point of contact, and in such conversations Father was always almost impressed with me, for I could depict an idea with a lively imagination and pursue it with a daring consistency': see *Letters and Documents*, p. 211.

p. 71     *The Mysterious Family*: *Kierkegaard's Journals and Notebooks, Volume 2: Journals EE–KK*, ed. and trans. Niels Jørgen Cappelørn,

Alastair Hannay, David Kangas, Bruce H. Kirmmse, George Pattison, Vanessa Rumble and K. Brian Söderquist (Princeton University Press, 2008), p. 174: JJ 147 (1843). For an intriguing philosophical and psychological exposition of Kierkegaard's journal entry on 'The Mysterious Family', see George Pattison, 'The Mysterious Family or Why Kierkegaard Never Wrote a Play: An Old Question Revisited', in *Kierkegaard and the Nineteenth Century Religious Crisis in Europe*, ed. Roman Králik, Abrahim H. Khan, Peter Sajda, Jamie Turnbull and Andrew J. Burgess (Acta Kierkegaardiana, vol. 4, 2009), pp. 187–201.

p. 71    *'A guilt must rest upon the entire family'*: Søren Kierkegaard's *Journals and Papers: Autobiographical, 1829–48*, eds. Howard V. Hong and Edna H. Hong, assisted by Gregor Malantschuk (Indiana University Press, 1978), p. 141: Pap. II A 805, 806 (1838).

p. 72    *we first learn to love*: Kierkegaard's niece Henriette Lund once saw for herself how highly Kierkegaard esteemed the ability to love: 'One day, when I met Uncle Søren in my early youth, he teased me by being unwilling to admit my right to have an opinion about some subject or other that was currently popular. In the ensuing debate, in which I attempted to demonstrate my dignity and maturity, there was just one argument that instantly overpowered him. I said "Yes, because I have learned to appreciate love." With a changed expression, and with a serious tone of voice, he replied: "That is another matter. Then you are right. I realize now that you really are grown up!" I still remember it. It was as if he had taken off his hat and bowed to me with enormous respect': *Encounters with Kierkegaard*, p. 170 – from Henriette Lund, *Eringringer Fra Hjemmet* (Copenhagen: Gyldendal, 1909).

CHAPTER 6

p. 74    *No, a Christian's task is to follow Jesus, to imitate him*: see S. Kierkegaard, *Practice in Christianity*, ed. and trans. Howard V. Hong and Edna H. Hong (Princeton University Press, 1991), 201–32.

p. 77    *Michael Pedersen helped to guide the Society's financial affairs . . . he was regarded as one of the group's most faithful members*: in a letter dated 28 August 1838 (shortly after Michael Pedersen Kierkegaard's death), the leader of the Copenhagen Society of Brethren wrote that, 'Our society loses in him one of the most faithful members, both for the outer and for the inner . . . He has certainly done in the quiet more good than many have thought, who declare and take him for a miser . . . In him I lose a faithful brother in the true sense of the word, who at each opportunity told me his opinion openly, but in a very plain way, and who in our society's affairs, which he covered with particular love and took to heart, has given us good advice for many a year.' Quoted in Christopher B. Barnett, *Kierkegaard, Pietism and Holiness* (Ashgate, 2011), pp. 60–61.

p. 77     *'We know we are sinners, great is our imperfection'*: from a discourse by J. C. Reuss, quoted in Barnett, *Kierkegaard, Pietism and Holiness*, p. 52.

p. 78     *Mynster's presence 'inspired reverence'*: see Andrew Hamilton, *Sixteen Months in the Danish Isles*, Vol. 2 (Richard Bentley, 1852), p. 187.

p. 78     *Michael Pedersen Kierkegaard went to Mynster for confession and communion*: see Niels Jørgen Cappelørn, 'Die ursprüngliche Unterbrechung', in *Kierkegaard Studies Yearbook 1996*, ed. N. J. Cappelørn and Hermann Deuser (Walter de Gruyter, 1996), pp. 315–88.

p. 78     *So it was Mynster who confirmed Kierkegaard in the Church of Our Lady*: on Kierkegaard's confirmation in 1828 and his mature view of confirmation, see Niels Thulstrup, 'Confirmation', in *Theological Concepts in Kierkegaard*, ed. Niels Thulstrup and M. Mikulová Thulstrup (Reitzel, 1980), pp. 247–53.

p. 78     *Kierkegaard remembers how, when he was a boy, his father promised him a rix-dollar if he would read one of these sermons aloud*: see *Kierkegaard's Journals and Notebooks, Volume 5: Journals NB6–NB10*, ed. and trans. Niels Jørgen Cappelørn, Alastair Hannay, David Kangas, Bruce H. Kirmmse, George Pattison, Joel D. S. Rasmussen, Vanessa Rumble and K. Brian Söderquist (Princeton University Press, 2012), p. 299: NB10, 59 (1849).

p. 80     *'The most fashionable place of worship in Copenhagen'*: Hamilton, *Sixteen Months in the Danish Isles*, p. 180.

p. 80     *In 1834, following the death of his father-in-law*: Mynster's father-in-law died in 1830 and was replaced by Peter Erasmus Müller; Mynster then replaced him in 1834.

p. 84     *For Luther, it was words like these that expressed the clear certainty of faith*: see Richard Rex, *The Making of Martin Luther* (Princeton University Press, 2017), for an analysis of certainty in Luther's theology.

p. 84    *Yet for Kierkegaard they contain endless questions*: Kierkegaard discussed this verse from Matthew several times in his authorship: see, for example, S. Kierkegaard, *Concluding Unscientific Postscript to the Philosophical Crumbs*, ed. and trans. Alastair Hannay (Cambridge University Press, 2009), pp. 361, 367, as well as S. Kierkegaard, *Christian Discourses / The Crisis and a Crisis in the Life of an Actress*, ed. and trans. Howard V. Hong and Edna H. Hong (Princeton University Press, 2009).

p. 84    '*The truth that divine governance embraces everything*': J. P. Mynster, *Betragtninger over de christelige Troeslærdomme* [*Observations upon the Doctrines of the Christian Faith*], 3rd edn, vol. I (Deichmanns, 1846), p. 311; quoted in Bruce H. Kirmmse, *Kierkegaard in Golden Age Denmark* (Indiana University Press, 1990), p. 107.

p. 85    '*certainty for the doubter, strength for the struggling, comfort for the sorrowful*': J. P. Mynster, *Prædikener paa alle Søn-og Hellig-Dage i Aaret*, vol. 2 (3rd edn, Gyldendal, 1837), p. 403. For more discussion of this sermon and Kierkegaard's response to it, see Christian Fink Tolstrup, '"Playing a Profane Game with Holy Things": Understanding Kierkegaard's Critical Encounter with Bishop Mynster', in *International Kierkegaard Commentary, Volume 20: Practice in Christianity*, ed. Robert L. Perkins (Mercer University Press, 2004), pp. 245–74.

p. 85    '*happiness and blessing*': Mynster, *Prædikener paa alle Søn-og Hellig-Dage i Aaret*, p. 414.

p. 85    '*Though he possessed the blessing, he was like a curse for everyone who came near him*': S. Kierkegaard, *Upbuilding Discourses in Various Spirits*, ed. and trans. Howard V. Hong and Edna H. Hong (Princeton University Press, 1993), p. 254.

p. 86    '*Christianity has been taken in vain, made too mild*': see *Kierkegaard's Journals and Notebooks, Volume 5: Journals NB6–NB10*, p. 57: NB6, 74 (July or August 1848).

p. 86    '*How quieting, how soothing – alas, and how much danger in this security!*': *Christian Discourses*, pp. 163–5.

p. 87    *On the first occasion he preached on Matthew 11:28*: this first sermon was not documented, but it probably took place on 18 June 1847. See Niels Jørgen Cappelørn, 'Søren Kierkegaard at Friday Communion in the Church of Our Lady', trans. K. Brian Söderquist, in *International Kierkegaard Commentary, Volume*

*18: Without Authority*, ed. Robert L. Perkins (Mercer University Press, 2007), pp. 255–94.

p. 87 *'I do not know what in particular troubles you'*: *Christian Discourses*, p. 266.

p. 87 *'like a flautist entertaining himself'*: *Kierkegaard's Journals and Notebooks, Volume 9: Journals NB26–NB30*, ed. and trans. Niels Jørgen Cappelørn, Alastair Hannay, Bruce H. Kirmmse, David D. Possen, Joel D. S. Rasmussen and Vanessa Rumble (Princeton University Press, 2017), p. 419: NB30, 41 (1854).

p. 88 *his 'exceedingly weak but wonderfully expressive voice'*: P. C. Zahle, *Til Erindring om Johan Georg Hamann og Søren Aabye Kierkegaard* (Copenhagen, 1856), pp. 9–10, quoted in Cappelørn, 'Søren Kierkegaard at Friday Communion in the Church of Our Lady'. Cappelørn suggests that Zahle did not hear Kierkegaard's first sermon in Vor Frue Kirke, and thinks it 'more likely that he heard Kierkegaard preach in the Citadel Church on Sunday May 18th, 1851': see ibid, pp. 285–6.

p. 88 *'openly before everyone's eyes, and yet secretly, as a stranger'*: *Christian Discourses*, pp. 269–70. This is from the second Friday communion discourse that Kierkegaard preached in Vor Frue Kirke, on 27 August 1847.

p. 88 *'with my father in mind I would very much like to do it'*: see *Kierkegaard's Journals and Notebooks, Volume 4: Journals NB–NB5*, ed. and trans. Niels Jørgen Cappelørn, Alastair Hannay, David Kangas, Bruce H. Kirmmse, George Pattison, Joel Rasmussen, Vanessa Rumble and K. Brian Söderquist (Princeton University Press, 2011), p. 263: NB3, 36 (November or December, 1847).

p. 89 *'never been closer to stopping being an author'*: *Kierkegaard's Journals and Notebooks, Volume 5: Journals NB6–NB10*, p. 262: NB9, 79 (9 February 1849): 'Stopping being an author was an idea that occurred to me from my earliest days; I have often said that there was still a place available for the author who knew when to stop. In fact, I actually had already thought of stopping as early as *Either/Or*. But I was never closer to stopping than I was with the publication of *Christian Discourses* [in April 1848].'

p. 89 *'Let us pay tribute to Bishop Mynster'*: see *Kierkegaard's Journals and Notebooks, Volume 4: Journals NB–NB5*, p. 252: NB3, 16 (November or December 1847).

p. 89    *he thinks that, for Jesus, becoming a monk or a hermit was a temptation*: see *Kierkegaard's Journals and Notebooks, Volume 5: Journals NB6–NB10*, p. 164: NB8, 29 (November or December 1848).

p. 90    *he wonders whether Jesus wanted his followers*: see *Kierkegaard's Journals and Notebooks, Volume 4: Journals NB–NB5*, p. 377: NB5, 14 (May to July 1848).

p. 90    *'an extremely unhappy man'*: see *Practice in Christianity*, p. 275; *Kierkegaard's Journals and Notebooks, Volume 5: Journals NB6–NB10*, p. 57: NB6, 74 (July or August 1848).

## CHAPTER 7

p. 92    *'alas, I would rather write a folio than publish a page'*: *Kierkegaard's Journals and Notebooks, Volume 5: Journals NB6–NB10*, ed. and trans. Niels Jørgen Cappelørn, Alastair Hannay, David Kangas, Bruce H. Kirmmse, George Pattison, Joel D. S. Rasmussen, Vanessa Rumble and K. Brian Söderquist (Princeton University Press, 2012), p. 19: NB6, 24 (July or August 1848).

p. 92    *this 'idolized' actress learned that her fame was 'empty'*: S. Kierkegaard, *Christian Discourses / The Crisis and a Crisis in the Life of an Actress*, ed. trans. Howard V. Hong and Edna H. Hong (Princeton University Press, 2009), pp. 304–5.

p. 93    *'When it comes to the feminine'*: ibid.

p. 94    *When Luise Pätges gave her first performance as Juliet*: on the life of Johanne Luise Heiberg and her connection to Kierkegaard, see Katalin Nun, *Women of the Danish Golden Age: Literature, Theater and the Emancipation of Women* (Museum Tusculanum Press, 2013), pp. 62–84.

p. 94    *He became a familiar figure in Reitzel's bookshop*: see Niels Thulstrup, *The Copenhagen of Kierkegaard*, ed. Marie Mikulová Thulstrup, trans. Ruth Mach-Zagal (Reitzel, 1986), pp. 41–60; *Encounters with Kierkegaard*, ed. Bruce Kirmmse, trans. Bruce Kirmmse and Virginia Laursen (Princeton University Press, 1998), p. 110–11: a translated extract from Otto B. Wroblewski's *Ti Aar i C. A. Reitzels Boglade* [*Ten Years in C. A. Reitzel's Bookshop*] (1889). Wroblewski, a bookseller at Reitzel's shop from 1843 to 1853, recalled that 'The peculiar figure of *Søren Kierkegaard* is the sort one does not forget even if one has seen it only once – even more unlikely that we would, we who saw him so regularly in the bookshop. He wasn't very forthcoming. With Reitzel, of course, he spoke only about press business, and with us at the bookshop only about buying books. But I, at any rate, was strangely moved by a friendly smile from the deep blue, melancholy eyes with which he could look at you, a look that occasionally was coupled with a satirical line near his mouth when a remark amused him.'

p. 94    *he took his new books, in their plain paper covers*: many of the books Kierkegaard owned are now in the Kierkegaard Archive at the Royal Danish Library in Copenhagen. A beautifully illustrated account of Kierkegaard as a lover and collector of books is presented in Niels Jørgen Cappelørn, Gert Posselt and Bent Rohde, *Tekstspejle: Om Søren Kierkegaard som bogtilrettelægger, boggiver og bogsamler* (Rosendahls Forlag, 2002), pp. 105–219. On Kierkegaard's preference for Møller's bookbinding, see Niels Jørgen Cappleørn, Joakim Garff and Johnny Kondrup, *Written Images: Søren Kierkegaard's Journals, Notebooks, Booklets, Sheets, Scraps, and Slips of Paper*, trans. Bruce H. Kirmmse (Princeton University Press, 2003), pp. 163–4.

p. 95    *'the demon debater from the North'*: see Thorkild C. Lyby, 'Peter Christian Kierkegaard: A Man with a Difficult Family Heritage', in *Kierkegaard and His Danish Contemporaries, Tome II: Theology*, ed. Jon Stewart (Ashgate, 2009), pp. 189–209.

p. 96    *every man, the poet Novalis urged in 1798, 'should become an artist'*: Novalis, *Glauben und Liebe* [*Faith and Love*] (1798), in *Novalis Schriften*, ed. Paul Kluckhohn and Richard Samuel, vol. 2 (Kohlhammer, 1981), p. 497. Novalis was the pseudonym of Friedrich von Hardenberg.

p. 96    *Modern life had become 'prosaic' and 'irreligious'*: Henrik Steffens, *Indledning til philosophiske Forelæsninger* [*Introduction to Philosophical Lectures*] (Gyldendals Trane-Klassikere, 1968), pp. 6, 134–5, 143; quoted in Bruce H. Kirmmse, *Kierkegaard in Golden Age Denmark* (Indiana University Press, 1990), pp. 82–4.

p. 97    *'the development of man's capacity for feeling'*: Friedrich Schiller, *Essays*, ed. Walter Hinderer and Daniel O. Dahlstrom (Continuum, 1993), pp. 107, 131–2.

p. 97    *'a feeling that is not sensual, but spiritual'*: Friedrich von Schlegel, *Dialogue on Poetry and Literary Aphorisms*, trans. Ernst Behler and Roman Struc (Pennsylvania State University Press, 1968), p. 99.

p. 97    the 'unconscious poetry that moves in the plant': ibid, p. 54.

p. 97    a 'feeling for that eternal and holy being': Friedrich Schleiermacher, *On Religion: Speeches to its Cultured Despisers*, trans.
Richard Crouter (Cambridge University Press, 1996), p. 3.

p. 97    'the quiet disappearance of one's whole existence in the immeasurable': ibid, p. 23

p. 97    'strive to awaken the slumbering kernel of a better humanity':
ibid, p. 7.

p. 98    everything 'is in God': see *The Collected Works of Spinoza, vol.
I*, trans. Edwin Curley (Princeton University Press, 1985), pp.
420–24 (*Ethics*, Part I, Proposition 15). Spinoza is more properly
described as a panentheist (everything is in God) than as a pantheist (everything is God) – but pantheism is the version of Spinozism
that the Romantics seized upon.

p. 99    H. C. Ørsted pursued research into 'the Spirit in Nature': Aanden
i Naturen [*The Spirit in Nature*] was the title of the collection of
papers H. C. Ørsted published just before his death in 1851. He
discovered electro-magnetism in 1820. On Kierkegaard's relationship to H. C. Ørsted, see Bjarne Troelsen, 'Hans Christian Ørsted:
Søren Kierkegaard and *The Spirit in Nature*,' in *Kierkegaard and
His Danish Contemporaries, Tome I: Philosophy, Politics and
Social Theory*, ed. Jon Stewart (Ashgate, 2009), pp. 215–27.

p. 100   in 1833 Heiberg set out his own manifesto: see *Heiberg's On the
Significance of Philosophy for the Present Age and Other Texts*,
trans. and ed. Jon Stewart (Reitzel, 2005), which follows the
scholarly debate prompted by Heiberg's essay.

p. 101   his philosophy professors Poul Møller and Frederik Christian
Sibbern: on Kierkegaard's relationships with these two important
philosophy teachers, see Finn Gredal Jensen, 'Poul Martin Møller:
Kierkegaard and the Confidant of Socrates', and Carl Henrik
Koch, 'Frederik Christian Sibbern: "the lovable, remarkable
thinker, Councilor Sibbern" and "the political Simple-Peter Sib-
bern" ' – both in *Kierkegaard and His Danish Contemporaries,
Tome I*, pp. 101–67 and 229–60.

p. 101   an 'unforgettable' teacher: in his memoirs, Hans Lassen Martensen remembers 'the genial, unforgettable Poul Møller, to whom
we looked up with admiration, and who, without trying, exerted
such a fruitful influence on us', in *Af mit Levnet* [*From My Life*],
vol. 1 (Gyldendal, 1882), p. 16.

p. 102   *When she confided her 'deep indignation' at how Kierkegaard had 'mistreated her soul'*: see *Encounters with Kierkegaard*, ed. Bruce Kirmmse, trans. Bruce Kirmmse and Virginia Laursen (Princeton University Press, 1998), pp. 213–16.

p. 102   *'the enthusiasm of my youth'*: S. Kierkegaard, *The Concept of Anxiety*, trans. Reidar Thomte (Princeton University Press, 1981), p. 178.

p. 102   *He wrote to Regine of the 'genie of the ring' within him*: see S. Kierkegaard, *Letters and Documents*, ed. and trans. Henrik Rosenmeier (Princeton University Press, 2009), p. 66 – letter to Regine Olsen, 28 October 1840. On Kierkegaard's connection to Oehlenschläger, see Bjarne Troelsen, 'Adam Oehlenschläger: Kierkegaard and the Treasure Hunter of Immediacy', in *Kierkegaard and his Danish Contemporaries, Tome III: Literature, Drama and Aesthetics*, ed. Jon Stewart (Ashgate, 2009), pp. 255–71. On the figure of Aladdin in Kierkegaard's own writing, see Jennifer Veninga, 'Aladdin: The Audacity of Wildest Wishes', in Katalin Nun and Jon Stewart (eds.), *Kierkegaard's Literary Figures and Motifs, Tome I: Agamemnon to Guadalquiver* (Ashgate, 2014), pp. 31–40.

p. 103   *'Never in her life had she seen a human being so deeply distressed'*: *Encounters with Kierkegaard*, p. 196: from Martensen's autobiography *Af mit Levnet*, vol. I, p. 79.

p. 104   *His first literary journal entries were on the master-thief*: on Kierkegaard's interest in the master-thief, see F. Nassim Bravo Jordan, 'The Master-Thief: A One-Man Army against the Established Order', in Katalin Nun and Jon Stewart (eds.), *Kierkegaard's Literary Figures and Motifs, Tome II: Gulliver to Zerlina* (Ashgate, 2015), pp. 111–20.

p. 104   *One day Kierkegaard tried out this 'youthful, romantic enthusiasm'*: *Kierkegaard's Journals and Notebooks, Volume 1: Journals AA–DD*, ed. and trans. Niels Jørgen Cappelørn, Alastair Hannay, David Kangas, Bruce H. Kirmmse, George Pattison, Vanessa Rumble and K. Brian Söderquist (Princeton University Press, 2007), pp. 128–30: BB 42 (1837).

p. 105   *'I have seen the sea turn blue-grey'*: ibid, pp. 7–8: AA 4 (1835).

p. 105   *'for I could spare it, and she needed it'*: ibid, p. 9: AA 5 (1835).

p. 105   *'the church bells call to prayer'*: ibid, p. 12: AA 7 (25 July 1835).

p. 105   *Still in character as a Romantic poet, Kierkegaard took an evening walk*: see ibid, p. 9: AA 6 (July 29, 1835).

p. 106     'I have often stood there and pondered my past life': ibid, pp. 9–10: AA 6 (29 July 1835); citation abridged.

p. 107     'What I really need is to get clear about what I must do': ibid, pp. 19–20: AA 12 (1835); citation abridged.

p. 108     Kierkegaard explored themes from the old legend of Faust: on Kierkegaard's interest in Faust, see Leonardo F. Lisi, 'Faust: The Seduction of Doubt', in Nun and Stewart (eds.), Kierkegaard's Literary Figures and Motifs, Tome I, pp. 209–28.

p. 109     'the unhappy relativity in everything': Kierkegaard's Journals and Notebooks, Volume 1: Journals AA–DD, p. 223: DD 30 (14 July 1837).

p. 110     'Søren these days is perhaps more than ever weighed down by brooding': see Encounters with Kierkegaard, pp. 142–3 – from P. C. Kierkegaard's journal, August 1837.

p. 110     'If an author who neither has a considerable fund of ideas nor is very industrious': Christian Discourses / The Crisis and a Crisis in the Life of an Actress, p. 316.

## CHAPTER 8

p. 112     nor does he want people to think that he started out as a daring aesthete, and then became a religious writer: see Kierkegaard's Journals and Notebooks, Volume 5: Journals NB6–NB10, ed. and trans. Niels Jørgen Cappelørn, Alastair Hannay, David Kangas, Bruce H. Kirmmse, George Pattison, Joel D. Rasmussen, Vanessa Rumble and K. Brian Söderquist (Princeton University Press, 2012), pp. 17–18: NB6, 24 (July or August 1848); pp. 45–6: NB6, 64 (July or August 1848); pp. 56–7: NB6, 74, 75 (July or August 1848); p. 66: NB6, 87 (July or August 1848).

p. 113     he tries to console himself with the thought of Rasmus Nielsen's friendship and loyalty: for an excellent summary of Kierkegaard's complex relationship with Nielsen, see Jon Stewart, 'Rasmus Nielsen: From the Object of "Prodigious Concern" to a "Windbag"', in Kierkegaard and His Danish Contemporaries, Tome I: Philosophy, Politics and Social Theory, ed. Jon Stewart (Ashgate, 2009), pp. 179–213.

p. 113     'But what is the worst thing about this is that I have managed to get the whole matter so muddled in reflection': Kierkegaard's Journals and Notebooks, Volume 5: Journals NB6–NB10, p. 24: NB6, 28 (July or August 1848).

p. 114   'it is reflection that wants to make me extraordinary': ibid, p. 19: NB6, 24 (July or August 1848).

p. 114   Orla Lehmann: on Kierkegaard's relationship to Lehmann, see Julie K. Allen, 'Orla Lehmann: Kierkegaard's Political Alter-Ego', in *Kierkegaard and His Danish Contemporaries, Tome I*, pp. 85–100.

p. 115   'Modern philosophy is purely subjunctive': *Kierkegaard's Journals and Notebooks, Volume 1: Journals AA–DD*, ed. and trans. Niels Jørgen Cappelørn, Alastair Hannay, David Kangas, Bruce H. Kirmmse, George Pattison, Vanessa Rumble and K. Brian Söderquist (Princeton University Press, 2007), p. 230: DD 51 (September 1837); p. 233: DD 62 (7 October 1837).

p. 115   he was casting about for a new project: see ibid, p. 231: DD 55 (20 September 1837), p. 232: DD 58 (25 September 1837), pp. 240–41: DD 87, 90 (7 and 10 December 1837).

p. 115   'Why I so much prefer autumn to spring': ibid, p. 236: DD 74 (29 October 1837).

p. 115   'Again such a long time has passed': ibid, p. 243: DD 96 (April 1838).

p. 115   Hans Christian Andersen's new novel: the literary novel was still a relatively new genre in Denmark in the 1830s, and H. C. Andersen was one of a few authors who – encouraged by the success of translations of Walter Scott's historical novels – tried their hand at prose fiction. On Kierkegaard's relationship to Andersen, see Lone Koldtoft, 'Hans Christian Andersen: Andersen was Just an Excuse', in *Kierkegaard and His Danish Contemporaries, Tome III: Literature, Drama and Aesthetics*, ed. Jon Stewart (Ashgate, 2009), pp. 1–32.

p. 115   the heavy, convoluted prose: Kierkegaard's schoolfriend H. P. Holst later described Kierkegaard's prose style as a 'Latin–Danish' full of participles and complicated sentences, and claimed to have helped Kierkegaard rewrite the review of *Only a Fiddler*: see S. Kierkegaard, *Early Polemical Writings*, ed. and trans. Julia Watkin (Princeton University Press, 2009), p. xxxi.

p. 116   'My father died on Wednesday, the 8th, at 2:00 a.m.': *Kierkegaard's Journals and Notebooks, Volume 1: Journals AA–DD*, p. 249: DD 126 (11 August 1838).

p. 117   'Our opinions nearly always differ and we are perpetually in conflict': *Early Polemical Writings*, p. 55.

p. 118   'You know very well, said he, that I consider writing books to be the most ridiculous thing a person can do': ibid, p. 57.

p. 118    *'an egg that needs warmth'*: ibid, p. 81.

p. 119    *'for genius is not a rush candle that goes out in a puff of air'*: ibid, p. 88.

p. 119    *'A life-view is more than experience'*: ibid, p. 76.

p. 119    *'It is only this dead and transfigured personality'*: ibid, pp. 75–85.

p. 120    he found it *'difficult to read with its heavy* Hegelian *style'*: see *Encounters with Kierkegaard,* ed. Bruce Kirmmse, trans. Bruce Kirmmse and Virginia Laursen (Princeton University Press, 1998), p. 28.

p. 120    *'an individual depressed by the world'*: see *Early Polemical Writings,* pp. 202–4.

p. 120    *Kierkegaard's preaching was judged to be*: see S. Kierkegaard, *Letters and Documents,* ed. and trans. Henrik Rosenmeier (Princeton University Press, 2009), pp. 19–20 – from the records of the Pastoral Seminary, winter semester 1840/41. On the pastoral seminary and Kierkegaard's time there, see Niels Thulstrup and Marie Mikulová Thulstrup, *Kierkegaard and the Church in Denmark,* trans. Frederick H. Cryer (Reitzel, 1984), pp. 107–11.

p. 121    *He focused his critique of Romanticism on Friedrich von Schlegel's experimental novel*: on Kierkegaard's analysis of *Lucinde,* see Fernando Manuel Ferreira da Silva, 'Lucinde: "To live poetically is to live infinitely", or Kierkegaard's Concept of Irony as Portrayed in his Analysis of Friedrich Schlegel's Work', in Katalin Nun and Jon Stewart (eds.), *Kierkegaard's Literary Figures and Motifs, Tome II: Gulliver to Zerlina* (Ashgate, 2015), pp. 75–83.

p. 122    *'Just as scientists maintain that there is no true science without doubt'*: S. Kierkegaard, *The Concept of Irony, with Continual Reference to Socrates,* ed. and trans. Howard V. Hong and Edna H. Hong (Princeton University Press, 1992), p. 326.

p. 122    *Kierkegaard's examiners*: see *Encounters with Kierkegaard,* pp. 29–32 – from the archives of the University of Copenhagen.

p. 122    *the magister degree*: Danish 'Magister' degrees became doctoral degrees in the 1850s.

p. 123    *'The only thing I can say I miss now and then are our colloquia'*: *Letters and Documents,* p. 102 – letter to Emil Boesen, 14 December 1841.

p. 124    *'I do not turn her into a poetic subject'*: ibid, p. 93 – letter to Emil Boesen, 16 November 1841.

NOTES

p. 124   'In the course of these recent events my soul has received a needed baptism': ibid, p. 93 – letter to Emil Boesen, 16 November 1841.

p. 124   'Whether my soul is too egotistical or too great': ibid, p. 95 – letter to Emil Boesen, 16 November 1841.

p. 124   He sent Henriette a sweet, funny letter: ibid, pp. 100–101 – letter to Henriette Lund, 13 December 1841.

p. 125   'that her family hates me is good': ibid, p. 102 – letter to Emil Boesen, 14 December 1841.

p. 125   In his letter to Sibbern he became a deferential, diligent student: ibid, p. 106 – letter to F. C. Sibbern, 15 December 1841.

p. 125   the big dogs which pulled carriages transporting milk: ibid, p. 99 – letter to Carl Lund, 8 December 1841.

p. 125   Wilhelm, aged ten, received an elegant letter: ibid, p. 110 – letter to Wilhelm Lund, autumn 1841.

p. 125   'We especially tried to cheer ourselves up': ibid, p. 111 – letter to Michael Lund, 28 December 1841.

p. 125   'just write freely about whatever occurs to you': ibid, pp. 112–13 – letter to Carl Lund, 31 December 1841.

p. 126   'I hold my life poetically in my hand': ibid, pp. 121–2 – letter to Emil Boesen, 16 January 1842.

p. 126   'Cold, some insomnia, frayed nerves': ibid, pp. 134–5 – letter to Emil Boesen, 6 February 1842.

p. 127   'My dear Emil, Schelling talks endless nonsense': ibid, p. 139 – letter to Emil Boesen, 27 February 1842.

p. 128   'An inexplicable presentiment took me there': Kierkegaard's Journals and Notebooks, Volume 5: Journals NB6–NB105, p. 83: NB7, 10 (August 1848).

p. 128   'At some point I must give a clear explanation of myself as an author' ibid, p. 50: NB6, 69 (July or August 1848).

p. 128   'I have been brought up and developed in the process of my work': ibid, pp. 48–9, 56: NB6, 66, 74 (July or August 1848).

p. 129   'How often haven't I had happen what has just now happened to me again?': ibid, p. 47: NB6, 65 (July or August 1848).

CHAPTER 9

p. 130   the spiritual life of 'the single individual . . . diametrically opposite to politics': S. Kierkegaard, The Point of View, ed. and trans. Howard V. Hong and Edna H. Hong (Princeton University Press, 2009), p. 121.

p. 131    'Now I can see my way to writing': Kierkegaard's Journals and Notebooks, Volume 5: Journals NB6–NB10, ed. and trans. Niels Jørgen Cappelørn, Alastair Hannay, David Kangas, Bruce H. Kirmmse, George Pattison, Joel D. S. Rasmussen, Vanessa Rumble and K. Brian Söderquist (Princeton University Press, 2012), p. 85: NB7, 13 (late August or early September 1848).

p. 132    'Christianity is not a doctrine': ibid, p. 39: NB6, 56 (July or August 1848).

p. 132    'every human being is equally near to God': ibid, p. 45: NB6, 63 (July or August 1848).

p. 132    'Compel a person to an opinion, a conviction, a belief – in all eternity, that I cannot do': The Point of View, pp. 47, 52, 50.

p. 132    the kind of reader who 'thinks he is a Christian': ibid, p. 54.

p. 132    'there is nothing that requires as gentle a treatment as the removal of an illusion': ibid, p. 43.

p. 132    'not to comprehend Christianity, but to comprehend that they cannot comprehend it': Kierkegaard's Journals and Notebooks, Volume 5: Journals NB6–NB10, p. 70: NB6, 93 (July or August 1848).

p. 132    'One does not begin directly with what one wishes to communicate': The Point of View, p. 54.

p. 133    'One can deceive a person out of what is true': ibid, p. 53.

p. 133    'the world has a thousand evasions and illusions': Kierkegaard's Journals and Notebooks, Volume 5: Journals NB6–NB10, p. 45: NB6, 63 (July or August 1848).

p. 133    'Life isn't like a romantic novel': S. Kierkegaard, Either/Or, Part I, ed. and trans. Howard V. Hong and Edna H. Hong (Princeton University Press, 1988), p. 45.

p. 134    'Marry or do not marry, you will regret it either way': ibid, pp. 38–9.

p. 134    'I have often sat beside a little running stream': S. Kierkegaard, Either/Or, Part II, ed. and trans. Howard V. Hong and Edna H. Hong (Princeton University Press, 1988), p. 144.

p. 135    'earnestness of spirit . . . you will miss out on the highest': ibid, pp. 6, 168.

p. 136    'Writing in the wake of the long revolutionary struggle in Haiti': see Susan Buck-Morss, Hegel, Haiti, and Universal History (University of Pittsburgh Press, 2009).

p. 136    'My mind roars like a turbulent sea in the storms of passion': Either/Or, Part I, pp. 324–5.

p. 138    '*There I go on Saturdays to prepare my sermon, and everything widens out before me*': Either/Or, Part II, p. 338.

p. 139    *Another powerful figure was Henrik Nicolai Clausen*: on H. N. Clausen and Kierkegaard's relationship to him, see Hugh S. Pyper, 'Henrik Nicolai Clausen: The Voice of Urbane Rationalism', in *Kierkegaard and His Danish Contemporaries, Tome II: Theology*, ed. Jon Stewart (Ashgate, 2009), pp. 41–8.

p. 141    '*Grundtvig looks on the development of Christian understanding*': *Søren Kierkegaard's Journals and Papers: Autobiographical, 1829–48*, ed. and trans. Howard V. Hong and Edna H. Hong, assisted by Gregor Malantschuk (Bloomington: Indiana University Press, 1978), p. 19: Pap. I A 62 (1 June 1835).

p. 141    *standing for election to Denmark's Constitutional Assembly*: In October 1848 Grundtvig won a seat on Denmark's Constitutional Assembly, where he sat alongside his old adversary Clausen, who was one of the unelected members of the Assembly appointed by the Crown. On Kierkegaard's relationship to Grundtvig, see Anders Holm, 'Nicolai Frederik Severin Grundtvig: The Matchless Giant', in *Kierkegaard and His Danish Contemporaries, Tome II*, pp. 95–151.

p. 141    '*Every once in a while a religious enthusiast appears*': *The Point of View*, pp. 47, 42.

p. 143    '*Perhaps my voice does not possess enough strength and heartiness to penetrate to your innermost thought*': Either/Or Part II, p. 354.

p. 143    '*One must imagine what it is like to have to have a newspaper ready*': *Encounters with Kierkegaard*, ed. Bruce Kirmmse, trans. Bruce Kirmmse and Virginia Laursen (Princeton University Press, 1998), p. 56 – this is from Hother Ploug, son and biographer of Carl Ploug: see *Carl Ploug. Hans Liv og Gerning*, vol. I (1813–48), pp. 110ff. On Kierkegaard's relationship to Giødvad, see Andrea Scaramuccia, 'Jens Finsteen Giødwad: An Amiable Friend and a Despicable Journalist', in *Kierkegaard and His Danish Contemporaries, Tome I: Philosophy, Politics and Social Theory*, ed. Jon Stewart (Ashgate, 2009), pp. 13–33.

p. 144    '*I think that no book has caused such a stir . . . all holy feelings*': see *Encounters with Kierkegaard*, pp. 57–8.

p. 145    '*there is much that must be forgotten*': see S. Kierkegaard, *Discourses at the Communion on Fridays*, trans. Sylvia Walsh (Indiana University Press, 2011), p. 119f.

p. 146    '*My listener, you, to whom my discourse is addressed!*': ibid, p. 125f.

## CHAPTER 10

p. 147    '*When the sea exerts all its might*': S. Kierkegaard, *The Sickness unto Death*, ed. and trans. Howard V. Hong and Edna H. Hong (Princeton University Press, 1983), p. 82, and see also pp. 14, 49, 131; S. Kierkegaard, *Eighteen Upbuilding Discourses*, ed. and trans. Howard V. Hong and Edna H. Hong (Princeton University Press, 1992), p. 399; S. Kierkegaard, *Upbuilding Discourses in Various Spirits*, ed. and trans. Howard V. Hong and Edna H. Hong (Princeton University Press, 2009), p. 121.

p. 147    *he leased another 'fine and expensive apartment'*: Kierkegaard's *Journals and Notebooks, Volume 5: Journals NB6–NB10*, ed. and trans. Niels Jørgen Cappelørn, Alastair Hannay, David Kangas, Bruce H. Kirmmse, George Pattison, Joel D. S. Rasmussen, Vanessa Rumble and K. Brian Söderquist (Princeton University Press, 2012), pp. 144–5: NB7, 114 (September to November 1848); see also pp. 450–51.

p. 147    '*when all the furniture of the town is exchanging quarters*': see Andrew Hamilton, *Sixteen Months in the Danish Isles*, vol. 2 (Richard Bentley, 1852), p. 170.

p. 148    '*Here, too, Governance came to my assistance*': Kierkegaard's *Journals and Notebooks, Volume 5: Journals NB6–NB10*, ed. and trans. Niels Jørgen Cappelørn, Alastair Hannay, David Kangas, Bruce H. Kirmmse, George Pattison, Joel D. S. Rasmussen, Vanessa Rumble and K. Brian Söderquist (Princeton University Press, 2012), p. 145: NB7, 114 (September to November 1848).

p. 148    '*What is most important often seems so insignificant*': S. Kierkegaard, *The Point of View*, ed. and trans. Howard V. Hong and Edna H. Hong (Princeton University Press, 2009), pp. 36–7.

p. 148    *that single individual*: see ibid, pp. 37, 69.

p. 148    *P. G. Philipsen, who ran a fairly new bookshop*: see Niels Thulstrup, *The Copenhagen of Kierkegaard*, ed. Marie Mikulová Thulstrup, trans. Ruth Mach-Zagal (Reitzel, 1981), pp. 50–51. Philipsen published Kierkegaard's dissertation *On the Concept of Irony with Continual Reference to Socrates* in 1841, and five collections of Kierkegaard's discourses during the 1840s.

p. 148    *One sermon was on 'The Expectancy of Faith'*: 'The Expectancy of Faith' is based on Galatians 3: 23–end, and 'Every Good and Every Perfect Gift' on James 1: 17–22. See *Eighteen Upbuilding Discourses*, pp. 1–48.

p. 149    'that single individual whom with joy and gratitude I call my reader': ibid, p. 5.

p. 149    'Quite strange, really. I had decided to change that little preface': Kierkegaard's Journals and Notebooks, Volume 2: Journals EE–KK, ed. and trans. Niels Jørgen Cappelørn, Alastair Hannay, David Kangas, Bruce H. Kirmmse, George Pattison, Vanessa Rumble and K. Brian Söderquist (Princeton University Press, 2008), p. 157: JJ 93 (April 1843).

p. 150    'I have a room looking out on the water': ibid, p. 162: JJ 109 (10 May 1843).

p. 151    'But the owner has married and therefore I am living like a hermit': S. Kierkegaard, Letters and Documents, ed. and trans. Henrik Rosenmeier (Princeton University Press, 2009), pp. 151–2 – letter to Emil Boesen, 15 May 1843.

p. 151    Since they parted he had prayed for her every day, often twice a day: See Kierkegaard's Journals and Notebooks, Volume 3: Notebooks 1–15, ed. and trans. Niels Jørgen Cappelørn, Alastair Hannay, David Kangas, Bruce H. Kirmmse, George Pattison, Vanessa Rumble and K. Brian Söderquist (Princeton University Press, 2010), p. 435: NB15, 4 (August to November 1849).

p. 152    'better coffee than in Copenhagen, more newspapers, excellent service': S. Kierkegaard, Letters and Documents, p. 97 – letter to P. J. Spang, 18 November 1841.

p. 152    'When one does not have any particular business in life, as I do not': ibid, p. 151 – letter to Emil Boesen, 15 May 1843.

p. 153    He used a notebook, labelled 'Philosophica': this is Notebook 13, which seems to date from December 1842, though in 1846 Kierkegaard added notes on Spinoza; see Kierkegaard's Journals and Notebooks, Volume 3: Notebooks 1–15, pp. 731–9. The notes from Tenneman's Geschichte der Philosophie continue in Notebook 14 (see ibid, pp. 767–8), which dates from the first months of 1843, and in Journal JJ (see Kierkegaard's Journals and Notebooks, Volume 2: Journals EE–KK, pp. 453–66), part of which was written during the spring of 1843.

p. 153    a series of unanswered questions: see Kierkegaard's Journals and Notebooks, Volume 3: Notebooks 1–15, pp. 409–11.

p. 154    'The secret of all existence: movement': ibid, p. 307: NB13, 34.

p. 155    his small, slanting hand: Kierkegaard's handwriting was unusually variable: it changed not only over the years, but over the course of single texts. Annelise Garde provides a graphologist's analysis of

Kierkegaard's handwriting (in Danish, with an English summary and some interesting specimens), in 'Grafologisk undersøgelse af Søren Kierkegaards håndskrift i årene 1831–1855', *Kierkegaardiana*, 10 (1977), pp. 200–238.

p. 157    '*The question of repetition will play a very important role in modern philosophy*': S. Kierkegaard, *Fear and Trembling / Repetition*, ed. and trans. Howard V. Hong and Edna H. Hong (Princeton University Press, 1983), pp. 131, 148.

p. 157    *the new tunnel under the Thames*: the first tunnel under the River Thames opened on 25 May 1843, just before Kierkegaard left Berlin.

p. 157    '*the possibility and meaning of repetition*': *Fear and Trembling / Repetition*, p. 150.

p. 157    '*Gendarmenmarkt is certainly the most beautiful square in Berlin*': ibid, pp. 151–2.

p. 159    '*My mind was sterile, my troubled imagination constantly conjured up*': ibid, pp. 169–70.

p. 159    '*handsome appearance, large glowing eyes, and flippant air*': ibid, pp. 133–5.

p. 159    '*It was obvious that he was going to be unhappy*': ibid, p. 136.

p. 160    '*A poetic creativity awakened in him*': ibid, pp. 137–8.

p. 160    '*Transform yourself into a contemptible person*': ibid, p. 142.

p. 160    '*for there was no trace of anything really stirring*': the first part of this passage was deleted from the margin of the manuscript, and did not make it into the published version. See ibid, pp. 184, 277.

p. 161    '*Humanly speaking I have been fair to her*': *Kierkegaard's Journals and Notebooks, Volume 2: Journals EE–KK*, pp. 164–5: JJ 115 (17 May 1843).

p. 161    '*quite irritable, like any melancholic*': *Fear and Trembling / Repetition*, p. 180.

p. 161    '*I am at the end of my tether. My whole being screams in self-contradiction*': ibid, p. 201.

p. 162    '*Make me fit to be a husband*': ibid, p. 214.

p. 163    That year he noted in his journal Socrates's '*very fine*' remark: see *Kierkegaard's Journals and Notebooks, Volume 2: Journals EE–KK*, p. 169: JJ 131 (1843).

p. 163    '*the main thing is that one is truly forthright with God*': ibid, p. 171: JJ 141 (1843).

p. 164    *'Because I would otherwise die'*: Kierkegaard's *Journals and Notebooks, Volume 5: Journals NB6–NB10*, p. 189: NB8, 87 (November or December 1848).

p. 164    *'are too wordy for me'*: ibid, p. 25: NB6, 29 (July or August 1848).

## CHAPTER 11

p. 165    *'I am still very exhausted, but I have almost reached my goal'*: *Kierkegaard's Journals and Notebooks, Volume 5: Journals NB6–NB10*, ed. and trans. Niels Jørgen Cappelørn, Alastair Hannay, David Kangas, Bruce H. Kirmmse, George Pattison, Joel D. S. Rasmussen, Vanessa Rumble and K. Brian Söderquist (Princeton University Press, 2012), p. 98: NB7, 36 (August to November 1848).

p. 165    *'After becoming an author, I actually have never once experienced'*: S. Kierkegaard, *The Point of View*, ed. and trans. Howard V. Hong and Edna H. Hong (Princeton University Press, 2009), p. 75.

p. 165    *'Then I become completely calm'*: ibid, pp. 71–3.

p. 166    *'the world, if it is not evil, is mediocre . . . this humanness'*: ibid, pp. 71–2, 88.

p. 166    *'It was my plan as soon as Either/Or was published'*: ibid, p. 162.

p. 166    *'I understood that my task was to do penance'*: ibid, p. 162.

p. 167    he has felt such a *'driving need'* for penance: see *Kierkegaard's Journals and Notebooks, Volume 4: Journals NB–NB5*, ed. and trans. Niels Jørgen Cappelørn, Alastair Hannay, David Kangas, Bruce H. Kirmmse, George Pattison, Joel D. S. Rasmussen, Vanessa Rumble and K. Brian Söderquist (Princeton University Press, 2011), pp. 139–40: NB2, 9 (1847).

p. 167    *'this is how I serve Christianity'*: Kierkegaard's *Journals and Notebooks, Volume 5: Journals NB6–NB10*, p. 44: NB6, 62 (July or August 1848).

p. 167    *'I showed the girl my confidence in her'*: *Kierkegaard's Journals and Notebooks, Volume 2: Journals EE–KK*, ed. and trans. Niels Jørgen Cappelørn, Alastair Hannay, David Kangas, Bruce H. Kirmmse, George Pattison, Vanessa Rumble and K. Brian Söderquist (Princeton University Press, 2008), p. 174: JJ 145 (1843). The entry was deciphered by modern scholars using a microscope.

p. 168    *'An individual with a sense of humour meets a girl'*: ibid, p. 176: JJ 155 (1843).

p. 169    'It amused him every day to see the sugar melt': Encounters with
          Kierkegaard, ed. Bruce Kirmmse, trans. Bruce Kirmmse and Vir-
          ginia Laursen (Princeton University Press, 1998), p. 208. On Israel
          Levin, see also Niels Jørgen Cappelørn, Joakim Garff and Johnny
          Kondrup, Written Images: Søren Kierkegaard's Journals, Note-
          books, Booklets, Sheets, Scraps, and Slips of Paper, trans. Bruce
          Kirmmse (Princeton University Press, 2003), pp. 150–58.

p. 169    Kierkegaard 'did not cut a particularly good figure on a horse':
          Encounters with Kierkegaard, p. 232 – from Hans Brøchner's
          recollections on Kierkegaard, written in 1871–2.

p. 170    True Christianity . . . went through more than a hundred editions:
          see Christopher B. Barnett, Kierkegaard, Pietism and Holiness
          (Ashgate, 2011), p. 12.

p. 170    Arndt urged generations of Protestant Christians to purify their
          souls: see Johann Arndt, True Christianity, trans. Peter Erb (Lon-
          don: SPCK, 1979), pp. 70–82 and passim.

p. 171    'A Christian is truly in the world but not of the world': ibid, p. 75.
          On Kierkegaard's reading of Arndt, see Joseph Ballon, 'Johann
          Arndt: The Pietist Impulse in Kierkegaard and Seventeenth-
          Century Lutheran Devotional Literature', in Kierkegaard and the
          Renaissance and Modern Traditions, Tome II: Theology, ed. Jon
          Stewart (Ashgate, 2009), pp. 21–30.

p. 171    Within his lifetime Copenhagen has acquired the features of
          urban life: see George Pattison, 'Poor Paris!' (Walter de Gruyter,
          1998), pp. 21–46.

p. 172    'a variety of black silk capes': see Niels Thulstrup, The Copenhagen
          of Kierkegaard, ed. Marie Mikulová Thulstrup, trans. Ruth Mach-
          Zagal (Reitzel, 1981), pp. 53–8. In her little book Lif i Norden [Life
          in Scandinavia], the Swedish writer Fredrika Bremer recounted her
          experience of walking along Østergade in 1849, and described the
          street as 'a kind of inferno', 'entirely hostile to humankind'.

p. 172    he recalls how he played the role of flâneur on the streets of
          Copenhagen: see The Point of View, p. 61.

p. 173    'nothing other than a very talented and well-read feuilleton
          writer': see George Pattison, Kierkegaard, Religion, and the
          Nineteenth-Century Crisis of Culture (Cambridge University
          Press, 2002), pp. 30–49.

p. 173    'No Grand Inquisitor has such dreadful torments in readiness as
          anxiety has': S. Kierkegaard, The Concept of Anxiety, ed. and trans.
          Reidar Thomte (Princeton University Press, 1981), pp. 115–16.

p. 173    'And this is the wonderful thing about life': ibid, pp. 78–9.

p. 174    'This is an adventure that every human being must go through': ibid, p. 155.

p. 175    'The more profoundly a human being is in anxiety': ibid, p. 156.

p. 175    When a human being 'passes through the anxiety of the possible': ibid, p. 158.

p. 175    'Then anxiety enters into his soul': ibid, p. 159.

p. 175    'With K. it frequently happened that when he reflected on some minor matter': see Encounters with Kierkegaard, p. 61 – from a letter from Hans Brøchner to H. P. Barfod, 10 November 1871.

p. 176    a character called Søren Kirk in Gjenboerne: 'I remember that one evening,' wrote Hans Brøchner, 'when I was on my way to a rehearsal for the play, I met Kierkegaard on Højbroplads and spoke with him. He said to me in a joking tone: "Well, so you are going to play me in Hostrup's comedy?" I related the contents of the role to him and told him my understanding of it. At the time I had no impression that Hostrup's joke affected him.' In his 1891 memoir, Hostrup recalled meeting Kierkegaard with Emil Boesen: 'the strange thing about this meeting was that he proved to be extremely friendly toward me, despite the fact that – according to his journals – he was extremely embittered about Gjenboerne. I looked at this strange man with the greatest of interest, and both before and since I have been deeply moved by several of his books.' See Encounters with Kierkegaard, pp. 61, 287.

p. 176    he deleted his own name from the title pages and gave each book a pseudonym: see S. Kierkegaard, Philosophical Fragments / Johannes Climacus, ed. and trans. Howard V. Hong and Edna H. Hong (Princeton University Press, 1985), pp. 176–7 (Pap. V B 39), The Concept of Anxiety, p. 177 (Pap. V B 42).

p. 176    'You are in a cocoon of thoughtfulness': S. Kierkegaard, Prefaces / Writing Sampler, ed. and trans. Todd W. Nichol (Princeton University Press, 1997), p. 9.

p. 177    'a book that does not owe its origin to an inexplicable inner need': ibid, p. 13.

p. 177    'for it would indeed be too bad if the public's gossip were to go to waste': ibid, p. 19.

p. 177    'lofty endeavour to restore lost souls to society': ibid, p. 178.

p. 177    'To be an author in Denmark is almost as troublesome as having to live in public view': ibid, p. 15.

p. 178   *he decided to stop writing upbuilding discourses*: see *Kierkegaard's Journals and Notebooks, Volume 2: Journals EE–KK*, pp. 194, 203: JJ 220, 255 (1844).

p. 178   *In his discourse 'To Need God is a Human Being's Highest Perfection'*: see S. Kierkegaard, *Eighteen Upbuilding Discourses*, ed. and trans. Howard V. Hong and Edna H. Hong (Princeton University Press, 1992), pp. 321–5.

p. 178   *'only the one who was in anxiety finds rest'*: S. Kierkegaard, *Fear and Trembling*, ed. C. Stephen Evans and Sylvia Walsh, trans. Sylvia Walsh (Cambridge University Press, 2006), p. 21.

p. 178   *'you gather everything together all at once and surround yourself with it'*: S. Kierkegaard, *Letters and Documents*, ed. and trans. Henrik Rosenmeier (Princeton University Press, 2009), p. 164 – letter to Emil Boesen, undated.

p. 178   *'See to it that you love yourself'*: ibid, p. 236 – letter to Henriette Kierkegaard, December 1847.

p. 179   *'He understood as few do'*: *Encounters with Kierkegaard*, p. 242 – from Hans Brøchner's recollections of Kierkegaard, written in 1871–2.

## CHAPTER 12

p. 180   *'1848 has raised me to another level'*: see S. Kierkegaard, *The Point of View*, ed. and trans. Howard V. Hong and Edna H. Hong (Princeton University Press, 1998), p. 207: Pap. $X^2$ A 66 (1849). This entry is titled 'On the Year 1848'.

p. 180   *'some of the best things'*: *Kierkegaard's Journals and Notebooks, Volume 5: Journals NB6–NB10*, ed. and trans. Niels Jørgen Cappelørn, Alastair Hannay, David Kangas, Bruce H. Kirmmse, George Pattison, Joel D. S. Rasmussen, Vanessa Rumble and K. Brian Söderquist (Princeton University Press, 2012), p. 144: NB7, 114 (August to November, 1848). In 1849 Kierkegaard wrote in his journal that 'My home has been my consolation, having a pleasant home has been my greatest earthly encouragement' – see *Kierkegaard's Journals and Notebooks, Volume 6: Journals NB11–NB14*, ed. and trans. Niels Jørgen Cappelørn, Alastair Hannay, David Kangas, Bruce H. Kirmmse, George Pattison, Joel D. S. Rasmussen, Vanessa Rumble and K. Brian Söderquist (Princeton University Press, 2013), p. 234: NB12, 143 (1849).

p. 180    *'Conditions are so wretched here in Denmark'*: Kierkegaard's *Journals and Notebooks, Volume 5: Journals NB6–NB10*, pp. 196–7: NB8, 106 (December 1848).

p. 181    *'it is perhaps my duty to God'*: ibid, p. 321: NB10, 105 (February to April 1849).

p. 181    *'in relation to God as a child to a father (mother)'*: ibid.

p. 181    *'nearly all my life has been so terribly wasted'*: ibid, p. 211: NB9, 8 (January or February 1849).

p. 181    *Kierkegaard was sitting in that church on the Sunday when the marriage banns were read*: see *Kierkegaard's Journals and Notebooks, Volume 3: Notebooks 1–15*, ed. and trans. Niels Jørgen Cappelørn, Alastair Hannay, David Kangas, Bruce H. Kirmmse, George Pattison, Vanessa Rumble and K. Brian Söderquist (Princeton University Press, 2010), p. 436: Notebook 15, 4 (August to November 1849).

p. 181    *'The keystone of her marriage is and will continue to be that I am a villain'*: *Kierkegaard's Journals and Notebooks Volume 5: Journals NB6–NB10*, p. 83: NB7, 10 (August to November 1848).

p. 182    *'The moment I die (which I have constantly expected will happen soon)'*: ibid, p. 91: NB7, 20 (August to November 1848).

p. 182    *'What a constant torment it has been to me'*: ibid, p. 90: NB7, 20 (August to November 1848).

p. 182    *'it remains my guilt nevertheless'*: ibid, p. 91: NB7, 20 (August to November 1848).

p. 182    *he was 'already betrothed' to Christianity*: see ibid, pp. 368–9: NB10, 191 (February to April 1849).

p. 182    *'the Christmas festival'*: ibid, p. 192: NB8, 97 (December 1848).

p. 183    *'there is an infinite difference between her and myself'*: ibid, p. 184: NB8, 76 (December 1848).

p. 183    *'I am constantly re-writing parts of it, but it does not satisfy me'*: see S. Kierkegaard, *Stages on Life's Way*, ed. and trans. Howard V. Hong and Edna H. Hong (Princeton University Press, 1988), p. 515.

p. 185    *'By now I have learned not too need night time in order to find stillness'*: ibid, pp. 16–17.

p. 185    *'Just one minute, my beloved, just one moment'*: ibid, pp. 183–4.

p. 186    *'a plain gold ring with an engraved date'*: ibid, pp. 189–90.

p. 186    *He also reproduced word for word the note he sent to Regine*: see ibid, pp. 329–30; also *Kierkegaard's Journals and Notebooks, Volume 3: Notebooks 1–15*, p. 433: Notebook 15, 4 (August to November 1849). Here Kierkegaard writes, 'If she should happen to see the book, what I want is precisely that she should be reminded of it.'

p. 186    *'June 18th.* Midnight. *Am I guilty, then?'*: *Stages on Life's Way*, p. 381.

p. 187    *'with all my power to remain faithful to my spiritual experience'*: ibid, p. 397.

p. 188    *'Only the one who seeks worthily finds it'*: ibid, pp. 16–17.

p. 188    *'He is, in truth, my body'*: *Encounters with Kierkegaard*, ed. Bruce Kirmmse, trans. Bruce Kirmmse and Virginia Laursen (Princeton University Press, 1998), p. 232 – from Hans Brøchner's recollections of Kierkegaard, written in 1871–2.

p. 188    *'One would think that Magister Kierkegaard possessed a kind of magic wand'*: see S. Kierkegaard, *The Corsair Affair*, ed. and trans. Howard V. Hong and Edna H. Hong (Princeton University Press, 1982), pp. 274–5.

p. 189    *'When it is the legitimate leader in Danish literature'*: ibid, pp. 24–7.

p. 190    *Inspired by the republican and socialist satirical press in Paris*: Honoré de Balzac's *Illusions perdues*, written between 1837 and 1843, gives a vivid account of Parisian journalism in the 1820s.

p. 190    *the Greek myth of Nemesis*: J. L. Heiberg published an essay on Nemesis in 1827. On Kierkegaard's own interest in the myth of Nemesis, see Laura Liva, 'Nemesis: From the Ancient Goddess to a Modern Concept', in Katalin Nun and Jon Stewart (eds.), *Kierkegaard's Literary Figures and Motifs, Tome II: Gulliver to Zerlina* (Ashgate, 2015), pp. 155–62.

p. 190    *Peder Ludvig Møller*: see Roger Poole, 'Søren Kierkegaard and P. L. Møller: Erotic Space Shattered', in *International Kierkegaard Commentary, Volume 13: The Corsair Affair*, ed. Robert L. Perkins (Mercer University Press, 1990), pp. 141–61; Troy Wellington Smith, 'P. L. Møller: Kierkegaard's Byronic Adversary', *The Byron Journal*, 42.1 (2014), pp. 35–47. P. L. Møller is sometimes cited as Kierkegaard's model for Johannes the Seducer: Roger Poole describes this theory as 'semi-canonical' in Kierkegaard research.

p. 190    *a review of* Stages on Life's Way: see *The Corsair Affair*, pp. 96–104.

p. 192    *'Would that I might only get into* The Corsair *soon!'*: ibid, p. 46.

p. 192    *He met Goldschmidt on the street, and they discussed these literary hostilities*: from an account in Goldschmidt's autobiography

*Livs Erindringer og Resultater* (Gyldendal, 1877): see *The Corsair Affair*, p. 146.

p. 193    '*It is really strange that a man does not have control of the book he buys and pays for*': ibid, pp. 132–3 (extract abridged).

p. 195    '*In the bitterness of that glance*': from Goldschmidt's autobiography: see ibid, p. 149.

p. 196    '*my beloved capital city and place of residence*': Kierkegaard's *Journals and Notebooks, Volume 2: Journals EE–KK*, ed. and trans. Niels Jørgen Cappelørn, Alastair Hannay, David Kangas, Bruce H. Kirmmse, George Pattison, Vanessa Rumble and K. Brian Söderquist (Princeton University Press, 2008), pp. 172–3: JJ 143 (1843).

p. 197    '*Out there in quiet activity, I shall breathe easier*': Kierkegaard's *Journals and Notebooks, Volume 4: Journals NB-NB5*, ed. and trans. Niels Jørgen Cappelørn, Alastair Hannay, David Kangas, Bruce H. Kirmmse, George Pattison, Joel D. S. Rasmussen, Vanessa Rumble and K. Brian Söderquist (Princeton University Press, 2011), p. 17: NB, 7 (9 March 1846).

p. 197    '*as correctly situated in literature as possible*': ibid, p. 12: NB, 7 (9 March 1846).

p. 197    '*in this way I can still avoid becoming an author*': see S. Kierkegaard, *Upbuilding Discourses in Various Spirits*, p. 356: Pap. VII$^1$ A 9 (February, 1846).

p. 197    *Thomasine Gyllembourg, Heiberg's mother*: see *Kierkegaard's Journals and Notebooks Volume 5: Journals NB6–NB10*, p. 38: NB6, 55 (July or August 1848): 'then I took [Heiberg's] mother and celebrated her'. On Thomasine Gyllembourg's anonymity, see Katalin Nun, *Women of the Danish Golden Age: Literature, Theater and the Emancipation of Women* (Museum Tusculanum Press, 2013).

p. 197    *Lusard is struck by the bright lights . . . in Tivoli Gardens*: see *To Tidsaldre*, in J. L. Heiberg (ed.), *Skrifter*, vol. XI (Reitzel, 1851), pp. 156–8. These translations are by George Pattison: see his *Kierkegaard, Religion and the Nineteenth-Century Crisis of Culture* (Cambridge University Press, 2002), pp. 54–61.

p. 198    *Heiberg's 1842 essay 'People and Public*': see J. L. Heiberg, 'Folk og Publicum', *Intelligensblade* 6, 1 June 1842, p. 137. Translation by George Pattison: see his *Kierkegaard, Religion and the Nineteenth-Century Crisis of Culture*, p. 65.

p. 198    'not for aesthetic and critical readers of newspapers but for rational creatures': S. Kierkegaard, Two Ages, ed. and trans. Howard V. Hong and Edna H. Hong (Princeton University Press, 1978), p. 5.

p. 198    'I cannot agree with that at all': ibid, pp. 95–6. The biblical reference is to Luke 23:28.

p. 200    He thought Adler was confused, but he felt inclined to support him: on Kierkegaard's relationship to Adler, see Carl Henrik Koch, 'Adolph Peter Adler: A Stumbling-Block and an Inspiration for Kierkegaard', in Kierkegaard and His Danish Contemporaries, Tome II: Theology, ed. Jon Stewart (Ashgate, 2009), pp. 1–22.

p. 200    'The merely human idea of self-denial': S. Kierkegaard, Works of Love, ed. and trans. Howard V. Hong and Edna H. Hong (Princeton University Press, 1998), p. 194.

p. 200    'persecution by the mob, the people, the public': Kierkegaard's Journals and Notebooks, Volume 4: Journals NB–NB5, p. 317: NB4, 62 (1848).

p. 201    'a form of evil': ibid, p. 111: NB7, 63 (September to November 1848).

p. 201    Denmark's 'demoralization', 'disintegration': see ibid, pp. 102–3: NB7: 46 (September to November 1848); p. 177: NB8, 57 (December 1848).

p. 201    'I feel no bitterness at all': Kierkegaard's Journals and Notebooks, Volume 4: Journals NB–NB5, p. 398–9: NB5, 61 (May to July 1848).

p. 201    in this life his trousers have received too much attention, and his authorship too little: Kierkegaard felt that his writings were ignored: it is true that, whereas Either/Or, Fear and Trembling, Repetition and Works of Love were reviewed extensively, other works – such as The Concept of Anxiety, Two Ages: A Literary Review and Christian Discourses – were not reviewed. See Kierkegaard's Journals and Notebooks, Volume 6: Journals NB11–NB14, p. 453.

p. 201    because 'they are envious': Kierkegaard's Journals and Notebooks, Volume 5: Journals NB6–NB10, p. 197: NB8, 106 (December 1848).

p. 201    he recalls how Peter responded to him: see ibid, p. 198: NB8, 108 (December, 1848).

p. 201    'They must be permitted to trample me down': ibid, p. 200: NB8, 110 (December, 1848).

p. 202    He imagines his future readers, 'who will be able to sit in peace and quiet': ibid, p. 191: NB8, 97 (December 1848); see also

Kierkegaard's entry from early 1849 on his 'martyrdom of laughter' – ibid, pp. 289–90: NB10, 42 (February to April 1849).

p. 202    *'Dying is the only thing that can clear the air'*: ibid, p. 11: NB6, 9 (July or August, 1848).

p. 202    *'truly unselfish'*: ibid, p. 181: NB8, 69 (December 1848).

## PART THREE

p. 203    *'How many times have I said that a warship doesn't receive its orders until it's out on the deep?'*: *Kierkegaard's Journals and Notebooks, Volume 5: Journals NB6–NB10*, ed. and trans. Niels Jørgen Cappelørn, Alastair Hannay, David Kangas, Bruce H. Kirmmse, George Pattison, Joel D. S. Rasmussen, Vanessa Rumble and K. Brian Söderquist (Princeton University Press, 2012), p. 300: NB10, 60 (February to April 1849).

## CHAPTER 13

p. 205    *'The question is: When should all the latest works be published!'*: *Kierkegaard's Journals and Notebooks, Volume 5: Journals NB6–NB10*, ed. and trans. Niels Jørgen Cappelørn, Alastair Hannay, David Kangas, Bruce H. Kirmmse, George Pattison, Joel D. S. Rasmussen, Vanessa Rumble and K. Brian Söderquist (Princeton University Press, 2012), p. 242.

p. 205    *'Humanly speaking, there is something pleasant about having secure employment'*: ibid, p. 14.

p. 205    *'a special ability to talk with ordinary people'*: see *Encounters with Kierkegaard*, ed. Bruce Kirmmse, trans. Bruce Kirmmse and Virginia Laursen (Princeton University Press, 1998), p. 109 – from H. C. Rosted, *Den gamle Postgaard in Hørsholm* (O. Cohn and E. Hasfeldt, 1925), p. 27. See also *Encounters with Kierkegaard*, p. 111, where Tycho Spang recalls Kierkegaard's 'quite remarkable and unusual talent for talking to people of every age and from every walk of life'.

p. 206    *in relation to* The Corsair, *a martyr*: on Kierkegaard's martyrdom at the hands of *The Corsair*, see for example *Kierkegaard's Journals and Notebooks, Volume 5: Journals NB6–NB10*, p. 349: NB10, 166 (February to April 1849): 'I am feeling indescribably weak and it seems to me that it can't be long until death makes an end of the matter. And truly a dead man is just what Copenhagen and Denmark need if there is to be any end to all this mean, envious, grimacing baseness.' Kierkegaard considered that he had offered himself as a sacrifice 'to guarantee that P. L. Møller and Goldschmidt were kept in line', though he thought it 'a heavy fate' that instead of earning wealth and renown for his art, 'as a result of being born in a demoralized market town' he was 'insulted by every street urchin, which envy followed behind and gloried in its victory'.

p 206     '*It is certainly true that I have been unspeakably unhappy*': ibid, pp. 259: NB9, 78 (February 1849).

p. 206     '*It is difficult to decide whether it is more humiliating*': ibid, p. 300: NB10, 60 (February to April 1849).

p. 207     *What should he do with* The Book on Adler?: on Kierkegaard's reworking of *The Book on Adler*, see ibid, p. 525.

p. 207     '*to introduce Christianity into Christendom*': ibid, p. 242: NB9, 56 (January or February 1849).

p. 207     '*Just as a cabinet minister steps down*': ibid, p. 237: NB9, 45 (January or February 1849).

p. 207     *a petitionary prayer*: see S. Kierkegaard, *The Lily of the Field and the Bird of the Air: Three Godly Discourses*, trans. Bruce Kirmmse (Princeton University Press, 2016), p. 5.

p. 208     '*in the place assigned*': ibid, p. 52.

p. 208     '*That you came into existence, that you exist*': ibid, pp. 78-9.

p. 208     '*the self runs away from itself*': S. Kierkegaard, *The Sickness unto Death*, ed. and trans. Howard V. Hong and Edna H. Hong (Princeton University Press, 1983), pp. 35-6.

p. 209     *he repented the 'melancholia' and 'hypochondriacal evasion*': see *Kierkegaard's Journals and Notebooks, Volume 6: Journals NB11–NB14*, ed. and trans. Niels Jørgen Cappelørn, Alastair Hannay, David Kangas, Bruce H. Kirmmse, George Pattison, Joel D. S. Rasmussen, Vanessa Rumble and K. Brian Söderquist (Princeton University Press, 2013), p. 8: NB11, 8; p. 55: NB11, 105 (May to July 1849). On how Kierkegaard's devotional reading influenced his decision to publish *The Sickness unto Death*, see Peter Sajda, '"The Wise Men Went Another Way": Kierkegaard's Dialogue with Fénelon and Tersteegen in the Summer of 1849', in *Kierkegaard and Christianity*, ed. Roman Králik, Abrahim H. Khan, Peter Sajda, Jamie Turnbull and Andrew J. Burgess (Acta Kierkegaardiana, vol. 3, 2008), pp. 89–105.

p. 209    '*I wanted to secure a comfortable future*': *Kierkegaard's Journals and Notebooks, Volume 6: Journals NB11–NB14*, pp. 8–14: NB11, 8–20 (May to July 1849).

p. 209    '*What makes my life so difficult is that I'm tuned an octave higher*': ibid, p. 101: NB11, 174 (May to July 1849).

p. 210    *The Danish State Church became the Danish People's Church*: see *Kierkegaard's Journals and Notebooks, Volume 8: Journals NB21–NB25*, ed. and trans. Niels Jørgen Cappelørn, Alastair Hannay, Bruce H. Kirmmse, David D. Possen, Joel D. S. Rasmussen and Vanessa Rumble (Princeton University Press, 2015), pp. 679–81.

p. 210    *Privately he now believed Mynster to be*: see *Kierkegaard's Journals and Notebooks, Volume 6: Journals NB11–NB14*, pp. 17, 35, 42, 45, 47: NB11, 25, 59, 61, 77, 80, 87 (May to July 1849).

p. 210    *He told Kierkegaard to come 'another time'*: see ibid, pp. 113: NB11, 193 (May to July 1849); p. 488.

p. 211    *He spent a restless night*: see *Kierkegaard's Journals and Notebooks, Volume 8: Journals NB21–NB25*, pp. 356–7: NB24, 54 (April to November 1851).

p. 212    '*I've been willing to ask God to free me*': *Kierkegaard's Journals and Notebooks, Volume 6: Journals NB11–NB14*, pp. 138–9: NB11, 233 (May to July 1849) – passage abridged.

p. 213    '*We are not twins, we are opposites*': ibid, p. 124: NB11, 204 (May to July 1849); S. Kierkegaard, *Practice in Christianity*, ed. and trans. Howard V. Hong and Edna H. Hong (Princeton University Press, 1991), p. 282: Pap. X B 48 (1849).

p. 213    '*Whereas from his central standpoint the brilliant Martensen*': see *Kierkegaard's Journals and Notebooks, Volume 6: Journals NB11–NB14*, pp. 550–51. Like Kierkegaard, Fredrika Bremer renounced marriage in the 1830s to become a writer; she was inspired by modern German philosophy and by English utilitarianism. When she left Copenhagen in 1849 Bremer sailed to New York and toured America: she wrote about slavery, prisons, Quakers and Shakers, and the Scandinavian communities of the Midwest. On her way back to Sweden she spent a few weeks in Britain, visiting Liverpool, Manchester and London, and meeting George Eliot and Elizabeth Gaskell.

     Fredrika Bremer's account of Kierkegaard was echoed by her English contemporary Andrew Hamilton, who travelled to Denmark around 1849 and later published a lengthy, two-volume travelogue. He did not meet Kierkegaard, but often saw him walking the streets, usually deep in conversation: 'He is a philosophical Christian writer, evermore dwelling, one might almost say harping, on the theme of the human heart. There is no Danish writer more in earnest than he, yet there is no one in whose way stand more things to prevent his becoming popular. He writes at times with an unearthly beauty, but too often with an exaggerated display of logic that disgusts the public . . . I have received the highest delight from some of his books . . . Kierkegaard's habits of life are singular enough to lend a (perhaps false) interest to his proceedings. He goes into no company, and sees nobody in his own house, which answers all the ends of an invisible dwelling; I could never learn that any one had been inside of it. Yet his one great study is human nature; no one knows more people than he. The fact is *he walks about town all day*, and generally in some person's company; only in the evenings does he write and read. When walking, he is very communicative, and at the same time manages to draw everything out of his companion that is likely to be profitable to himself.' Andrew Hamilton, *Sixteen Months in the Danish Isles*, vol. 2 (Richard Bentley, 1852), p. 269.

p. 214   *Martensen, the Professor of Theology, Court Preacher, Knight of the Dannebrog*: Martensen had followed Mynster's footsteps to become Court Preacher in 1845 and a Knight of the Dannebrog in 1847.

p. 214   *'Cruel I was, that is true. Why?'*: see S. Kierkegaard, *Letters and Documents*, ed. and trans. Henrik Rosenmeier (Princeton University Press, 2009), pp. 335–6 – letter to Regine Schlegel, 1849. For the series of draft letters to Regine and her husband, see ibid, pp. 322–37.

p. 215   *he was acquiring imitators and adherents*: see *Kierkegaard's Journals and Notebooks, Volume 6: Journals NB11–NB14*, p. 658. Peter Christian Kierkegaard also cited as one of Kierkegaard's 'imitators and adherents' the pseudonym H. H., under which Kierkegaard published *Two Minor Ethical-Religious Essays* – a drastically abridged version of his unpublished *Book on Adler*– in May 1849. As with his earlier pseudonymous works, Kierkegaard's friend Jens Giødvad had taken the manuscript to the printer to protect its author's identity. *Two Minor Ethical-Religious Essays* offered 'a point of view' on Kierkegaard's authorship by comparing the figures of poetic genius, apostle and

NOTES

martyr, and exploring their different relationships to the truth. It was much less personal than *The Point of View for My Work as an Author*, revealing only 'that I am a genius – not an apostle, not a martyr': see S. Kierkegaard, *Without Authority*, ed. and trans. Howard V. Hong and Edna H. Hong (Princeton University Press, 1997), p. 238.

p. 216   *a journal entry headed 'Protest Against Bishop Mynster'*: see *Kierkegaard's Journals and Notebooks, Volume 6: Journals NB11–NB14*, p. 385: NB14, 63 (November 1849 to January 1850).

p. 216   *'a little, cooped-up place, the homeland of nonsense'*: *Kierkegaard's Journals and Notebooks, Volume 7: Journals NB15–NB20*, ed. and trans. Niels Jørgen Cappelørn, Alastair Hannay, Bruce H. Kirmmse, David D. Possen, Joel D. S. Rasmussen, Vanessa Rumble and K. Brian Söderquist (Princeton University Press, 2014), pp. 120–21: NB16, 38 (February to March 1850).

p. 216   *St Augustine, he noted*: see ibid, p. 158: NB16, 92 (February to March 1850). Augustine was commenting on Matthew 5:39.

p. 216   *He found ammunition in Luther's sermons*: on Kierkegaard's reading of Luther and Tersteegen, see David Yoon-Jung Kim and Joel D. S. Rasmussen, 'Martin Luther: Reform, Secularization and the Question of His "True Successor"', and Christopher B. Barnett, 'Gerhard Tersteegen: Kierkegaard's Reception of a Man of "Noble Piety and Simple Wisdom"', both in *Kierkegaard and the Renaissance and Modern Traditions, Tome II: Theology*, ed. Jon Stewart (Ashgate, 2009), pp. 173–217 and 245–58.

p. 216   *'it is the great, unreasonable fool who runs out of the world'*: see *Kierkegaard's Journals and Notebooks, Volume 7: Journals NB15–NB20*, p. 528; see Martin Luther, *En christelig Postille*, trans J. Thisted (Wahlske Boghandling, 1828), vol. II, pp. 242; 246.

p. 217   *Emil was keen for him to visit Louise, but he was reluctant*: see *Letters and Documents*, pp. 344–6 – letter from Emil Boesen to S. Kierkegaard, 7 March 1850; and pp. 357–8 – letter from S. Kierkegaard to Emil Boesen, 12 April 1850.

p. 217   *he quarrelled with Rasmus Nielsen*: see *Kierkegaard's Journals and Notebooks, Volume 7: Journals NB15–NB20*, pp. 219–22: NB17, 71 (March to May 1850). Kierkegaard wrote several journal entries on Nielsen's book, which in his view 'battled mediocrity – in part with borrowed weapons' and 'spoiled the whole thing with all that scholarly apparatus and detail': see *Kierkegaard's Journals and Notebooks, Volume 5: Journals NB6–NB10*, p. 271: NB10, 9; p. 283: NB10, 33; *Kierkegaard's Journals and Notebooks, Volume 6: Journals NB11–NB14*, p. 28: NB11, 46.

p. 217    *'Each of us possesses the faith only to a certain limited degree'*: see *Kierkegaard's Journals and Notebooks Volume 7: Journals NB15–NB20*, p. 681. Martensen's book came out in May 1850.

p. 217    *a cheaper apartment on Nørregade*: see ibid, p. 695.

p. 217    *'In the afternoons I suffer so much from reflected sunlight'*: ibid, pp. 287, 324: NB18, 48, 92 (May to June 1850).

## CHAPTER 14

p. 219    *Most Danes 'longed and prayed for summer'*: see Andrew Hamilton, *Sixteen Months in the Danish Isles*, vol. 2 (Richard Bentley, 1852), p. 138. Hamilton also observed that 'Autumn is a glorious season, but the Danes scarcely seem to set the same value on it which we do in England' (p. 141).

p. 219    *an old man's 'noble wisdom' and a young girl's 'loveable foolishness'*: *Kierkegaard's Journals and Notebooks, Volume 6: Journals NB11–NB14*, ed. and trans. Niels Jørgen Cappelørn, Alastair Hannay, David Kangas, Bruce H. Kirmmse, George Pattison, Joel D. S Rasmussen, Vanessa Rumble and K. Brian Söderquist (Princeton University Press, 2013), p. 41: NB 11 (May to July 1849). On Kierkegaard's annual struggle between 9 August and 10 September, see ibid, p. 159: NB12 (July to September 1849).

p. 219    *it explored the difference between rigorous and lenient Christianity*: see S. Kierkegaard, *Practice in Christianity*, ed. and trans. Howard V. Hong and Edna H. Hong (Princeton University Press, 1991), pp. 233–57.

p. 220    *'Ah, a person can certainly proclaim leniency'*: *Kierkegaard's Journals and Notebooks, Volume 7: Journals NB15–NB20*, ed. and trans. Niels Jørgen Cappelørn, Alastair Hannay, Bruce H. Kirmmse, David D. Possen, Joel D. S. Rasmussen, Vanessa Rumble and K. Brian Søderquist (Princeton University Press, 2014), pp. 271–2: NB18, 27 (May to June 1850).

p. 221    *Kierkegaard visited Mynster*: see *Kierkegaard's Journals and Notebooks, Volume 8: Journals NB21–NB25*, ed. and trans. Niels Jørgen Cappelørn, Alastair Hannay, Bruce H. Kirmmse,

David D. Possen, Joel D. S. Rasmussen and Vanessa Rumble (Princeton University Press, 2015), pp. 68–9. See also Martensen's comment in a letter to his friend Pastor Gude, 26 Nov November 1850: 'This book has now caused the bishop to give up totally on K's work; naturally, the shameless pronouncements concerning the Church's sermons have made him indignant' – p. 787.

p. 222     *'You became a sword through the heart of your mother'*: *Kierkegaard's Journals and Notebooks, Volume 7: Journals NB15–NB20*, pp. 271–2: NB18, 27 (May to June 1850).

p. 222     *'For my part, I love being a human being'*: ibid, p. 276: NB18, 33 (May to June 1850).

p. 222     *Tersteegan – who gave away his inheritance and lived as a hermit*: see Christopher B. Barnett, 'Gerhard Tersteegen: Reception of a Man of "Noble Piety and Simple Wisdom"', in *Kierkegaard and the Renaissance and Modern Traditions. Tome II: Theology*, ed. Jon Stewart (Ashgate, 2009), pp. 245–57.

p. 222     *'Luther certainly possessed the inner truth'*: *Kierkegaard's Journals and Notebooks, Volume 7: Journals NB15–NB20*, pp. 329–30: NB18, 101 (May to June 1850).

p. 223     *'Shall we continue to force all members of the People's Church to undergo church wedding ceremonies'*: see *Kierkegaard's Journals and Notebooks, Volume 8: Journals NB21–NB25*, p. 682.

p. 223     *'defying Satan, the pope, the whole world'*: see ibid, pp. 371–2: NB24, 75 (April to November 1851).

p. 223     *'a clever and prudent man'*: *Kierkegaard's Journals and Notebooks, Volume 7: Journals NB15–NB20*, p. 376: NB19, 58 (June to July 1850).

p. 224     *'Surely the deepest and highest interest of the Church in our day'*: see S. Kierkegaard, *The Corsair Affair*, ed. and trans. Howard V. Hong and Edna H. Hong (Princeton University Press, 2009), p. 51.

p. 224     *'Simply because I have from the beginning understood Christianity to be inwardness'*: ibid, p. 53.

p. 224     *'For him it has long been settled that he is a Christian'*: *Kierkegaard's Journals and Notebooks, Volume 8: Journals NB21–NB25*, p. 212: NB23, 20 (January to April 1851). On Kierkegaard's connections to Rudelbach, see Søren Jensen, 'Andreas Gottlob Rudelbach: Kierkegaard's Idea of an "Orthodox" Theologian', in *Kierkegaard and His Danish Contemporaries, Tome II: Theology*, ed. Jon Stewart (Ashgate, 2009), pp. 303–33.

p. 224      *'one of our most talented authors'*: J. P. Mynster, *Yderligere Bidrag til Forhandlingerne om de kirkelige Forhold i Danmark* [*Further Contribution to Negotiations Concerning the Ecclesiastical Situation in Denmark* ] (Reitzel, 1851), p. 44; see *Kierkegaard's Journals and Notebooks, Volume 8: Journals NB21–NB25*, p. 759.

p. 225      *'I repeated again and* again': *Kierkegaard's Journals and Notebooks, Volume 8: Journals NB21–NB25*, pp. 337–9: NB24, 30 (April to November 1851); p. 759.

p. 225      *Towards the end of the summer he was back on Mynster's doorstep*: see ibid, pp. 402–4: NB24, 121 (April to November, 1851).

p. 225      *Kierkegaard preached a Sunday sermon on 'The Unchangingness of God'*: Kierkegaard published this sermon in August 1855 under the title 'The Changelessness of God: A Discourse': see S. Kierkegaard, *The Moment and Late Writings*, ed. and trans. Howard V. Hong and Edna H. Hong (Princeton University Press, 1998), pp. 263–81.

p. 226      *He had planned his sermon 'with the thought of "her"'*: see *Kierkegaard's Journals and Notebook, Volume 8: Journals NB21–NB25*, pp. 370–71: NB24, 74 (April to November, 1851).

p. 227      *'No one, either in life or in death'*: *The Moment and Late Writings*, pp. 277–81.

p. 228      *'When I went home, I felt well, animated'*: *Kierkegaard's Journals and Notebooks, Volume 8: Journals NB21–NB25*, pp. 370–71: NB24, 74 (April to November 1851).

p. 228      *'I have been told that you are gracious and kind to the young'*: S. Kierkegaard, *Letters and Documents*, ed. and trans. Henrik Rosenmeier (Princeton University Press, 2009), pp. 379–80.

p. 229      *'I have pricked up my ears and listened'*: ibid, pp. 381–4.

p. 230      *'You know that faith is a restless thing'*: S. Kierkegaard, *For Self-Examination / Judge for Yourself!*, ed. and trans. Howard V. Hong and Edna H. Hong (Princeton University Press, 1991), pp. 17–18.

p. 230      *'And this way, which is Christ, this narrow way'*: ibid, pp. 58–9.

p. 230      *gentle comfort, new life*: see ibid, pp. 75–85.

p. 230      *When Emil called on him they talked late into the night*: see *Encounters with Kierkegaard*, ed. Bruce Kirmmse, trans. Bruce Kirmmse and Virginia Laursen (Princeton University Press, 1998), pp. 100–101 – from a letter from Emil Boesen to Louise Boesen, autumn 1851.

p. 231    *sometimes 'every blessed day'*: see *Kierkegaard's Journals and Notebooks, Volume 8: Journals NB21–NB25*, p. 177: NB22, 146 (November 1850 to January 1851).

p. 231    'Perhaps it was coincidence': ibid, p. 532: NB25, 109 (May 1852).

p. 231    'Then came my birthday': ibid, pp. 532–3: NB25, 109 (May 1852).


## CHAPTER 15

p. 233    'New "Fear and Trembling"': see *Kierkegaard's Journals and Notebooks, Volume 9: Journals NB26–NB30*, ed. and trans. Niels Jørgen Cappelørn, Alastair Hannay, Bruce H. Kirmmse, David D. Possen, Joel D. S. Rasmussen and Vanessa Rumble (Princeton University Press, 2017), p. 250: NB28, 41 (1853).

p. 234    'quite literally letting go and giving up': ibid, p. 29: NB26, 25 (June to August 1852).

p. 234    'whether it was not all a fantasy': ibid, p. 290: NB28, 99 (1853).

p. 235    'Christianity is suffering to the end': ibid, p. 52: NB26, 51 (June to August 1852).

p. 235    'The closer to God, the more suffering': ibid, p. 151: NB27, 39 (August 1852 to February 1853).

p. 235    *For two years he has published nothing and written little*: apart from his journals, Kierkegaard's only substantial piece of writing between 1852 and 1854 was *Judge for Yourselves!*, a collection of discourses similar to *For Self-Examination*, which he left unpublished.

p. 235    'an enormous productivity': *Kierkegaard's Journals and Notebooks, Volume 9: Journals NB26–NB30*, p. 230: NB28, 16 (Easter Monday 1853).

p 235    'almost like foolishness': ibid, pp. 261–2: NB28, 54 (1853).

p. 236    'something like a plague to Bishop M.': ibid, pp. 262–3: NB28, 55 (2 November 1854).

p. 236    'Now he is dead': ibid, pp. 264–6: NB28, 56 (1 March 1854).

p. 237    'Now it must happen': ibid, p. 264: NB28, 56 (1 March 1854).

p. 237    *Martensen included a eulogy to the late Bishop in his Sunday sermon*: see Hans Lassen Martensen, 'Sermon Delivered in Christiansborg Castle Church on the Fifth Sunday after Epiphany, February 5th, 1854, the Sunday Before Bishop Dr. Mynster's Funeral', in S. Kierkegaard, *The Moment and Late Writings*, ed. and trans. Howard V. Hong and Edna H. Hong (Princeton University Press, 1998), p. 359.

NOTES

p. 237    'Bishop Mynster a truth-witness!': ibid, pp. 3–6; see 1 Corinthi-
          ans 4: 10–13.

p. 237    He blamed women for imposing on men 'all the nonsense of fini-
          tude': Kierkegaard's Journals and Notebooks, Volume 9: Journals
          NB26–NB30, pp. 353–4: NB29, 92 (May to June 1854).

p. 238    'He leads a withdrawn existence': ibid, p. 358–9: NB29, 95 (May
          to June 1854).

p. 238    a 'martyrdom of laughter': Kierkegaard's Journals and Notebooks,
          Volume 5: Journals NB6–NB10, ed. and trans. Niels Jørgen Cap-
          pelørn, Alastair Hannay, David Kangas, Bruce H. Kirmmse, George
          Pattison, Joel D. S. Rasmussen, Vanessa Rumble and K. Brian
          Söderquist (Princeton University Press, 2012), pp. 289–90: NB10,
          42 (February to April, 1849).

p. 239    Kierkegaard still held fire: around this time, April 1854, Kierke-
          gaard received a copy of Mynster's memoirs, Meddelelser om mit
          Levnet [From My Life], published posthumously by his son F. J.
          Mynster, a pastor. Kierkegaard returned the book to Pastor Myn-
          ster, explaining that he could not accept it: 'My relationship with
          your late father was of a very special kind. From the first time I
          spoke with him I told him privately . . . how much I disagreed with
          him. Privately I have told him again and again – and I shall not
          forget that he had so much good will that he listened to me with
          sympathy – that my principal concern was the memory of my late
          father. Now [Mynster] has died, I must stop. Now I must and intend
          to have the freedom, whether or not I want to use it, to speak out
          without having to take any such thing into consideration . . . As you
          in sending [this book] to me declare (and that was noble of you!) that
          everything is as it used to be, so, in accepting it, I would declare that
          everything is as it used to be – but that is not the way it is.' Kierkeg-
          aard also thanked Pastor Mynster for his 'affectionate' note, which
          he found 'in all sincerity, most touching'. See S. Kierkegaard, Letters
          and Documents, ed. and trans. Henrik Rosenmeier (Princeton
          University Press, 2009), p. 417 – letter to F. J. Mynster, 1854;
          Kierkegaard's Journals and Notebooks, Volume 9: Journals NB26–
          NB30, p. 672. We do not know whether Kierkegaard looked at
          Mynster's memoirs before he returned the book; if he did, he found
          no mention of his own name, and plenty of praise for Martensen.

p. 239    In 1855 Schlegel would take up this post – and Regine would
          leave Denmark: see Joakim Garff, Kierkegaard's Muse, trans.
          Alastair Hannay (Princeton University Press, 2017), p. 24.

p. 239    *Kierkegaard's article denounced him as a fraud*: see *The Moment and Late Writings*, pp. 3–8.

p. 240    *Martensen published a lengthy, supercilious response*: Hans Lassen Martensen, 'On the Occasion of Dr S. Kierkegaard's Article in *Fædrelandet*, no. 295'; see ibid, pp. 360–66.

p. 240    *tore it into little pieces*: see *Encounters with Kierkegaard*, ed. Bruce Kirmmse, trans. Bruce Kirmmse and Virginia Laursen (Princeton University Press, 1998), pp. 116–17 – from Mathilde Reinhardt, *Familie-Erindringer 1831–1856*, published privately in 1889.

p. 240    *'makes no impression on me at all'*: *The Moment and Late Writings*, pp. 9–10.

p. 240    *Martensen's 'blasphemy'*: see ibid, p. 25.

p. 240    *Rasmus Nielsen wrote in defence of Kierkegaard*: Nielsen's article was published in *Fædrelandet* on 10 January 1855: see *The Moment and Late Writings*, p. 651.

p. 240    *Kierkegaard encountered Regine on the street near his home*: see Garff, *Kierkegaard's Muse*, p. 9.

p. 241    *'kept up a brisk fire against official Christianity'*: ibid, p. 60.

p. 241    *'silk-and-velvet pastors'*: ibid, p. 43.

p. 241    *'A Thesis – Just One Single One'*: ibid, p. 39.

p. 241    *'In what did Socratic irony consist?'*: *Kierkegaard's Journals and Notebooks: Volume 10, Journals NB31–NB36*, ed. and trans. Niels Jørgen Cappelørn, Alastair Hannay, Bruce H. Kirmmse, David D. Possen, Joel D. S. Rasmussen and Vanessa Rumble (Princeton University Press, 2018), p. 371: NB 35, 2 (December, 1854).

p. 242    *beginning the first issue with an elegant preface*: see *The Moment and Late Writings*, pp. 91–2.

p. 242    *the 'enormous illusion' of contemporary Christianity*: ibid, p. 105.

p. 243    *'to glue families together more and more egotistically'*: ibid, pp. 248–9.

p. 243    *'One cannot live on nothing'*: ibid, pp. 204–5.

p. 243    *he no longer went himself*: see Niels Jørgen Cappelørn, 'Søren Kierkegaard at Friday Communion in the Church of Our Lady', trans. K. Brian Söderquist, in *International Kierkegaard Commentary, Volume 18: Without Authority*, ed. Robert L. Perkins (Mercer University Press, 2007).

p. 243    *These explosive pamphlets 'aroused a great sensation'*: see *Encounters with Kierkegaard*, p. 119 – from the diary of Hansine Andræ, October 18, 1855.

p. 243     *'I am in complete agreement with your judgement of Kierkegaard's behaviour'*: ibid, pp. 103 – from a letter from Carsten
Hauch to B. S. Ingemann, 25 March 1855.

p. 243     *he regretted that Kierkegaard's 'one-sidedness' now dominated
his philosophy*: ibid, pp. 103–5 – from a letter from F. C. Sibbern
to Petronella Ross, 26 March 1855.

p. 243     *Pastor Birkedal, felt 'the strong words cast a profound shadow'*:
ibid, p. 107 – from Vilhelm Birkedal, *Personlige Oplevelser i et
langt Liv*, vol. 2 (Copenhagen: Karl Schønbergs Forlag, 1890).

p. 244     *'it has been a continuing source of sorrow to me'*: ibid, p. 106 –
from a letter from Magdalene Hansen to Elise Stampe, 20 June
1855.

p. 244     *'quite his usual self in conversation'*: ibid, p. 111 – from Otto
B. Wroblewski, *Ti Aar i C. A. Reitzels Boglade* (1889).

p. 244     *When Hans Brøchner met him out walking one summer evening*:
see ibid, pp. 247–8 – from Hans Brøchner's recollections of
Kierkegaard, written in 1871–2.

p. 244     *'Until now it has not been clear whether or not K. was a noble
character'*: see ibid, pp. 108–9 – from *Nord og Syd* [*North and
South*], 15 September 1855.

p. 245     *'The only analogy I have before me is Socrates'*: *The Moment and
Late Writings*, p. 341.

p. 245     *'with a charming look'*: see *Encounters with Kierkegaard*, p. 117 –
from Mathilde Reinhardt, *Familie-Erindringer 1831–1856*.

p. 245     *'The patient cannot offer any specific reason for his present illness'*: see *Letters and Documents*, pp. 28–32 – from the medical
record at Frederiks Hospital. This record indicates the cause of his
death as 'Tuberculosis?'.

p. 245     *'a feeling of victory'*: see *Encounters with Kierkegaard*, p. 172 –
from Henriette Lund, *Eringringer Fra Hjemmet* (Gyldendal,
1909).

p. 246     *'his eyes shone like stars'*: ibid, p. 157.

p. 246     *'To be opened and read after my death'*: *Letters and Documents*,
pp. 33, 450. Kierkegaard's will was undated, but the editor of his
*Letters and Documents* suggest that it was written in 1849,
around the same time as Kierkegaard's letters to Regine and J. F.
Schlegel.

p. 246     *'It seemed as though he wanted me to come so that he could say
something'*: see *Encounters with Kierkegaard*, p. 121 – from a
letter from Emil Boesen to Louise Boesen, 17 October 1855.

p. 246     *'I therefore concluded that it was my task to be extraordinary'*: ibid, pp. 121–8 – from Emil Boesen's account of his hospital conversations with Kierkegaard, originally published in *Af Søren Kierkegaards Efterladte Papirer, 1854–55* (Reitzel, 1881), pp. 593–9.

p. 247     *he had alluded to this 'thorn in the flesh' several times in his journals*: see, e.g., *Kierkegaard's Journals and Notebooks, Volume 9: Journals NB26–NB30*, p. 207: NB 27, 88 (August 1852 to February 1853). The phrase 'thorn in the flesh' comes from 2 Corinthians 12: 2–7; Kierkegaard mentioned this in *Concluding Unscientific Postscript*, where he describes the thorn in the flesh as a 'religious suffering [that] becomes the mark of blessedness'. See S. Kierkegaard, *Concluding Unscientific Postscript*, ed. and trans. Alastair Hannay (Cambridge University Press, 2009), p. 381.

## KIERKEGAARD'S AFTERLIFE

p. 249     *a fierce debate about the Christian doctrine of immortality*: see Ludwig Feuerbach, *Thoughts on Death and Immortality*, ed. and trans. James A. Massey (University of California Press, 1980); István Czakó, 'Becoming Immortal: The Historical Context of Kiekegaard's Concept of Immortality', in *Kierkegaard and Christianity*, ed. Roman Králik, Abrahim H. Khan, Peter Sajda, Jamie Turnbull and Andrew J. Burgess (Acta Kierkegaardiana, vol. 3, 2008), pp. 60–65.

p. 249     *'strangely enough, while this is taking place, certitude declines'*: S. Kierkegaard, *The Concept of Anxiety*, trans. Reidar Thomte (Princeton University Press, 1981), p. 139.

p. 250     *Anders Westergaard once asked him*: this conversation was reported by Andreas Ferdinand Schiødte, who knew Westergaard, in a letter to H. P. Barfod in 1869: see *Encounters with Kierkegaard*, ed. Bruce Kirmmse, trans. Bruce Kirmmse and Virginia Laursen (Princeton University Press, 1998), p. 195. See also *Kierkegaard's Journals and Notebooks, Volume 7: Journals NB15–NB20*, ed. and trans. Niels Jørgen Cappelørn, Alastair Hannay, Bruce H. Kirmmse, David D. Possen, Joel D. S. Rasmussen, Vanessa Rumble and K. Brian Söderquist (Princeton University Press, 2014), p. 433: NB20, 58 (July to September 1850): 'A Socrates in Christendom. Socrates could not prove the immortality of the soul; he simply said: this matter occupies me so much that I will order my life as though immortality were a fact – should there be none, *oh well*, I still do not regret my choice, for this is the only matter that concerns me. What a great help it would already be in Christendom if there were someone who spoke and acted like that: I do not know whether Christianity is true, but I will order my whole life as though it were, stake my life on it – then if it proves not to be true, *oh well*, I still do not regret my choice, for it is the only matter that concerns me.'

p. 252     *Søren A. Kierkegaard Collection*: Kierkegaard's possessions were sold by auction after his death. A list of the 280 items and the names of their purchasers can be found in Flemming Chr. Nielsen, *Alt Blev Godt Betalt: Auktionen over Søren Kierkegaards indbo* (Holkenfeldt 3, 2000).

p. 252     *'for fear that too many people'*: see Niels Jørgen Cappelørn, Joakim Garff and Johnny Kondrup, *Written Images: Søren Kierkegaard's Journals, Notebooks, Booklets, Sheets, Scraps, and Slips of Paper*, trans. Bruce H. Kirmmse (Princeton University Press, 2003), p. 19.

p. 253     *he appointed a former newspaper editor, H. P. Barfod*: see ibid, pp. 22–9. Barfod found a slip of paper on which Kierkegaard stated his wish that Rasmus Nielsen edit his posthumous writings, in collaboration with Jens Giødvad and Israel Levin, which caused Barfod much concern.

p. 253     *The first volume of* Søren Kierkegaard's Posthumous Papers *appeared*: ibid, pp. 53–6.

p. 254     *a verse from an eighteenth-century hymn by Brorson*: see Christopher B. Barnett, 'Hans Adolph Brorson: Danish Pietism's Greatest Hymn Writer', in *Kierkegaard and the Renaissance and Modern Traditions. Tome II: Theology*, ed. Jon Stewart (Ashgate, 2009), pp. 63–79; Andrew J. Burgess, 'Kierkegaard, Brorson, and Moravian Music', in *International Kierkegaard Commentary, Volume 20: Practice in Christianity*, ed. Robert L. Perkins (Mercer University Press, 2004), pp. 211–43. There is no documentary evidence to show that Kierkegaard sang these (or any other) hymns, but he knew Brorson's hymns well and often referred to them in his writings.

p. 255     *'the whole burial plot'*: S. Kierkegaard, *Letters and Documents*, ed. and trans. Henrik Rosenmeier (Princeton University Press, 2009), pp. 26–7.

p. 256     *'The most dangerous part of his actions'*: see *Encounters with Kierkegaard*, p. 130 – from *Nord og Syd*, 15 November 1855.

p. 256     *'The crowd in the aisles was large'*: see ibid, p. 136 – from a letter from Hans Christian Andersen to August Bournonville, 24 November 1855.

p. 256    '*Today, after a large service at the Church of Our Lady*': see ibid, p. 135 – from a letter from H. L. Martensen to L. Gude, 18 November 1855.

p. 256    '*There was an enormous crowd present*': see ibid, p. 132–3 – from a letter from F. Sodemann to P. M. Barfod, 18 November 1855.

p. 257    *Henrik Lund's graveside speech*: see ibid, pp. 133–5 – from *Fædrelandet*, 22 November 1855.

p. 257    '*To me, the entire affair is a distorted picture of Søren K.*': see ibid, p. 136 – from a letter from Hans Christian Andersen to August Bournonville, 24 November 1855.

p. 257    *Bishop Martensen made sure Lund was prosecuted*: see Cappelørn, Garff and Konderup, *Written Images*, p. 10.

p. 259    *the birthday festivities*: reported in *Kristeligt Dagblad* on Monday, 6 May 2013.

p. 260    *Joakim Garff . . . spoke about the peculiar task*: I am grateful to Joakim Garff for showing me the text of his lecture. For a much earlier reflection on similar themes, see Garff's 'The Eyes of Argus: The Point of View and Points of View with Respect to Kierkegaard's "Activity as an Author"', *Kierkegaardiana*, 15 (Reitzel, 1991), pp. 29–54.

# Acknowledgements

This book was written in London, Philadelphia, Copenhagen and the Isle of Skye. I'm grateful to so many people in these places – in libraries and universities, yoga studios and cafés – for incalculable kindnesses, and for giving me time and space to think and write. King's College London, the Senate House Library, the University of Pennsylvania, the University of Copenhagen and the Royal Danish Library have provided resources to support my research into Kierkegaard's life. Skye, as usual, offered only itself: a place of rest and longing, and far horizons, in which to bring the book to completion.

Several people deserve special thanks: Daniel Crewe and Stuart Proffitt at Penguin helped to conceive this biography, and as its editor Stuart gave magisterial advice throughout; Richard Mason copyedited the text; Stephen Ryan proofread it magnificently; Amanda Russell researched the images; Ben Sinyor and Francisca Monteiro made sure text and image worked together on the page; and Richard Duguid oversaw production. Joseph Sinclair assisted me in compiling the index. Sarah Chalfant and Alba Ziegler-Bailey have helped to bring the book – and myself – into the world.

At Farrar, Straus and Giroux, Eric Chinski has been a warm, generous editor and his faith in the book a source of joy, while assistant editor Deborah Ghim was a delight to work with. June Park designed the cover, and Hannah Goodwin was the production editor.

In the spring of 2017 Joakim Garff generously welcomed me to the Søren Kierkegaard Research Centre, Ettore Rocca lent me his office, and Niels Jørgen Cappelørn gave late inspiration. At the Royal Danish Library, Erik Petersen brought me box after box of Kierkegaard's manuscripts and letters, and I was touched by his enthusiasm for my book. Luna Hvid provided a *hyggelig* home in Copenhagen, and made sure I saw the cherry blossom.

Alice Albinia, Noreen Khawaja, Kate Kirkpatrick, Simon Oliver, George Pattison and John Tresch read the manuscript at various stages and provided invaluable comments. John Callanan and Andy Cooper read parts of it.

Many wonderful friends and colleagues have supported me while I wrote the book – thanks especially to Rupert Shortt for his faithful friendship and unstinting encouragement; to Amy Merriman for her forebearance during my research leave; to Fiona Ellis, Sarah Coakley and Eddie Howells, for making me think and making me laugh; to John Cottingham for his wisdom and love. I am also eternally grateful to Russel Williams. Most of all I thank my husband John and son Joseph, for living the question of existence with me.

Clare Carlisle
London, Autumn 2018

# Index

# Illustration Credits

Clare Carlisle is a professor of philosophy and theology at King's College London. She is a regular contributor to *The Times Literary Supplement* and has written dozens of articles on philosophy for *The Guardian*. Her book *On Habit* was named an Outstanding Academic Title of 2014 by *Choice*, and she has recently edited George Eliot's translation of Spinoza's *Ethics*. Carlisle grew up in Manchester, studied philosophy and theology at Trinity College, Cambridge, and now lives in London.